THE COMPLETE HOW-TO-FIX-IT BOOK

ANDREW WAUGH

ILLUSTRATIONS BY JON PROSSER
AND BRUNO GRASSWILL

BONANZA BOOKS
A Division of Crown Publishers, Inc.
419 Park Avenue South
New York, New York 10016

CONTENTS

Guide
to
the book   6

Dictionary
of
contents A–Z   9

Illustrative
project
ideas   337

Glossary   397

Abbreviations   494

Index   497

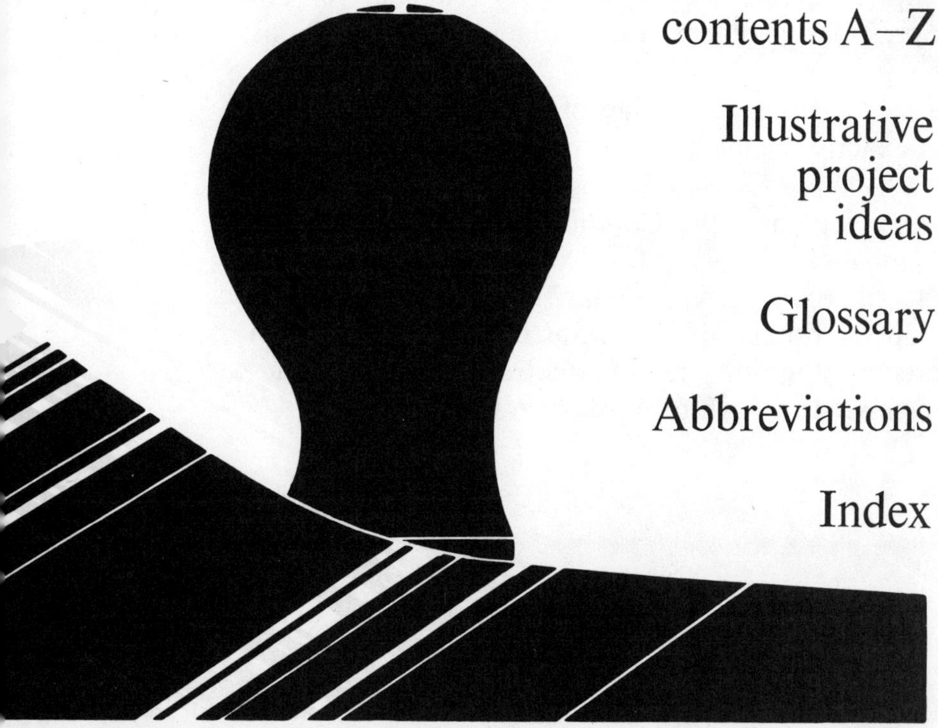

GUIDE

The *Complete How-To-Fix-It-Book* is divided broadly into four sections: the main body, the glossary, abbreviations and the index.

The first section deals basically with all repair, maintenance and painting jobs likely to be encountered in the average home.

The glossary supplements the main body of the book by enlarging and elaborating on various aspects of the job. It also provides interesting background knowledge to give a greater understanding of the subject.

The abbreviations provide a quick and easy reference for those terms and expressions commonly used in building specifications.

The index gives a complete listing of everything in the book and tells you exactly where to find it.

Like most encyclopedias, the *Complete How-To-Fix-It Book* is laid out alphabetically; so, for example, if you are confronted with borers or termites gnawing at your footings or floors, look up B—borers. If you want to convert feet to meters or pounds to kilograms, see M—metric conversion, and to replace a worn window sash or cord, turn to W—windows (replace cords).

DICTIONARY OF CONTENTS A.Z

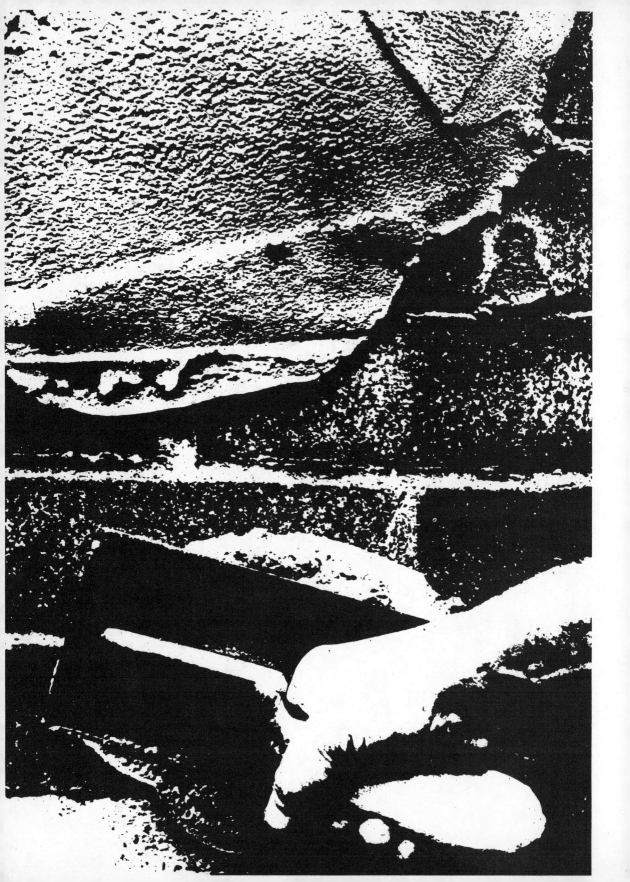

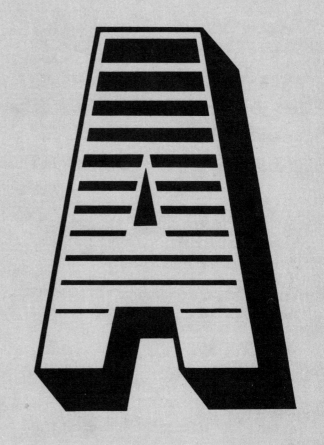

ABRASIVES	For Sanding
ABRASIVES	Using Sheets
ABRASIVES	Wire Wheels
ACCIDENTS	Avoiding
ACCURACY	In Measuring
ACOUSTICS	In Home
ADHESIVES	Practical Hints
ADHESIVES	To fix Laminates
ALLEN SCREWS	Keys
ALUMINUM	Assembly Methods
ALUMINUM	Edgings, Strips, etc.
ALUMINUM PAINT	Uses
ALUMINUM	Soldering
ALUMINUM	Tools Needed
ANCHORS	Wall Plugs
ANGLE DIVIDER	Use
ANGLES	Compound Cuts
ANT CAPS	Placing
ANTIQUE	Finish
APPLIANCES (Electrical)	Running Costs
ARCH BAR	Use
ASBESTOS CEMENT ROOFING	To Fix
ASBESTOS CEMENT SHEET WALLS	To Clean
ASPHALT	Paving
AXES	Types, to Sharpen

ABRASIVES — For Sanding

To get an attractive, smooth finish on wood you must rub it down with an abrasive paper of some kind after planing and possibly scraping the surface.

Ordinary sandpaper—which is actually glasspaper—is only one of a variety of abrasive papers and cloths, all of which are suited to particular jobs.

Sandpaper is used widely for preparing wood for painting or staining and especially for rubbing down exterior paintwork. It is comparatively cheap, but has a short working life and is unsuitable under damp conditions.

For a little extra cost, garnet paper gives a much better all-round result. It has a harder and sharper cutting surface than sandpaper, and lasts longer. All these abrasive papers are made in various grades of coarseness.

Wet or dry paper or waterproof paper is also more effective than sandpaper for many jobs, especially furniture finishing.

It has a waterproof backing paper to which the abrasive grit is fixed with a waterproof adhesive. It is used for either dry or wet rubbing.

When used wet, it is dampened by immersing in water, and produces a fine finish without clogging the pores of the paper. The water acts as a lubricant, giving the paper longer life and a finer cutting action. It also eliminates dust which could be inhaled.

For really heavy sanding and rubbing down, aluminum oxide paper will do a really good job on hardwood. For metal, use emery cloth.

Steel wool is a very effective abrasive for wood. It is made in three main grades—fine, medium, and coarse—and is useful for rubbing down paintwork on furniture to prepare it for a new finish.

Steel wool is also excellent to use in conjunction with a liquid paint remover when removing paint from around turned or curved sections of furniture or other woodwork. It won't dig into the wood like a scraper or knife. Fine-grade steel wool is used to flatten a too-glossy oil paint or enamel finish.

Pumice stone is another good abrasive for rubbing down paintwork. It is used with water. Powdered pumice is used for rubbing down finer work, especially for toning down the luster of plastic finishes or varnishes that are too glossy.

ABRASIVES — Using Sheets

It is a recognized fact that a block of some kind must be used with the sandpaper when rubbing a surface.

If the paper is used without the block, in much the same way as a piece of cloth it won't cut effectively, and the surface will be uneven.

The proper size for a sanding block is about 5 in. long by 3 in. wide.

The paper should fit this neatly without any overhang on the ends, and just sufficient turn-up on the sides to provide a grip for the fingers. This point is shown clearly in Figs. 1 and 2.

Sanding blocks in either plain cork or rubber can be bought.

On the other hand a couple of scrap ends of ¾ in. thick cork mat glued together then rasped and sandpapered neatly make an excellent block.

Alternatively, a piece of ¼ in. thick cork linoleum could be glued to one side of a ⅞ in. thick block of wood which is rounded or chamfered neatly on the top edges.

Plain pieces of wood do not make good sanding blocks.

There is no "give" in them, as is found in cork. Besides, it is easy to damage adjacent work with the corners of a solid wooden block.

For the most economical way of dealing with sandpaper, take a glance at Fig. 3.

It will be seen here that by folding an ordinary 12 in. by 10 in. sheet as indicated by the dotted lines it is possible to get six equal pieces, each 5 in. by 4 in.

There is a certain way of tearing the paper, too, to avoid ragged, uneven edges.

Place the sheet face side up on the bench, fold it over across the center of the 10 in. width until both edges meet neatly, and then crease the fold with the edge of the hand.

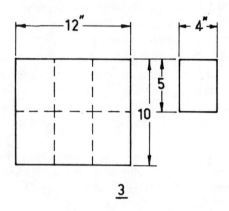

3

Bend the folded portions the opposite way, and press down with the hand.

The other two folds are carried out across the length in the same way, and after this is done, the portions can be torn off easily.

It is sometimes necessary to clean up a small hollow-shaped edge or hole with sandpaper.

One way is to glue a strip of sandpaper to a dowel rod and use this.

The disadvantage, however, is that the sandpaper wears out rapidly, necessitating gluing on another strip with the unavoidable delay while the glue sets.

A fine saw kerf is made at the end of a dowel rod at an angle of about 45 degrees, Fig. 4.

The dowel should be slightly smaller in diameter than the hollow shape into which it has to fit.

A strip of sandpaper is torn off and the end cut at about 45 degrees.

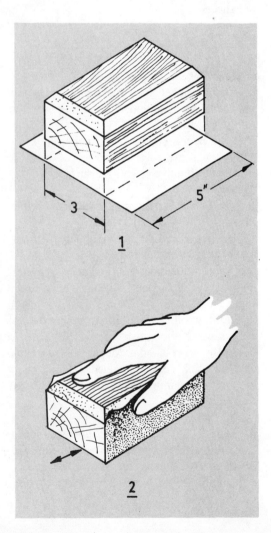

1

2

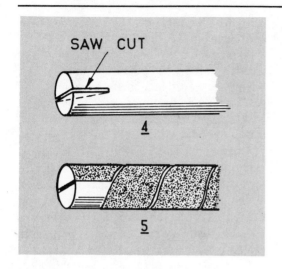

The pointed end is tucked into the saw kerf and the length is wrapped in a spiral around the dowel, Fig. 5.

It will be found to stay in position quite well, and as it becomes worn it is easily replaced.

ABRASIVES — Wire Wheels

Much of the effort can be taken out of cleaning and polishing metal, and cleaning woodwork if an abrasive wheel or scratch-brush is used on your power tool.

The work is simple enough provided you select the right brush for the job.

Here is an illustrated guide to the most popular types and their uses.

Fig. 1. Scratchbrush 3 in. diameter. A general purpose brush for cleaning rusty or dirty plain and ornamental cast iron prior to painting. Suitable for garden gates, door knockers, water tanks, conduit pipes, black iron fire grates, garden tools and metal window frames.

Fig. 2. Soft Bessemer steel wire filled scratchbrush, 3 in. diameter. Removes light rust deposits especially where items are to be re-plated. Will finish off items

previously cleaned with a 3 in. wire scratch-brush. Ideal for cleaning up dirty chrome, doorknobs and knockers, letter flaps or any brass parts that need burnishing.

Fig. 3. Brass wire filled brush 3 in. diameter. For finishing off items of brassware previously cleaned with soft scratch wheel, ready for polishing. Will remove deposits from switch covers, doorknobs, stair rods and candlesticks.

Fig. 4. Wire cup brush $1\frac{1}{4}$ in. diameter. Having a flat surface, is useful for removing old paint, especially when blistered, or for cleaning large areas of ironwork, stew and frying pans when heavily burned, oven plates, grills and garden spades.

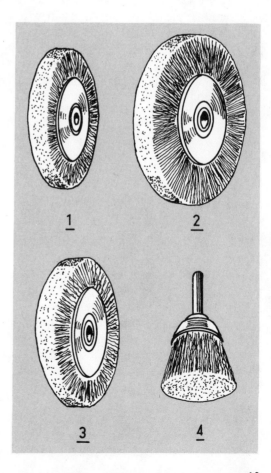

 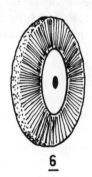

5 6

Fig. 5. Buffing wheel 3 in. diameter. Will give all the items so far mentioned a final polish. It has a fine cutting action when suitably dressed with an emery or polishing compound. It may also be used dry or with a chrome polish to polish nickel or chrome-plated finishes.

Fig. 6. Bristle wheel 3 in. diameter. Having a short cut, it will polish ornamental carved woodwork without scratching.

ACCIDENTS—Avoiding

Most accidents in and around the home workshop can be avoided if care and certain safety precautions are taken.

Fire can happen in the most unlikely places, and to anyone. Many fires start with accumulations of waste and rubbish. Keep this in metal cans with metal covers, and if it is to be burned, use an incinerator so placed that sparks cannot ignite anything nearby.

In the workshop, never store old paint or oil cleaning cloths in a drawer or box. There is a definite risk of spontaneous combustion here.

Also in the workshop or garage, don't store drums of gasoline or methylated spirits and be careful with that cigarette butt, which could set wood shavings from the bench afire.

In many houses the indiscriminate use of electric cords is a perpetual fire hazard. Never use a cord in a position where it may be damaged by furniture being pushed over it, and replace it as soon as it becomes frayed or damaged.

Fires are caused by overloading electrical wiring, as, for example, when a number of appliances run from one point. Your house wiring should be inspected at least once in ten years. Get a competent electrician to see if out-of-sight wires and connections are in good condition.

Be especially careful with portable electric heaters and radiators. People often plug them into an adaptor into which something else like the radio or television is also plugged. One member of the family leaves the room and pulls the adaptor out, carefully moving the heater behind a piece of furniture like an armchair.

Another member of the family later comes in to listen to the radio for a few minutes, plugs in the adaptor, and when he has finished, switches the radio off only at the set.

This situation arises frequently, and furniture or drapes are blazing before anyone realizes what has happened.

Clothing which catches fire is the story behind some of the most serious injuries. It is worth noting that woolen material smolders with a red glow, and when withdrawn from the source of heat, goes out.

Flannelette or cotton fabrics ignite easily, and the material is usually completely destroyed within a few seconds. Nylon melts; rayon is moderately flammable.

Fabrics containing a mixture of wool or cotton burn fairly easily, though are slightly slower to ignite.

Be sure that any type of blowtorch or burner you may be using to burn off old paint is used with extreme care. Keep the flame away from curtains, and if working outside around the eaves, first clear away any birds' nests.

Double-insulated power tools, standard in most countries, are helping to reduce the high accident rate due to electric shock in this country.

This is a type of appliance destined to become widely used in the home, where work often has to be carried out in damp and difficult situations. It is the only infallible safety guarantee.

Double insulation is self-explanatory. The normal primary insulation covering all conductors is supplemented by a second insulating barrier which completely encloses all live parts.

This isolates them from all parts handled by the user. The user is thereby further protected against electric shock if the primary insulation should break down.

Apart from the actual tool itself the various attachments need careful checking to see that they are adjusted properly.

It is surprising how often drill chuck keys are left in the chuck after tightening. This results in their flying out with great force when the drill is started.

Also see that the blade in the circular saw attachment is tightened properly and that the spring-loaded guard is always in position over the revolving blade.

For the home handyman the power drill, with its many accessories is a must. But with this, as with many other electric-powered units, accidents can happen

Authoritative records show that the main general causes of accidents in the use of portable electric tools are:

1. Faulty cords and tools, due to lack of proper periodical maintenance and to rough and careless usage.

2. Repair and adjustment of tools and cords by inexperienced and foolhardy persons.
3. General apathy of users to the very real danger in the misuse of tools and equipment—familiarity can breed contempt.

A power-operated grinding wheel is one of the most useful tools in any workshop, and provided reasonable precautions are taken to operate it safely there should never be any risk of injury. Here are essential points to note about the use of grinding wheels:

CHOOSE RIGHT WHEEL. Don't grind rough castings on a wheel intended for sharpening drills or other precision tools. On the other hand, don't try to sharpen tools on tough, coarse-grit wheels. Misuse can make wheels wear rapidly and may burn or otherwise spoil work.

HANDLE WHEELS CAREFULLY. Grinding wheels are breakable. They should not be dropped, jarred, or carelessly handled.

Before mounting any wheel, suspend it on a cord and tap lightly with some small implement. It should give forth a clear, metallic ring. If it doesn't, don't use it, as it may be fractured.

MOUNT WHEEL CAREFULLY. The wheel should fit the arbor freely but not loosely. Never force a wheel on, as expansion of the lead bushing may crack it.

Use compression flanges—not common washers—on both sides. Clean flanges and arbors of all foreign matter so that they do not bind, at any one point. Tighten the nut firmly but not so hard as to distort the flanges. Don't use loose bushings to make a wheel fit an arbor for which it is not intended.

After mounting a wheel, turn it by hand to make certain the spindle turns freely and the wheel clears the guard and grinding rests.

RUNNING WHEEL. Turn on power only when satisfied that these precautions have been taken and, even so, stand out of line of the revolving wheel for at least a minute before starting to grind.

COMMONSENSE PRECAUTIONS. It isn't clever to grind without guards or goggles. Even a very small particle can seriously damage the eye.

Finally, long ties or flapping shirt-sleeves are a definite hazard when grinding.

ACCURACY — In Measuring

If the handling of such basic tools as the rule and square seem a little obvious, it should be remembered that accuracy in their use is essential to good work.

No piece of work can be successful if its testing and subsequent marking have not been carried out accurately.

In woodworking the first essential is a rule, and a three-foot folding type marked in sixteenths of an inch is the one in general use.

For close work hold it on its edge so that the calibrations actually touch the wood. Unless this is done there is room for considerable error in accordance with how you happen to be sighting the work.

The thicker the rule the greater the possible error. This is why a beveled rule is an advantage; but even so the edge transference of sizes is advisable.

When you have to measure the thickness of a piece of wood, don't try to use the end of the rule. For one thing, it is awkward to place the end precisely even with the corner of the wood; and for another, the rule frequently wears at the ends, so leading to error.

The best way is to place the rule on edge with an inch mark even with one corner or edge and note the size. See illustration.

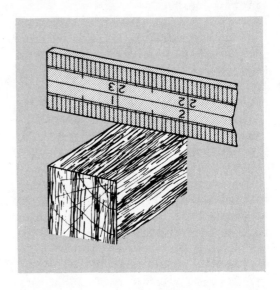

Although the woodworker's rule has no smaller divisions than sixteenths, measurements are taken with far greater accuracy than just sixteenths.

Actually, the woodworker measures to within a sixty-fourth of an inch, although he speaks only in terms of sixteenths. He does it in a curious way which has probably a lot of trade tradition in it.

If a measurement does not exactly equal a sixteenth he uses the terms "full" or "scant," or so many "and a half" sixteenths.

Thus he fixes his sizes within a sixty-fourth of an inch by dividing the odd sixteenths into four with his eye, and with practice he gets within extraordinarily fine limits.

For the preliminary rough marking out of wood the rule can be used as a sort of gauge, with the pencil held against the end of the rule with the right hand while the left hand acts as a guide against the edge of the board as the rule and pencil are drawn along.

ACOUSTICS — In Home

The way your radio, stereo set or television sounds, depends quite a lot on the room in which it is placed—and where it is placed in the room.

Put a radio in a completely bare room—no furniture or drapings—and switch it on. It sounds loud and harsh, and there's a pronounced and not very pleasant echo.

This is because the sound bounces back from the bare walls, ceiling and floor. Put the furnishings back, and the radio sounds normal again.

The same effect, even in a furnished room, can have quite a big influence on the apparent quality of music, and even on talking. The quality of the sound may be lost by **too much absorption in soft surfaces**, or too much bouncing-back from the walls, or too much amplification because of bare floors or walls.

Sometimes merely moving the radio or other instrument to a different spot in the room improves the quality of the sound. What determines this is how the music instrument is placed in relation to "live" walls and "dead" walls.

A live wall is one which bounces sound back, such as plaster or wood. A dead wall is one which absorbs sound—one which is draped, or covered with acoustical material. Curtains hung across a wall make it dead.

To get the best sound reproduction, you should have a dead wall opposite a live wall. The radio or other instrument is best placed against a live wall, and facing a dead wall.

A carpeted floor helps to get the right acoustic effect if you have a plaster or other hard ceiling—one is dead and the other live. But if your floors are hard-surfaced (plain wood, for example) put a rug under the radio, or "isolate" it by mounting it on rubber feet.

A large window draped with soft fabric helps to deaden the bounce-back of a live wall.

The best position for a stereo set with two or more speakers is in a corner of the room between two live walls, and facing two dead walls. This gives a forward bounce to the sound, with the live walls acting as a sounding board.

ADHESIVES — Practical Hints

Adhesives of all kinds should be used according to maker's directions, however here is a group of practical suggestions.

1. Keep adhesive tightly sealed when not in use and don't let it get dirty when in use.

2. See that you use a glue suited to the job and read the maker's instructions carefully.

3. Make sure the surfaces you are sticking are perfectly clean and dry.

4. If possible, work in a warm and airy room.

5. Leave the work to dry in a warm atmosphere if you want the quickest results.

6. In very cold weather, warm the surfaces before applying adhesive.

7. Roughen polished surfaces by lightly sanding them to obtain good key for the glue. Likewise, sand greasy timbers.

8. Make as good a fit as possible and test the fit before gluing.

9. Spread adhesive thinly but not so thinly that you "starve" the joint.

10. If you use a water-resistant glue, remember that wood and many other materials distort under alternate wet and dry conditions—this may seriously affect the glue line.

11. Apply enough pressure to hold glued surfaces close together, but not so much that you squeeze out most of the adhesive.

12. A panel or veneer pin, or a thin screw, can often be used to hold glued parts together until the glue grips.

13. Other temporary and useful clamps include cellulose tape, bulldog clips and, for flat surfaces, bricks or piles of books.

14. Apply pressure evenly on large surfaces if bubbles are to be avoided.

15. When using a glue of liquid consistency, make sure the surfaces are still wet when you come to join them.

16. If you are using an adhesive that can't be stored, mix only as much as you can use at one time.

17. Most glues have the same effect as size on surfaces that will eventually be painted or polished, so wipe off immediately any glue that is spilled on the work.

18. If you are gluing to a painted surface, test it by sticking cellulose tape firmly to the paint and then stripping off the tape. If the paint comes with the tape, the surface is not sound enough to glue to.

19. Use two brushes for the base and hardener of a two-part adhesive. Don't mix the brushes and don't let any hardener get into the base or it may solidify.

20. When using contact adhesive, make sure the two surfaces will fit exactly, as there is no second chance once the two surfaces have been brought together.

21. On non-porous surfaces make sure that contact adhesives are touch dry before bringing them together. And don't let dust settle on the adhesive film.

22. Most contact and rubber adhesives can be softened with gasoline which should, of course, be used with extreme care, being highly inflammable.

23. Many glues and solvents are based on toxic substances. Don't use them in unventilated rooms where there is danger of inhaling them. Don't use glue while smoking, or near a flame or electric heater.

24. Most glues can be used as fillers by adding fine sawdust, plaster of Paris or a similar inert compound.

25. If hanging paper or cloth-backed vinyl, or heavy wallpaper, use a mixture of four parts of wallpaper paste to one of PVA glue. Unbacked vinyl can only be stuck with a specially designed glue. Backed vinyl also needs a mold inhibitor added to the glue—otherwise you may get black mold spots appearing on the surface within three months of hanging the vinyl.

26. Epoxy resin glues can be used for gluing metal, glass, plastic and other non-porous materials. The glue is in two parts which are mixed together and then applied to the surfaces.

27. Latex rubber glues are used for sticking fabrics and are suitable for mending tears in clothing and for joining and binding carpets. When used on carpets hammer down the binding to help expel the air.

28. Dextrine pastes are suitable for sticking paper, cardboard and heavy wallpapers. When mounting pictures make light registering marks and smooth out all air bubbles with a clean cloth.

29. Paper backed veneers can be stuck with dextrine or one of the many other glues as long as they are fairly thin and that the setting time is sufficiently slow to allow the paper to be smoothed out.

ADHESIVES — To fix Laminates
Plastic laminates are usually fixed with a contact-type adhesive.

There are a number of precautions to note when fixing the laminated material to table tops or shelves.

Always fix them to a sound, well reinforced surface.

Check that the surface is dry and has been "aged" in the conditions of temperature and humidity to which it is expected to be subjected; a few days could be sufficient.

Items like doors and thin shelves should be covered on both sides with a plastic laminate to resist a tendency to curl. A cheap

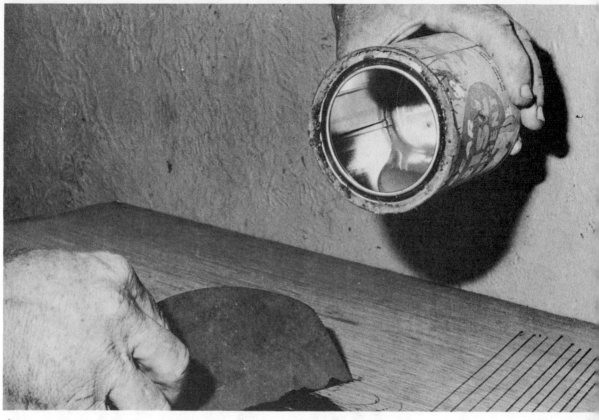

A

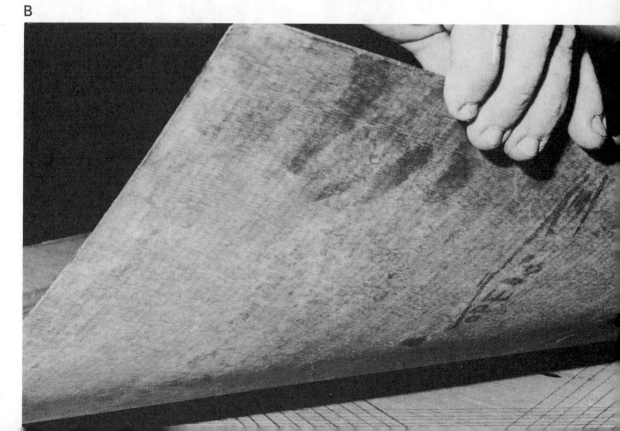

B

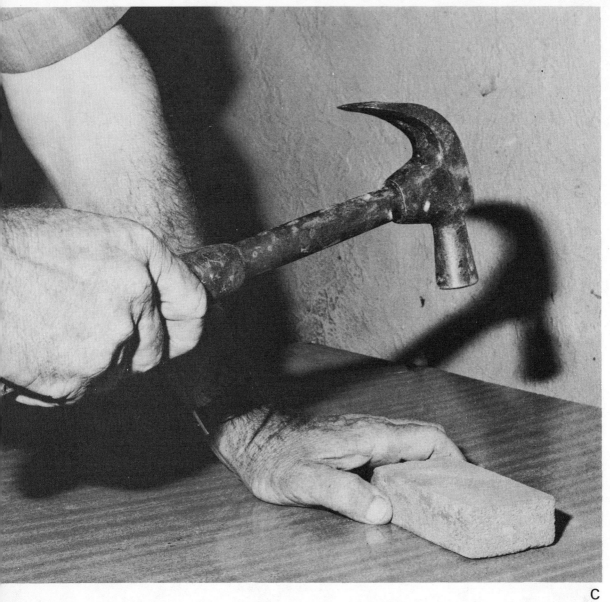

C

laminate on the inside face is quite satisfactory.

Make sure that the surface and edges, particularly the corners, are free from large
chips and blemishes; you just can't glue to
air.

The surface must be smooth and free from
hollows, bumps and waves; the highly
polished surface of the laminate will show up
such defects more than you realize.

Always support the laminate on board.
This support board can be quite thin, if well
battened. The laminate is not strong enough
to be supported on battens by itself and may
pucker or break if subjected to changes of
temperature, excess weight, or rough treatment, knocks and bumps.

All screws and nails should be punched
below the surface. It is disconcerting to have
nails popping-up again while the laminate is
being tapped down, for this prevents it bonding on to the surface correctly.

Remember that thinner laminates are less
likely to distort a thin table top or door
panel. Thick laminate should only be used
where exceptionally heavy surface wear is
expected.

Check the size of the laminate before
coating it with adhesive. Mark one end with
a china marker, just in case the area to be
covered is not a true rectangle.

When marking out the laminate, don't
place it face downwards on the surface to be
covered; if the edges are out of true, the
error will be doubled.

Do not attempt to apply adhesive to an
excessively porous surface. It should be
sized after removing any loose paint.

Don't be in a hurry; the adhesive must be
allowed to become touch dry. Wait the
appropriate amount of time, as indicated by
the manufacturer. When applying several
pieces, do not forget the order in which they

have been coated. It is a good idea to mark
the time at which the coating was commenced so that you do not suddenly realize,
after coating part No. 6 that part No. 1 has
been dry for half an hour.

When fixing laminate to wood, apply the
adhesive to the laminate first then to the
wood. This ensures that both surfaces are dry
at approximately the same time.

Do not work over a dusty area. Sawdust,
for example, will spoil the closeness of the
bond and with very thin self-adhesive film
coverings, it shows through as rough
blemishes.

Do not apply to a surface in humid conditions; condensation will prevent the
adhesive bonding as it should.

Avoid the adhesive becoming over-dry. If
this happens, use a warm household iron to
melt the adhesive by ironing over the finished surface.

In areas of heavy wear, do not put the
plastic laminate edging strip on after applying the top. This will leave a joint facing upwards which can lead to the edge being
broken away more easily than if the top were
to overlap the edge.

Do not file roughly when trimming excess
material from the edging laminate; work in
towards the shelf or table. This reduces the
chances of the surface becoming damaged
or the strip being displaced.

Here are the practical details of cutting
and fixing melamine-faced laminated plastic
sheets.

They can be cut with an ordinary hand
or tenon saw, although there are special
sheet-cutting saws available which are ideal
for the job.

When cutting a plastic-faced panel, score
through the plastic with a sharp knife or the
corner of a chisel.

This will act as a guide line and will prevent the plastic chipping when being sawn.

The knife or chisel must be really sharp, because of the material's high scratch-resistance. The plastic face should be upper-most, so that the downward, cutting stroke of the saw pulls the plastic down on to the backing board.

For small pieces, use a tenon saw. A fine-toothed panel saw, or the special sheet-saw is best for larger sheets. The sawn edges can be smoothed off with a file or a finely set plane.

Kitchen tables and work-tops that have grown shabby with use can be given a bright new wipe-clean surface with a colorful lami-nated plastic. The method of fixing this sheet material is shown in illustrations (A), (B) and (C).

After the table-top is smooth and even, apply special contact adhesive to back of plastic sheet and to table surface. Comb to an even coat with notched spreader, carry-ing adhesive right to edges (B).

When adhesive is touch-dry, line up the plastic panel with one edge and corner and roll the sheet down into place, pressing out air bubbles. The contact adhesive bonds instantly, so work carefully to line up the sheet accurately. Note the drawing pins in the end of the table which serve to position the panel.

Ensure good contact over the whole sur-face by going over it with a wood block and hammer, tapping from the center of the table outwards as in (C). Afterwards trim over-hanging edges with a plane or rasp, then file and sand smooth.

ALLEN SCREWS — Keys

The Allen or socket-head screws are a very effective method of joining and securing metal parts, and they are used extensively on all types of machinery and equipment.

In the home workshop such screws are almost certainly used on various parts of power tools such as the circular saw, jigsaw drill and many others.

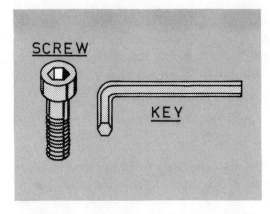

However, the use of these screws necessi-tates having the correct key at hand when required. An easily made holder which will keep the keys handy can be made from a piece of solid scrap metal.

Simply clean it up and drill and tap a series of holes to correct size and depth to take a set of the sizes usually worked with. A screw fitted in each hole forms a con-venient housing for its corresponding key as shown at (A).

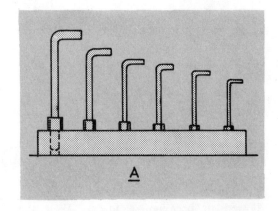

An alternative arrangement can be pro-vided by brazing a suitable washer to each key as shown at (B). The keys can then be hung on a hook above the bench where they will be available whenever required.

This arrangement is also suitable for such workers as maintenance mechanics, when a selection of the keys fitted with washers can be clipped together with an ordinary key ring. In this way they are convenient for use, and not so likely to be misplaced.

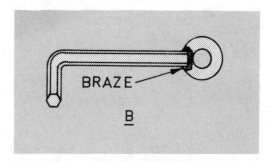

After long use the corners on the working ends of the keys become worn and it is difficult to get a firm grip in the recessed head of the screw. By carefully grinding off the worn portion of the key—see (C)—it can be given a new lease of life.

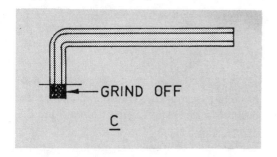

When the Allen screw has to be inserted in an awkward position keep it attached to the key with adhesive tape until thread engages around end.

ALUMINUM—Assembly Methods

Aluminum parts such as sheets, bars, and frame components may be assembled in a number of ways.

For example, when joining sheet aluminum with self-tapping screws, it is recommended that holes be punched in the parts for the screws, in preference to drilling.

Place the sheet on a block of softwood and punch with a sharp nail as indicated in Fig. 1. The punched hole provides more metal for engaging the threads of the self-tapping screws, so giving a much stronger connection.

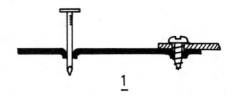

To bend bar aluminum about ⅛ in. or ¼ in. thick, simply clamp it securely in a vice and hammer with a heavy rubber mallet while applying bending force with the free hand. Cover the jaws of the vice with leather or scrap plywood to avoid marring the surface of the bar.

For a sharp 90 degree angle where strength is not especially important, notch the bar with a shallow saw slot as in Fig. 2 at the point where the bend is to be made.

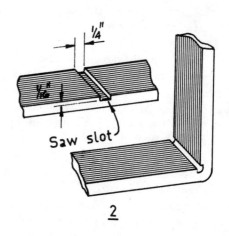

This not only ensures that the bend is made easily but it also prevents unsightly bunching or distortion of the metal around the area of the bend.

To form bar in small diameter bends, hammer bar around a sturdy piece of iron pipe held in a vice. The $\frac{5}{8}$ in. or $\frac{3}{4}$ in. wide bar can be curved around iron pipe if the partially bent bar is clamped to the pipe before the forming is completed. See Fig. 3.

RIVETING—offers a permanent, tight fastening that is easy to make, is inconspicuous and reliable.

To avoid sideways movement in the join, drill holes only just big enough to take the rivet. When several rivets are used in a join, drill the hole for one rivet at a time. Insert and head up each rivet before drilling the next hole and completing that rivet. This assures correct hole alignment. Be sure the pieces to be joined are firmly clamped together before riveting.

After each drilling, clean off surplus metal which may have come from the drill's action. Then insert the rivet, place the formed head against a vice or metal block, and hammer the "driven" head to form a flare.

To obtain the correct amount of metal to make the driven head, be sure that the rivet shank extends through the work a distance $1\frac{1}{4}$ to $1\frac{1}{2}$ times the rivet diameter.

To start to form the driven head, use the flat of the hammer directly in line with the rivet shank for the first few blows. Then use the ball face of the hammer to tap around the edge of the rivet to force the metal down and around the work. In this way, make the driven head look like the original formed head.

It is essential to use only aluminum rivets.

To remove rivets which have been badly driven, center-drill through the head of the rivet, using a drill the same size as was used for the original hole. To locate the hole

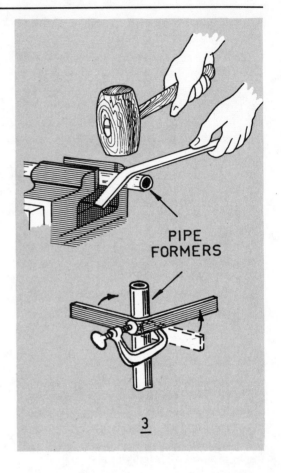

PIPE
FORMERS

3

accurately through the center of the rivet, file a flat area on the rivet head and center-punch on the exact center to start the drill properly.

Slots and tabs can be employed to join sheets at right angles. Cut slots with a $\frac{1}{4}$ in. chisel as shown in Fig. 4. Use snips or strong scissors and chisel for cutting the tabs which will fit neatly into the slots of the opposite sheet.

Insert the tabs and lock the joint by bending the tabs in opposite directions.

One of the most practical jobs that can be done with aluminum is the making of fly-screen window and door frames.

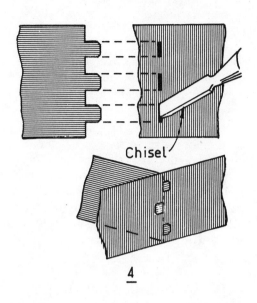

Chisel

4

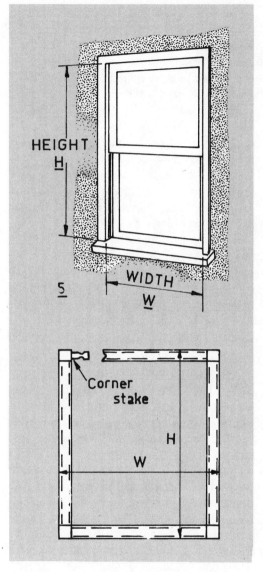

HEIGHT
H

WIDTH
W

5

Corner
stake

H

W

Special extruded sections together with corner pieces, hinges, etc., are available.

The first stage in such a job is to take the measurements for the frame and this is done in the way shown in Fig. 5.

If the screen is to fit over the win-frame (using flush type hinges) deduct 1/16 in. from the width and height of the window opening for clearance.

If the screen is to stand proud of the window frame (using offset hinges) add at least ½ in. to width and height of the window opening to give sufficient cover.

For the miter corner, assemble frame using miter, corner staking pieces and while still loose, check corners to ensure satisfactory mitering.

Cut framing members using a fine tooth hacksaw. Smooth sharp edges with a file or sandpaper. Assemble frame using corner staking pieces, checking with a square to ensure a right angle assembly.

The corner pieces should require only moderate pressure to make a tight fit. How-

ever, if too tight they may be eased by gently sandpapering or filing.

If corners are too loose, gently squeeze in the end of the frame member.

Corners may be permanently fixed by dimpling the frame section with a nail punch.

For best results use only aluminum or fiberglass insect screen mesh.

Cut mesh to the same size as the outside dimensions of frame. Tensioning of the screen may be effected more easily if several inches of screening are left extended at one end and then trimmed off after the PVC beading has been inserted.

Place frame on a cleared table, groove side up. Scatter small pieces of frame section in center area to hold mesh level, then line up mesh with outside edges of frame.

Press the screen mesh into the groove starting at one corner and working down the long side of the frame. Use a flat instrument or a rounded tool such as a wooden clothes pin so as not to mark the frame or damage the PVC. Press in PVC beading after inserting 12 to 18 in. of mesh. It may help to soften the PVC by soaking in hot water prior to its insertion. Repeat the procedure around the frame, trim off the excess and your frame is ready for fitting.

AVOID CONTACT WITH OTHER METALS. Where other metals contact aluminum for extended periods with moisture present, electro-galvanic reaction may result. For this reason, it is wise to use only aluminum fasteners, hinges and joining materials. However, should it become necessary to use iron or steel accessories, or to join aluminum with iron or steel, it is necessary to paint, enamel or lacquer the hardware first before fastening to the aluminum.

Aluminum paint is ideal for this purpose. This precaution is essential in any area where moisture may be present.

Contact between aluminum and copper, brass or copper alloys should also be avoided.

In perfectly dry conditions, aluminum does not need special protection when in contact with concrete. Some reaction may occur under wet conditions.

It is recommended that the embedded portions of aluminum should first be treated with a good bituminous paint.

Mortar, plaster and exterior stucco finishes may cause staining to the aluminum and care should be given to the storage and use of these materials near aluminum.

If aluminum is used in contact with zinc, it will be the zinc which will corrode in a damp atmosphere.

Contact with the ground over long periods may cause damage to aluminum, depending on the amount of moisture and free alkali in the soil. If aluminum is used for trellis work, garden markers or decorative garden borders, apply one or two coats of aluminum or bituminous paint to those areas to be covered with earth.

ALUMINUM—Edgings, Strips, etc.

Aluminum has become very popular for building purposes and has a variety of uses in that field.

Apart from flat sheets, aluminum is also obtainable in sections—moldings, edging, strips, etc., which are useful for fixing around the exposed edges of panels made from fiberboard and similar materials.

They conceal the edges, form a protective lipping, and have a high decorative value, giving a distinctive modern touch.

Some take the form of an angle strip which overlaps the surface as well as the edge, and is useful for fitting around the edges of shelves, cabinet framework, bed headboards and so on.

They should be selected to suit the thickness of material being used.

Some have one wing wider than the other. Other sections form easy-to-clean corners; some are parting beads for doors and there are plain strips.

Screws are the simplest and most satisfactory method of fixing. Generally, countersunk screws are used, though some may prefer roundhead.

Plated screws are preferable as they are not liable to rust, and the color matches that of the aluminum.

The holes are best drilled with a morse drill of the type used by metal workers.

It is necessary to make an indentation at the position with a center punch.

This forms a socket in which the drill can be started. Without it the drill is liable to wander.

Those having an electric drill will find this ideal, but otherwise the normal breast drill can be used.

As aluminum is comparatively soft, certain precautions in handling it are essential.

It bends easily—indeed, if gripped strongly in the hand the angle section is liable to be bent out of shape.

It is, therefore, necessary to support it adequately, and the simplest way is to place the strip along a flat piece of wood as in Fig. 1.

To countersink the holes the normal snail countersink used in woodwork is more satisfactory than the rose type intended for brass.

The latter is liable to choke owing to the softness of the metal. The snail type keeps its edge surprisingly well.

It will be found after drilling that the metal all round the underside of the holes has been bent downward owing to the pressure of the drill.

This is easily removed with an ordinary wood chisel.

The hacksaw is the best tool for cutting, and a blade with fairly large teeth is advisable to allow space for the chips.

Fine teeth are liable to clog.

Take precautions against accidental bending by screwing a wood strip to the bench and placing the aluminum over this, Fig. 2.

Small sections can be held steady with the left hand while the saw is used with the right.

Larger sections are best held by a wedge driven between the metal and a dowel bored into the bench. This enables the saw to be used with both hands.

A miter box is a handy appliance for cutting miters.

The angle is placed over a square strip of wood. This supports it, prevents accidental bending and keeps it square in the right position for sawing.

On all your aluminum projects, use aluminum nails, screws, and other hardware made of aluminum.

If these materials aren't available, then use chrome—or cadmium-plated hardware to avoid unsightly rust or corrosion.

Before you tackle any original designs or ideas, draw and lay out the project on heavy paper or light cardboard.

The paper or cardboard can be bent or folded to follow your design.

In this way you will avoid wasting any metal and can make corrections before a single piece of metal is measured and cut.

ALUMINUM PAINT—Uses

Several unusual properties of aluminum paint make it especially adaptable to household use, both indoors and out.

Practical tests show that aluminum paint prolongs the life of finishing paints applied over it. It forms a seal against moisture and has remarkable durability and covering power. This is due to the "leafing" action of the individual metal flakes which comprise the pigment.

The flakes are flat and overlap like leaves or shingles on a roof. Due to this leafing action, one coat of aluminum paint, properly applied, will hide any color—even black.

However, because of its nature, it is essential to keep aluminum paint constantly stirred when using.

It is especially effective over woods that do not hold paint well. The formation of a "toothed" surface bonds the succeeding coats of standard oil paint or enamel and prevents scaling and peeling.

Two jobs where this paint is extremely useful are for covering tar or creosote stains on timber that is to be painted in light colors, and also as a primer-sealer over stains or plaster walls. The main purpose is to prevent the stains bleeding through and spoiling the finishing coats of paint.

On metal exposed to the elements, aluminum paint is often used as a brilliant silvery finishing coat over a high-grade red lead or iron-oxide primer.

Although aluminum paint can be used as a primer under enamel or exterior metal work, it can be used as a final coat over metal primers because of the attractive finish it produces.

ALUMINUM—Soldering

Soldering an article made of aluminum is often regarded as a difficult job, but if care is taken, and the correct procedure followed, the result should be satisfactory.

The work is done with a special aluminum solder sold by hardware stores. No flux is needed, but the surfaces to be joined should be cleaned thoroughly with fine grade abrasive paper.

The two joining surfaces are first "tinned" or coated with the special solder. The usual method of doing this is to heat each piece with a gas flame or blowtorch until the solder melts when pressed against it.

To make the solder "take," spread it with a piece of stiff wire or by rubbing it with clean steel wool. This removes the oxide film and enables the solder to adhere.

It is sometimes easier to cut off small pieces of the solder and feed them on to the surfaces as you go.

An alternative method of tinning on small jobs is to use an ordinary soldering iron, the point of which has been filed down to the bare copper to remove all traces of the old solder. Heat the iron until it will melt the aluminum solder, then rub the iron over the surface to spread the molten solder.

After the surfaces to be joined have been tinned, press them together and heat until the solder melts and the joint becomes solid. If necessary, the joint can be smoothed with a spatula just before the solder hardens.

Where it isn't practicable to tin or cover the meeting surfaces before joining—for example when soldering a joint where two pieces of aluminum are riveted together, to make it watertight—the solder can be flowed straight on to the joint as in ordinary soldering.

The same general method is used. First heat the work with a blowtorch flame or—on small jobs—by holding a cleaned hot soldering iron against it. When the solder is in contact with the work, it melts, and is spread as before with a piece of wire, steel wool, or the point of the soldering iron.

An alternative bonding method for aluminum which does not require heat is to use an epoxy-resin cement. This is mixed from a two tube pack as required. However, the parts to be joined must be clamped together for at least twelve hours until the cement sets and hardens.

ALUMINUM—Tools Needed

More and more aluminum is being used around the home and cutting tools for aluminum projects will depend upon the thickness and shape of the stock being used.

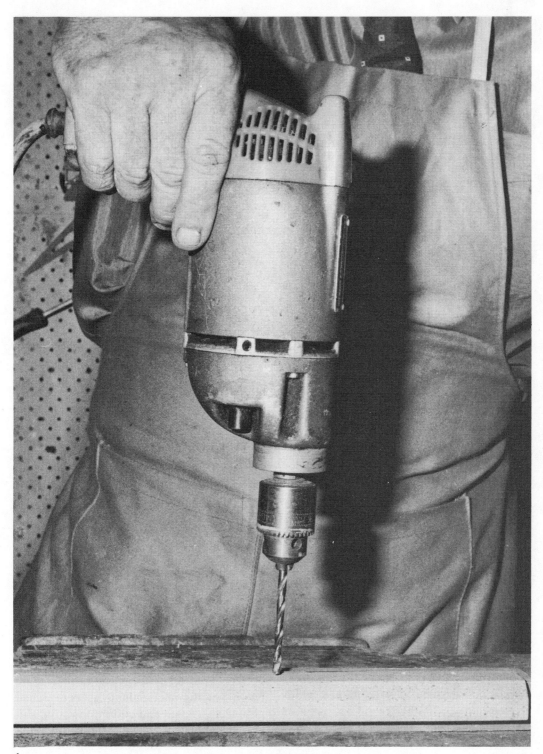

1

2

For tubes, rods, bars and extruded shapes, a good wood saw or hacksaw will do.

The more teeth per inch on the saw blade the finer and neater the cut.

Irregular curved lines can be cut with precision and fine edges with a coping, scroll, or jeweler's saw.

A pocket knife will remove burrs from inside tubes and can be used for small interior cuts on the plain and embossed sheets.

An ordinary pair of household scissors or combination tin snips will cut the plain and embossed sheet aluminum easily and accurately.

Small interior areas can be cut cleanly and neatly with a sharp cold chisel or a wood chisel. The metal should be laid over a piece of smooth scrap wood to save the tool edge when using a wood chisel.

Long-toothed single-cut files which do not clog up are effective cutting tools. A file card or steel brush will keep the teeth clean.

Auger bits in a carpenter's brace or a hand drill with twist drills will cut screw and rivet holes and also enlarge existing holes. All sheets must be backed with scrap wood for neat, clean holes.

Drilling accuracy in sheet, bar, tube or angle stock will be guaranteed if you use a center punch or nail tapped lightly to give the bit a resting place.

Your regular woodworking planes are suitable for dressing down the aluminum stock of sheet, bar or angle material. Always make a light cut and repeat cuts to get greater depth of cut.

A wood-cutting expansion bit backed up with smooth scrap wood will cut the large holes efficiently and cleanly in sheet stock.

Various hammers and mallets are useful in bending and forming aluminum sheet metal, bars and angle stock. Plastic tipped, rubber, wood and rawhide mallets will prevent marring and marking your projects.

ANCHORS — Wall Plugs

Shown here are various methods of securely fastening articles to a wall surface where it is not possible to screw directly into the wall material.

Fig. 1. For most fastening jobs, the fiber plug is suitable. In solid brick, stone or cement, it proves an extremely strong hold and needs only a small hole drilled in the wall.

Fig. 2. Where the hole has become enlarged or the brickwork has cracked, use asbestos filling compound. A tool is sold with the compound for pressing it well into the hole, and piercing a start for the screw.

Fig. 3. All-metal wall plugs resemble fiber plugs, but obviate the necessity to center the screw onto the plug, as both are inserted as one unit.

Fig. 4. Where a hole drilled for a fiber plug or filling compound breaks through into a cavity, use U-clips. They prevent the compound from being pushed through the hole.

Fig. 5. Ideal for lath and plaster walls is the spring toggle. A spring opens the "wings" inside the wall, and they provide a large load-bearing surface.

Fig. 6. The bolt with rubber sleeve is an adaptable method of fastening to partition walls, wallboards, plaster boards, etc. It is soundproof, vibration-free and waterproof.

Fig. 7. Rawl anchors are another type of fastener for wallboards, cavity walls, etc. The action of screwing in the bolt bends the arms of the rawl anchor behind the wall, which hold the nut permanently in position.

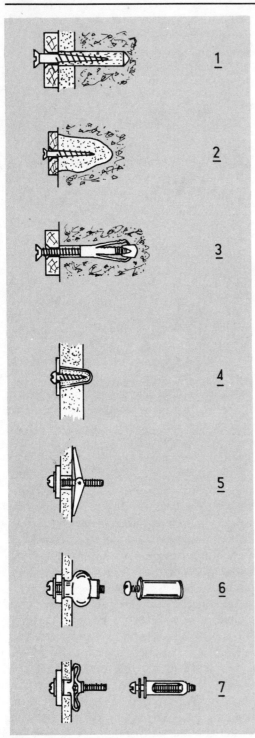

1

2

3

4

5

6

7

Fig. 8. For pictures, mirrors and other light fixtures use an angle-drive. Held by either one or two steel pins, they are strong and neat.

8

ANGLE DIVIDER — Use

In woodworking there are many occasions when it is necessary to lay out a cut dividing an angle.

Doing this with an ordinary bevel generally calls for the use of dividers when transferring the proper angle to the work.

However, with an angle divider it is possible to take the correct angle directly from the work and automatically the handle is in position for obtaining the miter for the angle.

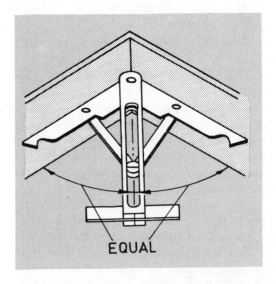

EQUAL

This tool is designed for bisecting or dividing any angle. It is especially handy for fitting trim, molding, and flooring into corners and odd angles.

The blades of the angle divider are adjusted to fit properly into the corner of angle to be fitted, see illustration. The angle formed by the two arms is divided perfectly by the position of the handle at all times.

Thus, by placing the handle along the work which is to fit in the corner, the correct angle is obtained and the work easily marked for making a perfect fit.

The handle is graduated on one side for laying out 4, 5, 6, 8 or 10-sided work. Used with the 'T' blade it makes an accurate try square.

ANGLES — Compound Cuts

The dished or flared type of modern picture frame is a good example of the application of compound angle cutting. That is, instead of the miter joint at the corners being a plain, flat 45 degrees it also protrudes outward.

Cutting such compound miters or angles give many woodworkers considerable trouble, especially when working from a complicated formula.

Here is a very simple but practicable method which can be adapted for use on most average-size home workshop circular-saw benches fitted with a miter gauge.

The saw table is not tilted but left square to the saw blade. A guide block of convenient size and ripped to the desired angle is then prepared.

As a guide this angle could be the one between the dished frame and the surface of the wall—usually 30 degrees.

The procedure, then, for a standard four-sided picture frame would be to set the miter

gauge to 45 degrees, place the guide block next to the miter guide, then the frame material on top of the block and make the cut. All these points are shown clearly in the illustration.

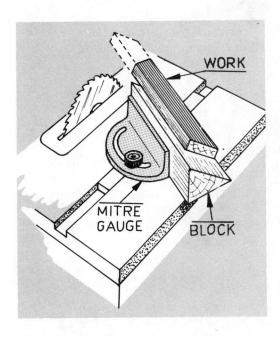

An advantage with this method of cutting is that it is not confined to cutting four-sided frames. Pyramids or hoppers of any angle and any number of sides, tapered flower-boxes and tapered footstools may be cut and assembled.

Two typical examples which will serve as a guide are three-sided and five-sided plaque frames.

As with the orthodox four-sided picture frame both the odd-sided frames have a 30 degree angle of tilt.

But for the five-sided frame the miter gauge is set at 36 degrees (180 degrees divided by 5), with a 60 degree miter set-up for the three-sided frame.

ANT CAPS — Placing

In the section dealing with the eradication and control of white ants (termites), reference is made to the necessity of fitting ant caps.

The placing of galvanized iron caps over all piers, walls and around fireplaces is also vitally necessary, and even here an occasional inspection is needed, as the pests have been known to build their runs out beyond the lip of the cap, over the top, and so into the timber.

Many people are under the impression that such capping is a sure protection against white ants, but such is not the case. The value of using caps lies in the fact that they are a barricade, which, combined with vigilance, helps to keep the white ants away.

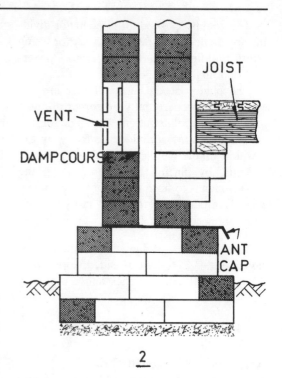

2

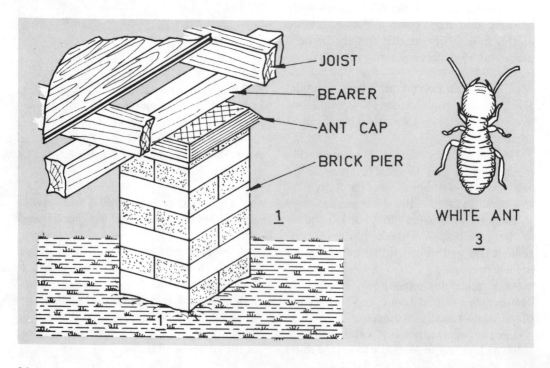

1

WHITE ANT

3

Fig. 1 shows an ant cap fitted over a pier with bearer, joists and floor above. Without this barrier these timber members and other timber would be wide open to white ant attack.

But it is not only the piers that need attention. Note that in Fig. 2 continuous ant capping is used between foundations and outer walls. Fig. 3 gives some idea of the appearance of the troublesome white ant.

ANTIQUE — Finish

Many homeworkers are keen to try their hand at producing an antique finish, and this can best be done on an old piece of furniture which is in reasonably good condition.

First remove old varnish or paint with a stripping solution, then rub with sandpaper until the surface is smooth. Start with a medium-grade paper, and finish with very fine grade.

Next apply enamel undercoat, being careful that grooves in carvings or other ornamentations are not filled with paint.

After the surface is completely dry, paint a coat of light colored enamel over it. The color should depend on your decorating theme, but you may use the lightest tones of either buff, grey, green, blue, pink, or even white.

Glazing of the surface comes next. In a shallow dish mix together one and a half teaspoons of burnt umber, three tablespoons of turpentine, and one tablespoon of clear varnish. With a small, soft brush apply this glaze to the surface of the furniture.

Work slowly and don't cover more than about a three-square-foot area at a time. Keep a clean soft cloth handy, and after you glaze an area, wipe over it with delicate strokes to produce a grained effect.

This is, more or less, a trial-and-error operation, but quite fascinating. If you are not pleased with the result, quickly wipe off the glaze with a rag dipped in turpentine. Then go over the area again with the glaze and repeat the light wiping action.

Continue this operation until the entire surface has been treated, but take care to merge the sections so that there are no distinct breaks between them.

The appearance at this stage should be one suggesting age, with suggestions of the undercoat appearing through and below the darker glaze.

Clear varnish is used as a final coat, and this operation should be left until the weather is fine and warm. Allow the varnish to flow without excessive brushing. When thoroughly dry, the surface is ready for rubbing down.

Use a soft cloth dipped first into light oil—sewing-machine oil is very good—then into finely powdered pumice. Rub the cloth gently over the surface. This will produce a satiny finish. The final touch is to remove any dust from the surface with a dry, clean cloth without exerting any pressure.

APPLIANCES (Electrical) — Running Costs

Electrical appliances are the modern householder's servants—they do the work and they don't make work.

Electricity sheds light and gives comfortable warmth unobtrusively and without causing the slightest effort to the user.

It is, in fact, so unobtrusive that you probably don't notice it unless by some unusual mischance it fails to function, or until the monthly bill comes in.

When the bill seems beyond all reason do you stop using your vacuum cleaner regularly? Do you switch off lights and grope about in semi-darkness? Or do you study just how much current your lighting and electrical appliances use?

LIGHTING. Economy is not worthwhile. A 100-watt bulb costs about a tenth of a penny an hour. Good lighting is essential to avoid undue strain on eyes and nervous system and for safety in the home. But remember you will need higher powered lamps if your shades, upholstery or decorations are dark.

FLUORESCENT LIGHTS. There is no real economy in switching off these lights for short periods. They use far less current than tungsten lamps but their highest consumption is when they come on. Frequent switching on shortens the life of the tube.

APPLIANCES OPERATED BY MOTOR. A vacuum cleaner, polisher, washing machine, refrigerator or mixer use very little current. Their size and the fact that they make some noise may be misleading. They are far less costly to run than a small electric heater.

HEATING. Any appliance that uses a heating element, whether it is a small room heater, an iron, a kitchen stove or hotplate, a water heater, a kettle or a washing machine, is more costly to run than the motorized appliances.

It is very easy to run up bills by using heating appliances extravagantly. Extravagance is caused by choosing the wrong appliance for the job; using the appliance in the wrong way; having it incorrectly installed; or not making use of thermostat control.

THE STOVE. An antiquated stove uses far more current than a modern one and produces results more slowly, so think twice about clinging to your old friend (the same

applies to old refrigerators). Use pans with level bases; on the old-fashioned, flat, solid hotplates use machined-base pans.

ARCH BAR — Use

An arch bar—also known as a chimney bar —is basically a bonding agent across an opening in a brick wall.

This opening could be a doorway, chimney breast, or a passageway entry.

As shown in the illustration, the bar has a bow or camber and the ends of the bar rest securely on each side.

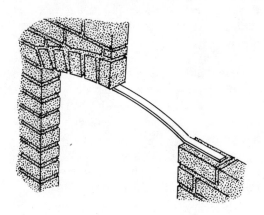

ASBESTOS CEMENT ROOFING —
To Fix

Corrugated asbestos cement sheeting is a very popular roofing material for garages, annexes, outbuildings and workshops. When properly laid, it provides a sound, watertight roof covering, but being a rather brittle material it must be handled and used with care.

The sheets are normally fastened to purlins, which can either be metal angle irons or timber beams. When fastening the sheets to angle irons, special hooked bolts are used as shown in Fig. 1.

The hooked part is slipped around the iron and secured with a fixing nut on top of the sheet. When making the holes in the asbestos sheets to receive the fixing bolts, use a brace and drill. Don't try to punch the holes with a sharp tool. This tends to break away the lower surface, thus reducing the effective thickness of the sheets. Always ensure that the fixing nuts are positioned on top of the corrugations—never in the hollows.

To spread the pressure imposed by the fixing nuts over a larger area, metal washers of diamond shape should be used. These are generally curved to suit the corrugations on the sheets. Bituminous felt washers are also used in addition to metal washers so that each hole is made watertight.

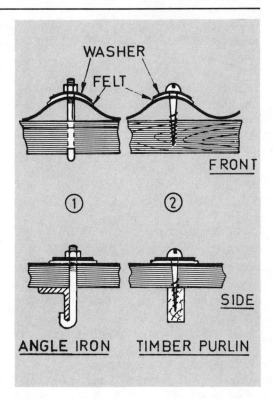

When securing asbestos sheets with hooked bolts, it is best to work with an assistant. One can then be inside the building, pushing the bolts through the holes in the sheets and hooking them round the angle irons, while the other is on top of the roof attaching the washers and tightening up the nuts.

If the sheets are to be fixed to timber purlins, then special screw nails are used. Holes are bored in the sheets as before and the screw nails are driven home with a hammer. The threads on the nails cause them to twist as they are being inserted, thus giving a firm grip of the wood. Care must be taken not to drive the nails in too far, otherwise the sheets will fracture. This type of fastening is shown in Fig. 2.

Corrugated asbestos sheets are obtainable in a variety of standard widths and lengths, so that the handyman should have no difficulty in getting material to span the full extent of the roof. If the roof is double

pitched, that is, two slopes meeting at a central ridge, then special ridge pieces must be used.

It is most probable that the sheets will have to be cut to size and this can be done with an old fine-toothed handsaw. Don't use a good saw for cutting cement asbestos because it will play havoc with the teeth. A special type of hacksaw is used for cutting these sheets.

It takes ordinary sized hacksaw blades and is designed so that the top bar does not get in the way when cutting.

If you are not too keen on their natural grey color, then why not paint the sheets? Special paints are now manufactured for this purpose, and can be obtained from most paint stores. Ordinary paint is not satisfactory.

ASBESTOS CEMENT SHEET WALLS —
To Clean

The asbestos cement sheets used widely for building garages and sheds sometimes become dirty and stained when left unpainted.

Cleaning the surface is usually fairly simple, and here are details for dealing with the various types of stains that occur.

Iron rust stains from gutters, nails, hinges, etc., may be brushed with a very weak solution of hydrochloric acid—about one part acid to seventy parts of water. These parts are by volume.

Take care when using this solution. It is very poisonous and corrosive, and should be handled carefully and kept away from skin and clothing, and out of the reach of children.

After use, rinse down thoroughly, as any residue on the surface could have an etching effect on the cement surface.

Wood stains caused by tannin usually respond to scrubbing well with a solution of household cleaner or with household bleaching solution.

A weak solution of cleaning powder sold for cleaning down domestic paintwork may also be used.

For soot and dirt, first try brushing with a stiff brush. If necessary, scrub with household bleaching solution, then rinse thoroughly with water. In extreme cases use the fine jet from a garden hose.

Asphalt or tar stains will usually respond to rubbing with a cloth moistened with mineral turpentine. Here several applications are usually necessary.

ASPHALT — Paving

When contemplating paving work around the house we usually think in terms of concrete, and there is no doubt that well-mixed concrete makes a permanent job.

However, concrete entails considerable work and expense, and for certain jobs asphalt gives very good results—for example, paths in the backyard or between garden beds.

Asphalt paths can be laid in two ways. The first is to get the solid bitumen, make it into a liquid by heating, then mix fine metal with the liquid bitumen to form the body of the path. This is the method used in most big jobs.

The second method is quite different, and is the one which has a definite appeal to the home worker. Here we use what is called a bitumen emulsion. It is used cold, and is simply a solution of water and bitumen.

In consistency, the emulsion is not much heavier than water, and is normally a deep brown color.

Broadly speaking, the main purpose of the bitumen emulsion is to act as a binder for the fine metal forming the bulk of the paths, and here, briefly, is the procedure.

First and foremost, have the foundation of the path solid and well drained. This may call for the excavation of soil or clay to a depth of say 4 in. and filling with hard broken bricks or similar rubble which is well rammed. This could be covered and leveled off with clean boiler ash.

Sweep any loose dust away from the path area and roll in a base of ½ in. grade metal screenings to a thickness of 1½ in. This should be consolidated well, but not too tightly packed, as the first application of the emulsion should be able to penetrate the surface of this metal base and surround the pieces.

Two applications of the emulsion and metal over the base are usually sufficient to produce a hard-wearing surface.

AXES — Types, To Sharpen

Every tool needs care in use and sharpening, but naturally the method will vary with different types of tools.

For example Fig. 1 shows an axe and two hatchets. The broad hatchet (A) is a very useful carpenter's tool for rough trimming, and the half-hatchet is a good general purpose tool to have in the home tool kit.

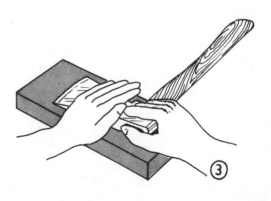

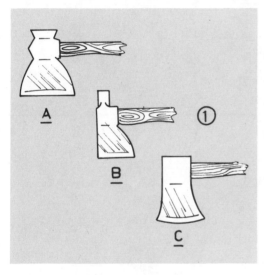

It is often necessary to grind an axe or hatchet to remove nicks and gaps in the cutting edge. This is best done by holding the edge horizontally against an abrasive wheel and moving it back and forth across the revolving edge as shown in Fig. 2. Follow this by grinding the cutting edge to the correct bevel.

Careless grinding will ruin any axe through heat caused by friction, or by making the edge so thin that it will not stand up under the force of a swinging blow. It is never advisable to grind an axe or hatchet on a high speed dry abrasive wheel. Grind slowly on a large diameter wheel which should be kept wet.

Start to grind about 2 in. back from the cutting edge and grind to about ½ in. from the edge. Work for a fan-shape effect, leaving reinforcement at corners adequate for sufficient strength. Then "roll off" on a convex bevel.

Remove all scratches with a whetstone or hone. A scratch or score on highly tempered steel will sometimes cause a break.

For sharpening a straight-edged blade, such as the hatchet (A) in Fig. 1, place the tool on a lightly oiled oilstone. Then tilt so that the bevel lies flat on the stone as in Fig. 3.

Hold the right wrist rigid—no sidewise twist—and move the tool back and forth on

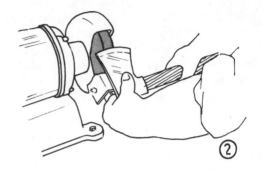

the stone. If the tool is ground with a double bevel, turn it over and repeat the operation.

For curved-edge tools such as the axe (C) Fig. 1, a different procedure is followed. Place the stone flat on the bevel of the blade with the tool itself held stationary. Apply light pressure, and move the stone with a circular motion.

Detail (A) Fig. 4 shows a side view of the stone being used on a tool with a double bevel cutting edge. Here an equal amount of honing is needed on each side.

In detail (B) Fig. 4, the stone is held flat against the back of a single-bevel hatchet and rubbed lightly several times to remove the slight wire edge or burr produced when honing the bevel to produce a cutting edge.

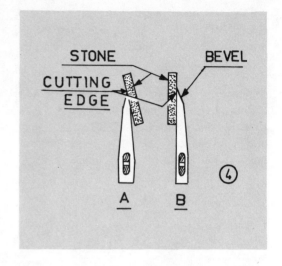

BELTS	V-Type
BENCH ACCESSORIES	To Make
BENCH	For Workshop
BLEACHING	Of Timber
BOLTS	Door Fitting
BORERS	Eliminating
BRACE & BITS	Selection
BRASS	To Clean
BRICK FIREPLACE	Restore Color
BRICKLAYING	Guide
BRICKWORK	Repointing
BRICKWORK	Stained
BRUSHES	Care
BRUSHES	For Painting
BUILDER'S SQUARE	To Make
BUILDING PAPER	Uses
BUTT GAUGE	Use

BELTS — V-Type

Until an appliance or electrical device breaks down in your home you probably aren't aware of just how the motor operates.

Usually the motor transmits its power by means of pulleys and V-belts. Many cleaners make use of them, as do washing machines, refrigerators, many power tools, and countless other appliances.

Since most belts are out of view—being concealed behind a guard in most cases—their condition is generally overlooked until they break or cease to function.

The first precaution with any V-belt is to adjust and maintain correct tension. First, measure the distance from center to center of the pulleys. Then apply light pressure downward with thumb at the half-way point. For each two feet between the pulley centers, the belt should be deflected half its own thickness. See illustration.

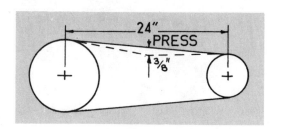

Here are some common causes of damage to V-belts with suggested remedies:

SPLIT ALONG THE TOP. This indicates that the belt has been used on a pulley that was too small. The remedy is to use a larger pulley or a smaller belt.

BROKEN BELT. There could be several causes of a broken V-belt, but having it so loose that it slips is perhaps the most common.

Loose belts often develop a crack—caused by a whip-like action. This could cause them to break. In such cases there is obviously a need to adjust the tension.

TORN FABRIC. Torn fabric covering the sides of most V-belts could be the result of roughness on the inside faces of the pulley track; but more often than not it is caused by a screwdriver being used to pry or lever the belt onto the pulley.

Torn fabric wears rapidly, so trim off any loose sections or cement them down with a rubber adhesive and move the motor to adjust the tension.

OIL ON BELT. When oil drips onto the pulley or belt it will cause slipping and eventually the belt will deteriorate until it is weakened and snaps, so stop any oil leaks.

FRICTION. Uneven wear and friction can be caused by faulty alignment of the pulleys on the motor and the appliance. Burning may even result. One sure indication is the smell of burning rubber or fabric.

Along with other regular household inspections, double check your V-belts—with machinery shut down and power switched off, naturally—and replace those with obvious signs of wear.

BENCH ACCESSORIES — To Make

Apart from a kit of standard hand tools, every woodworker needs the items detailed below.

They are concerned mainly with timber cutting on the bench and in all cases fairly hard, dry timber should be used.

MITER BLOCK. Fig. 1 shows a miter block which is ideal for small work. In construction, the top kerfed piece is glued down to the base.

It is quite a good plan to fix another strip beneath the front edge and steady the whole block.

Exact sizes need not be followed. Those given in the illustration may be taken as an approximate guide.

Mark out the 45 and 90 degrees cut on the top of the guide block and square them down at the edge.

To ensure that the saw follows the lines exactly, they can be cut in with chisel or marking knife and a sloping groove cut at one side. This will form a channel in which the saw can run.

It will be noted that the saw kerfs do not run quite to the bottom of the guide block. The reason for this is that if they did they would sever the guide block entirely.

In use, a strip of wood is placed along the base of the block and the saw is thus able to reach right to the bottom of the molding.

The 90 degrees cut, of course, is useful when it is necessary to cut the end of a piece of wood perfectly square.

In addition, a fourth cut at $67\frac{1}{2}$ degrees **is sometimes made. This is the true mitering** angle for 135 degrees which consists of a right angle plus 45 degrees, an arrangement which often occurs in cabinetmaking.

MITER BOX, Fig. 2. This is required for the larger moldings such as cornice moldings, etc.

It is essential that it be made from a sound timber because the cutting of the miter kerfs weakens the sides considerably and they might be liable to curl.

Plane up the three parts and fix the two sides to the base with glue and nails. It is, of course, essential for the top edges to be perfectly parallel with the bottom.

Across the top edges mark out the 45 degrees and the 90 degrees lines and square them down across the outside faces.

For cutting the kerfs you should use the

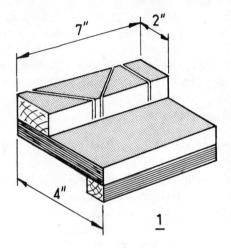

1

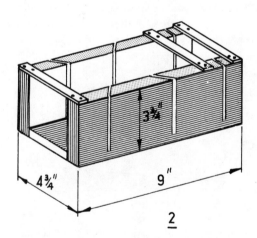

2

same saw that you will normally use for **mitering, either the tenon saw or a finely** toothed panel saw.

Fix the work down on the bench and, placing the saw on the line, begin to cut. The toe of the saw must be exactly on the line at the far side of the box, but it should not cut in far.

The sawing should be mainly on the near side. The handle of the saw just drops considerably as the cut progresses. Afterwards the box is reversed and the cut completed down the other side.

It is far easier to control the saw when it follows the front cut only and all risk of the saw wandering at the far side is avoided.

Note that the cuts stop short about ¼ in., from the bottom of the box. Strips of wood can be glued and nailed across the top afterwards to prevent any tendency for them to curl.

BENCH HOOK, Fig. 3. The uses of this are fairly obvious. It simply serves to hold wood while it is being sawn on the bench.

Once again sizes can vary considerably.

One essential point is that the piece fixed beneath the front edge must be doweled on, not screwed or nailed.

It is inevitable that after considerable use the wood of the base becomes deeply furrowed with saw cuts, and eventually the nail or screw might be uncovered and the saw jarred upon it. The use of dowels prevents this.

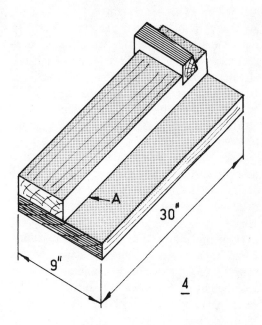

4

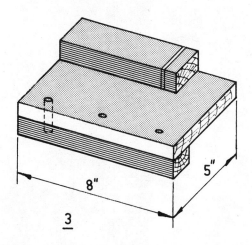

3

SHOOTING BOARD. A shooting board is used mainly for trimming the ends of timber pieces and can be made as shown in Fig. 4.

Here a fairly soft wood is suitable if sound and seasoned.

It is advisable, however, to have the heart side on the two pieces facing in opposite directions so that any tendency in the one piece to cup is countered by that in the other.

The edge of the top piece must be perfectly straight, but is planed over at a very slight angle, otherwise when the plane is used the cutter will remove shavings from it.

Note that the lower corner (A) is planed off at about 45 degrees. This is to form a dust groove. If it is not made dust is liable to accumulate in the corner and this will prevent the plane from running true.

The stop is best if tapered somewhat. It fits in a groove, the front edge of which is perfectly square with the running edge of the board. It is then tapped tightly home and the projecting end sawn off.

BENCH — For Workshop

A bench is an essential piece of workshop equipment, and the one described here is extremely strong and sturdy. The bench top should be as level as possible, and the front board at least should be sufficiently thick to absorb heavy blows as, for instance, when mortising. Well-seasoned hardwood could be used for the bench.

There are no rigid rules about the size of a bench. A lot will depend on the size of the workshop and the amount of space available. Suggested sizes for this particular bench are 6 ft long by 2 ft wide. A good average height is 2 ft 11 in. though this could be adapted to suit the height of the user. A good guide for determining the correct height is to make the surface of the bench level with the hip bone of the person likely to be using it most.

MAIN FRAMEWORK. The two main leg frames are made first, and the method of construction is shown clearly in Fig. 1.

The lower rail or each frame should be about 6 in. from the floor; these rails are tenoned into the legs, the tenons being glued and wedged. The top rails are secured with open mortise and tenon joints, the joints in this case also being glued and doweled. As it is imperative that the frames be square, a careful test should be made diagonally from corner to corner before placing them aside until the glue hardens.

As in Figs 1 and 2, the front apron piece is housed into a recess cut into the front top edge of each leg frame, and screwed into place to finish flush with the front edge of the bench top and face of the legs.

TOP. As most of the heavy work is done towards the front of the bench, the front board can be thicker than those towards the back, and one measuring 11 in. wide and 1½ in. thick is quite satisfactory. Obviously, care must be taken to see that the top boards especially are perfectly straight and free from loose knots or gum veins.

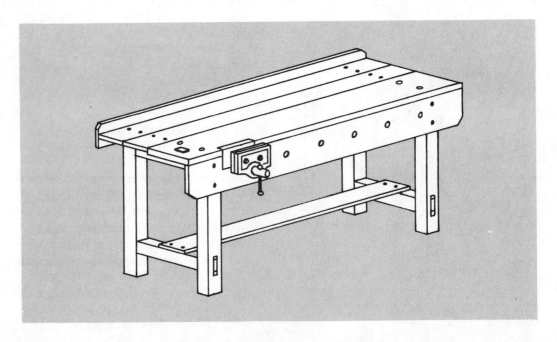

It is a good idea to bolt the front board to the frames as shown in Fig. 2 as this allows the board to be more easily reversed when the surface becomes worn. The heads of these bolts are recessed deeply, and the appearance of the bench is improved if the recesses are plugged with a short end of dowel glued into place. The width suggested (2 ft) is about the minimum for a bench, but if it can be made wider, so much the better.

As the two boards at the rear are thinner than the main front board, it is necessary to provide packing pieces underneath to build the boards up flush. These packing pieces are nailed to the frame, Fig. 3, and the boards screwed through them into the frames. The heads of the screws should be well countersunk below the surface. The back board is screwed in place, Fig. 2, and its purpose is to prevent tools or other articles being pushed over the back. Of course, if two workers are likely to use the bench, the back board could be removed and another vice fitted to the opposite end.

To complete the construction work, a spacing piece is cut and screwed to the bottom rails of the leg frames.

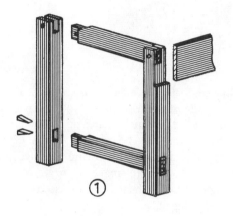

①

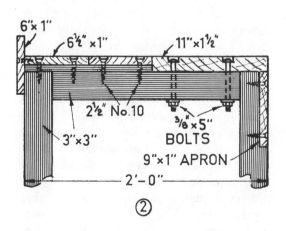

③

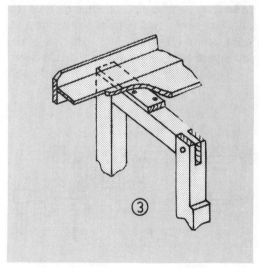

6″ x 1″
6½″ x 1″   11″ x 1½″
2½″ No. 10
⅜″ x 5″ BOLTS
3″ x 3″
9″ x 1″ APRON
2′-0″

②

FIXING THE VICE. The best type of woodworker's vice is that shown in Fig. 4, and one with an opening of at least 7 in. with 7 in. jaws is ideal. A larger size of vice is recommended where extensive work is involved. Two types of models of this particular vice are available, one with an ordinary screw action, and the other with a quick-action release and setting arrangement. The latter speeds up the work con-

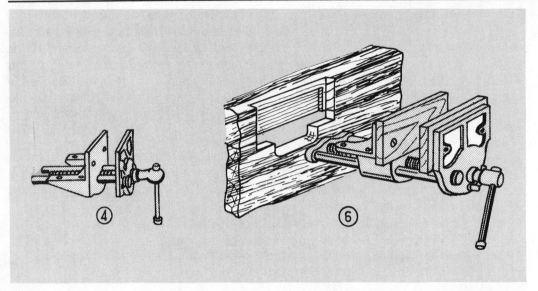

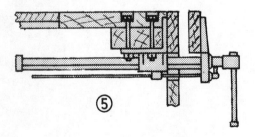

siderably, although, for home use, the ordinary screw type is quite satisfactory. As exposed metal parts are liable to cause damage to the tools, wooden cheeks which are fitted inside the metal jaws of the vice must project above the top edge of these metal jaws, see Fig. 5.

In fitting the vice, it is necessary to recess the front edge of the bench to receive both the metal jaw and its wooden cheek so that when the vice is fitted both cheeks are level with the top of the bench and the back metal jaw is entirely recessed as in Fig. 6. The opening in the front apron must be sufficiently large to allow the flange, two guide bars, and screw of the vice to pass

through, after which it is bolted to the underside of the top board. Note the packing piece in Fig. 5 which makes up the difference between the top board and flange of the vice. It is advisable to secure the vice with bolts and nuts to make it firm, and, as before, the bolt heads are recessed and the holes plugged.

When a long board is gripped in the vice for edge shooting, it is necessary to support the projecting end in some way. This can be done by resting the end on a hardwood plug which is inserted in one of a series of holes made in the apron piece, the holes being level with the vice screw (see drawing of finished bench).

BENCH STOP. Special metal bench stops having an adjustable flap with a serrated edge, Fig. 7, may be bought at any hardware store. These are recessed into the bench top so that they can be screwed down out of the way when not needed. However, there is always the danger that damage will be done to planes by accidental contact with the stop, and a simple but effective bench stop is shown in Fig. 8. It consists of two folding

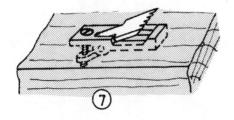

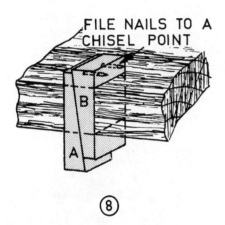

FILE NAILS TO A CHISEL POINT

off, and the top filed to a chisel edge. For cabinet work, however, it is better to omit them, as they are liable to leave marks which may be difficult to remove.

BLEACHING — Of Timber

Bleaching of timber can be done in several ways, and there are a number of commercial bleaches available.

Some of these produce very satisfactory results, and they will save quite a lot of trouble.

For those who prefer to prepare their own, there are a number of one-solution bleaches that can be used, such as oxalic acid (3 oz. to one quart of hot water), chloride of lime, and hydrogen peroxide (100 volume).

None of these is easy to control, and the results are at times unsatisfactory.

There is little doubt that the two-solution bleach is the best and the most easily controlled. The first solution is alkaline and the second is usually a high percentage of hydrogen peroxide.

Aqueous ammonia—made by diluting one part of 0.880 ammonia with five parts of water—is used for the first solution.

The second solution consists of hydrogen peroxide in the concentrated form (100 volume), or if the material is bleached readily it may be diluted up to four times with water.

All alkalis tend to darken wood, consequently there is usually a preliminary darkening effect with the No. 1 solution. Don't let this worry you, for the purpose of No. 1 is to cause the chemical reaction with the No. 2 solution, which does the actual bleaching.

wedges with a very slight taper. They are fitted to a hole about 2 in. square cut in the top of the bench in the planing position.

To lower the stop, piece (A) is tapped with the hammer to release it, and (B) is then knocked down to the required level. It may be necessary to knock up (A) from beneath to tighten the whole. To raise the stop, (B) is knocked up the required amount and tightened by tapping up (A). It is advisable to leave the ends at unequal levels—underneath at any rate—as this enables the two to be located more easily. Some may prefer to drive in a couple of nails near the top of B to prevent the wood slipping. They are knocked in, the heads are snipped

No. 1 solution is applied to the prepared wood with a mop or swab, and is immediately followed with solution No. 2 in a similar manner. The timber is allowed to dry thoroughly, after which the process is repeated if necessary.

Some timbers do not bleach readily, and in such cases the treatment may have to be repeated three or even four times before the desired result is obtained.

Hydrogen peroxide deteriorates if left standing, so buy only as much as is needed to do each job.

The ammonia fumes make it advisable to do the bleaching in the open air; if in a room see that all doors and windows are open before starting the bleaching operations.

When a satisfactory bleach has been obtained it is advisable to remove any chemical residue by wiping with warm water or methylated spirit.

BOLTS — Door Fittings

Various types of bolts are used for securing doors and hinged windows, all similar in operation, with a bolt sliding inside a metal tube or frame, though slightly different in design.

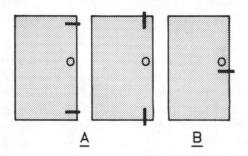

A   B

Barrel bolt, tower bolt, and pad bolt are three of the names used to describe them.

Bolts should be so placed that there is an even strain on the door, either by having a pair at top and bottom (A) or by using a single one near the middle (B).

Normally the bolt is on the door, but sometimes as with a wide jamb and the door opening towards the bolt, it is safer on the jamb.

Set the bolt square, and have it about ⅛ in. back from the door edge (C). This gives clearance, and allows the edge of the door to be planed off if it becomes necessary.

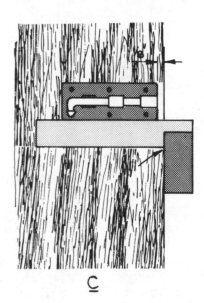

C

Fit the keeper plate over the end of the bolt, and screw it down while in this position.

If, on the other hand, the bolt is to be shot home into a hole, rub the end with chalk or pencil and press it into place to mark the jamb in the right place for drilling.

Drill the hole a little oversize to allow free entry of the bolt but not so big that there will be any movement or "play" in the door.

As a safety measure it is advisable to fix bolts on exterior doors with threaded coach bolts and nuts rather than screws.

BORERS—Eliminating

Borers in furniture and other woodwork can do a vast amount of damage unless checked. The holes and little piles of dust which they leave behind only indicate where borers have been, and not how many still remain.

In the spring and summer, the borer beetles swarm and lay their eggs in timber which will provide suitable food for the young grubs when they are hatched.

It is these grubs which do the damage. They travel into and through the timber and cause it to become honey-combed.

During all this time, there is no indication on the outside of what is going on below the surface. It is only when the grubs develop into mature beetles and emerge to start the cycle all over again that the trouble becomes apparent.

To eradicate the furniture borer the timber should be saturated with some kind of liquid cure so that it reaches the borer grubs and destroys them before they have a chance to bore their way out.

In the case of unpainted woodwork—say the backs or insides of pieces of furniture—repeated applications of the cure can be made with a brush. This is not possible, however, when the holes appear on painted or polished surfaces. Here, the liquid must be introduced into individual holes by means of a very fine syringe.

There are a number of effective commercial cures available, and a mixture consisting of 1 oz. of the fumigant para-dichlorobenzene dissolved in 1 pint of kerosene is also very good for treating furniture. For rough timber, such as floor joists and certain types of unpainted fences, creosote is a good preservative.

BRACE & BITS — Selection

When it comes to making holes with a carpenter's brace there is a vast array of drill bits from which to choose.

The brace itself can be bought in various sizes which are measured by the sweep or turning circle of the handle. A 10 or 12 in. sweep is best as smaller sizes may not give enough leverage when boring deep holes or using large-size bits. The brace illustrated at (G) is the best of all-purpose variety as it also allows ease of operation in a confined space.

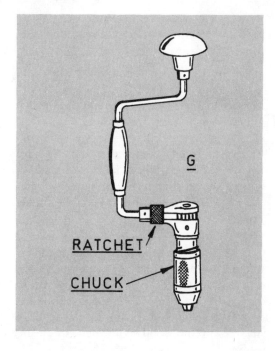

G

RATCHET

CHUCK

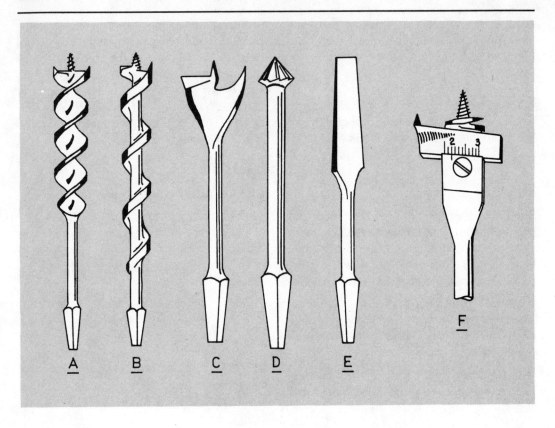

A   B   C   D   E   F

The most popular bits for boring deep holes are the twist bits, of which there are two main types. Both types have a square end to fit the brace chuck and a threaded screw point to draw the bit into the timber. The main difference lies in the twisted shank. Irwin pattern bits as in illustration (B) have one spiral which winds its way around a central shaft. A Jennings pattern bit (A) has no central shaft, the shank having a double twist.

The center bit is an old type which is not often used now. It has a square shank and one cutter with one side cutter (twist bits have two cutters and two side cutters). The center point has no screw thread to draw the bit into the wood so its speed of cutting is in direct relation to the hand pressure which is applied. It is suitable for shallow holes and for use in thin wood.

A modern version of this bit is the improved center bit (C), sometimes known as the quick-cutting bit. This bit has a screw thread at the point, and the twist from each of the two cutters takes only about half a turn. The remainder of the shank is straight. In spite of only having one side cutter, this bit cuts a clean hole. It also cuts quickly, but the straightness of the hole depends on the skill of the operator.

All these bits are available in sizes from $\frac{1}{4}$ to $1\frac{1}{2}$ in. You may find it possible to get center bits up to $2\frac{1}{2}$ in. and the improved type up to 2 in.

For larger holes, generally up to 3 in., you can get an expansion bit (F) (you may even find this type of bit for holes as large as 4 or 5 in. but they would be very difficult to turn with a brace of less than 12 in. sweep). The expansion bit usually cuts holes from $\frac{1}{2}$ to $1\frac{1}{2}$ in. or $\frac{7}{8}$ to 3 in.; you can set the cutter yourself to any size between those listed.

Countersinking screw holes in timber can be carried out with a carpenter's brace using either a snail countersink or a rose bit (D), the latter can be used on soft metal as well as wood. For more general use in metal there is a plain countersink bit.

A useful addition to your collection of bits for a carpenter's brace would be a screwdriver bit (E). These are made to suit most sizes of screws, though you would only need one for large-diameter, long-length screws which would be difficult to turn with an ordinary driver.

Finally, for pin holes there is the Archimedean drill. This is a little tool with a spiral shaft and a loose bobbin which slides up and down the shaft making it turn backwards and forwards. The little drill-bit used with this tool cuts in either direction and soon makes a fine hole. It is used mainly in toy making.

BRASS — To Clean

Brass household ornaments and fittings often can be picked up quite cheaply at auctions or second-hand shops, but they usually are tarnished badly.

If the following procedure is adopted there shouldn't be any trouble in cleaning and polishing them.

The first stage is to clean the brass thoroughly to remove dirt and grime. Rub with a cloth dipped in a kerosene or grain alcohol. Then scrub in warm water containing soap or detergent, plus a little household ammonia.

That initial treatment cleans off all the surface dirt.

To tackle the tarnish you rub vigorously with a cloth dipped in a mixture of vinegar and common salt. Use a stiff bristle brush to reach awkward spots.

Rinse with water and dry. Then polish with a household metal cleaner or a cutting compound of the type used on car paintwork. Repeat the polishing if necessary.

This treatment usually will restore brass provided its surface is sound and not pitted with corrosion.

It should be used only for solid brass—not for articles which are plated or colored to resemble solid brass.

BRICK FIREPLACE—Restore Color

A faded, dusty looking brick fireplace can be restored quickly and easily to its original attractiveness.

Turn back the carpet and cover the furniture, and then brush the fireplace with a wire brush. If you have a vacuum cleaner, hold the hose—minus rods and nozzle—in one hand and the wire brush in the other, keeping them close together so that the powdered brick and cement is sucked up before it has an opportunity to fly into the room.

Now go over the bricks again with the vacuum cleaner or a hand brush to ensure that loose particles are removed.

Add a small quantity of tile-red linoleum paint or other suitable color to some mineral turpentine and stir until thoroughly mixed.

Test for color by brushing onto an old newspaper. This should be a dull pink which should freshen the surface of the brickwork without giving the suggestion that it has been painted. In fact, the thinned down paint acts as a stain.

Each brick must be treated separately by brushing, and if necessary, wiping with a cloth if the color appears too dark or uneven.

BRICKLAYING — Guide

The homeworker is not likely to be called on to do any large bricklaying jobs, but the building of small retaining or garden walls, fence foundations, or maybe a sand or compost bin is well within the scope of the average handyman.

The main thing is to have some idea of the basic rules of bricklaying procedure.

For all types of brick walls a foundation or footing is needed. Usually this means laying a concrete pad.

The first stage, then, is to mark out the position of the wall and dig a trench 12 in. deep, 15 in. wide, and, if possible, about 1 ft longer than the intended length of the wall.

Ram the bottom of the trench until it is hard and firm.

On this will go a 4 in. thick layer of concrete to carry a single (4½ in. wide) brick wall.

Along the middle of the trench drive in wooden pegs about 3 ft apart, leaving 4 in. of each peg above the ground.

Place a long straight edge across the first two pegs, and test with a spirit level. In this way adjust the pegs all along the trench so that their tops are all perfectly level.

The concrete mixture for the foundation could consist of metal (4 parts), sand (2½ parts), cement (1 part).

Pour the concrete into the trench until it is flush with the tops of the pegs, and allow to set hard.

The mortar used for laying the bricks could be five parts of clean sharp sand to one part of cement, plus about ten per cent hydrated lime for ease in laying.

The foundation course is the layer of bricks placed immediately on top of the foundation base concrete.

On this job the course is the length of one brick wide (9 in.) and the bricks are laid flat.

Spread a ¼ in. thickness of mortar on the concrete base, and on this lay the bricks crossways to the run of the wall, Fig. 1.

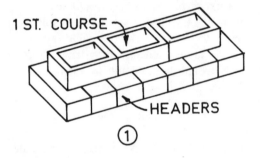

Such brick are called "headers." Those running in the same direction as the length of the wall are called "stretchers."

Use a straight edge and spirit level to level up the foundation course, and, where necessary, use the handle of the trowel to tap the bricks into place.

In Fig. 1 is shown the method of placing the first course of bricks in a single wall, and Fig. 2 shows the essential arrangement.

Each brick overlaps the joint immediately above and below it.

To do this, start all odd-numbered courses with a whole brick, and all even-numbered courses with a half-brick.

To cut a brick in half use a tool called a bolster. Mark the brick on each side, place the bolster on the mark on each side in turn, and give it a blow with the hammer.

A heavy blow in the center of the brick should break cleanly along the line of the cuts.

The layer of mortar between each course and the dab of mortar at the end of each brick should be a ¼ in. to ⅜ in. thick. Wet the bricks beforehand, and when laying them build up the ends first to six courses, then work to the middle of the wall, Fig. 3.

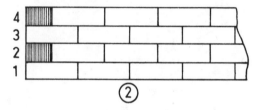

Fasten a length of string to two nails or, **better still, use proper flat bricklayer's pins.**

Push these into a mortar joint at the level of the first course and close to the outside of the built-up corners. The line must be taut, and is indicated by the dotted line in Fig. 3.

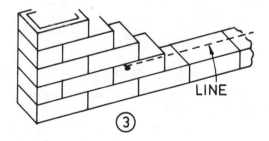

As each course is completed move the guide line up to the level of the next one.

When the sixth course has been completed, start on the ends again. Build them up to the required height—10 to 12 courses —then build in the middle portion again.

Be sure to check the corners frequently as the work proceeds to see that the brickwork is plumb or vertical.

This is best done with a plumb rule, which is a length of straight timber fitted with a plumb-bob attached to a length of strong chalk line.

An alternative is to use a level fitted with a plumbing bubble and straight edge.

If this type of narrow brick wall is to be built higher than 10 to 12 courses, or if it is a foundation wall set out for floor bearers, it must be strengthened by means of piers built at regular intervals.

For this job increase the thickness of the foundation concrete to 6 in. and widen the trench wherever a pier is to be built.

Fig. 6 shows the arrangement of the bricks for the foundation courses and for the odd and even-numbered courses.

The completed pier is shown in Fig. 5, and Fig. 4 shows clearly how the corners are made.

Where increased strength or bulk is required, a nine-inch wall will be needed, and here the foundation concrete will be 30 in. wide and 6 in. thick.

On this is laid the first foundation course, Fig. 7—two bricks wide; second foundation course, Fig. 8—one brick and a half wide; first main course and subsequent odd-numbered courses, Fig. 9.

The shaded brick in Figs 9 and 11 is called a closer and is only 2¼ in. wide. These closers are used to make the headers fall across the joints between the stretchers.

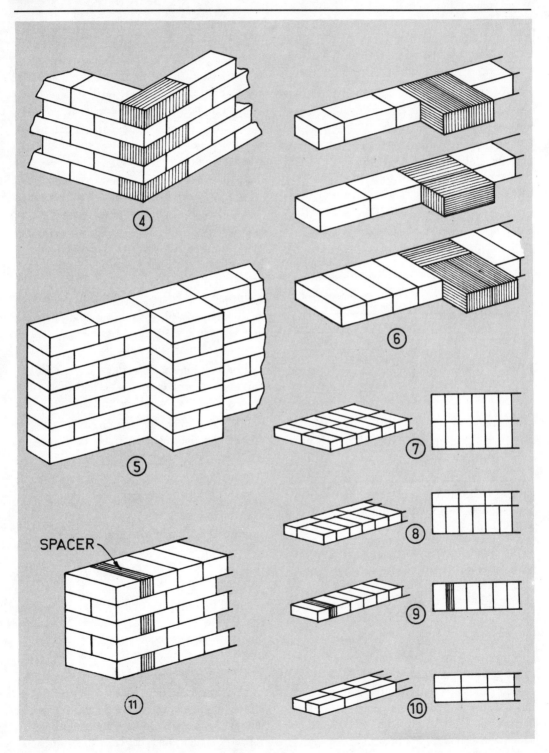

SPACER

The second course and all even-numbered courses consist of two rows of stretchers, Fig. 10. The finished wall is illustrated in Fig. 11.

Where the face of a wall is exposed to the weather it must be treated so that the water cannot lodge in the joints.

Put the trowel flat against the top of a joint, pressing the mortar in at the top and flush with the brick at the bottom.

The main tools required for bricklaying work are the standard trowel and a smaller pointing trowel, bolster, hammer, plumb rule or level, and the leveling line and flat pins.

The rule favored by most bricklayers is the wooden folding type.

BRICKWORK — Repointing

Repointing of brickwork means the re-conditioning of the mortar courses between the bricks. A good mix for the purpose could be three parts fine sand, one part cement, plus a little hydrated lime.

When water is added the result is an easily worked paste. Be careful, however, to mix the ingredients well together dry before adding water.

This mixture dries fairly light in color. If a grey look is required to match existing joints, mix vegetable black with the cement before adding the sand. A yellow color or the popular red shade can be achieved by the addition of yellow ochre or red oxide respectively.

You will also need a hawk to hold the mortar and a small pointing trowel. The hawk can be made from a piece of wood 7 or 8 in. square and 1 in. thick, screwed to a vertical handle about 6 in. long, Fig. 1.

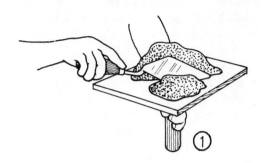

The first step in repointing is raking out. This means scraping out the joints to a depth of $\frac{1}{2}$ in. or more, if the mortar is in bad condition. All loose mortar must be raked away so the vertical and horizontal edges of the bricks are left clean to let the new filling bond well. Fig. 2 is a sectional view of a repointed joint.

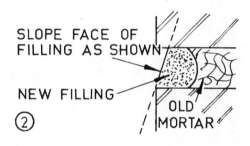

SLOPE FACE OF FILLING AS SHOWN

NEW FILLING

OLD MORTAR

Dampening the wall down well with water before beginning the raking will make it a less dusty job; also the new mortar will adhere better.

There are several ways in which the joints may be treated. Four suggestions or patterns are shown in Fig. 3.

The weather struck joint is perhaps the most effective and easy to form (A) Fig. 3. Take some cement on the hawk and press it down into a flat layer about 1 in. thick. A strip of cement is next cut off with the back of the trowel. Using a rapid stroke, sweep this length of cement into the raked-out joint, pressing it well home. Fill vertical joints first, then horizontal ones.

In finishing the horizontal joints, press in more firmly at the top than at the bottom so that the layer of cement slopes backward slightly, flush with the lower brick, but with the upper one overhanging a little. This slight backward slope helps the run-off of rain.

The concave joint (B) Fig. 3 is a pleasant one and is made with a round tool of suitable size. Flush pointing (C) is the term used when the joint is raked out as the laying is done so that colored mortar can be pointed-in later to improve the appearance of the brickwork.

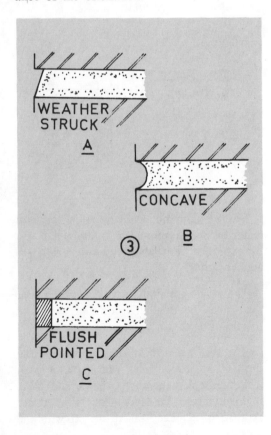

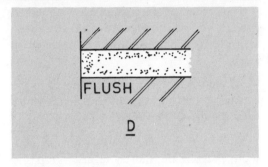

The flush joint (D) is the one used where no definite pattern on the work is required, and this is finished simply by cutting off excess mortar when the joint is made.

BRICKWORK — Stained

When brickwork becomes stained with tar or oil, the task of removal is usually difficult, but these suggestions will help.

In the case of fairly heavy splashes or deposits of tar on the face of brickwork, the bulk can be removed with a hot blade. Heat the blade of a wide paint scraper sufficiently to lift the tar without it sticking to the knife, but not hot enough for it to spread further.

After the heavy deposit has been removed, the stained brickwork may be amenable to treatment with mineral spirits, gasoline, kerosene, or carbon tetrachloride.

It is usually best to make preliminary trials to find the best method. Sometimes sponging with the solvent will do the job, but a poulticing method is often needed to draw the oil from the pores of the brickwork.

This method consists of making a stiff paste of whiting with the solvent. Working on a small area at a time, wet the surface thoroughly with the solvent, then apply the paste and allow it to dry.

Evaporation of the solvent will carry the dissolved oil to the surface of the whiting, which, when dry, is removed with a stiff brush. For deep-seated stains the operation may have to be repeated.

Any whiting remaining in the pores can be removed by hosing with a strong jet, although on occasions it may be difficult to restore a completely satisfactory surface to the brickwork immediately. This is especially so in the case of textured bricks.

Traces of whiting will, however, weather away or become obliterated in a comparatively short time.

These points emphasize the need for preliminary trials before starting to clean a large area stained by tar or oil.

As an alternative to the whiting, finely powdered brick dust to match the wall color could be mixed with the solvent to make the poultice.

Splashes of paint on brickwork can usually be removed by rubbing with a piece of brick similar in color to the wall bricks.

BRUSHES — Care

For the best painting results buy only best quality brushes.

Such brushes are made of pure hog bristles and they are not cheap.

Check a brush for quality by examining the bristle ends to see if they are "flagged" as in the detail Fig. 1.

A new brush will almost certainly have a few loose bristles and possibly some dirt in the bristles.

Remove this by spinning the brush between the palms of the hands as suggested in Fig. 2.

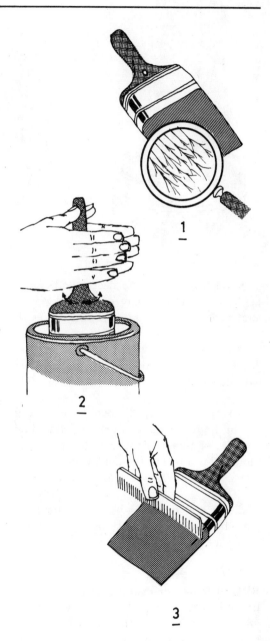

1

2

3

Follow this by combing the bristles, Fig. 3, to remove any kinks or curls.

Never soak a new brush in water. This makes the bristles flabby and ruins the sharp chisel edge.

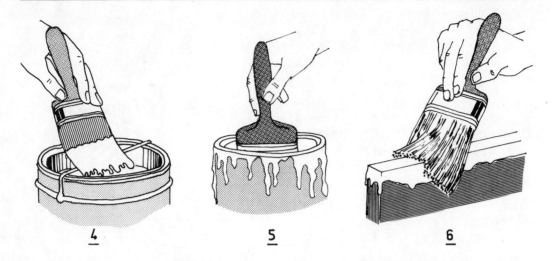

4   5   6

Never dip a brush too deeply and before application wipe off any excess on a wire stretched across the can as shown in Fig. 4.

The result of dipping the brush too deeply or careless loading of the brush is indicated in Fig. 5.

A very common fault when using a brush on furniture painting work is straddling the edge of a door or rail, Fig. 6. This wears the bristles down at the center and distorts them.

Either use a narrow brush or apply the paint by stroking crosswise lightly along the whole length.

BRUSHES — For Painting

Every homeworker is faced with a painting job at some time, and it is remarkable how many things can go wrong unless various precautions are taken.

Apart from selecting the best type of paint for a job, and preparing the surface thoroughly, there is the matter of correct procedure when applying the paint.

In themselves, these points may not appear very important, but they make a great difference when the job is finished.

For example, it is essential to brush into the wet area and so blend each stroke into the wet paint as indicated in Fig. 1. This will avoid ridges and lap marks when the paint dries.

Then again, always follow the grain of the wood when applying paint with a brush. Wood grain is composed of tiny ridges and if paint is brushed on crosswise, it may ripple slightly when dry. The correct procedure is shown in Fig. 2.

Except for overhead work, never tilt a brush upward. The paint will run down into the heel of the brush, harden, and swell the ferrule. This in turn will flare the bristles and cause them to lose their straight chisel edge.

Never paint with the sides of your brush. Angle it into the corners as shown in Fig. 3. This protects the bristles, gives a smoother, more even finish, and avoids the common defect in paint brushes known as fingering, as illustrated in Fig. 4.

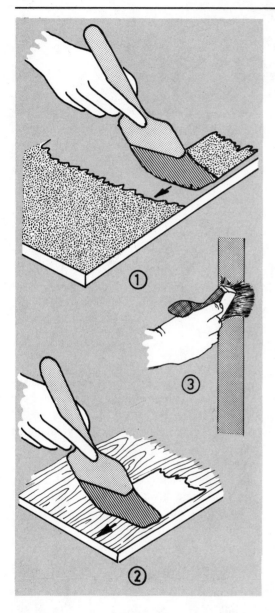

You can control the thickness and smoothness of a paint coat by the amount of paint carried in your brush. Dip bristles no more than half way into the paint. Deeper dipping may cause paint to accumulate in the heel of the brush, and the excess paint will almost certainly result in paint "runs" on the surface.

Three very important suggestions for achieving a smooth-painted finish are shown in Fig. 5. After the brush is removed from the can daub the paint on several spots before stroking (detail A). Then use long leveling brush strokes to spread it out thoroughly as in detail (B). Afterwards complete the section by brushing in the direction indicated by the arrows.

All trimming woodwork such as skirting boards, architraves, and picture rails should be painted last after ceilings and walls have been finished. Use the widest rim or sash brush practical for the job.

You can avoid messy after cleaning if you place a cardboard or sheet metal guard alongside the area being painted to catch any spattering paint or splashes.

At points where two different shades or colors are to meet, paint one color first; then after it has dried, mask the dividing line before applying the second color (Fig. 6).

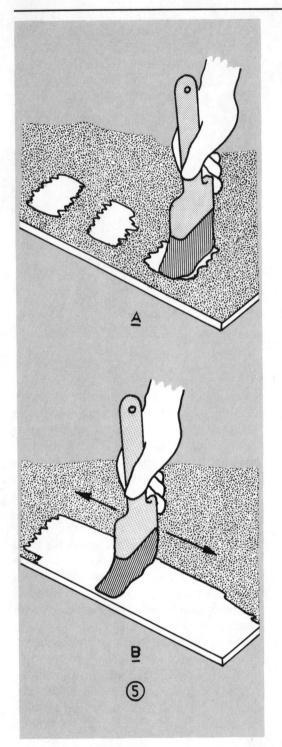

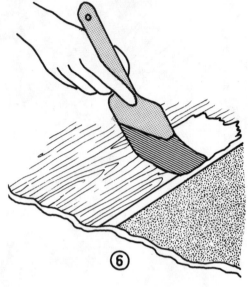

As a general rule, it is best to clean brushes out immediately after use and store them carefully, but where a painting job is to extend over several days, no great harm can come to the brushes if they are stored overnight in a suitable thinner or solvent. The main precaution is not to allow the brush to stand unsupported in a container.

Four methods of supporting a brush so that the bristles are suspended in the solvent are shown in Fig. 7.

At (A) a thumbtack has been driven into the handle a short distance and the protruding head is caught on the edge of the container.

In detail (B) small holes have been drilled in the handles to take a light rod which stretches across the can.

The brush handle passes through the container lid in detail (C) and is secured by a piece of wire passing through the handle above the lid.

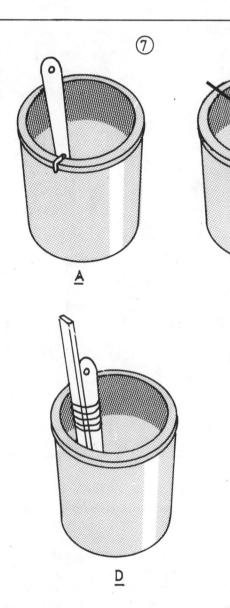

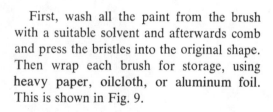

First, wash all the paint from the brush with a suitable solvent and afterwards comb and press the bristles into the original shape. Then wrap each brush for storage, using heavy paper, oilcloth, or aluminum foil. This is shown in Fig. 9.

Be sure that the bristles lie straight and that the brush is not compressed by the wrapping. Don't just lay the wrapped brushes flat on a shelf but suspend them with the bristles down. If it is a fine-quality brush used in oil paints, saturate the brush with raw linseed oil before wrapping.

A brush storage rack can be made by driving short nails part way into a panel of ¾ in. thick plywood so that the brushes can rest on the handles as in Fig. 8. Mount the panel in a workshop cabinet or behind a door.

The fourth method shows a stick being tied to the brush so that it extends slightly beyond the bristles, detail (D). In this way the brush can stand upright without resting on the bristles.

Where brushes are to be stored, the procedure shown in Figs 8 and 9 will pay dividends.

Apart from the standard paint brushes in various widths a number of others are designed for some specific job related to painting. Two of these are shown in Fig. 10.

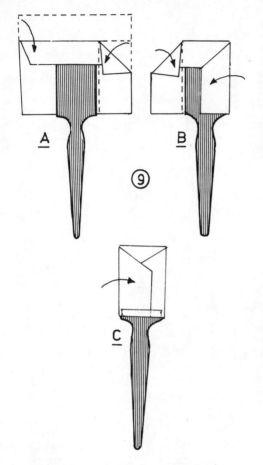

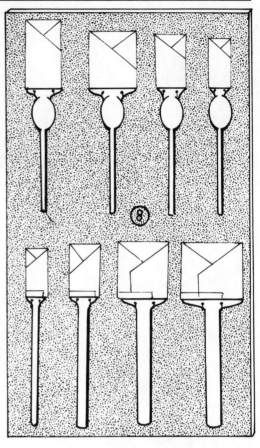

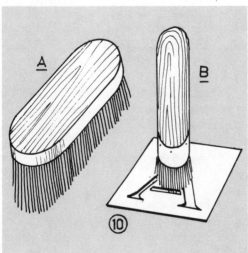

The wire brush (A) Fig. 10 is used mainly for removing rust from metal surfaces before applying paint. It is especially useful on rusted wrought iron gates and handrails. It should be noted, however, that it is not advisable to use such a brush on old rusted corrugated iron because of the risk of enlarging existing holes. It is usually better to use an ordinary scrubbing brush to remove all rust, then to apply a chemical rust inhibitor to the remainder.

The stencil brush (B) Fig. 10 has quite a number of uses apart from its main function of marking stencils. With a little experience it is possible to produce some striking textured effects with such a brush.

BUILDER'S SQUARE — To Make

When setting out any building or frame, it is essential to have a square of some kind, and the triangular set-square frame shown in the illustration is the simplest and most effective.

It is made on the 3-4-5 principle and is intended for setting out a job at right angles and, of course, for checking the angles.

Battens 2 in. wide and 1 in. thick may be used to form the frame, and the corners are half-lap jointed and then screwed. For extra strength screw plywood braces to the corners as shown. The three sides are exactly 3 ft, 4 ft, and 5 ft long, respectively.

In all setting-out work there is a base line, usually the front alignment, and if the set-square has its three-foot (or four-foot) side set accurately on this base line, the four-foot (or three-foot) side is exactly at right angles to the base.

These sides may be extended to any length to suit the building or frame being set out, and here is the way to check for squareness over extended distances.

From a point where the right-angled lines meet (A), measure, say, 15 ft in the direction of (B) and mark this point accurately. Next measure 20 ft from (A) to (C).

If the angle of the extended line is a right-angle the measurement from (B) to (C) should be exactly 25 ft. If it is not, the line (A-C) should be adjusted. Of course those lengths of 15 ft, 20 ft, and 25 ft may be any other group of multiples of three, four and five.

Measurement of all long lengths should be done with a steel tape.

BUILDING PAPER — Uses

Building paper is the name given to a number of light sheet materials which have an almost unlimited number of uses in building construction and in the home.

The basic material in most cases is kraft paper, in itself a very tough material. This is combined with bitumen to make it damp-proof, and sisal fibres to serve as reinforcement.

Ordinary building papers come in two grades—light and heavy. Then there are several special types which have advantages for particular uses.

Polyethylene-coated papers are used as vapor barriers, the thin coating of polyethylene on each face giving additional protection against dampness. These are used for damp-proof courses and flashings.

Reflective papers are faced on one or both sides with bright aluminum foil to reflect heat rays and so are used for thermal insulation.

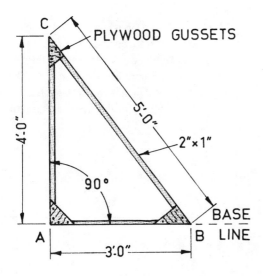

In construction work these papers have a valuable part to play for lining, damp-proofing, flashings, moisture barriers, and concrete curing, among many other uses.

Temporary uses in construction include partitions during building alterations, emergency weather protection after gale damage, and coverings for door and window openings.

Building papers can also be used as a substitute for tarpaulins and canvas in covering timber and other materials stacked outside, for example.

In the home, standard building paper serves as an underlay between floors and floor coverings. For this use it stops draughts through open joints in floorboards, reduces wear over raised board edges, and makes the floor and room warmer.

During wet, muddy weather a sheet of building paper on the hall and kitchen floor will give protection to a clean, polished surface. The paper also makes an ideal dust sheet for covering floors and furniture during a painting job.

If you are making a lawn with grass seed, covering with building paper for the first week will help germination by keeping the ground surface moist and at the same time keeping the birds off. Also in the garden you can cover shrubs and plants which have just been planted and protect them from frost or drying winds. Here a few light stakes and a length of the building paper will form a temporary screen or canopy.

Fixing building paper to timber is a simple job. Use galvanized broadhead clouts. Never use ordinary wire nails as the heads will pull through.

BUTT GAUGE — Use

When hanging a number of doors a most useful tool is the butt gauge, see illustration.

It is a small, all metal gauge used by carpenters and joiners for marking the butt recesses of room doors, three separate marks being required: (1) the thickness of the butt, (2) the depth of the door and (3) the depth on the jamb.

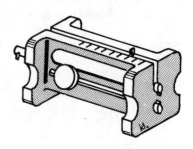

The two latter markings are necessary as allowance has to be made for the thickness of the paint on both door and jamb (about $\frac{1}{16}$ in.). There are thus three markers on the gauge, and when that giving the door depth is set, the second cutter is set automatically to the jamb.

Butt gauges have other uses, one of which is the marking of lines close up to the corner of a rabbet.

CABRIOLE LEGS	Uses
CALIPERS	Some Types
CARPETS	Care
CASTERS	Types
CAULKING	For Comfort
CEMENT WASH	Walls
CENTER PINS	For Dowels
CENTERS	To Mark
CHEMICALS	Uses
CHINA REPAIRS	Methods
CHISELS	Using
CHROME	On Cars
CIRCLES	Put to Use
CIRCULAR CUTTING	Ply, Plastics
CIRCULAR SAW	Using
CLAMPS	Uses
COACH BOLT & SCREW	Uses
COLOR	For Concrete
CONCRETE	Penetration Methods
CONCRETE	Ready Mixed
CONCRETE	Reinforcing
CONCRETE PATHS	To Lay
CONCRETE WALLS	Solid
CONDENSATION	In Roof
CREOSOTE	Preservative

CABRIOLE LEGS — Uses

The cabriole leg is a curved leg used originally in William and Mary, Queen Anne, early Georgian, and Chippendale furniture see (A).

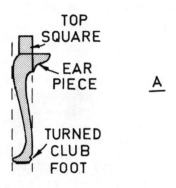

TOP SQUARE

EAR PIECE

A

TURNED CLUB FOOT

The leg is cut from a square, and as a rule there is a top square into which rails are jointed, though it is sometimes omitted in special designs.

Ear pieces are generally glued on at each side, and the leg terminates in the turned club foot, claw and ball, French scroll, lion's paw, eagle's claw, hoof, or some other device.

In a well-shaped leg the knee is high and flat, and from the knee downwards the leg should taper until the ankle is reached no matter from which angle it is viewed.

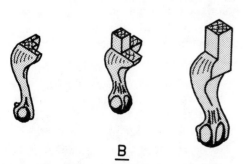

B

Often the knee is carved with acanthus leafwork, shell, husk, lion head, mask, and so on.

Detail (B) shows a ball and claw carved foot used on some cabriole legs, particularly in Queen Anne, Early Georgian and Chippendale furniture. It represents a bird's claw gripping a ball.

CALIPERS—Some Types

Calipers are essentially small precision tools used for accurate measurement of dimensions which cannot readily be obtained by laying a normal scale alongside the work.

Basically there are two types—the caliper gauge (A), which gives direct readings on a scale and is like a scale with fitted jaws; and adjustable calipers with divided legs which can be manipulated rather like compasses or dividers. Normally two separate operations are required to determine a measurement, first setting the calipers over the dimension required and then transferring the points to a scale in order to read off the measured dimension. Some calipers of this simple type are, however, self-indicating.

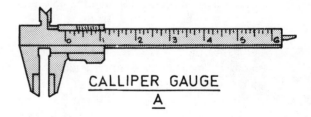

CALLIPER GAUGE
A

General-purpose calipers are of either outside (B) or inside (C) type. The former have bowed legs, and are intended for setting around external surfaces, such as a shaft, etc. Inside calipers normally have straight legs with the faces turned slightly outwards at the tips and squared off.

These are for setting to inside dimensions. In some cases the legs are still further narrowed or cut away to reach down into deep holes. With either type the dimension is first established by setting the points to the correct spacing, from which the measurement can be transferred or read off as a second operation.

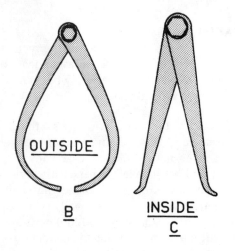

OUTSIDE

B

INSIDE

C

Simple calipers are of the type with a stiff joint, relying on friction to hold the legs set to any one position. Care must be taken in handling not to disturb this setting.

For most accurate work spring-bow calipers are to be preferred. In these the legs are sprung towards the open position by the spring-box top and adjusted to any particular setting by means of a knurled knob.

Toolmaker's calipers (D) are of this type.

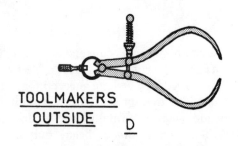

TOOLMAKERS

OUTSIDE   D

Usually, however, toolmaker's calipers are not made in the larger range of sizes. Stiff-jointed calipers are obtainable in sizes up to 18 in. or longer.

CARPETS — Care

Your carpet, however old, may have to serve for a long time yet, and the carpet beetle is one of its greatest enemies.

If your carpet, area rug or wall-to-wall carpeting is showing ominous signs of sparseness of pile, don't be misled into thinking that moths are responsible. The culprit, you may be sure is the devastating, tiny brown grub of the carpet beetle.

It is one of the worst kinds of saboteur, and scientific estimates show that about forty per cent of carpets are attacked by this grub. It feeds avidly on carpet pile, eating it for at least a foot in from the edges.

It is a strong flyer and is attracted by the pollen of garden flowers, particularly white flowers. If doors and windows are not screened, it can be found resting on window ledges and curtains after flitting in from the garden. It looks guileless enough, but don't be deceived by its looks. Its part in the destruction of your carpet is in the distribution of eggs, so kill it when you see it.

This little beetle lays at least one hundred eggs, depositing them in cracks in flooring boards and skirting boards, and in gaps in corners. So for this reason it is most important that these cracks should be filled in with cold-water putty.

Within fourteen days of laying, the grub is hatched from the egg, and it wastes no time in getting on with its work of destruction.

It begins feeding immediately and will continue to feed greedily for about three months. In warm climates there are two generations of the pest each year.

Frequent brushings around the edges of the carpet, beatings in the open air, and exposure to bright sunshine do a great deal of good to control the grub menace.

Vacuum cleaning destroys the eggs, Naphthalene flakes can be placed under the edges of the carpets to safeguard them from attacks, while the dusting of sodium-fluoride under the edges and around the skirting boards is an excellent form of control.

But this powder is poisonous and should not be allowed to contaminate the fingers or be placed within the reach of children.

Sodium-fluoride may be obtained from one of the large drug supply houses if your local druggist is unable to supply you.

If there is a space between your carpet edges and the walls, scrubbing with very hot water and soap will destroy the eggs, which may be in the cracks of the boards.

CASTERS—Types

These are made in many forms.

Chief fastenings are; round socket, square socket, screw, spring peg, plate.

The wheel may be metal, china, wood, plastic, or rubber.

There is also the ball caster.

For tea trolleys a special large size wheel is made for riding over carpets, and often a spring is incorporated to help the movement.

For heavy duty a ball-bearing type is used.

There are also special spherical types which give extremely easy movement.

Shown are various casters in general use. (A) round socket; (B) square socket; (C) tripod socket; (D) screw-plate; (E) peg and sleeve; (F) trolley table; (G) ball; (H) ball-bearing; (I) screw plate; (J) easy movement swivel ball or Shepherd type.

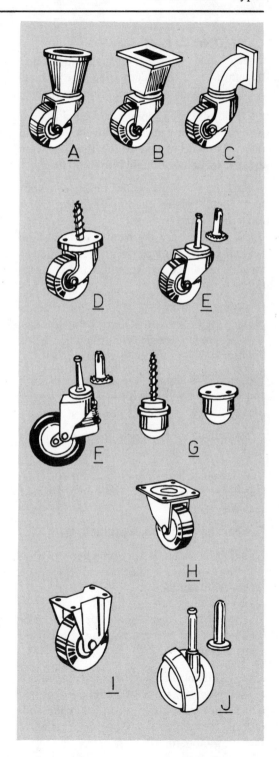

71

CAULKING — For Comfort

Wintry winds blowing through cracks and openings are a reminder of the many points around the home that need filling or sealing.

Obvious starting point is an outside door with a big gap between door bottom and floor. Any one of several weather strips on the market can be bought and fitted here.

Few gaps and cracks in masonry, woodwork, and plaster cannot be closed with modern sealing or caulking preparations. These products are designed to retain some flexibility after application to counteract any movement caused by expansion and contraction.

Sealing compounds are in three main types. One is in plastic strip form, another is of a similar consistency to putty and is applied with a putty knife or trowel.

The third is slightly thinner in consistency, and may be applied with a gun not unlike that used for greasing a car.

Some makers also supply the thinner grade in plastic tubes fitted with a nozzle.

When selecting a caulking compound it is very important to know the type of base material.

Some have an oil base, others tar.

While the latter is very effective for sealing and caulking, it must never be used on work to be painted.

The oil-base type should be the choice here, as it has no reaction on subsequent coats of paint.

It is available in black, grey and cream.

And now to ways of caulking the gap which appears at the back of a kitchen sink or bath, where it meets the wall covering of tiles or wallboard.

First be sure that the gap is clear of grease and grime by wiping first with a cloth dampened with white spirit.

Then press in a length of strip sealer or feed in a strip from the nozzle of a gun or tube.

Smooth off to shape if necessary with a knife which has been dipped in water, and leave undisturbed for a few hours to allow a tough film to form on the surface.

An alternative method of sealing here is to fix lengths of quarter-round molding with contact or latex-based adhesive.

CEMENT WASH — Walls

When a brick garage or other type of brick outbuilding is completed it is very often finished on the inside with a cement wash. This process is much cheaper and quicker than rendering or plastering the walls in the normal way.

Of course, concrete garages can also be treated in this way, and the process is often referred to as bagging. This is because a cloth bag or piece of burlap is used to apply the cement wash.

When using a cement wash over brickwork or concrete, the main precaution is to see that the wash or slurry does not dry out too quickly.

During warm, dry weather especially, the surface to which the wash is applied must be dampened to avoid too much evaporation before the cement has hardened.

Moisture is needed for the chemical reaction which occurs during the setting, so the wash application, like all types of concrete work should be kept damp for at least several days so that it will harden and cure properly.

An effective method here is to set the hose to give a very fine mist spray and go over the surface night and morning for a few days. Cement wash is a creamy mixture of Portland cement and water, just liquid enough to be spread by the burlap or applied with a stout whitewash brush.

The usual procedure is to cover one or two square yards with the wash, using the brush, and then to even it out with the burlap pad.

If so desired, fine dry sand can be included in the wash mixture in the proportions of one part of the sand for each part of cement.

The actual surface of the brickwork should be even and uniform, and any open joints or holes should be pointed up with a trowel at least a day before using the wash.

The purpose of the cement wash is not to apply a layer of cement mortar over the brickwork, as in rendering, but merely to create a uniform surface by filling in small cracks and indentations.

The burlap is used like a floor cloth to even the wash out. It should hide the distinct brickwork joints and give an overall grey cement color to the wall.

After several weeks the wall should have dried out sufficiently for the application of water or emulsion paint, although it is advisable to wait at least three months before applying an oil finish.

CENTER PINS — For Dowels

In furniture repair work involving turned sections it is often necessary to locate the center of the member. This can be done easily with center pins.

In Fig. 1 is shown the simple method of making center pins for dowels. A $\frac{3}{64}$ in. diameter hole is drilled in the center of the disk

and then a mild steel pin of $\frac{1}{16}$ in. diameter driven through the hole. This pin is then sharpened to a point on both sides of the disk in such a way that it does not protude more than $\frac{3}{16}$ in.

Fig. 2 shows a proposed dowel-jointed job, taken apart, so as to indicate how it is marked out for the positioning of the dowel holes. In actual fact, either piece could be marked out but, for convenience, the lower piece of timber has been shown set out for the hole positions.

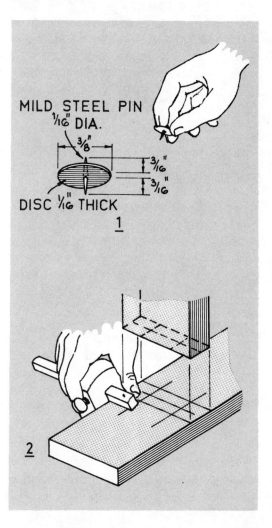

MILD STEEL PIN
$\frac{1}{16}$" DIA.
$\frac{3}{8}$"
$\frac{3}{16}$"
$\frac{3}{16}$"
DISC $\frac{1}{16}$" THICK
1

2

The marker is now pressed into position as in Fig. 3 the point piercing and entering the wood exactly in the center of the setting-out marks. In this particular example two markers will be required to each dowel hole.

After positioning the markers, both pieces of timber are carefully adjusted to each other and pressed together.

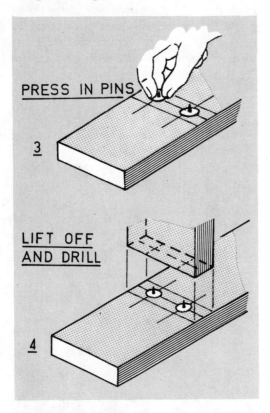

This action of pressing the parts together produces identical marks on the second piece of timber and ensures perfect register of the holes which are then drilled in the positions now indicated by the indentations, Fig. 4, produced by the markers.

CENTERS—To Mark

There are many occasions in woodworking when it is necessary to locate the center of square or round work.

In wood turning especially this is a routine job when turning between the two lathe centers. It is also necessary when fitting new dowels into broken rails or legs of damaged chairs and tables.

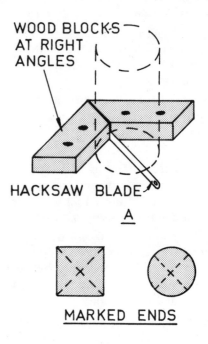

A simple tool for the purpose is shown in the sketch. It is very accurate and will save considerable time, especially on repetition work.

Two blocks of wood are screwed at right angles on a bench or block of timber, and a slot is cut in this block at the corner to make a 45 degrees miter. In this slot a short length of hacksaw blade is wedged tightly with the teeth facing up.

The work to be centered is set over the saw blade and pressed firmly into the angle formed by the two blocks of wood. Tap the upper end of the work lightly with a hammer to sink the teeth into the end grain. A circular rod in position is indicated by the dotted lines at (A).

Then turn the work around at about right angles and make a similar mark. The point at which the marks intersect will be the center. This is shown clearly in the end views of both square and round stock in the sketch.

This center-finding jig will be effective on timber ranging in size from ½ in. diameter upwards.

CHEMICALS — Uses

The home worker is often confused by the names of various chemical preparations referred to in do-it-yourself instructions. Here are a few explanatory details about some of them.

GOLD SIZE: Is a quick-drying varnish normally used to apply goldleaf and gold paint used in signwriting. It is also a useful binder for colors, ground-in-turpentine and paste wood fillers.

COPPERAS (green). Is another name for sulphate of iron. These crystals dissolved in water give a pale blue-green shade, and the solution can be used as a water stain on timber or as a chemical agent to produce a natural stone appearance on a cement surface.

For coloring cement, the surface is finished off with a trowel, and before it is completely set the copperas is dashed on with a brush. This produces a green appearance at first, which gradually changes to a brown or sandstone color, depending on the strength of the copperas solution.

ACETIC ACID. Is used in some furniture revivers. Household vinegar is an impure form of acetic acid and may often be used as a substitute when the pure acid is not available.

CONDY'S CRYSTALS. Comes in crystals of a deep purple shade. It is mixed with water to produce a dark brown stain on timber. It is often used as a stain on floors before applying a hard-wearing, clear finish to the boards.

CAMPHORATED OIL. Is a mixture of four parts of olive oil and one part of camphor. Apart from its medicinal uses, it is used for the removal of heat marks from a polished surface. Water marks left by vases also respond to gentle rubbing with a cloth dampened with camphorated oil.

CARBONTETRACHLORIDE. Is a very good solvent for all greases and oils and has the advantage of being non-inflammable. It is, however, very toxic and care must be taken to have adequate ventilation when working with it.

ACETONE. This can be used as a solvent for cellulose lacquers and paints, nail varnish, soft resins and certain glues. It will not, however, dissolve synthetic resins to any extent.

CHINA REPAIRS — Methods

Many pieces of china and glassware that are broken or chipped can be repaired and made almost as good as new. With a good vase or perhaps a cup or saucer from a very expensive set, it is especially important to do the job properly.

Use a transparent heat and waterproof adhesive cement; they are made and sold under various trade names, usually in tubes.

The first rule to note is that the broken edges should be mended as soon as possible.

If they are left exposed to the air, they get dusty and greasy, and will not join up properly.

For the same reason avoid touching the edges with the fingers.

If it is not possible to do the repair job straight away, gather all the fragments together carefully and wrap them in paper until the work can be started.

When using the cement, apply it to the edges to be joined with a small paint brush —the type supplied with a common school painting set is ideal.

Do not use too much of the adhesive cement, otherwise the joint will show, and it will not be as strong as it would be if a thin film were used.

After applying the cement to both edges of the sections to be joined, allow them to stand for a minute or two before pressing them together.

This allows the cement to become slightly tacky, and it will grip better.

When the edges have been brought together, it is essential to hold them firm and rigid until the cement becomes dry and hard.

It is no use just sticking them together and leaving them, as even the slightest movement in the parts after assembly will break the joint or throw them out of position.

The method of holding or clamping will depend to a large extent on the article itself and the nature of the repair.

Fig. 1 shows a typical job and the method of holding the parts of a plate together.

A length of fairly stout twine is looped over the edges of the plate and then twisted firmly with a pencil in the centre of the back. Of course be careful not to twist too hard and possibly break the joint.

All that is needed is sufficient pressure to hold the edges in firm contact.

Much the same result can be achieved by using stout rubber bands arranged in the same way.

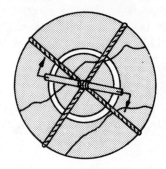

BACK OF PLATE
①

Where there is only a simple break or a crack, adhesive tape can often be applied over the joint after applying the cement as shown in Fig. 2.

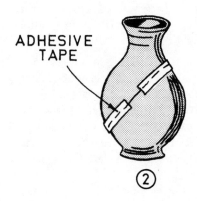

ADHESIVE TAPE

②

On the other hand, if a vase or bowl is broken into a number of pieces, a very effective repair method is to use a sand box.

Here the first thing to do is to get a box or container slightly larger than the article to be repaired.

In this is placed the base or main solid section of the article to be repaired and sand is poured around it to a point just below the edges. Cement is then applied to the edges as before, and the various parts are placed in position.

As the work proceeds, gradually filter sand both inside and outside the article so that when the top is reached, and the last fragment is fitted back into place, the article is completely buried in the sand where it will remain rigid.

The main precautions to note when using this method are to keep any grains of sand off the cemented edges, and to be extremely careful when pouring the sand—which must be dry—around the assembled parts of the article.

Repaired objects must be given plenty of time to set. They may appear to be set hard after a day or two, but the joints will be much stronger if they can be left for a week or more before use.

CHISELS — Using

Like any keen-edge woodcutting tool, wood chisels are designed to be used in a specific way. Knowing how to handle them correctly not only will produce better work with less effort, but will also make for greater safety.

KINDS OF CHISELS. There are three popular types of wood chisels—butt, firmer, and gouge. Although chisels are available from ⅛ in. to 2 in. wide, the four sizes that meet most homeowners' requirements are ¼, ½, ¾ and 1 in. widths.

The cutting edge of a chisel is straight across the end of the blade, at right angles to its axis, and for easy and accurate cutting the edge must be kept razor sharp. The cutting edge is beveled on one side only. The sides of the blade may be square or the top sides may be beveled as in (D). Fig. 1.

The beveled type is the lighter and is especially adapted for undercutting and for getting into V-shaped grooves having an angle of less than 90 degrees, detail (E). Fig. 1. The name of chisel parts is detailed in Fig. 1.

Detail (B) Fig. 1, shows the difference between a firmer chisel, with a blade about 6 in. long, and a butt chisel, which has a 2½ to 3½ in. long blade. The firmer chisel has the longer reach, but the butt type is handier for close-up work.

Short, thin-bladed chisels for delicate cutting are called paring chisels.

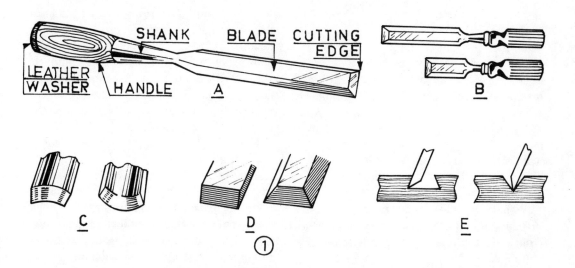

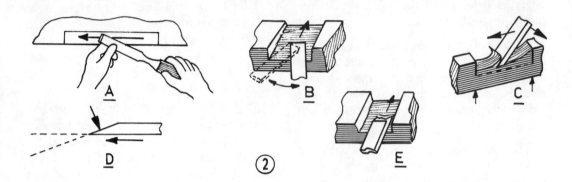

Gouges have curved cutting edges of various radii for rounding edges, bottoms of grooves, and for cutting flutes and beads. They are ground with the bevel either on the outside or the inside as in detail (C) Fig. 1.

As shown in (A) Fig. 1, the handle of a chisel, or gouge, generally slips into the end of a hollow, tapered socket which is a continuation of the blade. Some types have a tang on the blade that slips into a handle, the end of which is reinforced with a ferrule.

Handles may be of hardwood or plastic and are replaceable. Most wooden handles are capped with leather washers.

HOLDING A CHISEL. For light cuts and delicate work employ both hands in using a chisel. One hand guides the blade while the other applies the pressure.

For rough cutting, particularly across grain, use a mallet to drive a chisel. Light taps permit better cutting control than heavy blows.

Use of an ordinary hammer instead of a mallet will soon "mushroom" a chisel handle and may even split it unless the blows are cushioned by a rubber crutch tip slipped on the hammer head.

When using chisels, always follow safety precautions, directing the sharp edge away from you and keeping both hands behind the cutting edge.

POINTERS ON CUTTING. Work to be cut with a chisel should be rigidly supported. Small work can be held in a vice or by means of a bench hook.

When chiseling lengthwise along the edge or surface of wood, always cut with the grain.

If possible, hold the chisel at an angle toward one side as in (A) Fig. 2, which makes cutting easier and keeps the edge sharp longer than when the thrust is straight ahead.

Another method is to move the chisel from side to side while pushing it ahead as in detail (B) Fig. 2.

For roughing cuts—the removal of waste wood to within a short distance of the finish line—you hold a chisel with the bevel down, detail (C) Fig. 2. This gives better control and prevents digging too deeply into the wood. With the bevel up, as shown in detail (D) Fig. 2, the wedging action of wood against the bevel tends to divert the direction of cutting away from a straight line.

With the bevel down, a chisel tends to cut progressively more shallowly. This is caused by a slight downward pressure on the handle which makes the rear edge of the bevel serve as a lever fulcrum.

In roughing cuts, the most common mistake that beginners make is to attempt to remove most of the waste with one or two deep cuts. This usually produces rough edges extending beyond the finish line and often causes the wood to split.

For light finishing or paring cuts hold a chisel with the bevel up as in (E), Fig. 2. Press the flat side of the blade against the surface already finished, which will help to guide the tool in a straight line.

When cutting dados, grooves, or rabbets across the grain, as at (A) Fig. 3 it is best to make the outside cuts with a tenon saw. Then you chisel out the waste between them from both sides of the stock toward the centre to prevent splintering at the edges.

Wide recesses across the grain should have several saw cuts, as in detail (B) Fig. 3, so that the chips will be short and easy to remove, resulting in a uniformly flat surface.

The start of the cut should be made along the edge where the chips will split upward toward the surface if the grain runs at a slant. Starting at the wrong edge produces an uneven surface and may cause splitting beyond the depth required.

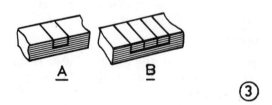

chisel and a mallet to make the shallow end-cuts, steps (A) and (B) of Fig. 4. It is best to use a chisel or suitable width so the cuts can be made in one or two passes instead of several successive ones not likely to be perfectly straight.

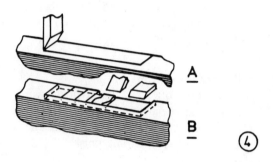

CHAMFERING WITH A CHISEL. While a block plane or a spokeshave generally is used to cut plain or continuous chamfers along the edges of stock (a spokeshave also for stopped chamfers), there are occasions when only a chisel can be used, as, for example, to cut short, stopped chamfers on inside edges of panel framing, where another tool cannot be manipulated.

Usually a chamfer is cut at a 45 degree angle. You first mark penciled guidelines on both edges of the stock as indicated by the dotted lines at (A). Fig. 5.

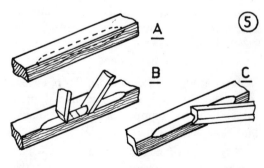

CUTTING HINGE GAINS. Shallow recesses, or gains, to accommodate hinge leaves so that they come flush with the wood, usually are cut entirely with a chisel.

(Sides of such a gain can be sawn only when the hinge leaves are as wide as the wooden pieces to which they attach.)

After marking the outline of the gain with a knife, or a carpenter's butt gauge, use a

Next rough out the ends, then the portion between them. This is done with two or three roughing cuts, with the cutting bevel down (B) Fig. 5, and working with the grain. Be especially careful at the end where the chisel will go against the grain when leveling off.

A paring cut at the ends first, then the flat portion finishes the chamfer (C) Fig. 5.

CHROME — On Cars

Car handbooks often say that frequent washing with soapy water and drying-off with a soft cloth or a chamois leather is all that's needed to protect a chrome finish.

Excellent advice, perhaps—in ideal conditions. But in practice chrome is under constant attack by water, mud, grit, salt (especially in winter) and atmospheric pollution. And, unfortunately, the chromium itself is porous.

When moisture charged with salt or acid from the air penetrates the chrome it attacks from below. Starting with the iron or zinc-based alloy components, it passes through the copper, then the nickel and finally pierces the chrome. When this stage is reached a crop of pimples appear.

If the minute pores in the chromium plate are sealed, corrosion can be largely prevented. The easiest way is to apply a good hard wax or silicone polish (the same as that used on the bodywork) whenever the car is washed and to make sure that this protective film is maintained.

Pay particular attention to sharp edges, where the chrome is often very thin. Watch the area of the bumper above the exhaust pipe, too.

The exhaust fumes contain sulphur, which combines with condensed moisture from the air to form corrosive sulphuric acid.

Cars that have to stand in the open all the year round, often in corrosive city atmospheres, need special protection. First clean any steel parts thoroughly, wipe them over with gasoline to remove any grease and then swab them with a rust preventive. Allow about 10 minutes for this to soak into the pores, wipe off the surplus and then apply the wax or silicone polish.

In winter dispense with the polish and coat the chrome with a transparent protective lacquer. When the lacquer becomes dulled remove it with thinners and apply a fresh coat.

On neglected, scratched or badly tarnished chrome, use only a polish specially intended for chromium. Even a mildly abrasive metal polish will quickly remove the plating.

CIRCLES — Put to Use

Circles can often be used to advantage in the workshop. A good example is shown at (A).

To determine the center of a broken pulley or gear when you have only a segment to work with, trace an outline of the outer circumference on a sheet of heavy paper.

Then adjust a small compass so that its span is less than the radius of the work, swing two pairs of arcs across the circumference, and draw a line exactly through each pair, as shown in the detail (A).

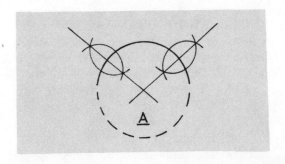

The point at which the two lines join is **the center of the circle and marks the distance from the axis of the rotation to the** outer circumference—that is, the radius.

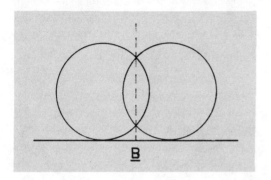

B

The diagram (B) shows an easy, accurate way to square across a wide board when a try square is not available or when the panel is exceptionally wide.

Use a paint can, or any cylindrical object, and draw two circles that touch the edge of the board. Draw a line through the two points where the circles intersect.

The line will be at right angles to the edge of the board or panel.

CIRCULAR CUTTING — Ply, Plastics

The woodworker is often faced with the task of cutting a large circular hole in such material as three-ply, plastic, or other thin sheet material, and finds that even an adjustable expansion-bit is not large enough.

He then usually marks the hole with a compass or dividers, and cuts the hole out with a keyhole saw, or possibly a coping saw.

This certainly does the job, but it is rather slow and leaves the edges a little ragged.

Time and energy can be saved and a much better result achieved by using a

washer or gasket cutter similar to that shown at (B).

It is a metal frame with a center point, a square-tapered shank to fit a standard brace, and a central set screw to lock the cutters in position.

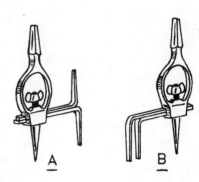

A **B**

For a circle up to 4 in. in diameter, one cutter only may be used, the other being turned up out of the way as shown at (A).

For larger circles the cutting is made much easier by using both cutters, one on each side, but care must be taken to see that **the radius of each one from the center is** exactly the same so as to give the required diameter.

The inner core of timber or plastic produced by cutting circles in this way can often be used for toy wheels or other purposes.

In addition to cutting plain circular holes the two cutters may be clamped together and used for cutting washers or gaskets, so this also makes it a handy tool for car-owners.

In soft wood and other material the point of the cutter will form its own hole, but for harder wood it is advisable to give it a start with a ³⁄₁₆ in. hole.

Always keep the cutters sharp and turn the brace with a fairly slow, steady action with plenty of downward pressure.

CIRCULAR SAW — Using

One of the most useful power tools in a workshop is the circular saw, and the ideal type for the home woodworker is one fitted with a back guide, blade, and operated by a ¾ h.p. electric motor. Additional desirable features are a rise-and-fall table and a tilting arrangement.

Although nearly all bench or table saws are fitted with a back guide this often does not guide long boards accurately when these are being ripped into strips. The trouble is due to the inability of the worker to keep the board against the fence.

To remedy this, provide an additional guide on the other side of the saw table, as shown in Fig. 1.

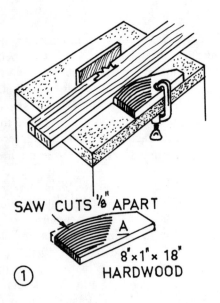

SAW CUTS ⅛" APART

A

8" x 1" x 18"
HARDWOOD

①

The extra guide consists of 18 in. by 8 in. by 1 in. thick straight-grained hardwood in which a number of saw cuts are made about ¼ in. apart, as indicated in detail (A) Fig. 1, to form a spring.

This block is clamped to the saw bench with a G-clamp, as shown, to bear against the edge of the timber being cut.

There are different types of blades for various cutting work in a circular saw bench, and shown in Fig. 2 is a clean-cutting saw blade. These are sometimes referred to as novelty blades.

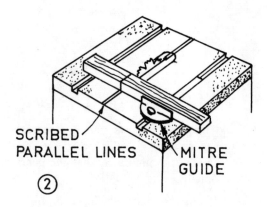

SCRIBED
PARALLEL LINES

MITRE
GUIDE

②

Unlike ordinary rip or crosscut blades, the clean-cutting type is slightly hollow ground so that the thickness of the blade is slightly greater at the teeth than in the center.

There is no "set" on the teeth, and it is this feature which produces a perfectly clean cut, especially across the grain.

Also shown in Fig. 2 is the operation of using the miter guide to support timber which is being cross-cut. The guide is also used to push the timber forward in complete safety.

Another idea is to mark two parallel lines on the table in line with the saw blade to indicate the blade thickness. This makes for more accurate cutting.

Mark the lines by laying a carpenter's square against each side of the blade. Note that the lines are carried along the tables both in front of and behind the blade.

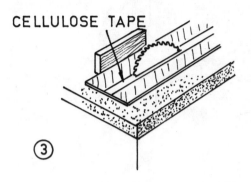

CELLULOSE TAPE

③

In Fig. 3 is shown a very simple precaution that can prevent plywood and veneer splintering when being cut on a power saw, especially a saw fitted with a standard blade.

Just lay a length of clear cellulose tape along the line of the cut. After making the cut, peel the tape remnants off gently in the direction of the grain.

CLAMPS—Uses

Clamps are very necessary when making glued joints, and there are several types under such names as handscrews, G-clamps, and bar clamps. Bar clamps are also referred to as sash clamps.

The actual mechanics of working and applying these clamps is usually obvious, yet there are certain tricks in operation that save time and help produce better results.

For edge to edge gluing of boards, alternate the direction of the grain. Grain direction can usually be seen clearly on the ends of the boards in sections of the annual rings, and the idea is to have the heart side up in one board and down in the next when assembling.

When this procedure of matching the grain is followed, there will be much less chance of the finished job being twisted or warped.

Some styles of bar clamps will stand alone on feet which also make provision for screwing down. Others will need supporting blocks to maintain an upright position as in Fig. 1.

Use paper at points where the clamp bars cross glued joints to prevent sticking or staining of the timber.

The boards or frames to be clamped are laid flat on the clamps, after which tightening should be done gradually, and in rotation where two or more bar clamps are being used.

The tendency of work being clamped is to hump or rise as the pressure is applied by turning the screw. This can be eliminated by fitting clamps on both sides or by attaching a temporary batten to the top surface of the work being clamped together.

After medium pressure has been applied, go over the joints with a hammer or mallet and a wood block and pound them flat.

A rubber hammer of the type used for changing car tires is ideal for this operation.

When assembling a frame it is essential to see that it is square. Fig. 2 is an exaggerated view of a frame which is out of square.

Adjustments can be made by loosening the clamps off and tapping the outside of the frame in one direction or another until it conforms to the try-square placed inside the frame as shown in Fig. 2.

This method is suitable for small frames, but for larger frames use the diagonal method of squaring shown in Fig. 3. Measure diagonally in both directions, as indicated by the dotted line, and, when both measurements are the same the frame is square.

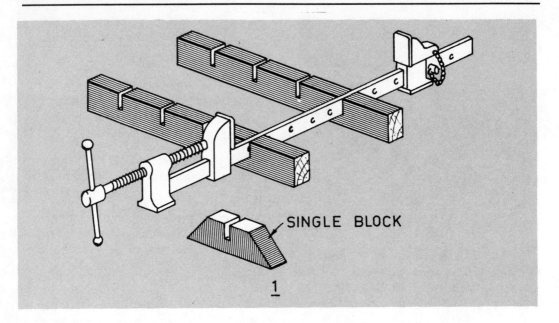

SINGLE BLOCK

1

If necessary correct the shape with a bar clamp placed diagonally across the frame, as shown in Fig. 3.

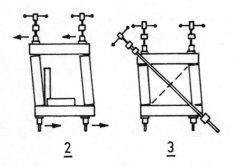

2   3

Extensive use should be made of dry setups to check fitting and accuracy of all joints. This will ensure that when the work is finally assembled and glued the job can proceed smoothly without annoying delays caused by taking apart the joints and refitting them.

COACH BOLT & SCREW — Uses

There is often some confusion when reference is made to coach bolts and coach screws.

The illustration makes the difference between the two perfectly clear.

The coach bolt has an oval head with a square shank section directly under the head.

The purpose of this square section is to prevent the bolt turning as the nut is tightened.

However to be effective, the hole drilled for the bolt must provide a firm fit without being too tight.

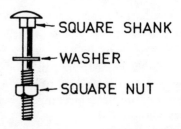

SQUARE SHANK

WASHER

SQUARE NUT

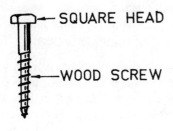

← SQUARE HEAD

←WOOD SCREW

The coach screw is used extensively on exterior work such as gates and fences. Such screws have great holding power and strength.

It is essential to drill pilot holes of suitable size to suit the diameter of the screws.

Normally the hole diameter should be approximately ⅛ in. less than the screw diameter. To some extent this will depend on the type of timber.

For example, the holes for the coach screws in hardwood should be slightly larger in diameter than those in softwood.

It will be seen that the coach screw has a square head which permits it to be driven in firmly with a spanner.

COLOR—For Concrete

Some people prefer colored concrete to the usual white for paths and drives. It is also used sometimes for concrete mower strips on garden edgings.

If you're doing a concreting job like this yourself, it's easy to put color in it by adding coloring pigment to the topping mix.

The coloring is added only to the mortar topping. Special pigments for this purpose are sold by hardware shops and builders' suppliers.

It is important to mix the coloring thoroughly with the dry cement before adding the sand, until the mixture becomes a uniform color.

It's also important to measure the quantities of coloring and cement accurately, and repeat the same proportions in mixing later batches, so that one part of the job won't be of a different shade from the rest.

Best method of mixing the coloring pigment and cement, some experts say, is to pass them through a fine sieve several times.

The amount of coloring to use varies from about 5 to 12 lb. for each bag of cement, depending on the depth of color you want and also to some extent on the color being used.

Some coloring pigments such as red and blue are fairly strong and not so much of them is needed, but if you're mixing a black concrete topping you'll need a larger proportion of coloring.

The method of finishing the concrete also affects the color to some extent. A steel floating-trowel gives a darker color than a wooden float. Keeping the new concrete covered and damp helps to darken the color.

It is possible to obtain ready-mixed colored cement (Portland cement colored with pigment) in several colors, which makes the job easier.

CONCRETE — Penetration Methods

What can you do with a concrete path or floor that is badly cracked or damaged—so badly that it's not worth while trying to patch it up?

One solution is to remove the old concrete and put down new. That means a lot of work and expense—and there's really no need for it in most cases.

What you can do instead is break up the concrete, then pour over it a thin mortar of Portland cement and sand, which binds the old concrete together and, in effect, makes a new path or floor.

This saves a lot of the expense and work of laying down new concrete.

This is a variation of what is called the penetration method of laying concrete. It is satisfactory for the average path or floor which does not have to stand very heavy traffic.

In the case of a path, you first lay boards evenly along each side of its whole length, just as you would if you were putting in a new concrete path.

The top edges of the boards should be about ¼ in. above the existing path, and you hold them in place with wooden pegs driven into the earth.

Then you break up the old concrete into small pieces with a heavy hammer or pick.

Mix up the mortar—one part cement and three parts sand, with water. It should be fairly thin, so that it will pour.

Dampen the broken-up concrete well, then pour on the mortar, which will penetrate between the pieces and bind them together in a solid mass.

Keep pouring on the mortar until it's level with the boards. Level it with a wooden straight-edge, and finish smooth with a wooden float.

Remove the boards when the concrete has set. Cover the new mortar with bags or other suitable material and keep it damp for a week, to let it cure and harden.

CONCRETE — Ready Mixed

Ready-mixed concrete very much simplifies, at a little extra cost, major concreting jobs around the house such as a garage drive.

Ready-mixed concrete is concrete produced at a central batching and mixing plant, and is supplied ready for use.

The concrete should be used within half to one and a half hours of delivery, otherwise setting will start before it is all worked into place, and the unworked material will be wasted. The working time is governed by the weather, and a hot summer day will reduce it to half an hour.

Ready-mixed concrete is supplied in cubic yards. The area to be filled should be measured and converted to square feet, then multiplied by the depth in inches. Divide this figure by 12 x 27 (that is, 324). The answer is the number of cubic yards of concrete to be ordered.

The standard truck carries three cubic yards. This is enough for a path about 80 ft x 4 ft x 3 in.

The quantity in a cubic yard always refers to the volume of concrete after pouring and compacting. One cubic yard is usually the minimum order accepted. If less than three yards are taken there is usually a small extra charge.

Most companies supply private customers, such as a householder, on a cash-on-delivery basis. The price will depend on the type of mix required, the quantity ordered, and the distance from the plant to the delivery address. If the price is acceptable, your order should be placed three to four days before delivery is required.

When using ready-mixed concrete the essential precautions are:
(1) Have all forms and framework ready to receive concrete on delivery.
(2) Have easy access to site.
(3) Have covering material handy to protect the finished surface.

CONCRETE — Reinforcing

To assure yourself of a concrete job that will take years of the hardest wear without cracking or breaking up, reinforce it with welded wire fabric at the time of pouring.

As concrete cures after the initial set, slight shrinkage often develops stresses which, under certain conditions, may crack the concrete.

A steel mesh made specially for the purpose and placed at the center of the slab tends to absorb and distribute these stresses and thus control the formation of cracks which are not only unsightly but may admit water, dirt and termites.

Exposed flat work, such as driveways, paths and patios, may warp and crack due to temperature variations between the top and bottom surfaces of the slab itself, or to structural stresses which develop due to settling of the soil or fill under the slab. Wire reinforcement adds the tensile strength necessary to control cracking of the slab under all these conditions.

For average purposes the mesh usually comes in rolls 60 in. or 72 in. wide and of various gauges. Your supplier will advise you about the gauge needed for your particular job.

The mesh is easily cut with wirecutters or small bolt-nippers for the larger sizes.

Placing the reinforcement in position in the freshly poured concrete can be done in either of two ways. By the first method concrete is poured to about half the finished thickness of the slab and leveled off. Then the wire fabric is placed and the final batch of concrete is poured without delay.

A second method often used for home projects involving slabs of considerable size, such as driveway sections, eliminate the need for two pours.

As the material comes from the ready-mix truck, a quantity of it is placed in small piles about 3 ft apart and equally spaced over the area to be covered. These piles are leveled so that their height is about half the thickness of the finished slab. Then the wire fabric is placed and the slab poured to full thickness. The piles of concrete will keep the fabric in the correct position in the center of the slab.

CONCRETE PATHS — To Lay

Of all the jobs the handyman does around the home, none is more necessary or practical than the laying of concrete paths.

Cracking is the worst fault in a concrete pavement. This can be the result of various factors, but the most likely cause is a faulty base or foundation.

It is better to excavate for a path than to place it on made or filled ground. If this is impracticable the earth should be rammed with a heavy tamper or well rolled until the bed is uniformly solid over the whole area. This precaution is necessary to prevent uneven settlement.

Next comes the sub-base. This is the term applied to a layer of material placed between the ground and the concrete. It must also be well consolidated by ramming or rolling.

Sand or ashes make the best sub-base by not only providing an even bearing surface for the concrete slabs, but also by draining off soakage water. Sodden ground means uneven settlement and cracking of the concrete.

The side forms or framework to hold the concrete should consist of fairly stout timber—say 4 in. x 2 in.—and must be carefully set with sufficient pegs on the outside to prevent bulging, with the resulting wavy edge to the pavement. See illustration.

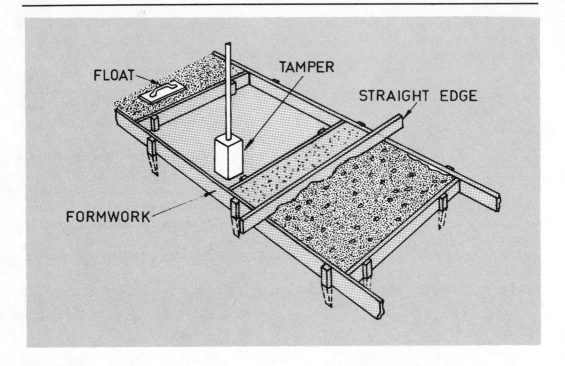

FLOAT

TAMPER

STRAIGHT EDGE

FORMWORK

Before pouring the concrete, the inside faces of the forms should be oiled so that they can be stripped or removed easily after the concrete has set.

The choice of materials for concrete work is most important. Apart from the cement there are the coarse and fine aggregates. The fine aggregate is usually sand, but for certain jobs may be finely crushed metal.

The coarse aggregate may consist of a number of materials. The best is blue metal of approximately ¾ in. gauge or screening, but other kinds of hard-broken stone, crushed slag, river gravel, coke, or washed boiler ash may be used, their relative value being roughly in that order.

Aggregate should be clean and free from vegetable matter. A loamy sand should never be used, but coarse sand or fine gravel is ideal, and for many jobs is preferable to finer sand. The latter, however, provides a smoother finish when used with cement to provide a topping mortar as described later.

The ideal method of laying a concrete path is to divide the total length up into sections about 3 ft long. Alternate slabs should be laid first and allowed to set, and then after a period of say twenty-four hours the cross forms are removed and the remaining slabs poured.

The first laid slabs should have the sides against which the others are to rest covered with a strip of bituminous roofing felt slightly less in width than the thickness of the slab.

The reason for laying slabs in this way is that concrete contracts when drying, and is liable to crack. A change in temperature will also cause expansion or contraction, and the joints formed by separating the blocks with the felt strip allows a little movement and so prevent cracks in the main slabs.

Joints should be placed at all sharp angles in the path, and if a pavement or floor is over 6 ft wide, down the center as well.

Before placing the concrete in position, the sub-base or foundation should be hosed lightly, but there should be no standing pools of water. A dry sub-base causes the concrete to dry out too quickly.

One of the basic rules of concrete mixing is that the proportions used should be sufficient and strong enough for the type of work being done and the purpose for which the concrete will be used.

The best proportions as far as strength and durability are concerned are three parts of coarse aggregate, two parts fine aggregate (sand) to one part of cement. Such a mixture is ideal for car drives and other parts subjected to heavy traffic.

However, for most paths and floors around the home, the proportions could be stretched to a mixture consisting of four parts coarse aggregate, two and a half parts fine aggregate and one part cement.

Mixtures weaker than this should be avoided because any small saving in cost is lost if the concrete starts to break up after a short time. In all cases the thickness of the path should not be less than 3 in.

When mixing, use as little water as possible. The dry materials should be first well mixed and the water added, after which the whole mass is turned over thoroughly at least three times to make sure that the metal, sand, and cement form a uniform mixture.

Those instructions assume that the mixing is done by hand on a flat platform, using a square-mouth shovel, but there are several alternative mixing methods.

A hand operated mixer is effective for most small jobs, and for the big job it is possible to hire a power operated machine at reasonable cost. Another very convenient way to get the job done with the minimum of hard work and time is to prepare all the framework first and then buy ready-mixed concrete.

Irrespective of the method of mixing, the concrete must be worked and spaded well into the forms or framework and firmly consolidated.

After packing, the concrete should be screeded level by drawing a board across the side forms and moving it forward with a sawing motion. This removes surplus concrete, and afterwards the surface is finished off with a wooden float.

Instead of troweling the main bulk of concrete in this way to finish the surface, a sand and cement topping mortar approximately half an inch thick is often used and screeded off in the same way as before.

The proportions of the topping are three parts of sand or fine metal screenings to one part of cement.

The main advantages to be gained from using the mortar topping are that it makes the job of coloring the path or floor much easier, and also results in a much more uniform surface after troweling. However, it is advisable to apply the topping as soon as the main bulk of concrete has been poured so that the two sections will bond together in one unit.

After troweling, the concrete should be covered or protected from damage for at least twenty-four hours, after which it must be kept damp for several days so that it will cure and harden. A good way to do this is to cover the surface to a depth of 2 or 3 in. with sand, which is kept wet for some days.

CONCRETE WALLS — Solid

Walls are often built of easily-handled and quickly-placed concrete blocks.

However, such blocks may not be suitable for some types of building, such as where a very dense surface is required that will take frequent washing down or where the wall must carry very heavy loads or will be subject to hard knocks.

Under these conditions dense concrete placed 'in situ' is necessary. As everyone knows, this type of wall is almost indestuctible.

Construction is relatively easy and depends primarily upon two things for a sound and good-looking result: proper well-constructed forms to hold the concrete until it has hardened sufficiently to become self-supporting, and the correct proportioning of materials.

Before any materials can be mixed or placed it is necessary to work out how much formwork will be required and how it is to be constructed.

Building forms is not just a matter of putting together some odd pieces of wood or sheet metal to hold the concrete; wet concrete is heavy, as anyone who has mixed it by hand knows, and consequently the forms must be solid and rigid if they are to do their job without bulging.

For all practical purposes, the weight of wet concrete can be taken as 145 lb. per cu. ft. To withstand this weight the formwork must be made of either 1¼ in. thick boards or ⅝ in. plywood.

The boards should be planed on the inside face and on both edges so that they will fit closely together and prevent fine materials in the concrete from leaking through the cracks. In this respect plywood is easier to use and also, since it can be purchased in larger sheets, easier to erect.

If plywood is used it is essential for it to be of the resin-bonded type to resist the moisture in the concrete.

Bracing for formwork is very important and should be made with not less than 2 in. x 4 in. timbers. The amount of bracing depends upon the size of the form and the quantity and speed of the concrete placing.

For normal small-scale construction with hand placing, it is not advisable to place concrete in heights, or lifts as they are called, greater than about 4 ft at one time. For such height bracing needs to be provided at about 2 ft intervals. See illustration at (A).

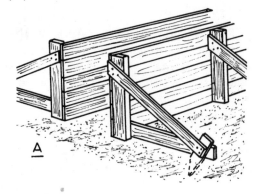

A

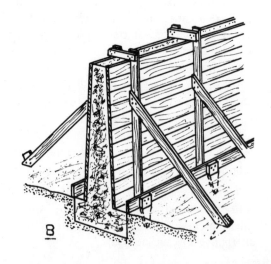

B

A lift of 4 ft does not, of course mean that concrete cannot be placed to greater heights, but that the first lift must harden before the second is placed. Also see at (B) that for higher walls a footing is provided together with extra bracing.

To ensure a good surface finish on concrete, formwork needs to be checked for cleanliness and to be oiled before placing begins. If the forms have been used before, traces of old concrete will cause blemishes. Protuding nails, wood shavings, etc., should be removed.

Oiling is necessary to prevent a close bond between form and concrete and allow the formwork to be stripped away easily. Proprietary brands of oil can be purchased from builder's supply merchants.

It is possible to use waste lubricating oil for coating forms. However, this does have certain disadvantages; the oil has a tendency to stain and the surface of the concrete becomes impregnated with oil and is then difficult to paint or plaster. If waste oil is used for formwork it should be applied as a very thin coat.

It is better to apply oil to forms before they are erected to avoid applying too heavy a coat, splashing of the steel reinforcement, or an accumulation of oil at the bottom of the form.

Oil must not be allowed to fall on the reinforcement or there will be no bond between steel and concrete and not only will the effect of the reinforcement be lost but also cracking may occur.

For walls, a standard 1:2:4 mix of concrete (by volume) is adequate; this means 1 part ordinary Portland cement to 2 parts sand to 4 parts coarse aggregate.

Care should be taken to keep the cement dry and to prevent it from 'air-setting' when it is delivered; this means that it must be protected not only from rain or direct moisture but also wrapped against moisture in the atmosphere.

Sacks of cement should never be stacked directly on the ground but always on a raised platform. Coarse aggregate can be either crushed stone or gravel, varying in size from ¾ to ³⁄₁₆ in.

While it is easy to calculate the size of a wall in cubic feet, remember that the volume of a quantity of concrete is by no means equal to the total volume of the ingredients used.

It is always better to try to use a whole bag of cement at one time; this avoids having part of a bag exposed to the weather during storage and also is often easier to calculate.

CONDENSATION — In Roof

One trouble you may be having, if your house has an iron roof, is condensation of moisture on the underside of the roof. This causes water drips which fall on the plaster ceilings, soaking through them and causing disfiguring stains and, in bad cases, deposits of mold.

Improving the roof ventilation helps to prevent this trouble. If there are no ventilation louvers, or other vents in the roof, they should be fitted; or existing louvers or vents may be inadequate, or may be blocked up and need cleaning.

Roof ventilation is particularly important if the rooms have ceiling vents which open into the roof. For example, a vent in the kitchen or bathroom ceiling to get rid of steam.

Apart from this preventative treatment, you can protect the ceilings from moisture drips by getting up into the roof and laying sheets of waterproof building paper, or aluminum-faced insulation, over the ceilings.

The sheets should be cupped in between the ceiling joists, forming hollows into which the condensed water will trickle and form pools instead of running through the joints between the sheets.

A layer of sawdust spread in the hollows will soak up the moisture and let it evaporate during the day. Softwood sawdust is better than hardwood sawdust.

Ceiling stains can be treated by scrubbing with a special paint-cleaning preparation, or household detergent. Let the ceiling dry thoroughly, then paint over the stained areas with cement sealer or a special sealer-undercoat.

After this you can paint over the stained area without fear of the stains coming through the paint.

CREOSOTE — Preservative

Timber decay is largely due to attack by fungi and similar growths. If timber is kept either thoroughly wet or thoroughly dry, this decay is almost impossible.

In the majority of cases of outdoor woodwork neither of these conditions is practicable, so that resort must be made to some preservative which will penetrate into all cells and fibers and act as a strong poison against destroying fungi.

It is obvious that to be thoroughly effective the liquid used must penetrate right through the timber, and to do this some form of vacuum impregnating plan is essential.

The only practical way, however, for the average home worker is to coat the surface of timber—such as bottoms of fence posts—with a brush. This has only limited penetration and therefore a limited preservative action.

The best known and one of the most effective preservatives is creosote, sometimes called wood preserving oil. The waterproofing qualities of creosote are negligible; it only prevents the attack of fungoid growths due to dampness.

Creosote dries slowly and tends to creep, so care should be taken that it is not close to any plaster or similar painted absorbent surface.

For thorough impregnation of posts buried in the earth the following method is recommended. Immerse timber in tank of creosote and heat up to 180-200 degrees F.

After maintaining this heat for about an hour it is allowed to cool and the timber removed. It is in the cooling period that the absorption takes place.

Heating can be done in a metal tank or drum, but be careful to keep the fire well confined.

DAMPCOURSES	Details
DAMPNESS	In Walls
DEPTH GAUGES	Two Types
DOOR	Adjust to Close
DOOR	To Hang
DOORS	Various Types
DOOR (Warped)	To Straighten
DOVETAIL JOINTS	To Make
DOWEL JOINTS	In Woodwork
DOWEL JOINTS	Jig
DRAWERS	To Ease
DRAWERS	To Make
DRAW KNIFE	Use
DRILLING	Pointers
DRILLS	Some Points
DRILLS	To Sharpen
DRY ROT	Details

DAMPCOURSES — Details

It is doubtful whether the average person realizes just how important it is to have efficient dampcourse in all buildings.

Faulty dampcourse is the cause of practically all damp-wall problems.

In most cases the work of repair is a job for the bricklayer, although, with a minor fault, it is often possible for the home handyman to put things right himself.

The main point to keep in mind is that the dampcourse is a layer of some impervious material which extends right around a building without a break.

It is built into the brickwork below floor level with the idea of preventing dampness soaking up from the ground.

Figs 1 and 2 show just how and where dampcourse is used for two different types of wall or conditions.

In Fig. 1 we see the average type of dampcourse as used in buildings which need such protections only above the ground level.

It illustrates clearly the protection afforded by such dampcourse to both walls and floor.

Note that the layer of dampcourse—it could be sheet lead—marked by the dark black line runs right under the floor bearer.

When, as sometimes happens, it is below the level of the ground outside, it is obvious that something must be done about dampness which could soak through the wall from the outside, in addition to seeping up from below.

An effective method is shown at Fig. 2 where three dampcourses are combined.

We see not only the lower horizontal layer, but a vertical course as well, and this is topped with a high level horizontal course.

Such dampcourses must cover the full width of the wall, and must reach down to under the lowest timbers and also up between 6 and 12 in. above ground level—no less.

DAMPNESS — In Walls

It is often difficult to locate or determine the cause of dampness in the walls of a building, so here are some pointers. See illustration on next page.

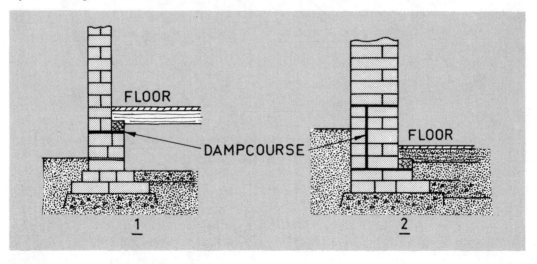

FLOOR

DAMPCOURSE

FLOOR

1

2

FAULTY DAMPCOURSES. If the dampcourse above the foundations is broken, dampness will gradually creep up the walls from below leaving unsightly stains on interior plaster. The only remedy is to renew the dampcourse. (See Dampcourses details.)

POROUS BRICKS. These will allow dampness from driving rain to soak through to interior walls.

The remedy is to render the outside wall surface with mortar containing a water-proofing agent, or to apply a water-proof solution to the bricks. Several coats of oil paint will also seal the surface.

CHOKED GUTTERING. This may allow water to overflow during very heavy rain. It runs down the wall and soaks through. Scoop out the dirt with a small trowel and flush well with water.

BROKEN GUTTER BRACKET. Can cause the same trouble by allowing the gutter to sag. Fit a new bracket or give temporary support with an ordinary shelf bracket.

CRACKED GUTTER OR DOWN PIPE. May produce damp patches on the wall. Fill with a bitumen sealing compound or epoxy cement.

BLOCKED DRAIN. Might prevent heavy rain from running away. Scrape dirt and leaves from grate and lift out. Pour down some strong disinfectant and then scoop out the dirt.

Use an old tablespoon with the handle bent at right-angles and bound to a wooden handle.

When the trap is clear, flush with two buckets of water and replace grate.

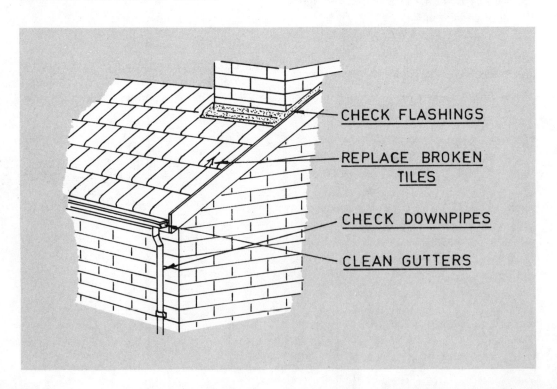

CHECK FLASHINGS

REPLACE BROKEN TILES

CHECK DOWNPIPES

CLEAN GUTTERS

DAMAGED FLASHING. A very common cause of dampness in walls is the result of faulty lead flashing under window sills.

In all cases the edges of such flashing should be turned up on both the sides and ends so that any rain driving under the window sill is trapped and unable to percolate inside the building.

DEPTH GAUGES — Two Types

When boring holes in wood, it is very often necessary to control the depth. One method is to count the revolutions of the bit in the brace, but this is unsatisfactory since the bit will cut slower in hardwood than in softer varieties.

A more satisfactory method is with the aid of a depth gauge. This is a device that may be clamped on the bit at any point to indicate the desired depth.

A number of these depths gauges in various patterns are on the market. However, gauges which are just as effective can be made quite easily.

The type illustrated is made of two pieces of softwood, 2 in. long, ¾ in. wide, and ½ in. thick. V-shaped grooves are cut on the inside faces of these pieces as shown in the sketch to keep the gauge at right-angles to the bit.

Two holes are bored in the blocks on either side of the V cut to take small bolts of, say, ⅛ or 3⁄16 in. in diameter. These are fitted with wing nuts so that they can be tightened easily to clamp the depth gauge to the bit in any desired position.

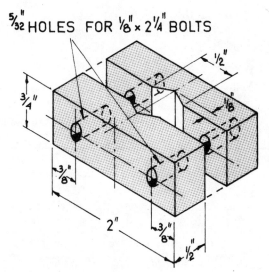

5⁄32" HOLES FOR ⅛" x 2¼" BOLTS
½"
¾"
⅛"
3⁄8"
2"
3⁄8"
½"

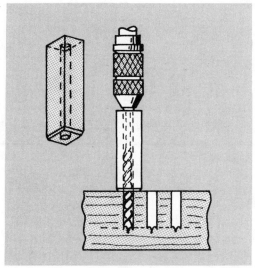

A second type of gauge is merely a block of $1\frac{1}{2}$ in. square stock, with a hole bored through the center.

The block of wood is slipped over the bit. When the block comes into contact with the surface being bored, the bit stops, and all holes bored will be of exactly the same depth.

However, blocks of various lengths are needed for each depth required.

DOOR — Adjust to Close

A door that refuses to close properly is a common home repair problem.

The trouble usually lies in the strike plate, see (A) in illustration. If you have to slam the door shut, a little filing on the edge (B) may do the job.

If it is obvious that filing won't help and that the strike plate must be moved either to the right or to the left, to ensure a close fit, take out the screws (D and D) holding the plate.

Then with chisel or pocketknife remove enough wood at (E) or (F) to move the plate the required distance. Screw back in place.

If the new hole is very close to the old, plug the old one with wood-patching compound or a whittled wood plug.

But first better give the screws a start in their new location with a push drill or simply by driving a nail.

After the plate has been securely fastened, fill in the leftover groove at (E) or (F) with the wood-patching compound or putty.

Now shut the door. Shut it again.

Don't slam it; don't lean on it; just shut it.

No crash, no rattle, instead a little click as the latch slips snugly into place.

Sometimes the scratches (C) made on the strike plate by the latch will indicate that the strike plate is out of line and must be moved up or down instead of to the right or left.

The procedure to be followed in this instance is, of course, the same.

Or you may find that there isn't a click because the latch sometimes sticks.

Usually this difficulty can be remedied by loosening the set screw on the doorknob and unscrewing the knob to the left away from the door until the latch moves back and forth easily.

Tighten the set screw at this place.

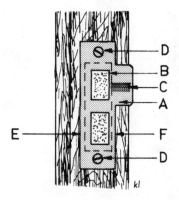

DOOR — To Hang

Many home workers are called on at various times to hang a door, so here are some simple instructions and sketches that should help.

Whether the door is small, large, or medium size, a standard size door for a room or one for a built-in-cupboard, the directions are the same—only the hinge positions will differ.

We will assume that we are going to hang an average domestic door measuring 6 ft 8 in. long x 2 ft 8 in. wide.

Test the width of door frame opening at top and bottom.

This is best done with a rod cut to fit neatly between the door jambs.

Check this rod with the door to see what amount needs to be planed off.

Both edges should be planed slightly off square from the outside face as suggested at (A) in the illustration.

This will prevent the door from binding in the frame.

Having done this, put the door into position and ease where necessary.

The thickness of a penny is a good-size joint to have showing down the two edges and at the top.

The bottom of the door should be parallel with the floor, leaving enough space for it to clear any fitted floor covering.

For holding the door steady when planing the edges or trimming ends, make the clamp shown at (B).

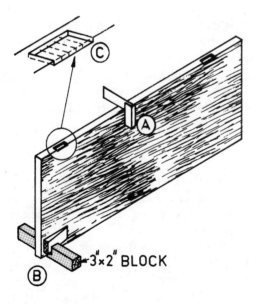

3″×2″ BLOCK

It is a block of wood checked out a little more than thickness of door so that a wedge can be slipped in to grip the door and block.

The position of the hinges can now be marked. Push door into frame opening and wedge in the position it will take when fitted.

Set one hinge 6 in. down from door top, and the other 9 in. up from the floor.

Mark these positions on the door and the frame with a sharp pencil, remove the door and fit in the wedge block as at (B).

This gives good working position for cutting the hinge recesses.

To ensure the hinges being square to the door and frame, set a marking gauge or butt gauge to slightly wider than the leaf of one hinge and mark; reset the gauge to the leaf thickness and mark again to give depth of hinge recess.

Pare out the recess as shown in insert (C) for each hinge, making sure that it is a neat fit.

The matching recesses are then cut in door jambs, and when this is complete, screw the hinges to the door.

Position the door at right-angle open position, and insert two screws only in the jamb, in case any adjustments are necessary.

Test the door to see whether it swings and closes without catching.

If it doesn't perhaps the hinges have been recessed too much, causing the door to become hinge bound, or the bevel of the door edges is fouling the frame.

The first fault is easily cured by inserting a slip of cardboard behind the hinge, and the second by taking off a few shavings.

Finally, drive in remaining hinge screws, and remove all sharp edges from door with a plane or glasspaper.

DOORS — Various Types

More and more home builders are realizing that doors can make or mar the appearance of a new home. In selecting doors the three points to watch are the cost, the function to be performed, and the type of home.

Here are some details of three of the more unusual door types:

DUTCH DOOR, Fig. 1. This type of door is unusual in the United States but extremely versatile. Built in two sections—upper and lower—the top can be opened while the bottom stays closed.

Dutch doors are made in several designs—either solid raised paneling, matched tongue and groove planks, or with glass panes set in the top half.

Convenient spots for their use are between kitchen and dining terrace, door to children's bedrooms, and between kitchen and dining-room.

LOUVERED DOORS, Fig. 2. Built much like slatted window shutters, louvered doors provide a pleasant combination of ventilation and privacy.

If you have a problem room that has windows in only one wall, a louvered door can give you a system of cross ventilation.

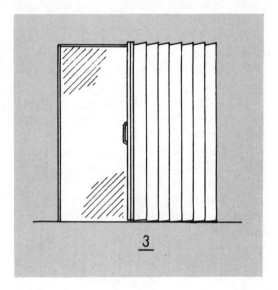

3

ACCORDION DOOR, Fig. 3. Not a door in the true sense of the word, the accordion door usually is a flexible, folding partition of real or imitation leather or plastic.

This type of door can be pushed out of sight into a recess or merely folded back against the wall.

DOOR (Warped) — To Straighten

The doors of a house naturally come in for a great deal of use, and in time certain faults will develop.

Of these, the most annoying, and often the most difficult to correct is a warp or twist in the door itself.

This often results in the door lock failing to operate and drafts probably find their

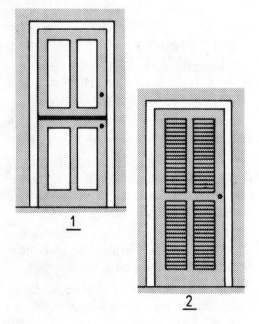

1

2

way inside the house through gaps between the door and the door frame.

There are several methods of repair, and the simplest should be tried first.

This is to remove the door from the frame and lay it on a flat surface in the sun with the round side up.

An open porch or patio can be used as a platform for the door providing it is perfectly flat, Fig. 1.

If, as is probable, dampness is the cause of the trouble, the sun will dry the timber in the door and possibly cause the twisted or warped section to fall back into shape.

Of course, hinges and doorknobs must be removed so that the door can lie flat.

A second method is to place the door on a pair of stools or similar supports with the bowed or round side up as in Fig. 2. Weights are then placed on top to force it back into shape.

Keep it in this position for two or three days. Bricks, concrete masonry blocks, or sandbags can be used for weights.

The third method as shown in Fig. 3 is especially effective when the door has warped diagonally.

Heavy screw-eyes are placed in opposite low corners and then connected by a length of steel clothes line with a turn-buckle inserted in it.

In addition, a 4 in. by 2 in. piece of stout timber is placed near the center as a kind of pivoting point for the pressure and tension as the turn-buckle is slowly tightened to pull the door frame back into shape.

The final method of straightening that can be tried is shown in Fig. 4. Here, a length of straight solid timber—6 in. wide by 2 in. thick is ideal—is secured to the twisted side with G-clamps to pull it straight.

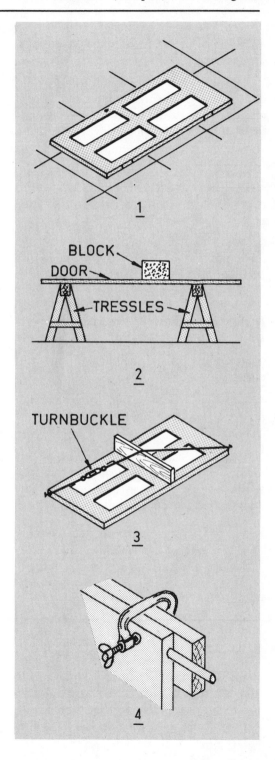

Then a ½ in. diameter hole is drilled as deeply into the center of the vertical stile as possible.

A ½ in. diameter hardwood dowel is then coated with woodworker's glue and driven into this hole. Allow the door to remain in the clamps until the glue dries. This usually takes about twenty-four hours.

Once the door is straight, and also on doors that are apparently not affected, it is advisable to paint the top and bottom edges.

This is rarely if ever, done, but it is a precaution which may prevent dampness entering the door and causing it to twist.

DOVETAIL JOINTS — To Make

An ambition of most home woodworkers—often thwarted—is to be able to cut neat dovetail joints.

Such joints, because of their strength and neatness, are the best for many wood-working jobs.

There are many variations of the dovetail joint, but the two dealt with in this article are the most used. They are the through and lapped dovetails.

For making such dovetails, the tools required are a tenon saw, marking gauge, rule, paring chisel, square, pencil, and a dovetail gauge or template. The latter can be made from a scrap end of thin sheet metal.

Both sides of the dovetail pins are cut at an angle, and this produces the wedge-shape appearance of the finished joint.

The two essential requirements for a neat result are to mark and cut the dovetail pins and sockets accurately so that they fit together firmly without forcing or being too loose.

The first operation should be to make a gauge or template, and details for this are shown in Fig. 1. To obtain the correct slope for dovetails suitable for average furniture construction, follow the method shown in detail (A) Fig. 1.

A piece of timber 6 in. long by 1 in. wide is marked off along the edge with diagonal lines as shown. The thickness of this block should be slightly more than one inch.

Detail (B) Fig. 1 shows a blank strip of thin sheet metal such as aluminum or copper bent at right-angles to the sizes indicated. The metal is then placed over the end of the wood as in detail (C) and the lines transferred to the long top edge of the template blank. The surplus metal outside these lines is then cut away with a pair of tinsnips and the edges filed smooth to produce the finished template shown in detail (D) Fig. 1.

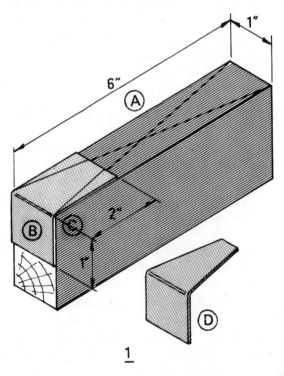

1

Fig. 2 shows the first stage in the making of a joint. A marking gauge is set to the thickness of the wood being used in the article, and a line marked around the end. Mark this line very lightly, as sections of it will have to be removed in the final cleaning-up after assembly.

Naturally, all pieces have been cut perfectly square on the ends. Next the metal template is used to mark out the dovetails as shown in Fig. 3. These are the pins of the through dovetail joint.

Use a sharp tenon saw to cut the dovetails—Fig. 4—being careful to cut on the waste side of the pins and not to allow the saw blade to cut any deeper than the gauge line.

After making the vertical cuts with the saw, the waste is chopped out in the manner suggested in Fig. 5.

To do this, the timber is clamped to the bench top and a sloping cut is made with the chisel at a point about $\frac{1}{16}$ in. from the gauge line. A second cut is made from the end, thus lifting out a small section of wood. Two chisels are shown in the illustration to indicate where the cuts are made.

The operation is repeated until the half-way stage is reached, when the wood is turned over and cutting commenced in a similar manner from the other side.

Final trimming up is done close to all lines when the bulk of the waste has been removed.

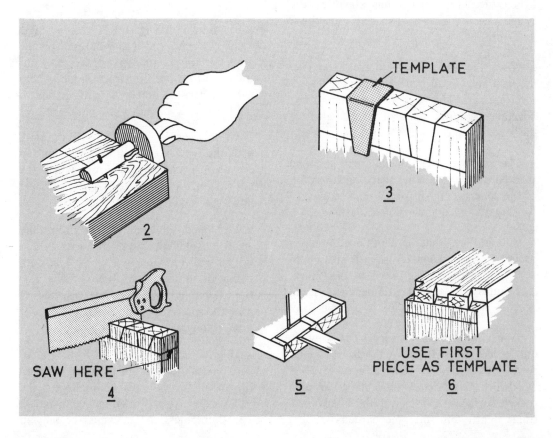

TEMPLATE

3

2

SAW HERE

4

5

USE FIRST
PIECE AS TEMPLATE

6

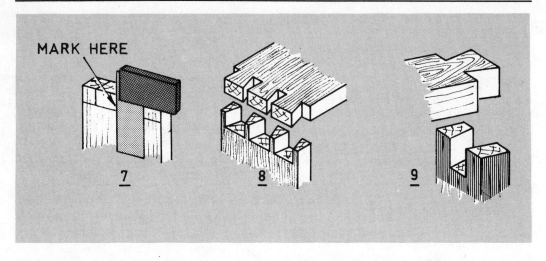

MARK HERE

7

8

9

An alternative method is to remove the bulk of the waste between the pins with a coping saw with the wood held upright in a bench vice. Final trimming down to the gauge lines is done with a sharp paring chisel as before.

When the dovetail pins have been cut, the next stage is to mark out the sockets to receive them. This is done by placing the dovetails on top of, and at right angles to, the matching piece of the frame.

The shape of the dovetails can then be marked off, so giving the shape and position of the sockets, Fig. 6. Use a pointed scriber or very hard lead pencil for marking.

Note in Fig. 7 that the depth line is gauged as before and that a try square is used to carry the cutting lines down to this mark. The removal of the waste timber to form the sockets is done in the same way as before.

Shown in Fig. 8 is a very clear view of one corner of a frame with the dovetails ready for assembly. Use a good quality woodwork glue brushed on to both pin and socket surfaces and clamp the assembled frame tightly until the glue hardens.

Afterwards, any surplus projections of the dovetail pins can be cleaned off with a steel smoothing plane.

An interesting variation of the dovetail joint is shown in Fig. 9. This is a single through dovetail, and it can be used on the top section of a wooden bracket and for many other furniture construction jobs where a narrow piece of timber is to be joined to a similar piece.

Next to consider is the lapped dovetail. This is the type often used in the making of a drawer, especially at the front where the drawer sides are joined to the solid drawer fronts.

The lapped dovetail differs from the through dovetail, because the sockets are blind, as will be seen in Fig. 9. The construction is similar, but there is one important difference and this concerns the setting of the marking gauge when setting out the length of the dovetails.

In Fig. 2 the gauge was set to the thickness of the timber, but for a lapped dovetail joint, an allowance must be made for the lap. Thus the gauge is set to the thickness of the timber less the thickness of the lap which is the distance from the drawer front to the back edge of the socket as in Fig. 10.

For example, if the timber is 1 in. thick and the lap is ⅜ in. wide, the gauge will be set at ⅜ in., which will be the length of the dovetail pins.

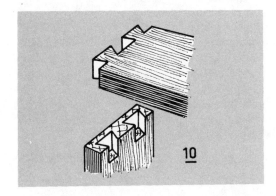

Finally, unlike other woodwork joints it is not advisable to try dovetail joints together before final assembly, as this is inclined to loosen them.

When all the joints have been cut, they should be glued and assembled in one complete operation and provided reasonable care has been taken to mark and cut carefully, there shouldn't be any problem of bad fitting.

DOWEL JOINTS — In Woodwork

No matter what article of furniture or woodwork we make, joints of some kind will be needed to assemble the various parts. These will range from plain butt joints to those secured with nails or screws, to the more complicated mortise and tenon, or dovetail joints.

One joint in common use for furniture making is the dowel joint. It is particularly useful when butting two boards together, as it gives added strength to the ordinary glued joint.

The dowels, or wood pins, as they are sometimes called, are best bought in various lengths and cut to suit.

On the other hand, there is a tool called a dowel plate which can be used for making dowels of various diameters.

Dowel rods that are to be used for jointing work should have a shallow groove along their length, as indicated at (A) Fig. 1.

This groove allows the escape of air and surplus glue when the dowel is driven home, so reducing the risk of splitting the timber being joined.

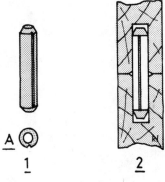

Note also in Fig. 1 that the ends of the dowels are chamfered so that they will enter the holes easily.

The general principle of the joint is that the dowels or pins are inserted into holes bored in the two surfaces to be joined.

It follows, of course, that these holes must be dead in line with each other so that they engage without distortion.

An important point to note is that the holes should be bored a little deeper than the actual length of the dowel, Fig. 2. The difference is only slight, but is necessary for a good joint.

105

The holes should also be countersunk slightly.

In Fig. 3 is shown the hole bored (B), then countersunk (C).

A typical dowel joint, with a rail being fitted into a leg or stile, is shown clearly in Fig. 4.

In Fig. 5 the same joint has been clamped firmly into place after gluing. The dowels are indicated by the dotted lines.

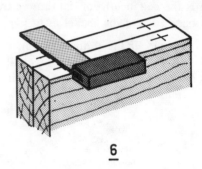

6

The first essential for a good joint is accurate marking out, and this operation is shown clearly in Fig. 6, where two boards are being prepared.

First mark the center of the edges to be joined with a marking gauge. (These edges, of course, have previously been planed straight and true.)

Then place the pieces face to face and grip them firmly together in a vice.

Keeping the ends level, measure the distance in from each end for the positions of the dowels, and mark across the two boards with a square as shown, Fig. 6.

When the center of the holes are correctly positioned, they should be bored and countersunk in readiness to receive the dowel pins, which are tapped into one edge as indicated in Fig. 7.

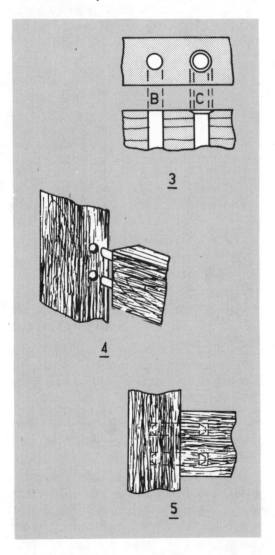

3

4

5

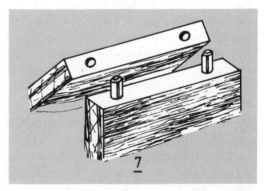

7

Bore the holes with a clean cutting twist bit, keeping the bit upright all the time. To help to keep the bit straight a tool is available called a doweling jig, which clamps onto the face of the timber and ensures accuracy in boring.

For most work, $\frac{3}{8}$ in. diameter dowels are suitable. This is assuming that the thickness of the frame timber is that used in most jobs, namely $1\frac{3}{16}$ inches or $\frac{7}{8}$ in.

The diameter of the dowels should never be more than half the thickness of the timber in which it is being used.

To illustrate the most common error to avoid when making a dowel joint, take a glance at Fig. 8.

8

The first joint (D) is accurate, the holes meeting perfectly, and square with the jointed surfaces.

The second one (E) is square, but the holes are not in line. If a dowel is already fixed in one piece, it will be practically impossible to force it into its corresponding hole in the other piece.

The third example (F) shows the result of not holding the bit plumb and square to the edge.

The centers have been correctly positioned, but the holes are not square with the jointed edges. It may be possible to force the dowel home, but it will be weakened in the process.

Of course all that has been said about boring accurately when looking from the face side applies equally looking from the end.

The first hole (D), for example, can look all right from one side—say the face—but may be out of line when viewed from the end. The most common result of this fault is that an assembled frame takes a twist or warp which is practically impossible to remove.

Hot woodworker's glue, liquid glue, or casein cold water glue may be used with dowels.

Put a little glue inside the holes with a small round stick, put a dab of glue on the ends of the dowels, and tap them into the holes.

Glue the inside of the opposite holes similarly. Then smear the projecting ends of the dowels with glue, brush a little along the edges of the two pieces being joined, and finally tap the two pieces together.

Use a sash clamp to draw the joints tightly together, and allow them to remain under pressure until the glue sets.

DOWEL JOINTS — Jig

Extensive use should be made of dry setups to check fitting and accuracy of all joints. This will ensure that when the work is finally assembled and glued the job can proceed smoothly without annoying delays caused by taking apart the joints and refitting them.

To make a good dowel joint, two things are essential.

First, the holes for the dowels must be accurately marked and bored straight and square to the face of the timber.

Secondly, the dowels must fit into the holes firmly.

Drilling the dowel holes straight and square to the face of the timber is not an easy job for the tradesman—for the home worker it is a difficult one.

The illustration shows a jig for boring dowel holes, and its use makes the job easy for the most inexperienced woodworker.

By the use of this jig, which is clamped to the timber as shown, holes can be easily and accurately bored in the end, edge and surface of the timber. The jig shown can take any thickness of timber up to 3 in.

Apart from the jig itself, there are a number of hardened steel guides and a depth gauge supplied with the jig.

The guides are in various sizes and when fitted in the jig ensure that the holes bored are square and true to the face of the timber. The depth gauge is shown in use on page 97. The gauge fits over the bit and regulates the depth of the holes to be bored.

It can be secured to the bit at any point by means of a small thumb screw.

DRAWERS — To Ease

In most cases, a faulty drawer requires only a little attention to put it right, but the job must be tackled properly.

Drawers that refuse to slide freely are most annoying, particularly if they are in constant use.

Don't rush for a smoothing plane and start removing a lot of shavings in a fit of pique. Remember, a drawer which is planed too small is worse than one which sticks a little.

Let us first consider a few of the faults commonly associated with drawers.

Sticking drawers can be caused by the wood swelling. This is quite common with new furniture if the wood has not been seasoned to the proper degree.

In such a case it is best not to try to remedy the matter right away. Leave the drawers as they are for a few weeks to see if the wood will shrink back to its original size once it has become acclimatized to the normal temperature of the room. A spell of damp weather can easily cause temporary swelling of the drawers.

If, however, the drawers refuse to return to their original free state after a fair trial period, then locate the actual sticking parts and remove a little of the wood with a scraper or a smoothing plane. Finish off with a rub of fine sandpaper.

Before easing a sticking drawer it is a good plan to first examine the dovetail joints on the front member. Sometimes these joints become loose, causing the sides to spread outwards and rub against the drawer runners.

If you find that these joints are loose, knock the members apart, scrape off the old glue and re-assemble, using a strong woodworker's glue. Once assembled, insert one or two nails as a precaution against further trouble.

In many cases a sticking drawer can often be eased simply by applying a little lubricant. The best lubricant to use is beeswax (or a candle). Don't use machine oil or grease, as these are messy and are likely to stain the wood.

Give the edges of the drawers and runners a liberal rub of beeswax, note the difference it makes. Do this regularly to all drawers whether they are sticking or not; it is well worth the time. Ordinary soap is another good lubricant.

Sometimes a drawer slides too freely, with the result that it frequently gets pulled right out and its contents scattered over the floor.

To prevent this happening, screw a **wooden tongue** to the back member of the drawer as shown in Fig. 1.

This can be turned upright whenever the drawer is inserted, and should be made so that it catches on the upper rail of the drawer opening when the drawer is pulled out. If you want to remove the drawer, then simply twist the tongue to the side.

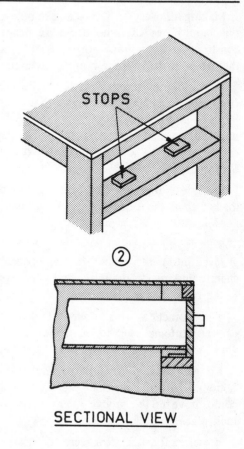

① STOPS

SECTIONAL VIEW

②

When a drawer can be pushed in farther than it is supposed to go, you will know that the drawer stops are missing.

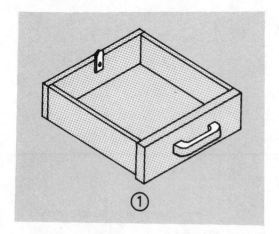

①

These stops are normally made from small pieces of plywood and are fixed to the lower rail of the drawer opening. Their function is to keep the drawer in a proper closed position by engaging behind the front rail as shown in Fig. 2.

Sometimes these stops become loose and it is quite a simple matter to nail them into position again.

DRAWERS — To Make

Thanks to modern materials and power tools, many jobs can now be done in a fraction of the time they used to take, and in most cases the result is much better.

Making drawers is a typical example of this, and if we examine orthodox drawer construction we can see how to adapt it to the needs of the average home craftsman.

First, the sides are dovetailed into the front and back, which means that these joints cannot be broken by the normal strain imposed on them—that is, in pulling the drawer front to drag the whole drawer forward.

Secondly, the drawer front is made thicker than the sides and back so that it does not distort when pulled.

The bottom—about ¾₆ in. thick—is grooved into the front and sides and projects slightly underneath the back, and is screwed to the bottom edge of the back.

This practice was followed because drawer bottoms used to be made of solid wood which was subject to shrinkage.

No glue was used in fitting the drawer bottom. This meant that the front edge could move in the groove if any shrinkage took place.

If necessary, the rear screws were removed after some time and the shrunken bottom pushed into its front groove again before re-screwing at the back.

These details of orthodox construction are useful to know, but with the advent of materials such as plywood and hardboard, which do not shrink, the necessity for a bottom grooved into the body or frame of the drawer has disappeared.

A hardboard bottom can be fitted quite simply as in Fig. 1. Thin strips or fillets are glued and pinned around the lower inside edges of the drawer, and the hardboard rests on, or is glued to these.

As an alternative to the fillet strips, grooved slips of the type shown in Fig. 2 can be glued and tacked to the inside bottom edges of the drawer to hold the hardboard or plywood bottom.

A simple feature of the orthodox drawer construction which is worth using is a low back. In other words, the back is not as wide as the front.

Fig. 2 which is a sectional view of the back of an old drawer fitted with dovetails, shows how the sides are chamfered off at the rear to meet the top edge of the narrower back.

This is a real advantage where the drawer is inside a close-fitting framework and where there is little chance of the air to escape as the drawer is closed.

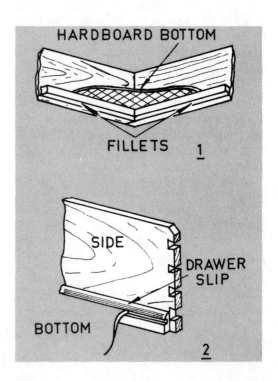

With a well-fitting drawer, air pressure can be quite a factor in easy closing, and a low back enables the air trapped behind at (X) Fig. 3, to flow over the top and out as indicated by the arrows.

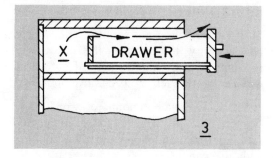

3

Drawers in cupboards and cabinets can be improved in a number of ways. For example, dividers or partitions in a drawer will separate the articles stored there and make them easier to find.

It is important to plan the layout carefully, so each article will fit easily into its own compartment.

A good idea is to make a pattern by placing all the articles on a piece of paper or cardboard the size of the bottom of the drawer. Mark on the paper the space required for each article. From this pattern it will be easy to measure the length of the partition pieces required.

For making the partitions, use plywood or hardboard, and the drawer will be easier to clean if you make dividers that are removable.

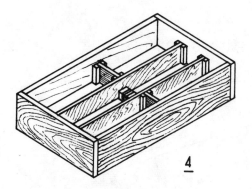

4

If a frame is not used, small cleats that are nailed to the ends or sides of the drawer as in Fig. 4 may hold removable divider strips in place.

To separate a drawer into equal sections, Fig. 5, cut one strip of hardboard or plywood the length of the drawer and two—or more pieces—the width of the drawer. Mark out and cut slots one-half the height of the dividers at the points where they cross each other so that they fit together as at Fig. 6.

5

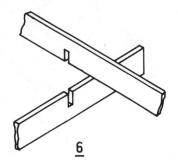

6

Shallow sliding trays may be made for both shallow and deep drawers to use the space to best advantage.

These trays may slide from side to side or from front to back. A tray generally covers one-third to one-half of the drawer area to permit access to the articles stored in the bottom of the drawer.

A tray or trays may be used for storing small articles that will not interfere with opening and closing drawers. In the workshop it is ideal for small items such as drills and punches stored in tool cabinets.

Fig. 7 shows a typical wide drawer fitted with a sliding tray. Determine the depth of the tray, allow some clearance at the top, and tack light runners (A), in place at back and front. Cut the bottom of the tray and fit it into the drawer to see that it slides easily. Then fit and cut the four sides of the tray.

Plan the sides so that the pull will be against the nails used for assembling the tray. This gives greater strength. For example, in the tray shown (Fig. 7) the front and back pieces overlap and are nailed into the side pieces.

indicating that friction, and therefore binding, has occurred (Fig. 9).

If the trouble is not serious, it may only be necessary to lubricate the drawer by rubbing the sides and bottom edges with a wax candle or stick of special dry lubricant.

Where a certain amount of wood must be removed to achieve free-running, try **rubbing with sandpaper and then rubbing** with the candle.

You will be surprised how little wood needs to be removed, and unless done gradually and carefully, the drawer may **become loose in the frame.**

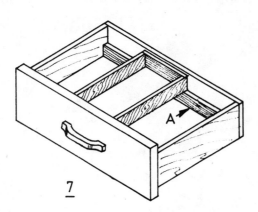

7

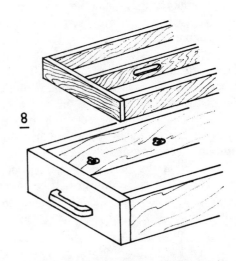

8

The idea illustrated in Fig. 8 is well worth noting. Screw-eyes are used to make easily **removable cleats for supporting a tray in** a deep drawer. Just turn two into each drawer side to support the tray.

When a sticking drawer is to be eased so that it can operate freely, the first step is to take it out and check where it is binding.

This is done by inspecting the drawer for polished areas on the top, bottom, or sides,

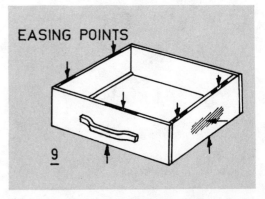

EASING POINTS

9

DRAW KNIFE — Use

Although the draw-knife is a tool which has fallen out of use to some extent, it still has many uses in woodworking.

One of its main uses is for removing surplus wood before sawing or planing down to an exact finished size or shape. For instance, if a panel is about an inch too wide and the waste strip will be of no use to you, it is quicker to cut it away with the generous chips of a draw knife than to plane or saw it away.

A draw knife is equally useful when working up to a shaped edge, and is much quicker than a bow-saw or keyhole-saw.

The illustration shows a draw knife being used.

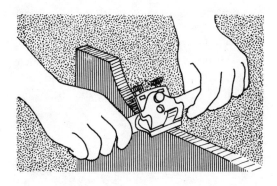

For chamfering or rounding over square sections, too, the draw knife is excellent, especially for large, heavy work.

The main precaution when using the draw knife is to watch the direction of the grain carefully. It is usually a wise move to make preliminary saw cuts in the waste area as shown, so as to stop any split that may develop from going too far.

The tool is sharpened on one side only, and the side which faces the wood when it is used depends upon the particular job.

When the bevel on blade is downwards, the tool has a tendency to rise from the cut, and this helps to prevent any risk of cutting the cut too deeply into the wood.

For finishing off, however, and when dealing with convex shapes as distinct from **hollow, or concave ones, the bevel on blade** is usually uppermost.

There are many jobs where the finish produced by a draw knife is good enough to leave without further attention. However, where a fine surface is necessary for paint or polish, finish off with a smoothing plane **or spokeshave, and finally, fine-grade sand**paper.

DRILLING — Pointers

A portable power drill has come to be accepted as an essential part of the home workshop kit. A few suggestions about the types of drills to use for various jobs will be useful.

When drilling wood, use special wood drills and lift them occasionally while in motion. This helps the drill to clear itself and prevents overheating. Never use wood drills on any other material.

For metal drilling, carbon-steel or high-speed steel drills give the best results. Lubrication of metal drills in use is necessary, and here are the most suitable lubricants for various metals:

HARD STEEL: Turpentine or kerosene.

SOFT STEEL: Lard oil or soluble oil.

MALLEABLE IRON: Soluble oil.

WROUGHT IRON: Lard oil or soluble oil.

BRASS: Kerosene, or dry.

ALUMINUM AND SOFT ALLOYS: Kerosene or soluble oil.

CAST IRON: Dry.

It is essential to keep metal drills ground to the correct angle in both directions. The main drilling angle is 59 degrees at the point, and various jigs or guides for holding the drills when grinding are available.

For masonry, brickwork, glazed tile, etc., use special masonry drills or bits. These are tipped with some super-hard material such as carbide or tungsten.

When drilling cement or concrete, you may encounter metal reinforcing rods which could damage a masonry bit, so it is advisable to lift drill frequently to inspect the material.

Another precaution when drilling brick or masonry walls is to check the positions of any electrical or water conduits recessed below the surface.

Where possible, masonry drilling work with a portable power drill should be done at low speed, and it is here that a dual-speed model drill has a distinct advantage.

DRILLS — Some Points

With a portable electric drill it is possible to drill holes in any surface in practically any position.

Where possible, greater accuracy in drilling is achieved by fitting the drill into a vertical or horizontal drill stand.

The four drill types shown will cover most jobs likely to be encountered around the home.

The average masonry drill, Fig. 1, looks like a twist drill but has a small tip of tungsten carbide brazed into the point. The hole diameter swept out by the carbide tip is larger than that of the fluted body.

Such drills are usually run at low speed and when drilling large holes in brickwork or masonry of any kind it is advisable first to drill a smaller pilot hole. Masonry drills should not be used to drill holes in glass or metal. Special drills for glass are available in a range of sizes.

Twist drills are available in a wide range of sizes in variations of ⅟₆₄ inch, and they can be of high-speed steel or the softer and

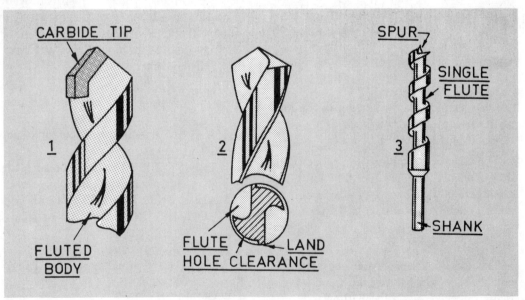

cheaper carbon steel. The latter type are quite suitable for most wood-drilling work.

A twist drill, Fig. 2, is a cylindrical piece of tool steel with opposed helical flutes machined along part of its length.

The flutes carry away the chips, and on the leading edge of each flute is a raised portion called a land, which is shown in Fig. 2. The distance across the lands is equal to the hole diameter produced by the drill.

The drill point includes the complete conical end. The drill cuts only with the point and the lands guide the drill in a straight line.

When twist drills become blunt and worn, it is essential that they be sharpened correctly. Sharpening is best done by holding the drill in an attachment called a sharpening jig which is fixed firmly to the frame of the grinding wheel so that the drill point makes contact with the revolving wheel at the correct angle.

Up to $\frac{1}{2}$ in. diameter you can use the twist drill for drilling in wood. Above this size, and up to $1\frac{1}{4}$ in. diameter use special wood boring bits.

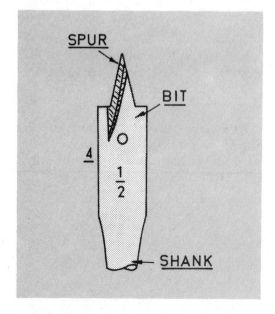

Fig. 3 shows a special wood bit in the size range between $\frac{1}{4}$ in. and $\frac{3}{4}$ in. diameter. This bit has a single helical groove, the spur point is tapered and unthreaded—unlike bits used by hand in a brace—and there is a vertical knife edge spur projecting below the horizontal cutting edge for severing the wood fibers before drilling actually starts. This feature ensures a perfectly clean hole.

Bits of this type are sold in sets with reduced $\frac{1}{4}$ in. diameter shanks which can be gripped by the chuck of even the smallest power drill. They are made of carbon steel and the cutting edges can be sharpened with a triangular saw file.

The type of wood-boring bit shown in Fig. 4 is suitable for boring larger diameter holes when used with a power drill. The cutting end is integral with a long, slender $\frac{1}{4}$ in. diameter shank. In addition to drilling a clean hole, ample clearance is provided for the waste timber, and there is no clogging.

DRILLS — To Sharpen

To do a good drilling job the first essential is to have the twist drill itself sharpened accurately.

This entails having the drill point ground to the correct angle in each direction.

To do this grinding work freehand calls for considerable skill and time. What is needed is a guiding attachment that will hold the drill firmly in position while being sharpened.

Such an attachment is shown in the illustration and the main parts are the base, setting disc, drill trough, clamp and adjusting screw.

The attachment is bolted through the base to a bench close to the grinding wheel, and the setting disc is adjusted according to directions supplied.

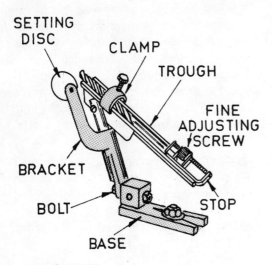

SETTING DISC
CLAMP
TROUGH
FINE ADJUSTING SCREW
BRACKET
BOLT
STOP
BASE

The drill to be sharpened rests in the trough of the attachment and is held firmly in place by the clamp.

Naturally, the drill is placed against the wheel in the approximate grinding position, then positioned accurately by means of fine adjusting screws at the bottom end of trough.

The attachment can be readily mounted for use with a standard bench grinder, lathe, or other equipment carrying a grinding wheel.

It is suitable for sharpening all standard straight-shank drills from $\frac{1}{8}$ in. diameter to $\frac{1}{2}$ in. diameter.

DRY ROT — Details

The term "dry rot" is a little misleading. It was probably given the name because the disease causes timber to fall into a dry, powdery state.

However, the fungus which causes the trouble does not like dry conditions, and timber which is perfectly dry is rarely attacked.

In order to flourish, the dry rot fungus must have timber and surroundings which contain a certain amount of moisture. That is why dry rot is often found in the floor timbers of old homes in which there is little or no ventilation, and in damp, humid basements.

Affected timber should be removed and burned as soon as the trouble is noticed, since dry rot is very contagious. If this is not done, the tiny seeds or spores and the roots of the fungus might be transferred to sound timber, and so keep on growing and multiplying.

These roots penetrate the wood, and then tunnel through the wood cells, feeding as they go. Under this attack, woodwork of all kinds quickly loses its nature, and instead of being strong and elastic, becomes weak and brittle.

Repair work must begin with the thought that dry rot cannot gain a hold on woodwork that is dry and well-aired.

Sufficient wall ventilators must be provided in the foundations, and any direct cause of damp, such as broken drain pipes or gutters, must be eliminated.

As a preservative on woodwork, creosote can be used. Copper sulphate dissolved in water also is effective, and the best method is to brush these on to the timber.

EBONIZING	**Process**
EDGE	**Attachment for Squaring**
EDGE GLUING	**Timber**
EDGES	**Treatment**
ELECTRICITY	**Home Maintenance**
EPOXY RESIN	**Cement**
ESTIMATING	**Bricks, Mortar**
ETCHING	**On Tools**
EXPANSION JOINTS	**Types**

EBONIZING — Process

The process of finishing woodwork black in imitation of ebony interests many wood-workers, and it is comparatively simple.

The main requirement is that the wood be reasonably hard and fine-grained.

The surface is stained first with a black stain, either proprietary or made with black aniline dye. Afterwards the grain is filled with a black paste filler.

It is then polished with an ebony polish made with one pint white french polish to which half an ounce of black spirit aniline dye is added.

To make the polish a still more intense black, a piece of washing blue wrapped in muslin is dipped into it and squeezed until a little of the blue is dissolved. Stir thoroughly, then strain the whole solution through muslin.

The entire polishing process is carried out with this black polish in the manner described in Furniture Finishing—French Polishing.

Finally, the polish is dulled by dipping a fine-haired brush into the finest pumice powder and drawing it along the surface, or using the finest steel wool lubricated with wax polish and rubbed in the direction of the grain.

EDGE—Attachment for Squaring

It's important in wood-working to keep edges square and true.

Fig. 1 shows a planing attachment of great help to the inexperienced woodworker.

It comprises a piece of flat board held to the body of a steel jack or smoothing plane by two small clamps to form a guide block.

Glued to the lower part of the wood is a spacer of sufficient thickness to bring the edge of the work near the center of the plane-iron's width.

The work is gripped in the bench vice and the plane with its attachment operated as shown in Fig. 1.

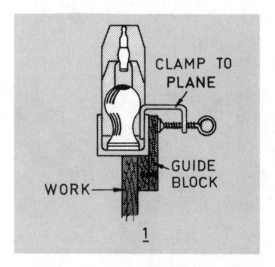

Assuming that the user is right-handed, the right hand pushes the plane along the edge of the work while the wooden attachment is pressed firmly against the vertical face of the work by the left hand.

Some sanding may be necessary on the planed edge.

It is useless to plane this flat and square, then round it or otherwise destroy the precision obtained by the indiscriminate application of a hand-sanding block.

Make up a tool similar to that shown in Fig. 2. This comprises two pieces of wood screwed or glued together to form an L shape.

The upper surface of the vertical piece has a shallow opening cut to accommodate a piece of sandpaper with the abrasive side downwards.

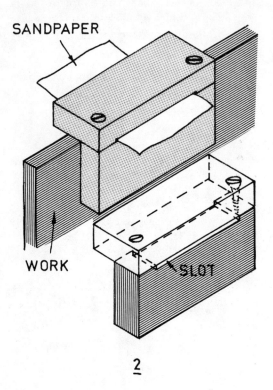

SANDPAPER

WORK

SLOT

<u>2</u>

boards are to be glued up to make say, a table top, the annual rings must be reversed on every other board to counteract the tendency of the glued-up panel to continue warping.

Stock glued up with the annual rings facing in the same direction will continue to warp and cup after gluing, see (A) in illustration.

On the other hand, when glued with the annual rings reversed in alternate boards as at (B), the stock tends to remain flat because each board reacts against any tendency of its neighbor to warp.

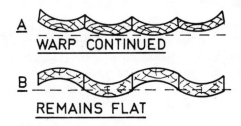

A

WARP CONTINUED

B

REMAINS FLAT

In use, the outer edges of the abrasive paper are folded around the edges of the top horizontal piece of wood with one hand and the complete assembly is rubbed along the work to produce the final finish.

If the vertical faces of the work and the sanding attachment are maintained in contact with each other, the edge of the work will be sanded flat and square.

EDGE GLUING — Timber

The gluing of timber edges may be done in a number of ways. The two methods in common use are the plain rubbed joint and the doweled joint.

However, one important precaution common to all methods is the arrangement of the various boards. For example, when several

The illustrations are exaggerated.

It is interesting to note that certain boards may show more distinctive annual rings than others. This is because of the procedure used when cutting boards from the log.

What is called quarter sawn has the short lengths of annual rings at right angles to the surface. Because of this, a quarter sawed board is less likely to warp or cup than one showing end grain annual rings as in details (A) and (B).

Sometimes reference is made to the heart side of timber. This refers to that side showing the smaller diameter annual rings.

EDGES — Treatment

Many different composite wood boards and other sheet materials are suitable for making table and cabinet tops.

However, most of them need beading or cover strips for the edges to protect the laminations from damage and to give a neat finish.

Here are some suggestions:

Fig. 1. For thin plywood tops use this **half-round molding** with a rabbet cut from the underside to fit over the panel. It gives a slightly raised edge, and is fixed with glue and panel pins.

Fig. 2. For thicker plywood or other composition board, use quarter-round beading to give rounded edges. As with all such **beadings, the corners are miter jointed.**

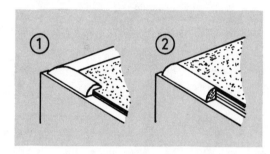

Fig. 3. This is a **flat lipping** with the top edge flush with the top. It is secured directly to the edge of the table or cabinet top.

Fig. 4. **This type of edge molding and the** others following are designed mainly for use with laminated plastic sheet material which has been fixed over a plywood or hardboard base on a table or cabinet. This particular section or shape is sometimes referred to as **hockey stick pattern.**

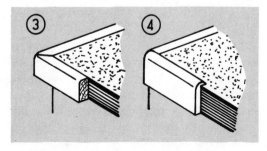

Fig. 5. This is called L section edging. There are many variations in both plastic and aluminum.

Fig. 6. This aluminum beading is screwed to the edge of the top and the plastic strip inserted in the channel.

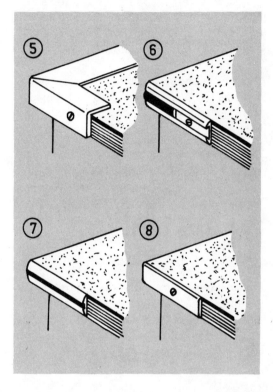

Fig. 7. Rounded aluminum or wood beading is plain but effective. It may be fixed with raised-head screws or with glue and panel pins.

Fig. 8. This is a flexible plastic strip, sometimes with a self-adhesive backing. It bends easily around corners and saves the trouble of cutting miter joints.

ELECTRICITY

The flick of a switch provides the electrical energy that household appliances, furnaces, lights, and workshop tools convert to thermal and mechanical energy. When something goes wrong, however—when the switch does not summon up the genie of the household or when a light fixture needs to be changed—the handyman needs a few basic facts at hand. A basic understanding of household electrical systems and of the operation of a few appliances and tools will prepare him to take care of several common minor electrical problems safely and easily —especially in emergencies.

THE DANGERS. First of all, serious mishaps are unlikely to occur in working with electricity if you understand that almost everything, including the human body, can conduct electric current. Even the insulation on electrical wiring and cords conducts current in negligible amounts. It is especially dangerous to touch electrical appliances, fixtures, or cords when your hands are wet or very moist or when you are standing on a damp floor. Moisture increases your body's conductivity. So, before you touch a lamp socket, a frayed appliance cord, or a malfunctioning light switch, shut off its source of power: unplug an appliance, shut off a circuit, or throw the main switch at your fuse box or circuit breaker box.

BASIC LANGUAGE. The second thing you need to know is the basic language of electricity.

A *circuit* is the path that electrical current follows through your house wiring from the source of supply to one or more outlets and back to the source of supply. Nothing happens in a circuit until you close the connections in it by flipping a switch to allow the current to complete the flow. Why worry about shutting off the current then? If you do not, you might close, or complete, the circuit by touching the wires with your fingers or with a tool. Remember, your body conducts electric current just as your house wiring does.

Volts measure the amount of force behind the current that moves along power lines and through the circuits of your house wiring.

Amperes measure the amount of current that flows through the wires, or "lines," as the result of the voltage push.

And *watts* measure the amount of current actually used by an electrical device.

Grounding is the connection of your household electrical system to the earth— often through a wire connected to a water pipe. New household wiring is supposed to provide for a "third prong" connection in each wall outlet as a protection against shocks in using electrical equipment.

HOUSEHOLD CURRENT. The current that power companies supply to households in this country is *alternating current*. That term is familiar to most of us because we know that battery cells provide *direct current* and that our household outlets provide alternating current. The difference between the two types can be stated very basically. Direct current is uninterrupted in the flow from power source to outlet. Alternating current flows in cycles—usually 60 cycles per second.

It is not especially important to understand that difference, but it is important to know that alternating current can be transformed from higher to lower voltages, and vice versa. Direct current cannot be transfomed. Since it is voltage that provides the push to transmit current through power lines, the higher the voltage in the lines, the greater the distance alternating current can be transmitted.

The possibility of transformance is most important to the handyman when it comes to knowing whether the house needs a new circuit to accommodate a high power user, like an air conditioning system. A simple formula will help here: amperes equals watts divided by volts.

Modern appliances have plates or embossed markings stating the wattage and voltage they require. You will have to find out whether your circuits carry 120 or 240 volts. With this information you can then figure whether or not the amperage of a circuit can handle the demands that will be placed on it. Naturally, if it cannot, your circuit breakers or fuses will shut off the current. The solution, in this case, is not a fuse of higher amperage, but a new circuit.

The formula given above, by the way, can be used in comparing the relative efficiency of appliances. Remember it when you go shopping for air conditioners.

Transposing the formula to *watts equals volts times amperes* leads to an important point. An appliance that uses 8 amperes at 120 volts (that comes to 960 watts) would give the same service if it had been designed to operate on 4 amperes at 240 volts (that, too, comes to 960 watts). Same performance, same cost to you, but the *line current* would be cut in half!

This reduction is part of the reason that a home appliance salesperson or the utility company may advise you to buy a 240-volt air conditioner or kitchen range if your house is already wired for 120/240-volt service.

Not only is line current reduced at 240 volts, but also there is less wasted wattage due to heat loss in the lines and voltage drops in connections. In short, 240-volt circuits make more efficient use of electricity —an important consideration in an energy-conscious society.

HOUSEHOLD WIRING. If you do not know what voltage your household wiring can carry, ask your utility company to send a representative to your home to inspect the wiring. This person will know the answer immediately and will be able to tell you what wiring is compatible with your needs and with your neighborhood's power lines.

Before calling an electrician to make any alterations in the household wiring system, you might also ask the local power company to send a service representative to your house to give you advice on the wiring. Tell the representative what appliances you have added or are planning to add to your household and ask for recommendations. If there are specific suggestions for alterations, make a careful note of them so that you will be able to communicate them accurately to your electrician. In case an electrician disputes this information, have him call the power company. These services are provided in most areas —and without cost. An electrical contractor can also advise you on wiring needs.

The alterations that may be needed to correct inadequate wiring affect three areas.

1. The service entrance, which is the wiring leading into the fuse or circuit breaker box, may need new wiring to provide greater capacity.

2. The fuse or circuit breaker box may have to be replaced to accommodate higher current loads, that is, higher amperage. As an alternative, a second box can be added if the original one is a modern, safe installation.

3. The circuits that serve various areas of your home may need to be rewired. These are the branch circuits.

FUSES AND CIRCUIT BREAKERS. The fuses or circuit breakers in your house are troubleshooters, though in older buildings they may seem like troublemakers because fuses are frequently "blown." The blown fuse or tripped circuit breaker is a protection against overloading a circuit, which would overheat the wiring and eventually cause a fire.

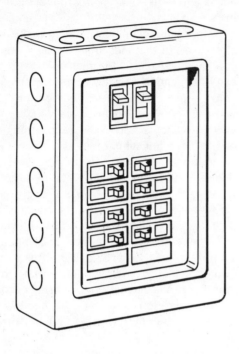

CIRCUIT BREAKER BOX

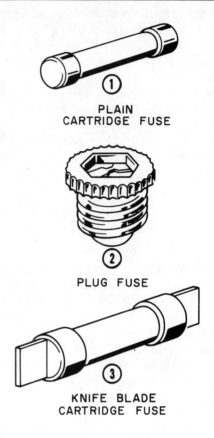

① PLAIN
CARTRIDGE FUSE

② PLUG FUSE

③ KNIFE BLADE
CARTRIDGE FUSE

Restoring the flow of current after a circuit breaker has tripped is a very simple matter—the flip of a switch. To replace a fuse, however, you *must* open the switch controlling the correct circuit or open the main switch—that is, turn off the flow of current to the circuit or to the house.

New fuses should have the same capacity ratings as the old ones—provided that the old ones matched the circuit amperage. To use a fuse of higher capacity would invite a circuit overload, which can lead to a fire.

Fuse replacement obviously demands that you know the amperage (current capacity) of the circuit that has blown. Screw-in or plug fuses can be used with circuits that carry up to 30 amperes. Cartridge fuses

are used in circuits that carry 60 to 100 amperes.

Tamper-free fuses can also be used in plug fuse sockets. They come with adapters that are screwed into the sockets. A tamper-free fuse of one size cannot be used with an adapter of another size. Since the adapter cannot be removed once it is locked into the socket, it provides protection against using fuses of the wrong size.

A handy innovation is a circuit breaker that screws into a plug fuse socket and can save the aggravation of a blown fuse. It is relatively expensive in comparison with fuse prices, but well worth the money. Naturally, it is foolhardy and dangerous to use one with a capacity too high to protect the circuit from overloads.

Before you attempt to restore the flow of current to the circuit, you should try to find out what caused the trouble. Disconnect the appliance or lamp that was plugged in or turned on just before the circuit went out of service. Then throw the circuit switch.

If the fuse or circuit breaker does not interrupt the flow of current again, then a temporary simple overload was very likely the problem. In this case it may be time to consider the adequacy of your house wiring. But if the circuit is one that services a high power user like an air conditioner or a washing machine, the solution may be to use a time-delay, or "slow-blow," fuse that will handle the current drawn by the motors of these appliances during their starting periods.

If you disconnect all plug-in equipment on the line and the circuit still goes out of service, then the problem may be faults in the wiring or insulation. This is the time to call an electrician. Do not even try to use the circuit until the problem is remedied.

It is more likely that you will find the source of trouble is a short circuit in a lamp switch or cord, an appliance cord, or a worn wall switch. Connect appliances to the circuit or turn lights on one by one until you find the one causing the trouble. To avoid blowing a fuse while you look for a short circuit, you can turn a 75-watt or 100-watt bulb into the fuse socket. It will begin to burn brightly when the defective item is plugged in or turned on.

Exposed wires in lamp and appliance cords can cause short circuits. If you find any exposed wires, tape them so that they do not touch. If a wall switch created the problem, take off the cover plate and examine the connections—with the power off, of course.

APPLIANCE WATTAGE CHART.

To avoid overloading your electrical circuits, it is necessary to know exactly what wattage each appliance and fixture draws when it is in use.

Most small appliances can be plugged into regular wall outlets, but it is a good idea to know the approximate amount of current each one draws. Some appliances, like refrigerators, require several times the normal wattage of their motors when they first switch on. This is the reason that the lights sometimes dim when a refrigerator or an air conditioner starts.

Following are the average wattages of several ordinary household appliances.

Broiler-rotisserie	1350-1650
Coffeemaker	up to 1100
Electric blanket	200
Electric skillet, saucepan	1100
Fan	100
Fluorescent light	15-40
Fryer, deep-fat	1350
Heater, portable	1000
Iron	1000
Ironer	1650
Lamp, floor	150-300
Lamp, table	50-100
Mixer	100
Radio	100
Refrigerator	150
Roaster	1650
Rotisserie	1100
Television set	300
Vacuum cleaner	125
Waffle iron, grill	up to 1100

Some electrical appliances draw so much current that they should be placed on individual circuits. Below is a list of some of these appliances with their average wattages.

Air conditioner, ¾ ton	1200
Cook top, built-in	4000
Dishwasher, waste disposer	1500
Dryer, 240-volt	4500-9000
Freezer	350

Garbage disposer	500
Heater, built-in bathroom	1000-1500
Oven, built-in	4000
Range	8000-16,000
Washing machine	700
Water heater	2000-4500
Water pump	700

INSTALLING WALL SWITCHES.

Faulty connections in a wall switch will often make sputtering noises or cause lights to flicker when the switch is used. This problem can be corrected before a short in the switch blows the circuit. You may also want to replace a switch because the lever or button is broken or stiff or because it is noisy. "Silent" switches are available, too, especially for bedroom installation.

Before you do anything to the switch, kill the circuit involved by throwing the circuit breaker or the switch on your fuse box. If you need power somewhere else in the house, remove the fuse for the circuit that services the switch you are repairing then turn the main switch on again.

Remove the switch cover plate, lay it aside, and remove the screws from the bracket that holds the switch in place. Carefully pull the switch out of the box—the wires are stiff and breakable—to the point where you can work with the connec-

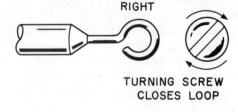

RIGHT

TURNING SCREW
CLOSES LOOP

WRONG

TURNING SCREW
OPENS LOOP

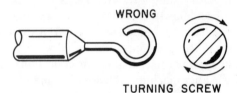

ATTACH WIRE
TO SCREW TERMINALS

tions and the wires. Then disconnect the wires, first loosening their screw connections and then unhooking the bare copper wire. You will duplicate this connection on the new switch. Attach the black wire to one of the screw connectors and the white wire to the other.

If one of the copper wires snaps off, you may have to trim off a bit more insulation to expose more wire. Shave the insulation off carefully with a knife blade and clean off any remaining bits with the back of the blade. With long-nosed pliers, bend the wire into a loop that will tighten around the screw as it is turned clockwise.

With the connectors tightened, ease the switch assembly back into the box so that the wires are not crimped. Replace the screws that hold the bracket to the wall and put the cover plate on again.

REPLACING OUTLETS. The procedure for replacing an outlet receptacle is similar to the one for replacing a switch assembly. The wire connections are made in exactly the same way for the usual "con-

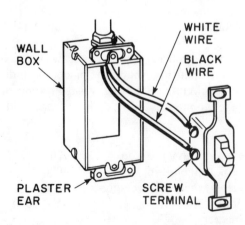

WALL BOX

PLASTER EAR

WHITE WIRE

BLACK WIRE

SCREW TERMINAL

venience" outlets that are found about a foot above floor level.

Control outlets and special-purpose outlets that are combined with switches are a bit more complicated to replace. But if you buy the right replacement parts and follow the pattern of wiring on the old receptacle precisely, you should have no trouble.

DOORBELLS AND BUZZERS. Electric doorbells or buzzers are operated either by transformers or by dry-cell batteries. There are several maladies they can suffer, especially those operated by batteries. The usual source of trouble is a worn-out battery. Other difficulties may be loose connections on the transformer, bell, or push-button terminals, a broken circuit wire, a short circuit, or corrosion of push-button, bell, or buzzer contacts.

To examine the connections in the push button, it is necessary either to unscrew it from the wall or to remove it from the outer shell, depending on the type of button. Sometimes the contact becomes dirty or corroded from exposure to the weather, in which case the contact points should be cleaned with sandpaper. Examine the connections in the button and tighten any that appear to be loose. Do the same with the connections on the bell, transformer, or battery.

A maladjustment of the bell parts sometimes occurs, but not frequently. When it does, tightening the adjusting screw or cleaning the contact may be all that is necessary. This screw is located inside the bell box and may need to be moved closer to or farther away from the spring. If the spring is too stiff, it should be bent slightly toward the coils.

If the bell refuses to work after all adjustments have been made, look for a short circuit or broken wire in the system. A piece of metal carelessly placed across the lead wires or terminals, or a staple touching both lead wires where the insulation is badly worn will produce a short circuit. Worn places in the insulation should be wrapped with friction tape. A broken wire is sometimes difficult to locate. To find the break, examine the wire with particular care where it is exposed, especially in places where it is fastened with staples or where there is a sharp bend.

LIGHTING. Light affects color, and it affects your vision. In living areas, improper lighting can cause eyestrain for readers and television viewers, and ill-chosen lighting can wreck a color scheme. In work areas, improper lighting is a hazard.

Fluorescent lighting is widely used because of its more efficient use of electricity (more light per watt of power used), but it has a greater effect on color than does incandescent lighting. The standard cool white (CW) or warm white (WW) fluorescent tube produces light that appears blue-white in combination with incandescent light, which is yellowish. Standard tubes are not recommended for home use, except in the workshop. Deluxe fluorescent tubes are recommended because they reduce color distortion.

Deluxe cool white tubes, which are marked CWX, are particularly well suited to the cool colors of blue or green color schemes. Deluxe warm white tubes, marked WWX, produce light that blends particularly well with incandescent light. Their light also enhances warmer color schemes and flatters complexions.

Once the lighting scheme for a living area is worked out, you can dramatically increase its flexibility by planning for the use of dimmer-control switches. These enable you to choose the level of light in a room—from full brightness to the dimmest glow.

A dimmer control for incandescent lighting is often simply mounted in a wall switch to replace the usual on-off switch. You need only make sure that the watt capacity of the mechanism equals or exceeds the total wattage of lights wired to it. Dimmer controls can also be installed on lamps. Stores that specialize in lighting needs can handle the installation for you.

For fluorescent lighting, you must plan for dimmer controls before installing the fixtures. The controls cost considerably more than do incandescent dimmer controls, and the fixtures have to be compatible with the controls.

Dimmers are excellent for use in the bedrooms of children and older people because they allow you to see while taking care of them at night, yet allow you to keep the light low so that they will not be bothered by glaring brightness.

What do you do when you need to get more light from an existing lighting scheme?

1. Add another lamp. Most living rooms probably need at least five portable light fixtures (lamps), and most bedrooms, three. For flexibility, choose one with a three-way switch or a dimmer control.

2. When you redecorate, use lighter colors for walls, floors, and draperies so that more light is reflected from these large surfaces.

3. Add structural (wall) lighting fixtures to brighten an expanse of wall—and create a feeling of spaciousness in a room of average size. This sort of installation often involves setting an 8-foot to 20-foot strip of fluorescent light at the junction of wall and ceiling and hiding it from direct view with cornice. The cornice directs light downward over a wall or draperies to highlight textures or works of art. Innovative variations on structural lighting are track lights and ceiling spotlights used near a wall.

Photographs courtesy of Lightolier

4. Replace bulbs now in use with bulbs of higher wattage, but do not exceed the rated wattage of a fixture. If you want more light from a fluorescent fixture, you will have to replace it with one made for tubes of greater wattage.

5. Replace outmoded bare-bulb ceiling fixtures with shaded or shielded ones. The new fixture will diffuse the light. If you do not want to pay for a new ceiling fixture, buy silver bowl bulbs, which will direct light against the ceiling to reduce glare and provide greater reflectance.

6. Replace all darkened bulbs and tubes. They produce 25 to 50 percent less light than do new bulbs, but they use the same amount of current. (Use the darkened bulbs in closets.)

7. Get new shades for table lamps, and choose translucent materials of light colors.

LAMP REPAIRS. When a lamp flickers, something is wrong with it. Unplug it and unscrew the bulb. If the bulb flickers in a socket or lamp that you know to be in working order, throw the bulb away and put a new one in the lamp. If the bulb does not flicker, then you have some work to do on the lamp.

Remove the socket shell from its base by inserting the blade of a small screwdriver into the toothed joint between them. The place to insert the screwdriver is near the switch. Twist the blade of the screwdriver slightly and press the socket shell sideways to open the joint. Wiggle the socket off carefully and examine the connections, making sure that no loose wires are causing a short circuit. Now examine the length of cord inside the lamp base to see if it is frayed. Tape all bare or frayed places. Wear is likely to appear where the cord bends or where it has been stepped on or crushed.

Buy a new cord if the old one is badly worn. It should be the same length as the old one—or even longer. In buying a new cord, be sure to allow for the length of the lamp base.

If you replace the cord, you will have to make a new Underwriters knot inside the socket cap. This double knot in the two insulated wires of the cord will ease any strain on the connection to the switch terminals.

If you do not find any problems in the wiring, look for dirt in the socket. Use an old paint brush to clean it.

If none of these investigations reveals the problem, then the switch may be faulty. Loosen the terminal screws and remove the wires from the old switch. Put in a new

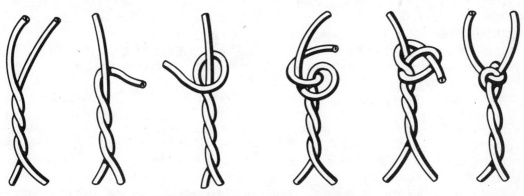

UNDERWRITERS KNOT

switch, making sure that the wire loops tighten around the screws as they turn clockwise.

APPLIANCE MAINTENANCE AND REPAIR. You should keep in mind several rules when you are looking for the cause of appliance malfunctions. Be sure not to rush the job. You should examine the appliance carefully before you try to pry it apart or cut through any of it. In most cases, the appliance has been designed so that it can be opened for repair, usually by removing screws or by taking off a snap-on panel. As a general rule, you will find that the access opening is in a part of the appliance hidden from view—the bottom of a toaster, the back of a clock, or the side of a radio.

If you are prevented from taking off a covering by the presence of a shaft or some long part, you will usually find setscrews holding it. By removing them, you will be able to remove the part and then the cover.

Some appliances have special parts sealed in a metal case. Simply replace the entire sealed unit if it seems defective.

It is almost always inadvisable to try to strip down and repair a large appliance like a refrigerator, an air conditioner, or a television set. There are simply too many things that may be wrong, and repairs are extremely complicated. If you are an expert repairman, of course, go ahead.

Before you call in a pro, however, be sure you check the plug, the cord, and the outlet. Incidentally, if any appliance does not operate, the very first thing to do is to make sure it is plugged in!

As with lamp cords, check for frayed or worn insulation, and tape the bad places. Have severely worn cords replaced unless you can get to the cord connections without damage to the appliance.

Check the prong end of the plug. The connections here may be loose. To find out,

you'll have to take the plug apart. Loosen the screw in the prong end and remove the seal. It is impossible to do this with modern molded plugs, of course. If you are going to replace them, you simply have to cut them off and proceed from there.

Examine the cord around the plug. In long use, the insulation normally becomes worn at this point. The cause of many plug failures is the hand that removes the plug from a wall outlet by tugging on the cord.

If the plug needs to be reattached, cut the cord above the worn insulation with wire cutters or electrician's pliers. Separate the two wires of the cord for about 1½ inches. You may be able to tear the thin segment of insulation between them easily, but with some cords, you'll have to use a knife. If you damage the insulation covering the wires, cut both of them again to get rid of the damaged section.

Scrape about ½ inch of insulation from each wire and twist the loose strands together. Clean the wires with the back of a knife blade and do not touch them again with your hands.

Now insert the wires through the plug and bend them into "eyes" with long-nosed pliers. Turn the eyes in a clockwise direction so that they will tighten as the screw connectors are tightened. Make sure there are no loose strands protruding from the twisted wire eye as you work it around the connector. With the screws tightened, replace the end seal.

Snap-on plugs simplify the job of plug replacement tremendously.

MOTOR MAINTENANCE. Large appliances are usually motor-driven, and there are three common symptoms of trouble with the motor: the appliance will not start, the motor runs hot, or the motor runs too slowly. Any of these difficulties may be caused by inadequate or defective power supply, unoiled or dirty parts, defects in wiring, or a defective belt connection.

You can at least locate the probable cause of trouble in a motorized appliance by using the following checklist.

1. Check the power supply. Be sure the cord and socket are in working order.

2. Check to see that the motor is properly oiled. If it is not, you may find that a good oiling will stop its running hot or slow. Pay attention to the oiling instructions that accompany the motor; some are self-lubricating. Never oil a part unless it is clearly marked OIL or unless a lubricating chart specifies it. If the proper grade and type of oil are not specified in the instructions, use light machine oil or an oil made for electric motors.

3. Check the motor to see if it needs cleaning. If so, clean all grease and dirt from the open windings with a clean, dry cloth or soft-bristled brush.

4. Check belt adjustments and clean all oil and grease from the belt and pulley. Be sure the belt is tightly installed. Most belts are controlled by wing screws or slot bolts. Turn the screw or bolt until the belt is tight to the touch.

Motor noise often is due to factors unrelated to proper functioning. Any motor produces vibration as it operates, and the solution to what may seem to be excessive noise can be to place the appliance on a sound-insulating pad made of a material like cork or rubber.

This insulating method works both with large appliances, such as refrigerators, and small ones, such as blenders. Wall-mounted or window-mounted appliances, such as fans and air conditioners, should be insulated from the wall or window with strips of plastic foam or flexible gaskets.

Refrigerator motors often perplex their owners because they know the machines have to be kept in good working order, yet they are reluctant to pay for service calls if things do not seem too serious. Some refrigerator malfunctions are not serious, but they can and should be quickly remedied.

If the refrigerator motor runs too much, the condenser may be dirty, the door may be leaking air, or the refrigerator may be too close to a wall or stove. A refrigerator with its condenser at the back should be at least 4 inches from the wall and 12 inches from the ceiling.

You should clean the condenser at least once a year. It is located at the back or bottom of the refrigerator. Disconnect the plug before you touch the unit, and follow the manufacturer's instructions for cleaning.

To check the door for air leakage, place a thin piece of paper between door and frame and close the door. If you can pull the paper out without any resistance, the door gasket probably needs to be replaced. It can be unscrewed, but have a new one in hand before you do it. Appliance dealers may have to order the gasket you need.

Check the door for air leaks, too, if your refrigerator needs defrosting too often or if it is a self-defrosting model that does not remain frost-free.

Make sure that the refrigerator thermostat is set at about 40° or 45°. Settings below 35° will cause frost to form too rapidly.

The time to avoid home diagnosis of refrigerator ailments is when the motor runs hot and gives off a pungent odor. Unplug it and call a repairman—and ask a neighbor to store your food if you cannot make other arrangements at home—portable coolers with ice, for example.

EPOXY RESIN — Cement

The handyman will find many uses around the home for epoxy resin cement.

It is bought in two containers. One contains the base and the other the hardener.

The two ingredients are mixed in equal parts to form a strong permanent material which, when cured, is claimed to be tougher than concrete.

The material can be used to fasten together almost any combination of materials, to fill holes, cracks, leaks or breaks.

On many repair jobs you can do both bonding and sealing with it.

It is claimed that it is easier, quicker, cheaper and more satisfactory to use than caulking or flooring compounds, putty, nuts, screws, bolts, rivets, welding or soldering.

This plastic repair material adheres quickly and easily to almost any material, and is easy to apply in small or large quantities.

It will form a fine edge and can be feather-edged by using water or oil on the spreader.

When cured it can be sanded, filed or machined smooth. Trowel and mixing surface can be cleaned easily and quickly under running water.

The base and hardener remain unchanged until mixed.

When they are mixed chemical reaction causes the setting or hardening of the product.

At room temperature, the normal curing time is several hours, although there are some "instant" types available which harden in a few minutes.

ESTIMATING — Bricks, Mortar

One of the most common questions asked by homeworkers concerns the method of estimating how many bricks and how much mortar will be needed for a particular job.

There is nothing especially difficult about making these calculations, and here are the details.

BRICKS. A $4\frac{1}{2}$ in. wall (where the wall thickness equals the width of a standard brick) takes about fifty bricks per square yard (that is 3 ft x 3 ft on the wall face), which allows a few for waste.

A 9 in. wall takes about 100 bricks per square yard allowing for waste.

MORTAR. For $4\frac{1}{2}$ in. brick walls, with $\frac{3}{8}$ in. thick joints, allow $\frac{3}{4}$ cu. ft of mortar per square yard of wall. For 9 in. brick walls allow $1\frac{3}{4}$ cu. ft of mortar per square yard of wall, which will include the extra interior joints. These figures are for wet mortar, which is about one-third less in bulk than the dry mix. Then allow for slight waste.

A cement mortar (of one part Portland cement to three parts sand) for a square yard of 9 in. brickwork takes nearly half a cwt. of cement and slightly more than $1\frac{3}{4}$ cu. ft of sand. For a square yard of $4\frac{1}{2}$ in. brick wall the amounts are slightly less than half. These are average figures and of course the thicker the joints the more mortar you use.

You cannot calculate exactly the quantities required as there are several variable factors. But these figures are a useful guide.

Use just enough water to make a stiff but workable mix. Too much water weakens the mortar and causes it to run down the wall.

If you find a cement mortar works harshly off the trowel you can buy a proprietary plasticizer from a builder's merchant. There are several brands and a little added to the mortar makes it work smoothly and easily.

A cement-lime mortar is easier to work than a one-to-three cement mortar. Take half a part Portland cement a quarter part hydrated powder lime and three parts sand for a general purpose mortar. But a plain one-to-three cement mortar is better below the damp proof course and for brick or tile sills and copings.

ETCHING — On Tools

A name neatly etched on steel tools adds a distinctive touch and shows pride of possession. Etching can be done quite simply and is more suitable for tools than a letter punch.

For example it is not easy to punch letters in a hard chisel or saw blade.

The theory of etching is simple. Coat the **metal with wax, scratch through the wax with a scriber and then apply acid.**

Where the metal is protected by the wax the acid cannot act but where it is exposed by the scribed lines the acid bites and so etches the name or initials.

If you have a lot of tools to treat, by far the best wax to use is an etching ball (dark). Paraffin wax from candles will also serve quite well except for a slight tendency to crack if small lettering or fancy designs are attempted.

Warm the metal slightly, apply the wax and dab lightly with a pad of rag until there is a thin layer all over. Scratch the initials or name with a needle or an engineer's scriber ground to a fine point.

Use one part nitric acid added to one part hydrochloric acid applied with a small feather to the exposed metal. Keep tickling it with the feather to brush away the bubbles that rise.

About ten minutes etching will be enough, but it is impossible to give exact times since a lot depends on the strength of the acid, type of steel, the room temperature and other factors.

Another etch can be made of four parts glacial acetic acid and one part alcohol to which one part nitric acid is slowly added.

Afterwards wash well, melt off most of the wax and clean off the remainder with kerosene or turpentine.

EXPANSION JOINTS — Types

When two masses are set next to each other and each is subject to expansion and contraction, a special joint is used between them.

This joint is flexible, providing space for the mass to move into when it expands. It is flexible enough so that when the mass contracts, the joint expands to fill the gap.

Expansion joints are generally used when laying concrete. A space is left between two large sections of concrete (using a board treated with oil or grease, or a metal divider for easy removal after the concrete has set). This space is filled with asphalt which, while it hardens on the surface, remains pliable inside.

Another method of adding an expansion joint is by using specially treated felt and setting it between the masses of concrete as each section is formed.

If an expansion joint is not used with large masses of concrete, there is a good chance it will buckle and crack. Should this happen, it is necessary to chop openings for expansion joints and to repair the cracked concrete.

It is always best to use an expansion joint when laying a concrete patio abutting the house.

This joint can be made by using a 4 in. by 1 in. piece of softwood set between the house and patio.

While the wood can remain and act as a cushion, it will eventually rot. Therefore, remove it after the concrete is cured and pour asphalt into the opening.

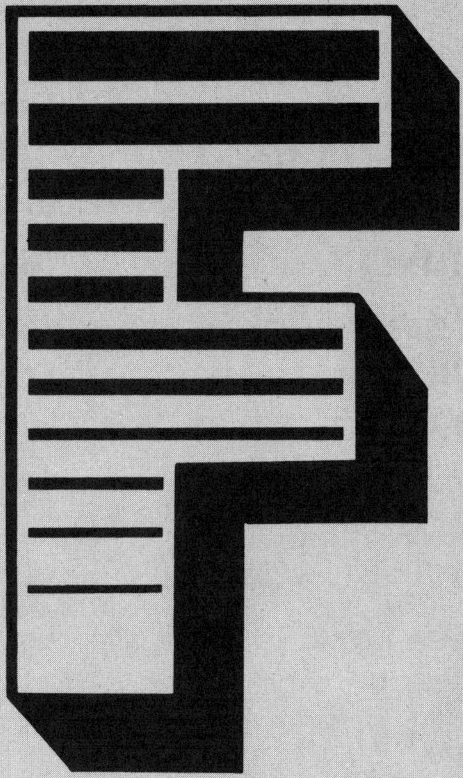

FENCE POSTS	Make Secure
FILES & FILING	Hints
FILES	Using
FILLISTER PLANE	Details
FINISH	With Sealer
FLASHING	To Waterproof
FLOOR BOARDS	Jointing
FLOORS	Eradicate Scratches
FLOORS	Faults Corrected
FLUXES	Types
FRAMES	Finishing Touches
FRAMES	In Brickwork
FUNGUS	On Walls
FURNITURE	Accidents
FURNITURE	Bruises
FURNITURE FINISHING	French Polishing
FURNITURE FINISHING	Lacquering
FURNITURE FINISHING	Preparation
FURNITURE FINISHING	Staining & Filling

FENCE POSTS — Make Secure

When erecting fence posts, every effort should be made to fix them so that they remain firm and upright.

Two methods often used to achieve this are to concrete around the base of each post, or to fix braces above ground level.

Both methods, however, have disadvantages. Concrete makes the job more costly, and any later removal is difficult. The brace method is unsightly.

Shown in the illustration is a simple way to ensure that a post remains firm and secure in the ground.

First allow that each post will go at least 2 ft 6 in. into the ground. Obtain two pieces of scrap hardwood—4 in. by 2 in. is a good size—and cut them approximately 2 ft 6 in. long.

Nail these two members to the base of the post at right angles to each other, keeping the lower piece about 6 in. above the bottom end of the post as shown.

It will be necessary to dig narrow trenches for the projecting ledges, after which the post is lowered into the hole and adjusted for height and plumb. Broken bricks are packed tightly around the supporting ledges.

Finish off by filling in the remainder of the hole with earth in 4 in. layers, taking care to compact each layer tightly by ramming before spading in the next.

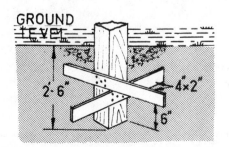

If the supporting ledges are well nailed to the post and the earth is fully compacted around the base, the post will remain firm.

It is advisable to apply two coats of creosote to the bottom of the post and also to the ledges before placing in the hole.

FILES & FILING — Hints

Every woodworker and home handyman has a file or two in his tool kit. Some are used for the conventional filing of metal, and others for smoothing timber surfaces. Fig. 1 is a typical type of flat file.

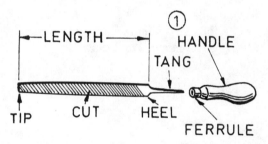

However, there are quite a few hints about files and filing that are little known. For example, a new file should be first used on brass, copper, and similar metal to prolong its life.

When it becomes dull, it can then be used effectively on steel and wrought iron. On the other hand, if a new file is used on this metal at the beginning, it becomes practically useless on brass and copper.

Thus, when a new file is bought, use it for filing brass and copper until a new file is wanted; the older file will then come in handy for filing rough bolt ends, wrought iron handrails, and the numerous other steel filing jobs.

Illustrated in Fig. 2 are eleven sectional views of standard files. Six are for relatively specialized work but the other five are extremely useful and necessary in woodworking. These are:

Half-round file, which is used for working on hollow and concave surfaces, enlarging holes, and so on.

Round, or rat-tail file. This is useful for enlarging holes and rounding slots neatly.

Square file. For filing square holes and slots. It is also useful for making V-cuts in edges.

Triangular or three-corner file. Is used mainly for sharpening the teeth of saws and filing grooves in metal and timber.

QUADRANGULAR ②

- MILL
- PILLAR
- SQUARE

TRIANGULAR

▶ TAPER
▮ CANTSAW
◀ KNIFE
◣ CROSSCUT

CURVED

● ROUND
━ HALFROUND
◗ PIT
◣ CROSSING

Flat file or hand file. It is principally used on flat surfaces and edges. A flat file with a plain edge—or safety edge—enables flat filing to be done in corners without risk of damaging adjacent parts.

Of course, all these files are metal-cutting, but they also serve for wood cutting and rasping, especially the half-round type.

There is a special half-round type called a cabinet file that is made exclusively for use on wood.

Files are made from hardened cast steel. Because of this they cannot be used on hard-tempered steel such as plane-iron cutters, chisels, axes, and other edge-cutting tools.

A brand new file used in a futile attempt to sharpen, say a twist drill or plane iron, is soon ruined. Indeed, it will make no impression.

The correct sharpening tool in such cases is a grinding wheel or oilstone or a combination of both.

Finally, files should always be fitted with handles over the tangs. File handles in plastic or wood are cheap, and the fitting of a handle is not only a safety-first measure against injury, but also makes for more accurate and comfortable working.

FILES — Using
When using a file, it is important to take up the correct position and stance. Ideally, the surface you are filing should be at elbow level.

Uphill or downhill filing makes it difficult to stroke the tool accurately and produce a surface that is either completely flat or uniformly curved.

If you are right-handed, plant your left foot about 2 ft ahead of your right. Left-handed workers of course will reverse this stance.

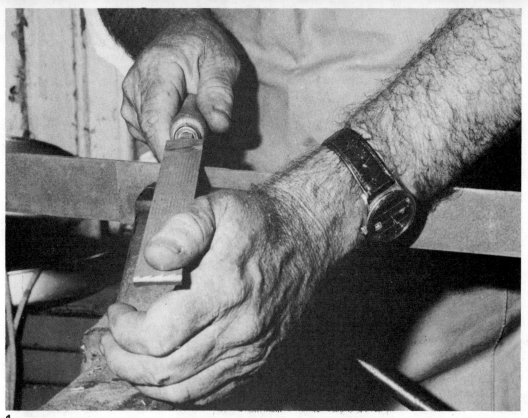

1

2

Cradle the handle in your right palm with your thumb resting on the top and your index finger along the side. This lets you keep the file level while applying weight to the forward end at the beginning of each stroke, to both ends of the file at the middle of the stroke, and to the handle as you conclude the stroke.

To remove large quantities of material quickly with a coarse file, grip its forward end as in Fig. 1. This way you can apply maximum downward pressure with the heel of your hand.

For accurate medium-pressure work, stretch your thumb and fingers wide apart to distribute weight evenly along the file, Fig. 2. With this method you can feel unevenness in the metal you are filing and use the full length of the file.

For very precise surfacing with small files, hold the tip of the file between your thumb and index finger Fig. 3.

Draw-filing finishes a job, and Fig. 4 shows how to hold the file (one with very fine teeth). Draw and push it along the surface with even pressure. The burr that will form along each edge should be removed with a few light, angled strokes of the file.

The main precaution is not to see-saw the file. Keep your body stationary and let your arms pivot from the shoulders.

When working on narrow surfaces, hold the file diagonally and stroke forward and sideways at the same time, reversing the diagonal and transverse direction of the strokes frequently. Because the file teeth face forward, exert pressure only on the forward strokes. During return strokes let the file glide across the surface of the work.

FILLISTER PLANE — Details

This is an extremely useful plane to have in a tool kit. It is really a rabbet plane fitted with a guide fence.

If the fence is a fixture, it is known as a standing fillister; if adjustable, the plane is called a moving fillister.

It may also have a depth gauge and tooth, the latter enabling the plane to be used across grain without previously sawing down to the depth.

The tooth works ahead of the main cutter and the plane should be moved backwards a few times over the wood to score the line of cut.

Wooden fillister planes, like most other wooden types, are becoming obsolete.

An adjustable metal rabbeting and fillister plane is the ideal type for the avid woodworker, especially if he is planning any furniture construction. It has two positions for the cutter—one for ordinary work, and the other up towards the front of the plane for bull-nose work.

The usual length of the plane is 8½ in., fitted with a 1½ in. wide cutter, spur, depth gauge, and adjustable fence.

It is imperative that fillister plane blades or cutters are ground and sharpened perfectly square so that the cutter edge is level with the side of the plane and does not scrape against the adjoining edge of a rabbet or groove.

FINISH — With Sealer

For finishing timber surfaces, you have the choice of three good clear natural finishes.

These are the waxed look, the semi-gloss which is a dull shine with more luster than the waxed finish, and the full gloss, which is the brilliant glass-like finish of fine cabinetry, pianos, and some other furniture finished professionally.

The waxed finish look seems to be the most popular today, but in fact few furniture pieces now are really wax finished. There are better and quicker ways of arriving at the dull luster of the wax finish.

The real wax finish was a laborious process. The ingredients were beeswax melted in turpentine, and a lot of elbow grease. The piece had to be polished repeatedly for many weeks before the luster was built up.

When the surface had been really sealed with the wax, it did not show scratch marks easily, stood up to heat better than French polish, was very easy to restore, and brought out the natural color and grain of the wood very well.

Its big defect was that it marked very easily with liquids. Today you can get the same appearance as wax finish simply by painting floor sealer on to the wood straight out of the can.

This sealed-waxed finish has several advantages over the old wax finish. It is impervious to water, resists alcohol and other spirits well, reinforces the surface of the wood so that it is much harder than it would be with wax alone, and it is just as easy to restore as when waxed.

The thing to be careful about when starting the job is to make sure you have an absolutely clean brush, preferably one 2 in. wide. You will also need a wiping rag. This should be old, soft, and absorbent, but not fluffy.

All floor sealers are very thin when you buy them in cans, because the purpose of the sealer is to penetrate right into the fibers of the wood. Thick mixtures would not do that.

Just brush on a generous coat and leave it to stand for a quarter of an hour. Any sealer that hasn't soaked into the wood at the end of that time is superfluous, so wipe it off with the rag. Give the wood two more coats of sealer with at least twelve hours drying time between each, and the job is finished.

If you want your piece to have that waxed feel and slight sheen, cut the surfaces lightly with steel wool, then rub a beeswax and turpentine wax compound, or ordinary furniture polish, over it.

FLASHING — To Waterproof

The term flashing describes the method or material used to make various points on a building weatherproof by preventing the entry of rainwater through a roof, around a chimney, or under windows.

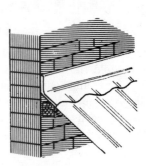

The illustration shows application of the flashing principle. Here a lean-to roof covering a veranda or house addition has been attached to the wall of an existing brick building.

A wooden plate is first secured to the wall to support the ends of the rafters to which the roofing material is fixed. The joint between the roof and wall is covered by a strip of lead or zinc flashing material.

As an alternative, bitumen-base roofing felt may be used, but the sheet lead is much easier to work and beat into shape around the corrugated sheet roofing or tile contours.

Especially where the roof slope or pitch is very low, the flashing should extend down the roof covering at least 9 in. and be dressed to the required shape.

The top edge is turned over at right-angles and fixed into a joint in the brickwork which has been raked out. Wedge the edge firmly into the open joint at various points, then use a strong cement mortar and a small trowel to repoint the joint along its length.

Much the same procedure is followed when flashing around a brick chimney, although here the raked-out joints in the brickwork will step down to suit the roof pitch.

FLOOR BOARDS — Jointing

There are two principal types of tongued and grooved floor boards. The one most in use is that shown in Fig. 1 detail (A). Several such boards can be laid at the same time, as the nails are driven into the joists through the face of the board.

The other type of board which is a little more expensive is shown at (B) Fig. 1. This floor board is laid by what is known as secret nailing.

The boards are laid separately, the nails being driven through the tongue into the floor joists as shown in Fig. 2. The groove in the next board covers the nails in the adjoining board and a floor is thus obtained without any nail-heads showing.

When several boards are to be taken up and used as a manhole or trap they should be battened together underneath and the bottom edge of the groove on the board at one edge of the manhole cover pared off with a chisel, Fig. 3.

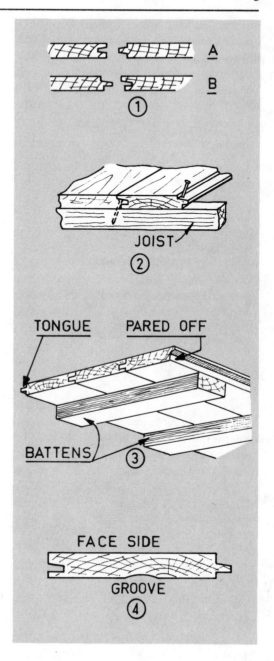

When placing this trap in position the tongue on the one edge of it is placed in the groove of the board fixed to the floor, the trap is gently lowered and will then slip easily into place.

When using tongued and grooved floor boards, especially new ones, care should always be taken to notice which is the face side, as the distance from the face side to the edge of the groove is greater than the opposite side, as indicated in Fig. 4.

The idea of this is to give greater thickness on the wearing surface. However, many floorboards are grooved on the underside as a precaution against twisting or cupping so here there won't be any difficulty in selecting the face side.

FLOORS—Eradicate Scratches

Scratches on a handsome hardwood floor spoil its appearance. However, they can be repaired.

The method used depends on how bad the scratches are. If they are only surface marks, which don't affect the wood itself, here's what to do:

Saturate a pad of fairly coarse steel wool with gasoline and rub over the area in the direction of the wood grain, to remove the varnish or other finish.

When the finish is off, smooth down with a pad of fine steel wool. Be careful of fire danger from the gasoline fumes.

Refinish the area by brushing on diluted shellac varnish, or ordinary varnish diluted with turpentine (if the floor is an oil-varnished one).

After waxing and polishing scratches will be practically invisible.

For deep scratches that go into the wood, remove the finish with steel wool as described then fill the scratches with wood filler, colored to match the floor.

Sand smooth when dry, clean with a rag dipped in gasoline and then finish as already described.

FLOORS — Faults Corrected

The floors in a house, or any other building, are likely to develop various faults after laying and being in use for some time.

These faults are not necessarily caused by inferior material or poor workmanship in actually fitting the boards. In most cases they are due to failure to take certain simple precautions.

For example, when floorboards are giving trouble by creaking when walked on, the cause is usually because of insufficient nailing.

The floor joists to which the boards are fixed are usually spaced at 18 in. centers, and the boards should be double-nailed at each point of contact between floorboard and joist.

Afterwards the nail heads are punched slightly below the floor surface with a nail punch.

Where this double-nailing and punching has not been done, a board may rise slightly and creak. Renailing as in Fig. 1 will usually overcome the trouble.

If floorboards shrink a little and rub against each other in the grooves between the joints this will also cause a creaking noise. Where this trouble occurs in a ground floor, thin wedges driven between the top of the joists and the underside of the boards will usually stop the creaking, Fig. 2.

Where there is a tendency to creak over a wide area rather than in one isolated spot a 3 in. by 1 in. batten or cleat nailed or screwed to the joist and forced tightly against the underside of the boards will help, Fig. 3.

A third possible cause of a floor being unstable is that the joists and bearers supporting the joists have shrunk or become loose.

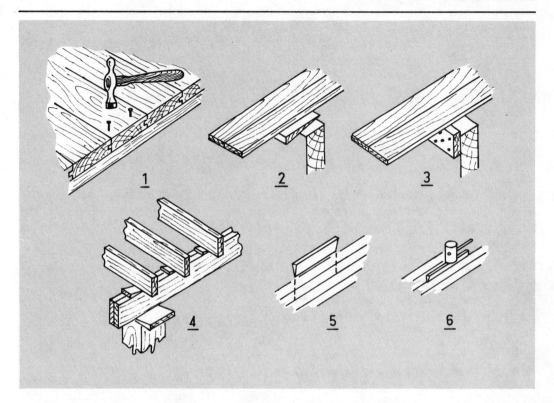

Piers or foundation walls also sometimes subside, leaving the bearers and joists suspended and likely to sag.

The repair procedure in these circumstances is shown clearly in Fig. 4.

Drive wedges under the joists where they rest on the bearer until the gap between the top edge of the joists and the underside of the floorboards is taken up.

If the foundation walls or piers supporting the bearers have subsided slightly, drive wedges under the bearers at the points where they rest on the walls or piers. If this wedging proves inadequate, install new piers or strong footings under the bearers.

Floors that vibrate when walked upon result from inadequate support over the whole area. This is a more serious problem than that of isolated loose boards and joists.

Some of the causes of this trouble are the use of joists which are too light—4 in. wide and 2 in. thick is the minimum—too long a span between the bearers which support the joists, an insufficient or improperly located bridging or bracing between the joists.

With second or other intermediate floors this bridging between the joists is especially important as it is the main method of keeping the floor rigid. When vibration becomes severe in a second floor, the ceiling of the first floor may have to be opened to install extra bridging.

However, several simple remedies can be applied when the floor is at ground level, and it is possible to get underneath.

Doubling the joists by nailing an additional member to each of those already installed is usually practical and effective.

Jacking up the floor from underneath and installing one or more extra bearers or piers is another method.

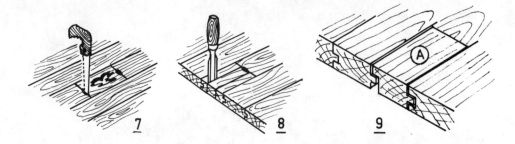

Apart from the various major floor faults described, there are also a number of smaller surface problems. The most common of these are cracks between the boards.

If the cracks are not big they can often be filled with a paste made from fine sawdust and hot woodworker's glue. Prepared plastic wood could also be used, but the sawdust paste is much cheaper.

For slightly wider cracks, an alternative method is to soak a length of cord in woodworker's glue and drive it into the crack along its entire length. Punch the cord slightly below the surface, then finish off flush, using the sawdust paste or plastic wood.

Of course there are times when the cracks are so wide and deep that it is not advisable to use either of these two filling methods suggested.

Where such cracks are more than $\frac{1}{4}$ in. wide, follow the procedure suggested in Figs 5 and 6.

Cut a wedge-shaped strip on which the top edge is slightly thicker than the width of the crack to be filled, and smear the faces with glue. Either hot woodworker's glue or the more convenient cold P.V.A. type may be used.

Hammer the strip in with a wooden mallet until it fits tightly and is protruding only slightly above floor level, Fig. 6. Allow to stand until the glue hardens, then plane and sandpaper the strip until it is flush with the rest of the floor.

Damaged boards can be repaired by removing the affected sections.

First drill holes with a brace and bit or power drill about 2 in. beyond the damaged part, insert a keyhole saw in the holes, and cut across the board. This operation is shown in Fig. 7.

If the flooring is tongued and grooved, chisel double-splits the length of the section between the saw cuts. Pry out the center chiseled piece first, then the two side pieces as indicated in Fig. 8.

Cut a new piece of flooring to the required length, chisel off the bottom section of the groove and fit it into place as at (A) Fig. 9.

If possible, have this new patching piece spanning one or more joists, although it should remain in place merely supported by adjoining boards.

FLUXES — Types

In soldering work a flux helps the solder to flow and unite with the metal. Here are details of the main fluxes.

1. Hydrochloric acid, also known as muriatic acid, used when soldering galvanized iron. It is a corrosive poison with a

cleaning effect on galvanized iron. Thus it will remove any oxide coating before you apply solder. However, being a poison, it should be clearly labeled and kept from the reach of children.

2. Zinc chloride, used for soldering tinplate, copper or brass—in fact, generally for metals which are not galvanized or coated with zinc. Zinc chloride is made by putting zinc or small quantities of galvanized iron clippings in a small pot of hydrochloric acid adding small pieces until effervescence ceases.

3. Sal ammoniac, a flux for copper, which is generally in block form for tinning soldering irons.

4. Soldering pastes and liquids, of which there are quite a few on the market. These are quite satisfactory for general repairs, provided that the working surfaces are perfectly clean.

5. Tallow, which is a good flux for lead, copper or brass. Electrine candle—don't use wax candle—can be used as tallow provided that the metal surfaces are cleaned bright before applying the flux.

6. Resin, a good flux for lead, copper and brass. The usual stipulation about clean metal surfaces is most important.

Keep your flux in a glass or porcelain jar. A baby food jar should prove quite suitable.

FRAMES — Finishing Touches

There are several ways in which a picture frame may be finished apart from the conventional painting or staining. Some methods are:

A natural wood frame can be polished with wax of the same color. Or it may be varnished and rubbed, when dry, with pumice and linseed oil, then waxed.

Pickling a frame highlights the grain. Rub white lead into natural wood, then wipe with a clean cloth. Clear varnish, in either a glossy or dull finish and white wax will prevent a yellow tinge.

Grey, black or green pickled frames are not likely to compete with a painting for attention. Apply dominant color first when mixing colors. When dry apply second color and wipe off most of it, allowing first color and tone of the wood to come through.

A little patience and work will resurrect an old gilt frame from a junk shop. If a patch of gold leaf or small ornament is missing, burnt sienna pigment will disguise the damage. Thin the pigment with turpentine and cover the frame, allowing color to flow into recesses and over broken edges. Wipe off excess with cheesecloth, starting at the center on each side and working toward corners. Wipe more pigment from centers than from corners. After about twenty-four hours soak a piece of cheesecloth in turpentine and rub highlights on the edge of frame and ornaments. Then coat the frame several times with orange shellac, thinned half-and-half with methylated spirits.

To spatter-paint a frame with oil color, or a combination of two colors, dilute paint with turpentine to watery consistency.

Dip a toothbrush into the paint and draw a knife blade across the brush to create a spray. Concentrate your fine spray of color at the corners for a tone graduation. Dry. Coat with wax varnish.

For replacing worn spots on gilt frames with gilt paint, don't attempt to repaint the entire frame because liquid gilt does not have the luster and richness of gold leaf. A second method is to use gold leaf which comes in sheets. Cut a piece to fit the space. Use small pieces of gold leaf rather than a single large one.

FRAMES — In Brickwork

When building with bricks or concrete blocks it is essential to secure window and door frames securely so that there is no possibility of movement or vibration.

This is usually done by nailing or screwing hoop-iron ties or brackets to the frame uprights at intervals, and extending along the mortar joints as the brick or block laying proceeds.

Such straps or brackets can be made from strips of hoop-iron cut from a roll to a length of about 12 in. and turned up at right-angles on one end for about 1½ in. Two holes for galvanized fixing clouts are punched or drilled in this turned-up section.

However, it is much more convenient and time-saving to buy such brackets ready made, and shown in the sketch is a good type.

They are galvanized and are much better than those fashioned by hand. Both edges are corrugated slightly and the end which fits into the brickwork is split or fantailed to ensure a very secure grip in the mortar joint.

FUNGUS — On Walls

Especially after a spell of wet, humid, weather it is not uncommon to find a type of fungus or mold appearing on walls or ceilings.

The cause of this trouble is excessive moisture, and the growths are dark in color and very disfiguring and damaging to paint. Removing them is usually quite easy, but making sure that they don't recur may mean some extra effort.

The first thing to realize is that there are several types of these fungus-like growths.

One of the most common is dark grey, or black in color, and there is another which is a bluish-green. The grey or black fungus is particularly disfiguring as it stains the surface and can penetrate deeply. The bluish-green variety, on the other hand, usually wipes off with a damp cloth, but may reappear.

All these growths can feed on certain types of wall finishes, including some kinds of water paint and calcimine. A wall painted with gloss paint or enamel is not so liable to attack.

Areas where the fungus growths appear should first be brushed down and then washed thoroughly. This treatment will sometimes cure the trouble, but the probability is that spores will remain and the fungus will start to grow again, so further treatment is advised before repainting.

The procedure is to use a special fungicide solution which can be bought from paint and hardware stores under various brand names. The action of this solution is to destroy the spores.

Silicone waterproofing liquids sold for treating masonry and similar surfaces which contain chemicals that resist organic growths can also be used. These preparations have the added advantage of waterproofing the wall surface, and paint may be applied over them.

In addition to actual treatment of the affected areas, it is always advisable to check up carefully on any faults causing dampness, and have them repaired.

Excessive condensation of moisture may be partially or wholly responsible for creating conditions suitable for fungus growth. If so, more efficient ventilation is indicated. Where the trouble appears around the skirting in a room the chances are that faulty dampcourse in the brick walls is allowing dampness to soak up from the ground.

FURNITURE — Accidents

Accidents will happen to your furniture.

A cigarette falls unnoticed from an ashtray, a piece of polished furniture becomes scratched, or a chair leg becomes loose.

More times than not there is a simple solution for hiding or repairing the damage once you know how to go about it.

Here is a simple guide which opens with a summary of basic precautions.

(1) Avoid using too much wax—it will only collect dust and produce a dull, smeary finish.

(2) Clean up any spills as quickly as possible so they won't have a chance to soak through the finish.

(3) Use coasters for glasses whenever you serve.

(4) Buy ashtrays with grooves that will put out a cigarette if you accidentally leave one burning.

(5) Glue felt matting to the base of lamps, ashtrays, or any rough-surfaced piece you keep on the tops of tables and sideboards.

(6) Follow the recommendations for care which the manufacturer of your furniture gives on his tag or label. These instructions are attached to help you keep your furniture new-looking for a long time.

(7) Before you use a cleaning or refinishing compound on your furniture, read the directions carefully. If you're in doubt, test the product on a small spot in an inconspicuous place.

With the passage of time, dust settling on polished furniture becomes trapped in the polish and the furniture gradually darkens in color. You can revive it by rubbing it over with a soft cloth dampened with mineral spirits (turpentine substitute).

Use a soft, clean polishing brush for dealing with crevices in moldings and carvings.

If the furniture is sticky and retains fingermarks, it should be washed. Use warm, soapy water, and rinse it with several changes of clean, warm water.

Dry it thoroughly with a clean soft cloth. Use the water sparingly—it is not necessary to swamp the surface.

Dry the surface very thoroughly and leave it for several days before repolishing with silicone furniture cream, wax emulsion, or silicone furniture polish.

Silicone furniture polish may also be used to clean dingy furniture. Dust it first, then wipe it over with a cloth dampened with mineral spirits and allow it to dry. Apply silicone polish with a clean cloth, allow it to dry, and wipe over it with a soft duster.

Apply a second wiping of silicone polish, leave it to dry and wipe it lightly with a clean soft duster. No rubbing is necessary with silicone polish.

We all know those disfiguring white marks that come from hot dishes or spilled water. They can usually be removed with cigarette ash and vinegar.

Sprinkle the ash on the mark and the surrounding area. Then dampen a clean, soft cloth with vinegar and use it to burnish the ashy surface.

Use the cloth lightly and always rub in the same direction as the grain of the wood.

If the mark does not respond to this treatment, wipe the surface clean, sprinkle a little silver-polish, Fig. 1, on a cloth and rub gently over and around the mark.

Medium scratches in a polished surface can often be hidden with colored shoe polish. Apply it with a soft stick, leave it to harden and then burnish across the scratch with a soft cloth.

A good filler for fairly deep scratches is wax crayon of a color matching the wood, Fig. 2. An alternative method is to use beeswax or plastic wood colored to suit.

Blisters sometimes rise on veneered furniture, usually as a result of spilled liquid being allowed to soak in. The repair is easy to carry out. Working carefully, slit the blister along the grain with a razor-blade.

Smear glue from a tube on to a thin piece of card, insert the freshly glued card under each half of the blister in turn, pressing the blister down onto the glue before withdrawing the card.

Rub briskly and firmly with a lint-free cloth to spread the glue thoroughly and remove all surplus exuding from the slit. Weight the repaired part with books and leave it overnight to dry.

If the slit is visible when the glue is dry, treat it as for medium scratches. Finish off with furniture cream or polish. All traces of glue must be wiped from the surface before the repair is weighted; this is important.

Much the same procedure is shown in Fig. 3 where a section of loose veneer or laminated plastic is being glued back into place.

Re-gluing joints is a common furniture repair job. Where possible, take the joint apart, and sand or rasp off old glue. Build up the joint with wedges or wrap one member with glue-soaked string to provide a tight fit, Fig. 4. Tap the joint into place, and hold with clamp for several hours.

FURNITURE — Bruises

When furniture has been in use for any length of time damage of some kind is certain to occur, and perhaps the most common blemishes are bruises on polished surfaces.

There are several methods of removing the disfigurement caused by such dents and bruises.

One is first to remove the polish from around the bruised area by rubbing lightly with very fine abrasive paper. Then prick the dent with a needle and apply a little hot water with a cloth.

Pricking with the needle opens the surface and allows the hot water to penetrate slightly. This in turn releases the compressed wood fibers and they swell back to regain their former level surface.

An alternative method, which has the same result, is to place a damp cloth over the dent and then apply a fairly hot iron for a few seconds. After this, the surface is allowed to dry and is re-polished.

For very severe dents in furniture or in cases where a section has been chipped out, a filler is the most effective way of getting over the trouble.

Prepared plastic wood, which can be bought in tins or tubes, does a good job. It is pressed firmly into the cavity with a knife or chisel and allowed to stand above the surface slightly to counteract any slight tendency to shrink while drying. When thoroughly dry, it may be papered down flush with fine grade abrasive paper.

If the base of the bruise or dent is smooth, roughen the area slightly with abrasive paper to provide a key for the plastic wood. It is also advisable to stain the plastic wood with a suitable pigment to match a particular timber color, since it is not always possible to stain the hardened plastic wood after sanding smooth.

Instead of plastic wood, a home-made filler which is quite satisfactory can be made by mixing an appropriate color pigment with beeswax. Just melt the wax and add the color.

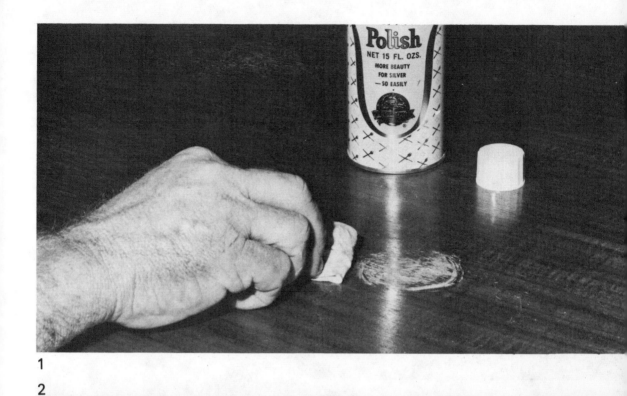

1

2

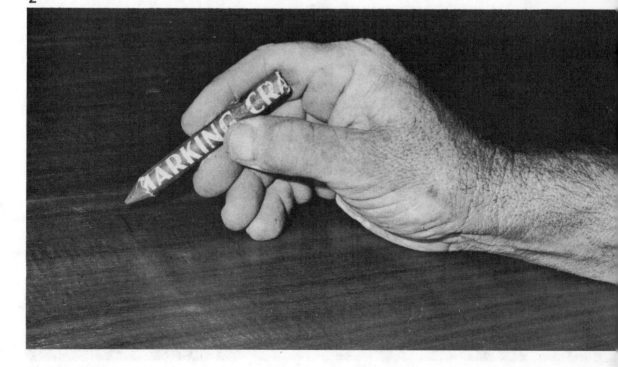

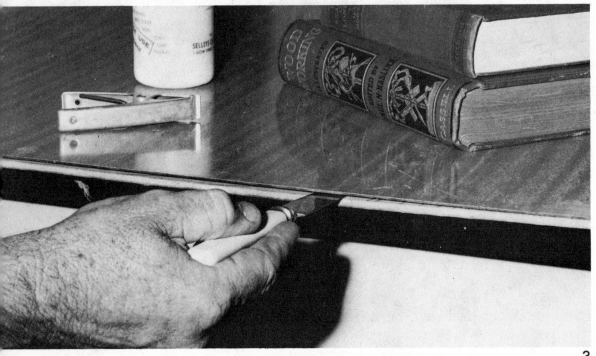

3

4

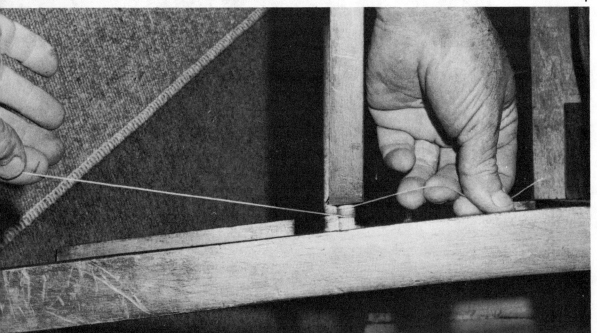

For timbers stained in various shades of red, or having a natural red color, such as cedar, use a pigment known as sienna, and for brown or oak shades use umber. While the colored wax is still warm it should be fashioned into a rod or stick.

When applying, melt with a soldering iron and allow the molten wax to drip into the dent or crack until a little more than full. After this the surplus is scraped off with a sharp chisel or knife, and the surface retouched with a little polish.

FURNITURE FINISHING
— French Polishing

After the furniture has been stained, the grain filled, the surface oiled, and time allowed for the oil to dry, the appearance of the wood should be completely dull and flat, the color more or less of the shade or tone required but rather lighter, and the wood free from all grain indentations.

At the same time, there should not be any pasty surplus filler on the surface as this will obscure the grain and produce a muddy effect.

Before actually starting to polish, make sure that the conditions and surroundings are suitable. These are simple, but vitally important for success. First, the workroom must be comfortably warm with a temperature of at least 65 degrees. The room must also be free of drafts since they carry dust and are inclined to leave the wood surface cloudy.

Naturally, the workroom must be clean, for dust and dirt make successful French polishing work impossible. Great care must be taken in this regard, because even in a clean room there is a tendency for a certain amount of fine dust in the air to settle on the surface to be polished.

At all times, try and work in a good, clear light, preferably daylight. The furniture should be placed between the handyman and the source of light. By adjusting the position of his head, it will then be possible for the handyman to sight along the surface frequently to note the progress of the polishing work and to make any necessary adjustments.

RUBBER—The pad or rubber through which the polish is applied consists of an absorbent cotton pad covered with a soft white linen or cotton fabric.

The various stages in forming a French polishing pad are shown in Fig. 1. After forming the inner pad of absorbent cotton (approximately 6 in. square) into a triangular shape, cover it with a piece of old linen, slightly larger than the original size of the piece of cotton.

Holding the pad and one corner of the rag in the left hand, stretch the opposite corner of the rag over the point of the pad, then turn first the left-hand corner and then the right-hand corner underneath the point, letting the right corner overlap.

Holding this taut with the fingers of the left hand, proceed to overlap the remaining rag backwards from left to right, using the right hand. Finally, twist the whole quite tightly and hold it in the right hand. The rubber should be roughly pear-shaped. In this form, it fits the hand comfortably, and the small pointed end is useful for working into corners.

POLISH—A polish made by dissolving flake orange shellac in methylated spirits will be suitable for most polishing work done in the home workshop. Where a perfectly clear polish is required, however, it will be necessary to use a bleached shellac with the methylated spirits.

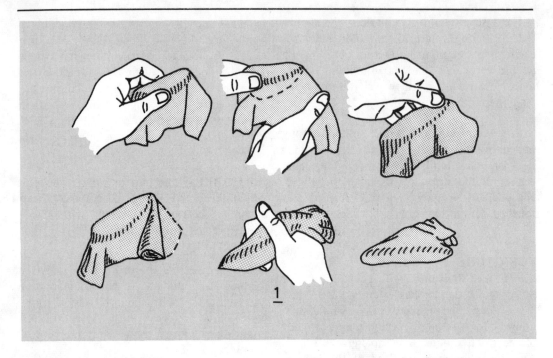

<u>1</u>

When mixing the standard orange polish, the usual proportions are 6 oz. of shellac dissolved in a pint of methylated spirits. With the bleached shellac used for making the clear polish, however, 12 oz. to each pint of spirits will be needed, as the bleaching process reduces the strength of the shellac.

Keep the polish in bottles, and cut a V groove in the side of the cork so that the polish can be shaken freely onto the rubber. Alternatively, whenever the rubber is charged, it should be placed over the open mouth of the bottle and the latter inverted once or twice.

Label all bottles, shake them thoroughly every time more polish is required, and keep them well corked. Incidentally, when charging the rubber, the polish is always applied to the inner pad of cotton by removing the outer covering and then replacing it as before. In this way, the polish can be squeezed out through the cloth covering as it is needed during polishing.

APPLYING THE POLISH—The first stage in actually applying the polish is often referred to as skinning in. This, as the term suggests, consists of putting a layer or skin of polish on the surface. It is done by charging the rubber with polish, starting at one edge of the work, and moving straight along with the grain, gradually covering the entire surface once (A) Fig. 2.

Allow a few minutes for the surface to dry out, and then rub over it with a piece of fine sandpaper. This will expose any traces of filler on the surface, which traces should be rubbed off immediately.

Charge the rubber once again, and repeat the process twice more. After this, a dull kind of gloss will start to appear. The surface should then be allowed to stand to harden for twelve hours.

The next stage of the work is referred to as bodying up, and its purpose is to build up the body of polish. As before, charge the cotton pad and replace the outer cloth covering of the rubber.

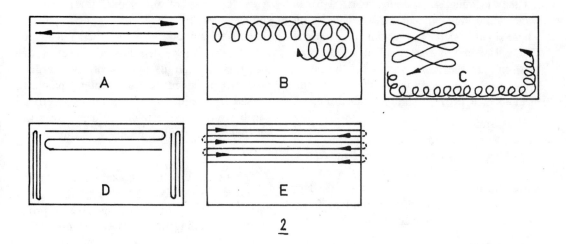

2

Practice will soon show how much polish is needed. When pressed with the fingers, it should exude slightly, but there should be no excess pressed out at the sides during actual use.

A little raw linseed oil placed on the sole of the rubber at this stage will act as a lubricant to prevent the rubber sticking. A spot or two dabbed on with the finger is all that is needed.

This time use a circular movement as in (B) Fig. 2, working gradually over the whole surface, and then back again. The oil will prevent the rubber from dragging, but at the same time will leave a dull smear in its path.

Do not use more oil than is necessary, however. By using a little oil, the pressure on the rubber can be increased; then when it becomes clear that a fair amount of polish is on the surface, change the movement to the figure eight pattern shown in (C) Fig. 2.

This rubbing helps to spread the oil over the whole surface, and its presence is apparent from the slight smears left by the rubber. As the rubber becomes dry recharge it with fresh polish and continue the work. This stage of the job requires patience and perseverance, and time must be allowed between applications for the polish to harden.

SPIRITING OFF—The final stage of polishing is "spiriting off," and its main purpose is to get rid of the oil smears left on the surface. A fresh cover on the rubber will be needed, and the polish used is thinned out progressively with methylated spirits as the work proceeds.

Use long, gentle strokes as in (D) Fig. 2, and continue until only a few smears are left. To remove the last few smears, change to the movement shown in (E) Fig. 2, in which the rubber is taken right through and off the work. This leaves a smooth, satin-like surface which will dry to a bright finish within a few hours.

FURNITURE FINISHING — Lacquering

Instead of using French polish for furniture and other woodwork, a very effective finish can be obtained in much less time by several applications of clear lacquer. As with French polishing, the surface must be prepared carefully and stained or filled where necessary.

Clear lacquer is generally referred to as water-white, and is ideal for wood finishing where it is desired to retain the natural shade. Lacquer is best applied by a spray gun, and, in the home workshop the spray attachment supplied with most vacuum cleaners will prove a suitable substitute.

For small jobs, the lacquer may be brushed on, but care must be taken to keep the brush moving and to use a light touch. Otherwise, there will be a tendency to dissolve the lower coats. The lacquer used in either spraying or brushing should be fairly thin, and three or four coats will be needed.

Each coat should be sanded down lightly when thoroughly dry, using very fine grade wet-or-dry sandpaper in conjunction with a lubricant consisting of soap and water.

After applying the lacquer, the surface is treated with a rubber similar to that used for French polishing, except that chamois leather is used instead of linen as a covering for the inner pad.

The rubber is charged with a special lacquer bodying-up solution sold by most paint stores; it is used with a circular motion. Keep the rubber moving all the time it is on the surface, otherwise it will leave a mark.

As a final operation, rub over the surface lightly with a pad of fine grade steel wool, and get a first-class finish by polishing with a flannelette pad dampened with a lacquer-finishing spirit.

FURNITURE FINISHING — Preparation
Irrespective of the type of finish desired for an article of furniture, the first essential is to have its surface carefully prepared. Defects that are scarcely visible in the bare, unpolished surface become more and more apparent as the finishing work proceeds.

In the case of softwoods, it is usually sufficient to dress the surface first with a sharp steel smoothing plane, then finish off with fine sandpaper used in the direction of the grain. When using any of the harder timbers, plane marks and rough patches caused by sections of the grain tearing out can be removed effectively by using a wood scraper and then finishing off with fine sandpaper.

The standard cabinet maker's scraper is a flat piece of steel about 5 in. long, 3 in. wide, and 1/16 in. thick. The cutting edge is produced by rubbing the edges at a slight angle with the round back of a gouge so as to produce a burr. The scraper is then pushed firmly along the timber surface in the direction of the grain and a fine shaving is removed. In addition to this flat scraper, there is also a special type fitted with a handle and detachable blades, and in most cases the amateur will find this tool more effective and easier to handle than the standard flat scraper.

After preparing the surface, the handyman is faced with the problem of deciding which finish to use. In most of the furniture described in this book, the choice is more or less restricted to clear lacquer and plastic or French polish. Before any type of final finishing material can be applied, however, it is necessary to decide whether or not the timber should be stained.

Staining is quite different and distinct from the polishing procedure in that the purpose of staining is simply to color the timber, whereas the polish or lacquer imparts a hard, lasting, gloss finish to the surface.

Where the natural color of the timber is attractive, a stain is not necessary and the finish is applied directly to the bare natural timber.

FURNITURE FINISHING
— Staining & Filling

Stains are used to change the natural color of wood. The two types of flat stain in general use are identified as water stains and oil stains. Of the two, the oil stain is easier to use than stain made from water-soluble pigments, although the latter gives a uniform color and is less expensive.

An effective water stain that will produce a walnut shade can be made by mixing 4 oz. Van Dyke brown, $\frac{1}{4}$ pint liquid ammonia, and 1-1$\frac{1}{2}$ pints of water.

Start by mixing the Van Dyke brown with the ammonia, add half the water, and test for depth of color on a scrap section of wood. Keep on adding water until the right shade is obtained.

A second water stain can be made quickly at home by dissolving ordinary Condy's crystals in water, and applying the mixture with either brush or cloth.

A matching oil stain can be made by dissolving black Japan in turpentine. This gives any shade of oak from very dark to light, depending on the amount of turpentine added to the pigment.

As a guide, start with the Black Japan thinned out with about four times its volume of turpentine. This gives a suitable warm brown shade which may be further warmed up slightly by adding a little burnt sienna. Burnt sienna is also soluble in the turpentine.

In all cases, the handyman should regard stain as merely a dye which is used to make the color of the wood more pleasing or more suitable for the purpose in view.

Stains which leave a solid residue and thereby obscure the natural grain of the timber are unsatisfactory, except where it is specifically desired to hide an unattractive surface.

Here is a summary of the important points connected with staining work in general:

1. If the natural color of the timber is suitable and attractive, a stain is not required.

2. Ready-made stains can be bought in various colors and shades, but it is not difficult to make and match stains at home. If, however, home-made stains are used, do the mixing only in clear daylight. Color is difficult to judge in artificial light.

3. Always make up sufficient stain to complete the particular job on hand. Allow it to settle, and pour it off into a clean jar. Sediment at the bottom of a container may get on the brush or rag and change the shade as the work proceeds.

4. Stains are tested for shade and depth of color on a scrap end of the particular type of timber being used. The test area of stain is allowed to dry, and then dampened with water.

5. It is easier to prepare the stain carefully and make one application exactly in the required shade than to stain two or three times.

6. Always allow a day for oil or water stains to dry out thoroughly before applying the finishing coats of polish, lacquer or varnish.

7. Where mixed timbers of varying colors are used, it will be necessary to stain all the lighter sections to match the shade of the darkest piece used in the article.

FILLERS—When the grain of the timber used is very open and coarse, it is necessary to use a filler of some kind to make the surface perfectly level and smooth. This must always be done with such timbers as oak.

Paste wood fillers can be bought in different shades and colors to match the particular timber or stain concerned. Homemade fillers are also effective. One that is used widely is made of a finely crushed whiting, colored to match the wood being polished or lacquered.

The whiting is first crushed, then placed in a suitable container and mixed with turpentine to form a paste, after which a suitable pigment to match the wood is added and mixed in thoroughly.

As a suggestion, Van Dyke brown may be added to the filler paste for walnut and oak, and yellow ochre for light oak. In all cases, the pigments are in powder form.

The filler paste, prepared to the consistency of thick cream, should be rubbed over the timber surface with a piece of rough cloth or burlap. After being allowed to stand for about fifteen minutes, surplus filler is rubbed off the surface across the grain.

It must be across the grain, because rubbing in the same direction would probably force the paste out of the open pores thereby completely ruining the filling operation.

Finally, when all surplus filler paste has been removed from the surface, a light brushing of raw linseed oil is applied and the article is placed on one side to dry and harden for twenty-four hours before polishing or lacquering.

GAUGES	Marking
GILDING	Methods
GIMLETS	Some Details
GLASS	Boring
GLASS	Cutting
GLASS FIBER	Repairs
GLASS	To Break
GLASS	Using
GLYCERINE	Is Useful
GRINDER	Sharpening Jig
GUTTERS	Making

GAUGES — Marking

There are two main types of gauges used in woodwork.

First there is the single-tooth marking gauge shown in the illustration at (A) and (B).

That at (A) has a fixed marking pin, whereas the pin at (B) may be adjusted by means of a small wedge.

In use, the block merely slides along the stem and is held in place by a thumbscrew.

The gauge shown at (C) is called a mortise gauge and is used mainly for marking out the parts of a mortise and tenon joint.

Note the two pins. The end one is fixed with the other moving to any desired position on a sliding bar.

Unlike the single-tooth marking gauge (A and B) the block on the mortise gauge is usually held firmly by a flush fitting screw.

Some mortise gauges are fitted with a single tooth on the reverse side of the stem for standard gauging.

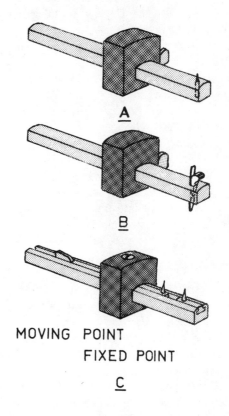

A

B

MOVING POINT

FIXED POINT

C

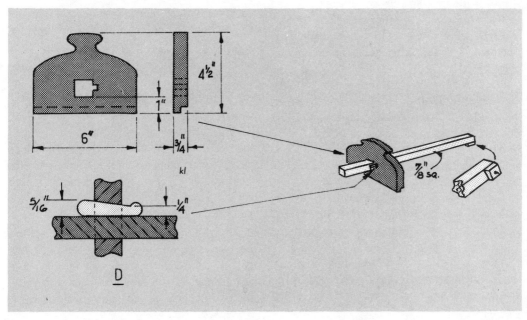

D

Shown also at (D) is a useful gauge for marking large panels.

It is easily made from scrap ends of timber.

Use plywood for the stock and rabbet the bottom edge as shown.

The stem fits through a hole in the stock, and this hole is checked out to take a wedge for locking the stem in position. The cutaway section shows this detail clearly.

Also note that the marking pin at the end of the stem is housed in a plywood block.

This brings it into line with the top edge of the rebate in the block.

GILDING — Methods

Gold leaf or gold paint can be used for gilding such things as picture frames or for producing various decorative effects.

Gold paint can be obtained in the form of a powder which is mixed with a special liquid medium.

Gold leaf is bought in book form, each book containing about twenty-five leaves. It is used with gold size as an adhesive.

When a frame or other article is to be regilded, clean thoroughly with lukewarm water to which a little washing soda has been added.

Putty or plastic wood can be used to fill any cracks. If the moldings have been damaged it is better to use plastic wood, as this will be easier to carve when hard.

When the complete frame is ready for gilding, wet a section with gold size and leave it until tacky.

Then, with a clean knife—don't touch with fingers—pick off a gold leaf, place it in position, and blow gently on it to force it into contact with the surface.

Using a pad of absorbent cotton, press the leaf down now so that it adheres firmly, and burnish with either an agate or bone burnisher.

If gold paint is to be used, clean the article as before, and mix the powder and medium thoroughly. Then apply the paint evenly with a clean camelhair brush.

For a first gilding on bare timber, see that the surface is perfectly smooth, then apply a coat of size or good undercoat of white paint.

After drying, the surface can be evenly coated with gold size and left until tacky.

If the surface is large it is best to gild only small portions at a time.

When gold leaf is used, place the work on a large sheet of paper to collect any unused scraps of leaf.

GIMLETS — Some Details

The gimlet is a tool which appears to have gone out of fashion in recent years. Still it is very handy on many occasions for jobs around the home.

The chief use of a gimlet is in making screw holes. It is threaded at the end so that as it is revolved it penetrates into the wood, so obviating the need for downward pressure.

In this respect it differs from the bradawl, which is also used for making screwholes. Furthermore, the gimlet makes a positive cut, the core or waste escaping along the spiral or groove.

It will be realized then that the gimlet is specially suitable for tough wood which would offer considerable resistance to the bradawl. It is also invaluable in positions where it would be awkward to apply the pressure that the bradawl needs.

For instance, if you had to bore a hole high up and were standing on top of a stepladder, it would be most awkward to exert any pressure with your arm extended. After the initial press-in, the gimlet needs only to be turned.

One fault of a gimlet is its tendency to split the grain of timber if used near an edge, so the safe rule is to take extra care in these positions, especially if the wood is thin and of a soft or brittle nature.

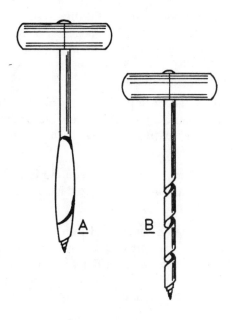

The most commonly used type is called the half-twist gimlet, see illustration at (B). It will be seen that there is a screw-end which bites into the wood and so feeds the tool along.

Above the screw is a spiral groove, the flat metal part between is tapered and so as the gimlet is turned, the top edge of the flat part projecting more than the lower part, cuts into the wood. The core escapes along the spiral groove.

A second type (A) is known as the shell gimlet. This also has the thread at the end, but in place of the spiral groove there is a straight one.

In this type all the cutting takes place at the end just above the thread, the straight groove serving only as a clearance passage.

Both the half-twist and shell gimlets run from very small sizes up to ¼ in. diameter. For larger holes up to ½ in. or more, the auger gimlet is needed. This is rather like the twist bit commonly used in hardwood. There are no clean-cutting nickers, only the cutters.

Consequently the hole it makes is inclined to be rather rough since there is no preliminary cutting of the grain.

GLASS — Boring

Boring a hole in a bottle or decanter can be done with a special glass-boring drill, or by using the improvised drill shown in the illustrations.

The tool can be made from a discarded 5 in. triangular file, normally used for sharpening handsaws. It has three equal sides which curve towards the top, and a power or hand operated grinding wheel is used to form the point. First flatten the tip of the file until each side of the triangle formed measures about ⁵⁄₁₆ in. see illustration at (A).

Use the flat side of the grinding wheel and hold the file horizontally. Grind each side of the triangular tip about 25 degrees so that a small triangular pyramid is formed (B).

GRIND TO POINT

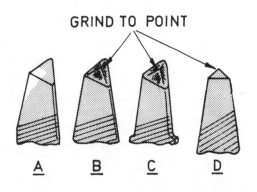

Grind off each corner to about 1¼ in. back, slightly undercutting so that the tip has the greatest section of this 1¼ in. length (C). Detail (D) is a frontal view of the point. The other end of the file will fit into the chuck of an ordinary brace or hand drill.

GLASS — Cutting

Anyone can cut glass if he tackles it confidently and remembers certain basic rules.

However, before anything is done, it will be as well to list the tools required for glass-cutting.

They are: A glass cutter; a straight-edge or T-square; a spring steel rule; and a flat bench or table. Now for some details of these items.

Any glass cutter should work well if handled correctly, but perhaps the one that most homeworkers will find most convenient is the metal shaft, single wheel type.

A glass cutter that is kept well oiled, and not left to rust on a shelf should last for many years.

The straight edge or T-square can be homemade or bought from a tool store.

Fig. 1 shows the head section of a T-square for glass cutting. The blade or stem is mortised into the cross piece and secured with screws.

Holes are drilled as indicated to counteract any warping in the timber. These holes could be ¼ in. diameter.

An important feature of the square are grooves or notches cut into the cross piece on each side of the straight blade. They allow the glass cutter to traverse the full length of the glass.

A pull-out spring steel rule is the most useful accessory for measuring off. This should be marked off in inches, usually up to seventy-two. The footage measure is not used in the glass trade and sizes should always be written down in inches.

The smallest unit of measurement is ⅛ in. So, should a job in hand demand a more accurate size, then a full or scant ⅛ in. is correct.

For example if the size required is 12⁵⁄₁₆ in., then the glass size required is a full 12¼ in. or a scant 12⅜ in.

The table or bench used for cutting glass should be flat, preferably covered with a blanket or felt, and kept fairly taut to avoid wrinkles. But whether covered or not, the bench must be kept clean.

Glass is made in various weights, and the grade used for average size house windows is 24 oz.—that is every square foot weighs 24 oz.

When a window exceeds 36 in. square, 32 oz. glass should be used, and it is also advisable to use this heavier grade glass in doors that are likely to be slammed.

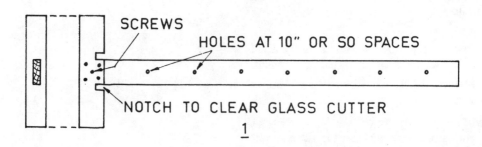

SCREWS

HOLES AT 10″ OR SO SPACES

NOTCH TO CLEAR GLASS CUTTER

1

Measuring correctly is more difficult than would appear at first sight. One must get the sizes right, and get them down on paper so that the cutter can understand them and cut the glass to the correct size.

Measuring should be tackled with the steel rule mentioned earlier. A tape measure tends to stretch with use, and is not reliable for accurate measuring.

A 2 ft or 3 ft wooden rule can be used where the sizes are less than the full measure of the rule but if two measurements have to be taken, added together, then an allowance made for a clearance between glass and window frame, a mistake can very easily occur.

First ascertain that the opening to be measured is square, and that none of the bars is warped.

If all is well, measure the exact distance between the top rabbet and the bottom rabbet, as indicated in the sectional view shown in Fig. 2.

From this measurement subtract $\frac{1}{8}$ in. to allow for a clearance between glass and frame, and write down the resulting size. Measure the width in the same way. Always measure height of the frame first to enable the cutter to distinguish one size from the other.

This is especially important when lining-up certain types of glass which have distinctive patterns.

Now to the actual handling and cutting of a piece of glass. First there is a correct way to lift and place the square of glass on the table. Pick up the square by placing one hand on each vertical edge, lift it off the floor, then tilt it sideways so that the right hand is at the bottom and the left hand at the top.

In this position, walk across to the bench and place the glass against the front edge

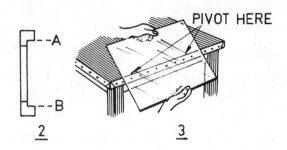

of the bench as near the center of the glass as possible.

The right hand should now be below the edge of the bench and the left hand should be about the same distance above as indicated in Fig. 3.

The right hand now lifts the bottom edge of the glass and pivots it on the front edge of the bench so that the top of the glass comes to rest flat on the bench.

It is then slid on to the bench, leaving about an inch overlapping.

If the glass is dirty, clean it thoroughly with a rag dipped in turpentine or a moist chamois cloth, and dry off.

Then lay the straight-edge or T-square on the glass, and measuring from the left hand edge, move the T-square along until it comes to rest $\frac{1}{16}$ in. short of the required size measuring to the right hand side of the T-square.

This $\frac{1}{16}$ in. is an allowance for the thickness of the shaft of the glass cutter.

To use the glass cutter, take it up between the first two fingers, with the first finger on the flattened place provided and the thumb underneath, as shown clearly in Fig. 4.

Now reach forward and place the wheel of the cutter as near to the top of the glass as is possible without it actually going over the edge, close up against the right hand side of the T-square.

The left hand should be pressed firmly on to the T-square, about halfway up the glass. Care should be taken to see that the fingers of the left hand do not get in the way of the cutter.

Now, taking care that the T-square does not move, exert a slight pressure on the cutter, and, keeping it pressed firmly against the T-square, draw it down towards you, completing the cut in one operation.

After cutting, there are several methods of opening the cut. The method used will depend on the size of the off-cut. If the off-cut exceeds 12 in. lift the T-square and slip it under the cut as in Fig. 5.

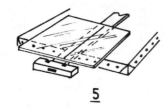

5

The piece of glass required should be pressed gently down on the bench. This will cause the off-cut to be lifted clear of the bench. Holding the cut size down firmly with the left hand, press the off-cut down firmly with the right hand held roughly central.

This will create tension over the surface of the glass and cause it to snap along the mark made by the cutter.

Where the off-cut is less than 12 in., use the method shown in Fig. 6. Place both hands under the edge of the glass with fists clenched—one hand each side of the cut.

The curled forefinger should touch the glass underneath and the thumbs press down on top.

Now move the knuckles of the two little fingers in towards one another at the same time exerting a slight upward pressure with the forefingers and keeping the thumbs held firmly on top.

This will cause tension, and the cut should open along the mark.

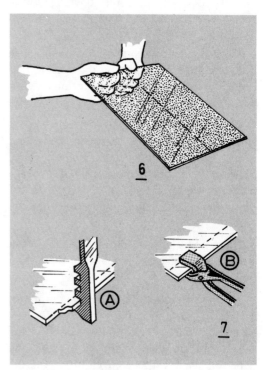

6

7

If only a small strip is to be cut off a square of glass, break it away after cutting by gripping and levering with suitable slot in glass cutter or by using flat-nose pliers, (A), (B), Fig. 7.

GLASS FIBER—Repairs

All sorts of repairs are made easier with glass fiber and a knowledge of how to use it will speed jobs which have always been tricky.

The surfaces to which it is applied must be absolutely clean. All dirt, rust, grease and wax must be removed.

Next, the surfaces must be roughened to form a key to which the glass fiber will bond itself. This presents no difficulty and, depending on the materials involved, you can use a file, a rasp or sandpaper.

In cold weather you should use an electric heater (or a similar heat source), to expedite setting. The same job, however, can be done by adding an accelerator to the resin in accordance with the manufacturer's instructions.

When you apply the glass fiber, allow a generous overlap on to the material to which, it is being applied.

Always follow the manufacturer's instructions implicitly, but the method of application is fairly general. The resin comes in the form of a powder and a liquid. These are mixed—and then you have to work fast, for the resin sets rock-hard in about half an hour.

First mix a fairly stiff paste and brush this thickly onto the overlap area of the material being repaired. Then thin the paste, and stipple this onto the glass fiber with a brush. Press the glass fiber into position. Repeat the process for a second layer, and again for a third if extra strength is required.

In half an hour the resin will be hard.

Use the scrim type of fibers, in the illustration at (A), for covering large areas, such as caravan roofs, boat hulls and the like.

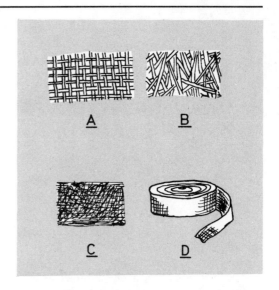

The chopped strand mat (B) is best used where reinforcing strength is needed. However it does not yield such a smooth finish.

Glass fiber tissue, shown at (C), can be worked into a really hard, smooth surface. The woven ribbon (D) is handy for binding edges to give a neat finish, and for places where local reinforcement is needed.

A plastic beaker makes the best mixing bowl. When the residual resin is hard the beaker can be flexed and the contents peeled out. Any brush can be used, provided it is fairly stiff,

In their tightly lidded containers, the ingredients of the resin will keep almost indefinitely in a cool, dark place.

GLASS — To Break

There are occasions when it is desirable to make tumblers, tankards or pencil holders from glass bottles, jars or any glass vessel.

The method of doing this is shown clearly in the illustration. Fill the vessel with light oil to the desired height and into this dip

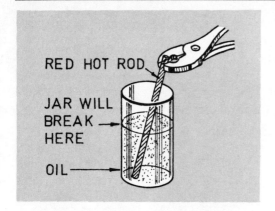

RED HOT ROD

JAR WILL
BREAK
HERE

OIL

a red-hot rod, a pair of pliers or pincers should be used.

This will result in a clean break around the circumference of the vessel at the height of the oil. The cut edge should be even although possibly a little sharp. This sharp edge can be smoothed off by grinding lightly on an abrasive wheel.

GLASS — Using

Glass is used for many jobs around the home apart from windows, and it is important to select the correct type and thickness for any particular job.

There are two main types of transparent glass—sheet glass (which is the cheapest to produce) with a fire-finished surface and never, as a consequence, perfectly free from distortion—and polished plate glass, where the two surfaces are ground flat, parallel, and polished.

SHEET GLASS is specified by weight, that is the approximate weight per square foot, with the exception of the two heaviest grades, which are $\frac{3}{16}$ in. and $\frac{1}{4}$ in. thick respectively. These two grades are called thick drawn plate glass. The weights for lighter

grade sheet glass generally used for glazing purposes are 18 oz., 24 oz., 26 oz., and 32 oz.

PLATE GLASS is specified by nominal thickness in inches. There is, however, a considerable variation in actual thickness for given nominal sizes. It is as well to check this if an exact match or fitting is essential. For example, $\frac{1}{4}$ in. plate may vary from $\frac{3}{16}$ in. up to $\frac{5}{16}$ in. thickness. Specifying $\frac{1}{4}$ in. exact, however, should guarantee that the thickness is within $\frac{1}{64}$ in. either way. Similarly with $\frac{3}{8}$ in. plate. Larger thicknesses— $\frac{1}{2}$ in. plate and above—are within $\frac{1}{32}$ in. of the nominal size either way.

Sheet glass is made in three different qualities; for general glazing, for better work, and for high-grade jobs. Plate glass is also made in three qualities—standard and selected grades, and silvering quality for mirrors.

SELECTING GLASS for the right purpose is important. Drawn glass is almost invariably used for glazing work in homes.

On the other hand, select plate glass should be used where clear vision is important. For example, ordinary small-pane sashes could have, say, 24 oz. drawn glass, but large picture windows would certainly call for select plate glass.

Usually 24 oz. glass is considered the most suitable weight for average domestic glazing work, although very small sashes may be fitted with lighter grade sheet glass.

FIGURED GLASS is available in a number of patterns under such names as Arctic, Flemish, Fluted, Crystalline, etc. Such glass should always be glazed with the rougher face inside the room. This is because it is easier to apply the putty to the smooth side and also if the rougher side faced outward it would collect considerably more dirt and grime.

GLYCERINE — Is Useful

Glycerine is invaluable in the home, and can be utilized in many different and simple ways.

If a white cloth should get stained with tea or coffee, soak the stain in equal quantities of glycerine and water adding a little ammonia as well.

Then rinse in hot soapy water and the stains will disappear.

Fruit stains can likewise be removed with glycerine. Cover the area thickly with glycerine and put the cloth aside for an hour or two.

Then stretch the material tightly over a basin and pour boiling water through it, afterwards washing it with soap in the usual way.

When woolen garments show signs of turning a bad color, or of getting "felted," add a tablespoon of glycerine to each pint of rinsing water. Then hang the garment up to dry, if possible in the open air.

If a little glycerine is added when starch is being used, the iron will run much more smoothly over starched things.

Apply glycerine at once to scorch marks and leave it to soak in, then wash out with soap and warm water.

Dry and cracked shoes will take on a new lease of life if treated in the following way. Dry them thoroughly, clean well, then rub glycerine into the leather, leaving it to soak for two or three days.

Later, polish with a good shoe polish.

The leather will be delightfully soft and glossy, and the shoes will look as good as new.

Glycerine is also excellent for whitening the hands and keeping them soft. Mix it with a little lemon juice and eau-de-Cologne, and apply at night.

People who do much rough and dirty work will find this treatment invaluable.

Hobbyists who make models from molds will find that the hardened plaster will come away easily if the inside surfaces of the molds, which come into contact with the plaster, are brushed over with glycerine before pouring wet plaster.

GRINDER — Sharpening Jig

Although one of the most frequent operations in the average workshop is grinding or re-grinding tool edges it is surprising how many workers find it difficult to hold such tools as chisels and plane irons at the correct angle when grinding them on a bench grinder, whether power or hand operated.

Not all cutting bevels are the same, and although a grinder may have a guide it may not be suitable in all cases.

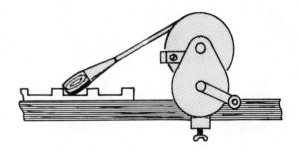

Here a simple jig of the type shown in the illustration will be useful. It is a notched strip of hardwood about 12 in. long and 2 in. wide.

The thickness could be 1¼ in. As a guide have the notches ¾ in. wide, ½ in. deep and spaced about 1 in. apart.

The jig is tacked or screwed to the bench directly in front of the revolving wheel. The end of the handle of the tool being ground is merely set in an appropriate notch to suit the bevel on the cutting edge of the blade.

Sometimes it is more convenient to attach both notched jig and grinder to a separate plank. This can then be clamped to the bench when needed and removed afterwards, leaving the bench clear for other work.

If the tool being ground is very narrow move it evenly across the revolving edge of the grinder so as not to cause excessive wear on one section.

Also dip the edge in cold water frequently to prevent overheating of the blade and possible loss of temper.

GUTTERS — Making

The most important part of making gutters is soldering the parts, and, apart from the corner joints, the lengths should overlap by about 6 in. and be securely soldered.

Most lengths should be joined and soldered on the ground. The assembly is then lifted carefully onto the brackets.

The outlet sections for downpipes are cut and prepared before the gutter is erected.

Brackets are fixed to the facia board or rafter ends by long galvanized nails, or clout nails, about three feet apart.

A slight fall must be allowed towards the downpipes. A chalk line from end to end of a section as a guide for positioning brackets, ensures a straight even line for the gutter.

Finally, after the work is complete it is well to coat the inside of the gutter with a bituminous roofing paint as a protection against rust.

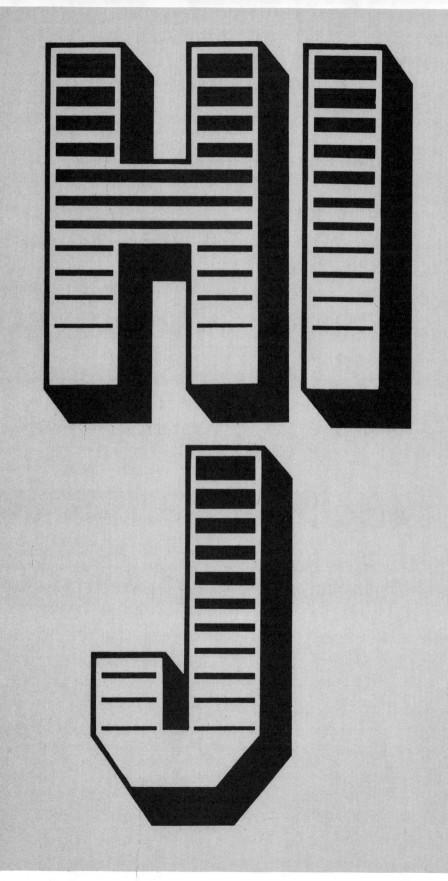

HIJ

HACKSAW	Using
HALVED JOINT	To Make
HAMMER	Secure Head
HAMMER	Using
HARDBOARD	Fix Sheets
HARDBOARD	Joints
HINGES (Butt)	Fitting
HINGES	Types, Uses
HOUSED JOINT	Stopped Type

INSULATION	For Comfort
ISOMETRIC	Projection

JOINTS	Tightening

HACKSAW — Using

For metal cutting of any kind, from cutting heavy bars to removing rusty bolts, your hacksaw will do a better job if you remember several fundamental rules about selecting and using the tool.

As with any tool, buy only the best quality hacksaw frame—preferably the rigid tubular type as in illustration at (A). Cheap, light frames become twisted and distorted under the tension required to tighten the blade.

When buying and using hacksaw blades, select the tooth pitch to suit the thickness and quality of the material. The main rule is to have at least three teeth of the blade in contact with the metal at all times. This means that the thinner the metal the finer the teeth.

Standard hacksaw blades are nine, ten and twelve inches long, and the frames are adjusted to suit.

Blades are available with 14, 18, 24, and 32 teeth an inch, and here are some details concerning the most suitable blades for various metals and materials.

Use 32 TPI blades for: Conduit tubing, cycle tubing, sheet metal of 18 gauge and thinner.

Use 24 TPI blades for: Angle iron mild steel up to ¼ in., brass piping, stainless steel up to ½ in. tubing over 18 gauge and wire rope.

Use 18 TPI blades for: Aluminum, heavy angle iron, brass, bronze, copper, steel.

Use 14 TPI blades for: Asbestos, cast-iron.

It might be argued that it would be safe to use nothing but 32 TPI blades, but this is not so because soft materials like aluminum and plastics have tooth-clogging tendencies, and the fine teeth would just ride over material without cutting.

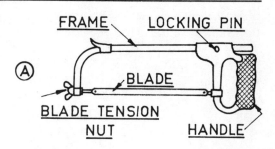

If you do a good bit of ferrous-metal hacksawing, you'll find it worthwhile to pay a little extra for special alloy-steel blades, which cut faster and hold up longer than ordinary blades.

Place the blade in the saw, teeth forward. It can be either in normal position in relation to the frame, or angled 90 degrees to meet special clearance problems (B).

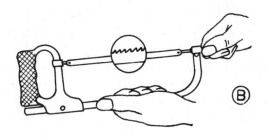

Then tighten the blade until it gives a pinging sound when plucked with your thumb. After a few cuts it will stretch a bit, so give it another turn of the screw.

To start an accurate cut, use your thumb as a guide, sawing slowly with short strokes (C).

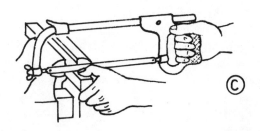

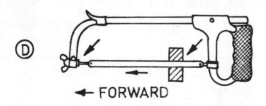

As the cut deepens, shift your hand to the front of the frame and equalize pressure at both ends of the saw. Apply this pressure firmly downward on forward strokes (D), and lift up slightly on back strokes (E).

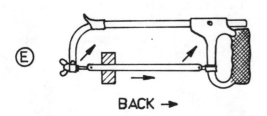

← FORWARD

BACK →

While sawing, stand with your feet at least 12 in. apart and flex your knees in line with the strokes to add a slight body sway to your arm motion. A good cutting speed is 50 strokes a minute.

Wherever possible, the work should be clamped tightly in the vice to prevent it moving. Always keep the hacksaw blade flat on the metal being cut.

The more teeth there are in contact with the work the better the saw operates, and the less chance of breaking the teeth, so don't hold the blade at a sharp angle.

If you break a blade while making a cut and have to use a new one, don't insert it into the old cut. Instead, turn the job over and start afresh. The new blade will be wider than the old one, and would probably jam in the old cut.

HALVED JOINT — To Make

One of the most useful woodworking joints is the cross-halved joint. It is used extensively when building cupboards and other framed woodwork.

The illustrations show clearly the method of setting out and cutting the joint.

Fig. 1. The pieces to be cut are marked out.

Fig. 2. As an aid to accurate cutting, chisel a shallow groove on the waste side of the marking-out lines. This will save time in the long run, and help to ensure an accurate joint.

Fig. 3. It makes removal of the waste wood very much easier if you make several saw cuts in it.

Fig. 4. Hold the piece of wood firmly in a vice for removing the waste. Start near the edge, chipping pieces out, and work down to the gauge line. With soft woods it will probably be possible to do this by thumping the handle of the chisel with your open hand, but with harder woods it may be necessary to use a mallet.

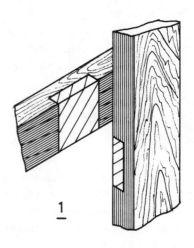

1

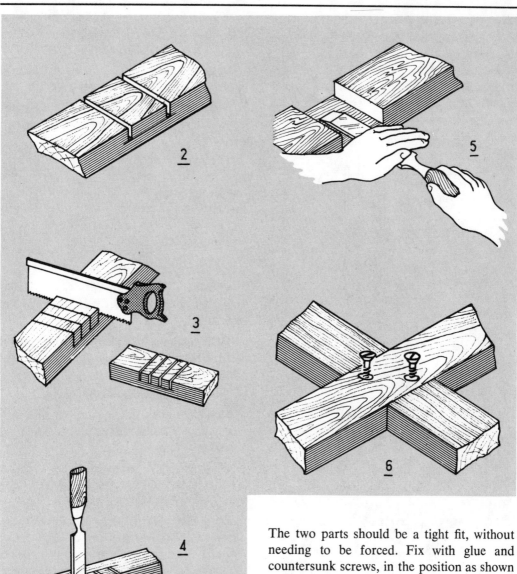

Fig. 5. Final smoothing off should be done by paring with the chisel, flat side to the wood. Finish by removing any high points by a slight slicing movement of the chisel.

The two parts should be a tight fit, without needing to be forced. Fix with glue and countersunk screws, in the position as shown in Fig. (6).

HAMMER — Secure Head

When a hammer head becomes loose, it is a simple matter to fix it. See Fig. 1.

Cut two short pieces of heavy wire, bend the ends and file them to sharp points.

Press the wires into shallow grooves cut in the sides of the handle so that the points bite in, and force the handle into the head.

The wires should project at the top about ¼ in. You complete the job by hammering the wires over.

A loose hammer head won't drive nails in properly. There's also the danger that it may fly off and cause damage.

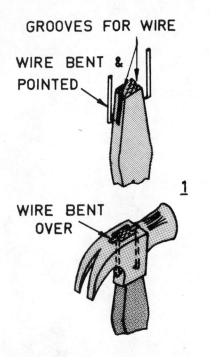

GROOVES FOR WIRE

WIRE BENT & POINTED

WIRE BENT OVER

1

If a plain steel wedge is used in tool handles, grind the thin edge to a point as shown in the cut-away illustration, Fig. 2.

Note also that a hole has been drilled at approximately the center of the wedge.

When treated in this way it will hold more firmly than even a notched or corrugated wedge.

The reason for this is that as the pointed wedge is driven into the handle, part of the displaced timber is forced into the hole in the wedge from each side and very effectively locks it in place with very little chance of working loose.

HAMMER — Using

Using a hammer properly is something of an art.

Hammer blows are delivered through the wrist, elbow, and shoulder, depending on the force you want to exert.

Swing rhythmically, in an easy arc.

Don't let the hammer head twist, and keep the handle parallel to the nail head at the moment of impact.

This way, the face will always deliver square blows.

Shown at (A) is the grip for starting a nail, and at (B) the grip for a full swing. Detail (C) shows that in driving a nail, allow a fraction of the head to protude for punching. This avoids bruising the timber surface.

When you use a hammer with a nail set to drive the nail heads below the surface of wood, strike the head of the set just as squarely as you would a nail.

At the same time, rest your little finger on the work in a position that steadies the set and prevents its slipping off the nail head.

These points are shown clearly in (D).

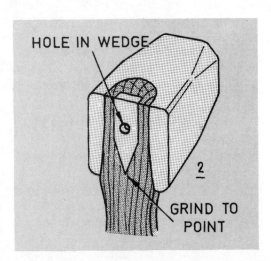

HOLE IN WEDGE

GRIND TO POINT

2

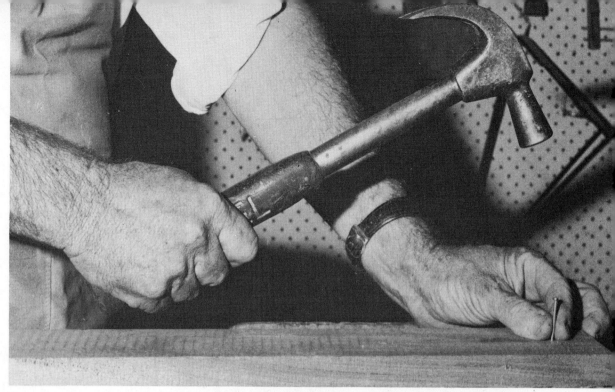

A

B

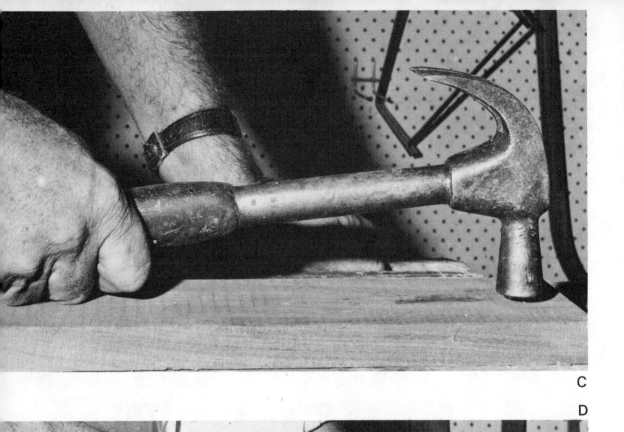

C

D

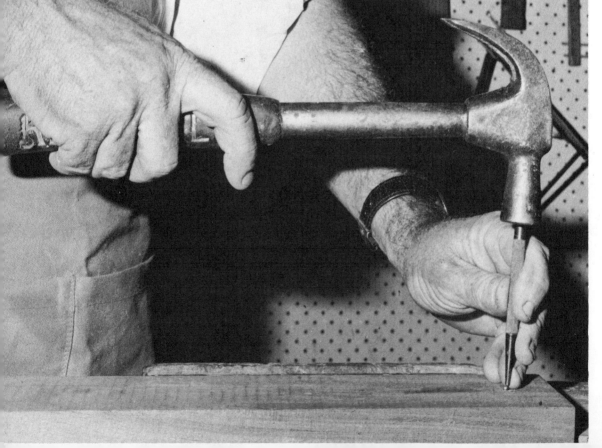

Here are some brief hints for using a hammer.

1. Always keep hammer heads clean and dry. A greasy face may slip off a nail and damage the work, or cause injury.

2. **Never hammer with the side or "cheek" of the head.** It is comparatively **weak and may crack.**

3. Always strike with the center of the face of the hammer head. It is especially hardened for that purpose.

4. Don't damage the face by striking steel harder than itself.

5. Never use a hammer with a loose head or tape up a handle that is even slightly fractured. Apply new wedges to re-tighten a loose head—a new handle if the old one is cracked.

6. Finally, don't use a hammer claw to pry heavy framing timbers apart, or open heavy crates. The correct tool for this job is a pinch bar.

HARDBOARD — Fix Sheets

If hardboard sheets are to be fixed to a brick or concrete wall they may be attached with adhesive if the wall is reasonably even and straight on the surface.

The alternative is to plug the wall and **screw in wooden furring strips about 2 in.** wide and ¾ in. thick.

The sheets are then nailed to these strips with special cadmium plated hardboard nails.

The nailing procedure for hardboard sheets is very important, and it is shown clearly in the diagram where the base is a timber stud frame with cross pieces called **noggings.**

Nails should be spaced at 4 in. centers on all edges of the sheets, and at 12 in. centers through the body of the sheets.

A basic principle is always to begin **nailing at the center of the sheet and work to the outer edges.**

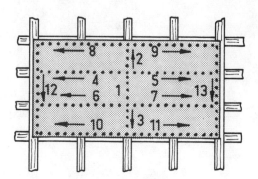

The numbered illustrations shows clearly the nailing sequence.

Remember also that the sheet edges should be brought into only moderate contact—not tightly butted together.

This is to avoid surface buckling if expansion of the sheets occur.

HARDBOARD — Joints

The use of hardboard for ceilings and wall panels is increasing, and close attention should be paid to the treatment of joints between sheets.

Such joints can add much to the appearance of a surface, but there is one precaution that should be noted.

Allow a slight clearance between adjoining sheet edges for any movement caused by atmospheric conditions. Detail (A) in the illustration shows a plain butt joint with a gap of about ³⁄₁₆ in. Here the joint could be covered with a strip. An alternative treatment is to V-joint the sheet corners by chamfering or by rounding them over. In such cases no cover strip is needed.

The treatment shown in detail (B) is very attractive. The edge of one sheet is **beveled completely, with the adjoining one** double chamfered to form a deep V-joint. The advantage of this joint is that the timber framework underneath is hidden.

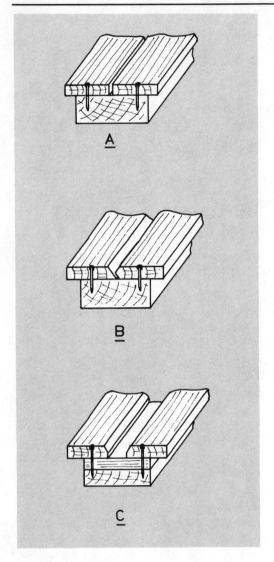

A

B

C

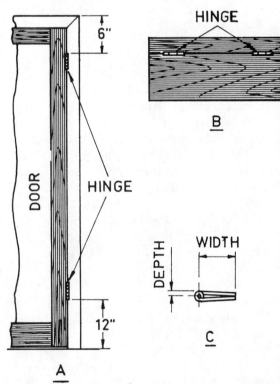

HINGES (Butt) — Fitting

When fitting narrow butt hinges space them correctly and evenly.

For instance, place door hinges below the top rail and above the bottom rail as in the illustration at (A). A long door may need a third hinge half-way between the top and bottom hinges.

On a box, place the hinge (B) about one hinge length from the end of box. For small boxes up to 18 in. long, narrow butt hinges ranging from 1 to 1½ in. long are suitable.

For fitting a standard butt hinge, cut a recess out of both the sections to be joined so that the hinge flaps will screw down flush with timber.

The depth of each recess is equal to half the thickness of the knuckle as shown at (C).

The same result is achieved in detail (C) where the upright frame members have been covered first with a strip of hardboard. Then the sheets are chamfered or rounded on the edges and spaced any desired distance apart.

In all cases it is advisable to use special cadmium-plated hardboard nails for fixing sheets. The heads of these nails are punched below the surface and stopped with a proprietary filler or a mixture of glue size and whiting tinted to the required color.

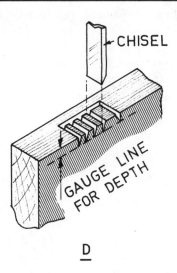

← CHISEL

GAUGE LINE FOR DEPTH

D

Gauge this depth, and mark the length and width (less the knuckle) of each flap.

Make a series of vertical cuts in the marked position with a sharp chisel as at (D), then pare down to the depth gauge line and trim the recess (E).

Fasten each leaf with one screw and try the fit. Make any necessary correction, and insert the other screw. If the recesses have been made a little too deep, pack with a slip of cardboard.

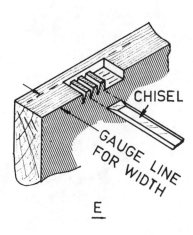

CHISEL

GAUGE LINE FOR WIDTH

E

The screw holes in butt hinges are countersunk, so always use the correct gauge screw so that screw head does not protrude.

HINGES — Types, Uses

The most common type of hinge is that shown in the illustration at (A), the narrow butt hinge seen on most room and cupboard doors.

Details (B) and (C) show two variations of the plain butt hinge. They are the rising butt hinge and the loose-pin hinge. When a pair of rising butt hinges is fitted to a door it rises on a helical joint when swung open, so clearing a thick carpet or unevenness in a floor.

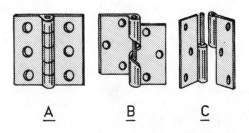

A   B   C

They are made right and left-handed. To determine which is required stand outside the door, and, if the sites for the hinges are on the right, right-hand hinges are called for, if the sites for hinges are on the left they must be left-handed.

The lift-off or loose-pin hinge (also for right or left hand) is useful when for any reason frequent removal of a door is necessary. Here it is just a matter of tapping the pin connecting the wings of the nut out of place and lifting the door down.

For hanging large doors and gates the Scotch tee hinge—so called because of its shape—is generally used. Tee-shaped hinges of smaller size are also frequently used for hanging outside ledge doors on sheds and out-buildings.

Strap hinges, not unlike tee hinges, are used mainly on the hinged flaps of step ladders and trestles.

Two unusual but very useful hinges are the parliament and piano type. The parliament hinge is used where a door has to clear a skirting or other obstruction and fold back flat against a wall.

The piano hinges are brought in long strips, and, apart from their specific job of securing piano lids, are ideal for many cabinet hinging jobs.

HOUSED JOINT — Stopped Type

Here are basic details of a woodwork joint as applied to the construction of a set of bookshelves, although it has other applications and variations.

In this particular case it is called a stopped housing, because it stops short of the front edge of the bookcase ends.

In effect, the joint is hidden, and the shelves and the ends of the bookcase meet flush, as shown in the illustrations.

The best type of timber to use for bookshelves is a softwood such as pine. The size of the complete unit and its individual pieces is a matter of individual needs. You could have two, three or four shelves, and the back may be closed in with plywood or hardboard or left open.

You will also have to decide the distance between the shelves. These may be spaced equally, or you might allow a depth of 10 in. at the bottom for taller and heavier books and about 7 in. for the top shelf if it is to hold small paperbacks.

The most important details are that you cut the grooves or housings accurately so that the ends of the shelves fit them firmly, and that you position them on the inner faces of both ends, so that the shelves are on an exact level.

Match the two ends first to make sure they have the same dimensions. Then fix them in a vise; see Fig. 1. Measure the distance from the tops down to where you want the first shelf, and mark its position as shown across the back edges of the two ends.

Square up these marks with a try square and use the sharp edge of a chisel to carry them right across the wood. Then move the ends along in the vice to mark them similarly for each of the other shelves.

Each time you do this make sure that all edges and previous markings are in line with each other and, if necessary, tap the untrue parts with a mallet until they are in line.

If the wood being used is very soft or inclined to bruise, protect it in the vice with some scraps of plywood.

The next step is to carry the trench markings around from the backs of the end pieces to the inner sides, where you will set out the exact lines to be cut, as shown in Fig. 2.

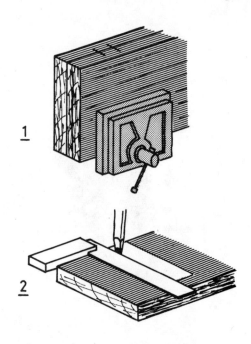

1

2

Make sure the pencil is sharp and produces a thin, clear line, or better still, use a special marking knife for setting out the guide lines.

This marking-out also defines the stopped part of the housing. Later on you will gauge the distance between the stop-line and the edge of the wood and transfer this measurement on the gauge to the ends of the shelves, so giving the size of the notch to be cut.

But in the meantime you are still at work on the trench or housings to hold the shelves. Having marked out a trench as shown, the next step is to cut it down to depth with the tenon saw (Fig 4).

What that depth is depends on the thickness of the end pieces. If they are an inch or ¾ in. thick, have the housing grooves ¼ in. deep. Fix this measurement on your gauge and mark is on the right-hand edge as indicated in Fig. 3.

Now, inside either of the longer lines make an indentation or V cut along which the saw blade can run. You can do this by scoring a deep line on the waste (inner) side of the pencil marks with a chisel as shown or by cutting with a mallet and chisel, Fig. 3.

Make the saw cut almost to the depth indicated by the line gauged on the back edge, and also stop just short of the stop line gauged in from the front.

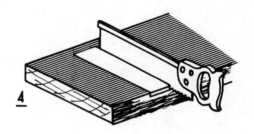

4

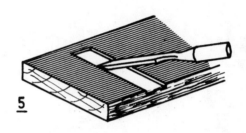

5

Then, with mallet and chisel, or chisel alone, depending on the softness of the wood, begin to ease the wood out of the groove as shown in Fig. 5. Start at almost the full depth and cut upward, so that you won't go the full length of the groove at first. Then, in the second stage, cut in toward the stopped end.

To cut the stopped end down to depth, mark this on your chisel with a pencil, and tap the chisel to the required depth along the inside of the stop-line. An alternative means of cutting a trench to depth is to use a router plane.

The next step is to mark out the dimensions of the notches on the ends of the shelves. This is best done in one operation so that the markings will be the same for all shelves.

As mentioned earlier, set the gauge to the distance between the stop-line and the nearest edge and transfer this measurement to the shelves held upright and together as shown in Fig. 6.

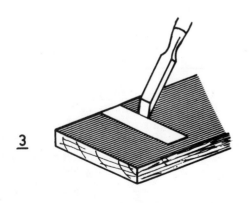

3

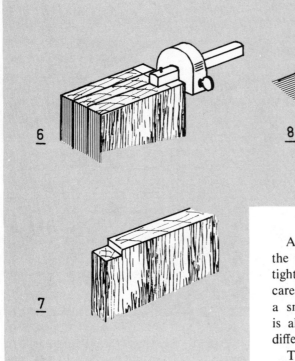

6

7

8

Depth of the notch, of course, will be equal to the depth of the trench. It can be sawn to depth and then cut back with mallet and chisel, or the job can be done with two saw cuts, inside the marked line. Figs. 7 and 8 show how the notched edges of the shelves will fit into the grooves or housings.

At this stage you will be ready to assemble the whole structure. If there is a shade of tightness in the trench this can be eased with careful use of the chisel. On the other hand, a small amount of looseness in the joint is all right as long as there isn't a gaping difference between the shelf and the trench.

The last step is to reinforce the joints with glue and perhaps nails. Use cold PVA type glue for assembly, and punch any nail heads below the surface if nailing is done through the bookcase ends.

After assembling the bookcase frame with glue a neat nailing method is to place the nails at an angle under the shelf, driving them in at a tangent so that they will bed in the wood of the end pieces without protruding.

INSULATION — For Comfort

The insulation of the roof area of a home is comparatively inexpensive, especially if the home handyman does the work himself.

Such insulation can keep a house up to 15 degrees cooler in summer, and warmer in winter.

In winter, the warmed air rises. If not retarded by insulation, it quickly escapes through the ceiling into the roof area.

There are quite a number of different materials used in home insulation, and all are easily installed.

Aluminum foil comes in sheet form and relies on reflective value to keep heat and moisture in during winter, and out during summer. It is sometimes combined with bulk insulating materials for further protection against both heat and noise.

Rigid batts are made from 2 in. and up to 6 in. thick from various insulating materials. They are easily cut with a knife to fit between ceiling joists or the vertical studs in a frame wall.

Loose fill comes from such materials as fiberglass, vegetable or mineral wool. It can be blown into ceilings or wall cavities or simply poured from bags passed into the roof area through a manhole.

Flexible blankets of the insulating material such as mineral wool or fiberglass may be laid quickly. They are also very easy to cut and fit between joists and studs.

There are also the rigid insulating boards, but these are usually used as a base or underlining for the other materials.

Apart from the advantages of protecting against heat and cold, all these materials form a very effective barrier against noise.

To understand the principles of insulation, it is an advantage to know the basic rules of heat transference, and here they are.

Heat travels towards the lower temperatures, and it does this in three different ways:

(1) CONDUCTION—Heat passes from one particle in a body to the next. For example, if one end of an iron bar is heated, the heat will travel along the bar by conduction.

(2) CONVECTION—This takes place when all gases and liquids are heated. Air next to the heat source expands, rises, and is replaced by cooler and heavier air which is in turn heated.

(3) RADIATION—Heat travels from a hot to a cold body without heating the space through which it passes. For instance, the sun heats the earth without heating the space between.

ISOMETRIC — Projection

This is a pictorial form of drawing in which one corner of the object is nearest the observer and is vertical, the two sides sloping away at 30 degrees with the horizontal.

Actual or scale sizes can be drawn on all three lines. The projection is satisfactory for small objects, but on larger ones such as sideboards, etc. it gives a somewhat distorted appearance and the proportions appear wrong.

It is used therefore on drawing intended to show working detail sizes, etc., rather than the actual appearance, though a compromise is sometimes made by drawing lines at 45 degrees, marking measurements on these, and dropping vertical lines to cut the 30 degrees lines.

Even so this does not allow for the fact that parts farther away appear smaller than those near, even though they are in fact the same size. For pictorial appearances perspective is better.

JOINTS — Tightening

Where two pieces of a structure—such as the mitered joint of a picture frame—butt against each other they sometimes loosen and gape open.

How to draw them together again without dismantling the entire frame is often a problem, but the method suggested here is simple and effective.

Detail (A) in the illustration shows the gap between two adjoining pieces of framework. On top is a piece of thin stiff brass plate bent as indicated and screwed down by a couple of screws on each end to the pieces to be drawn together.

Application of this method to a mitered joint is shown before hammering flat in detail (D.)

The strip may be of convenient width and length and cut from fairly thin-gauge rolled brass sheeting. For small ordinary tinplate may be used and will be found satisfactory.

In that case the holes for the screws—which should be small—are punched through with an awl.

Where possible an effort should be made to apply glue to the faces or edges which are to be drawn together so as to give maximum strength and holding power to the joint.

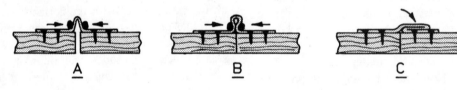

A   B   C

Then with a pair of pliers or pincers the plate is nipped together as in detail (B) where the two noses of the pliers are shown in sectional view.

This has the effect of drawing the ends together. Afterwards the loop can be hammered down flat as in detail (C). It will not then form an obstruction by projecting.

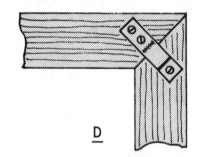

D

L

LADDER	**Aids**
LADDERS	**Use with Care**
LATHE	**Description**
LEATHERS, SPONGES	**For Cleaning**
LEVEL	**Improvised**
LEVELING	**Methods**
LINOLEUM	**To Lay**
LINOLEUM	**To Patch**
LOCK (Mortise)	**Repair**
LOCKS	**Security**

LADDER — Aids

If you own an extension ladder and use it regularly for window-cleaning, painting, gutter-cleaning, and so forth, you'll work in greater comfort if you add a few simple accessories.

Fig. 1 shows a useful crossbar which enables the ladder to rest against any part of the window at a convenient height.

You don't have to adjust it exactly to reach the sill or window head, and there is no risk of putting the ladder through the glass. It is made from a 2 ft. 6 in. length of ¾ in. electrical conduit, which passes through two holes bored through the ladder sides, approximately 1½ in. from the top.

The holes should be nearer the underside of the ladder to give the maximum clearance to the glass and an extra thickness of wood to take the strain. The fit should be fairly tight so that the tube will not slide about when the ladder is being moved.

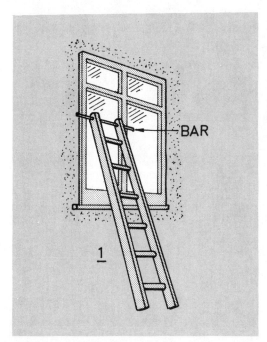

Fig. 2 shows another accessory, a light platform, which can be hooked on the ladder at any height. It enables the worker to stand in perfect comfort for prolonged periods, and can be moved up or down in a few seconds.

The constructional details of this accessory are shown in Fig. 3. The dimensions are given for a ladder with an internal width between the sides of 9 in. and the widths given should be adjusted for any variation from this figure.

A word of warning is necessary about the method of construction. The hangers from the back of the platform to the rung should be thick enough to ensure that the hooked ends will not in any circumstances open under the user's weight and anything heavy that he may be supporting.

Mild steel ¼ in. diameter is safe enough, but ⁵⁄₁₆ in. rod could be used for an unusually heavy man.

The hanger should be in one continuous piece, and should pass underneath the back of the platform, where it is fixed by cleats at each side.

The hanger can be swung round flat against the underside when the platform is not in use, and being underneath and not subject to any strain, the cleats cannot pull away. It is advisable to make the bends under red heat.

The second point to emphasize is the necessity of making the middle part of the platform wider than the space between the ladder sides. If this is not done, it is possible, by stepping on the extreme front edge, to tip the platform upwards, when the hooks may be lifted off the rung.

With the wider platform cut away only where it actually lies between the ladder sides, as shown in Fig. 3, the back of the platform cannot tip up, but the front can be lifted to attach or detach.

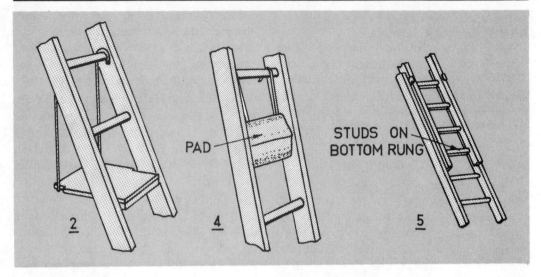

2   4   STUDS ON BOTTOM RUNG   5

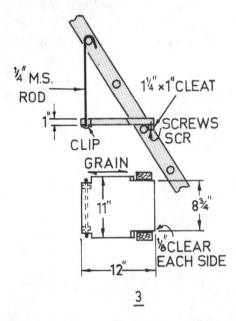

¼" M.S. ROD

1¼" × 1" CLEAT

SCREWS SCR

1"

CLIP

GRAIN

11"

8¾"

⅛" CLEAR EACH SIDE

12"

3

The length of the hangers should be such that the platform is level with the ladder inclined at its normal angle, but, as a guide, a 5 ft. length of rod will make the complete hanger with 1 to 2 in. to spare. If desired, the platform may be painted, and a tread of ribbed rubber sheet will ensure a good grip.

Another simple gadget—a foam-rubber support—which will give welcome comfort when working on the ladder for a long period, is shown in Fig. 4.

It is made from a piece of plywood, about 8½ in. by 6½ in. padded with ½ in. thick foam rubber and covered with waterproof cloth.

This may be hung on any rung. The hooks should be long enough to bring the pad centrally over the rung below.

And here is a safety hint. When stepping off the bottom rung of the top section of an extension ladder on to the lower section, the next rung will be found approximately 2 in. farther back.

A row of short, square-headed studs spaced at 1½ in. intervals along the tread of the lowest rung of the top section will warn the user when he must watch his next step see Fig. 5.

LADDERS — Use with Care

When choosing your ladder the length will be dictated largely by the type of house in which you live.

A good guiding principle is to aim at possessing ladders of sufficient length, either singly or spliced, and this includes extension ladders to reach the highest point of the building.

This will mean the gable apex on most houses, or the chimney stack where this is flush with, or near enough to, one of the walls so that the ladder will reach it from the ground.

The next thing to consider is the type of ladder most adapted to your particular requirements and in this connection it will be found that the extending ladder is becoming increasingly popular for several reasons.

The first is its manifest advantage of simple adjustment to a variety of heights.

These ladders can also be used singly, since they are easily detachable.

Extension ladders can be divided into different categories, governed principally by considerations of length and cost. Not only will a ladder needed to reach a considerable height, have to be of stronger section, but it also has a more complicated method of extension and locking devices.

When buying a ladder, the following points should be noted:
1. Are the sides free from knots or other defects?
2. Are the rungs well mortised and tenoned into the sides and securely wedged?
3. Are the rungs of good quality hardwood?
4. Are they reinforced, either individually or alternately, with metal rods riveted or bolted into the sides?
5. Is there any evidence that the wood was not properly seasoned?
6. Is the locking mechanism of sufficiently good quality to give complete reliability during years of wear?

Long ladders, either spliced or extension, can be weighty to handle, and the first job is to get them off the ground and properly erected. Where an assistant is available, he braces one foot against the bottom rung while the ladder is raised and pushed up rung by rung from the other end.

Failing this assistance, the foot of the ladder should be placed against a wall to prevent it from slipping.

The angle at which a ladder rests against the work is important. If it is too acute, there is a danger of sliding or of being pulled over backwards when the user leans out to reach an overhanging gutter.

If the foot is too far away from the wall a great strain is placed on the side members, especially if it happens to be a long ladder, and is even more dangerous if spliced.

The handyman should aim at getting the most comfortable angle for climbing, neither too vertical nor too sloping.

If much work is being carried out over lawns or soft paths, it will save time if a metal strip with a sharpened end is screwed to the inside of each side member in such a way that the point projects a couple of inches. It is essential to work safely with a ladder.

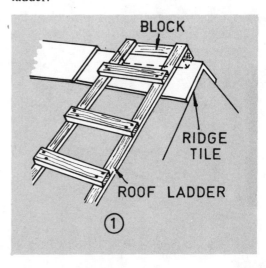

BLOCK

RIDGE TILE

ROOF LADDER

① 1

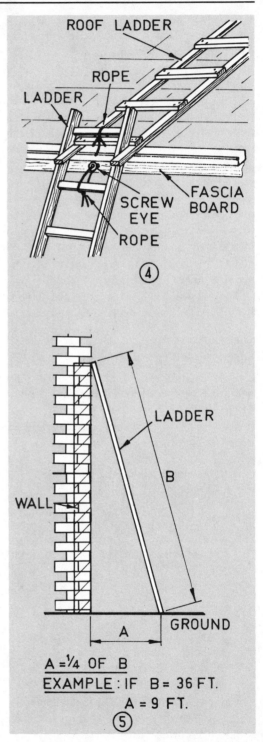

L

This is especially so when working from or around the roof.

Shown in Fig. 1 is a light ladder fitted with a block at the end and used as a roof ladder. The block fits over the ridge and permits work to be done, safely and with less risk of damage to tiles or other roof material.

Such a ladder can be made from light softwood battens.

ROOF LADDER

ROPE

LADDER

SCREW EYE

FASCIA BOARD

ROPE

④

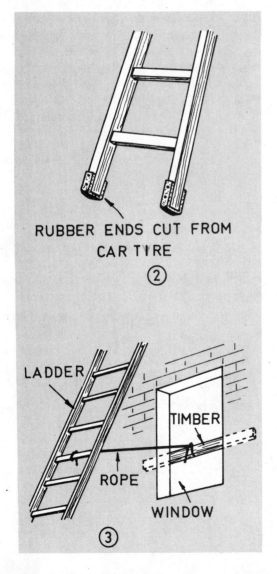

RUBBER ENDS CUT FROM CAR TIRE

②

LADDER

TIMBER

ROPE

WINDOW

③

WALL

LADDER

B

A

GROUND

A = ¼ OF B
EXAMPLE : IF B = 36 FT.
A = 9 FT.

⑤

As a further safety measure attach the bottom end of the roof ladder to the projecting end of the main ladder resting on the ground. This is shown in Fig. 4.

Especially if a ladder is resting on concrete a simple precaution against slipping is to fit strips of rubber to the ladder ends, Fig. 2. Also, where possible, keep the ladder firm in the center by means of a rope running from a batten inside a window frame to one of the ladder rungs as in Fig. 3.

Finally, have the ladder inclined at a convenient and safe angle to the wall.

Details of this are shown clearly in Fig. 5.

LATHE — Description
The lathe is a machine for turning wood to circular shape. Today it is invariably electrically driven. Size is known by the height of the centers above the bed.

Thus, a 4 in. lathe will turn wood to a maximum diameter of just under 8 in. (If one starts off with a square the measurement will have to be taken along the diagonal).

Another dimension required to be known is the maximum length between centers. Most modern small lathes range from 30 in. up to 54 in.

Spindle is usually hollow with morse taper, but outside is also threaded to take face plate and other chucks. Many lathes are made to take attachments such as circular saw, bandsaw, sander, and small surfacer.

Variation in speed is desirable as large diameter items require a slower speed. The following are optimum speeds, but there is nothing critical about it.

Wood diameter	R.P.M.
1 in.	3,000
2 in.	2,500
3 in.	1,500
5 in.	1,000
8 in.	650
12 in.	570
18 in.	300
24 in.	250

LEATHERS, SPONGES — For Cleaning
Chamois leathers are not cheap, so it pays to use them only for their proper purpose—and keep a few simple precautions in mind.

A leather can be used for washing down a surface with water, cleaning with soap, and most important of all, for thoroughly drying the surface.

Nothing compares with a chamois leather for absorbing all the moisture from a car after washing down, or after cleaning windows.

Here are a few precautions worth noting:

Never use detergents with a leather as they will immediately wash out the curing oils, leaving the leather coarse and brittle.

Never put a leather into water of over 115 degrees F.—use only warm water.

Never put a wet or dirty leather away as it will rot. Wash it with soap, rinse, squeeze out, and hang up to dry. Trim off any torn edges when they occur.

Sponges must be treated according to their type and the material from which they are made. There are genuine sea sponges and synthetic cellulose sponges.

When using a sea sponge, don't boil it, although it can be used in fairly hot water. Avoid rubbing soap into such a sponge, but if it is used with soap suds, rinse thoroughly afterwards and squeeze out.

Also, don't use the sponge with alkalis or strong disinfectants unless you rinse it thoroughly afterwards.

Cellulose sponges can be used in very hot water, and should be boiled occasionally for thorough cleansing. After use it helps to use a little disinfectant in the final rinsing water.

These sponges can be used with shampoos and detergents. However, no sponge should be wrung out, as this will twist and tear the fibers. You should just squeeze and manipulate it with the fingers.

LEVEL — Improvised

A carpenter's square and a plumb-line may take the place of the spirit level for some purposes if no level is available.

To level a wall, for example, the square would be set up in the following manner.

Use a two-by-four 3 to 4 ft long, depending on the height of the wall, and point one end to be driven into the ground.

In the other end cut a slot to receive the blade of the square, which must fit tight.

Drive the stake into the ground close to one corner of the wall and set the square in the slot.

Using the plumb-line as shown in Fig. 1, level the blade.

Now, by sighting over the blade, any irregularities can be seen.

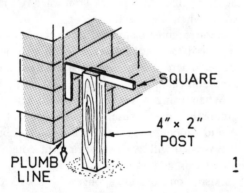

SQUARE

4" x 2" POST

PLUMB LINE

1

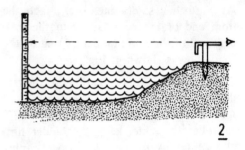

2

To find the fall in a sloping piece of ground, drive in the stake at the highest point and level the blade of the square as before.

Mark off the feet on a long stick.

Have someone hold the stick at the bottom of the slope and sight down the blade as in Fig. 2.

This will give a very close measurement of the amount of fall the slope has.

LEVELING—Methods

Sooner or later levels must be taken or determined. The home builder will need levels when he is building his fence, his paths, his terrace or when he is excavating for a septic tank, swimming-pool, or fish pond.

There are three methods of finding levels:

1. THE DUMPY LEVEL. This is usually beyond the means of the home builder.

2. THE LINE LEVEL. This is a common method used over long distances. The small glass tube with the bubble rising between two lines, hung onto the stretched string with two wire hooks, does its job satisfactorily, but when winds are blowing hard a correct reading is difficult to obtain. Also, it cannot be read around obstacles such as rocks, trees, and existing buildings. A refinement of this is the ordinary spirit-level on a straight-edge, but this is limited to the length of the straight-edge.

3. THE GARDEN HOSE. The garden hose filled with water will give levels exact to a minute fraction of an inch over any distance up to the length of the hose. It can be used around obstacles. It is simplicity itself, but to work it rapidly needs two pairs of eyes.

First fill the hose from the tap. When a gurgle-free flow is running stop both ends with fingers or corks. (Remove the nozzle for best results).

Carry the hose so that it forms a U with the two ends at the same level, and this will save you the trouble of having to refill the **hose when leveling operations begin. Take** one end and hold it level with the base height from which you are going to work. Leave it in the hands of your assistant with instructions not to move it.

Leave also a can of water so that it can be added to the hose as the spill occurs. Move off to the spot at which you want to place a mark level with the base height. You will have a stick erected perpendicular at this spot so that you can mark the level on it.

Place your end of the hose against this stick, and call for the fingers or corks to be removed. If the spot you have chosen with your end of the hose is exactly level with the base, no water will flow out of either end.

If water starts to pour out of your end of the hose you are lower than the base, so raise the hose until the flow stops and then re-top from the other end.

A refinement of this method could be found in the use of a piece of clear plastic or glass tube inserted into each end of a hose and sealed off to prevent loss of water.

LINOLEUM — To Lay

There are two main types of linoleum—printed and inlaid. The printed variety is the cheaper of the two, and with wear, the pattern will fade.

Inlaid linoleum, on the other hand, has the pattern right through to the backing. It will retain its pattern until the material is worn out.

Laying linoleum is not difficult, but unless care is taken it can be expensive.

It is always a good idea to take care and draw a plan of the area to be covered first. As an example, take a look at Fig. 1 and Fig. 2.

Measure the length and breadth in yards. For this room nine yards of two yards wide linoleum will be needed if laid as in Fig. 1. This will leave 4½ yds by ½ yd wide left over.

If laid as in Fig. 2 three pieces 3½ yds by 2 yds will be required—-that is 3 sq. yds more than for the first lay-out.

When the room is not a perfect rectangle, Fig. 3, further difficulties creep in. The extra piece of linoleum indicated by the dotted lines (A), should fit nicely into part (B). But unless the linoleum is plain, there could be trouble in matching a pattern.

In this case it is better to lay the linoleum as in Fig. 4, remembering to allow extra length on each strip for matching if **the linoleum is patterned.**

When ordering linoleum tiles, measure the area of the room in square yards, ask the salesman how many tiles go into each square yard, and order accordingly. For example, a room measuring 4½ yds by 3½ yds as in Fig. 1 is 15¾ sq. yds in area. Call this 16 sq. yds. With normal 9 in. square tiles you will get sixteen tiles to the square yard —a total of 256 tiles.

When roll linoleum is delivered, always examine the ends of the rolls before unwrapping. Damaged ends will make a bad and noticeable join.

Another simple precaution is to put the linoleum, unwrapped, in a warm room for at least twenty-four hours. This will save much trouble later when laying.

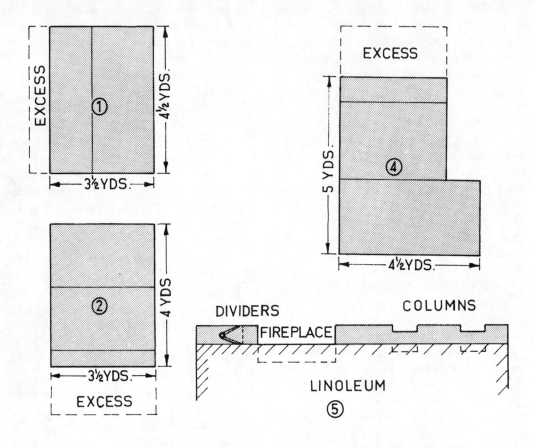

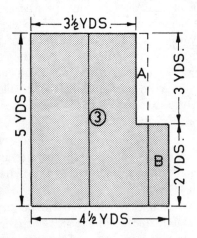

Fig. 5 shows the method of fitting linoleum around obstructions or irregular shapes, but first the floor surface should be prepared.

Sweep and clean the floor thoroughly, remove or knock down any protuding nails, and level off any raised boards. It is also advisable to provide a suitable underlay material.

Following your sketch plan, cut the linoleum with a special hooked knife and straight edge, making a deep score through the top surface along the required line. Then bend the linoleum and it will crack cleanly along the line, leaving only the backing to cut through.

Always lay the cut edges along the wall, leaving the selvages cut by the manufacturer to meet in the center of the room. Your own cutting is bound to leave a slightly uneven seam if you try to butt it against another piece.

To cut linoleum to follow the contours of a wall, press the edge up to any projections, set a pair of dividers to the distance (A) in Fig. 5 and draw the dividers along the wall.

When the dividers reach the fireplace obstruction they will be forced out, tracing a line or pattern. The same thing will happen when the door lintels are reached.

An accurate profile is obtained in this way, and the linoleum can then be cut and pushed into place. In some cases it is an advantage to cut patterns from cardboard and transfer these to the linoleum.

Your next step, after laying, is to bring the furniture back into the room and use it normally. The linoleum will almost certainly expand and this is generally indicated by heaving of the seams in the center of the floor.

Don't do the obvious thing and cut a thin slice off the edge of one of the strips along the seam. This will leave a ragged edge.

Move the furniture to one side of the room and do any cutting on the edge or edges adjoining the wall. Then move the linoleum so that the center seams fall back evenly into place.

It may be necessary to make adjustments of this nature several times over a period of several months.

An alternative method is to overlap the linoleum on a center joint for several weeks after laying it to allow for expansion when final fitting is carried out. The underlapping edge should be reversed and the surplus cut from the other edge. This method allows

for the removal of the edge that may have been damaged during the settling in period. It also saves having to shift the furniture again.

Linoleum is susceptible to damage from alkalis such as washing soda, ammonia, and harsh soaps. Polish new linoleum frequently with a liquid dry-bright polish to give it a coat of wax. Dirt will then not penetrate and can be removed by washing with a cloth and detergent.

Never scrub linoleum. One scrubbing equals a month's ordinary wear. If dirt and grime have really become ingrained, use a mixture of five parts mineral spirits and one part linseed oil—raw or boiled—and gently rub the dirty areas. This should remove the blemishes without marking the surface.

Rust stains are difficult to remove once they have penetrated below the surface. However, rubbing lightly with fine steel wool and the spirit-oil mixture will usually remove them.

LINOLEUM — To Patch

There are two parts of a room where linoleum or any other kind of floor covering will show excessive wear after a time. These are in the doorway and around work areas such as the sink and stove in the kitchen.

It's always a good idea to lay linoleum so that it can be turned around to equalize the wear, but of course this is not always possible. The only alternative is to use mats to reduce the wear and tear on certain spots.

It is easy enough to patch linoleum which has worn into a hole. To make such a repair you will need a piece of the original material left over from the time the linoleum was first laid. Wise people usually keep trimmings and odd lengths for such a time as

this. If this hasn't been done, it should be possible to cut a piece from some out-of-the-way corner or from under a permanently placed piece of furniture.

With a sharp knife, cut away a square containing the damaged or worn section, see Fig. 1. Make a neat job of this, otherwise your final effort will look like a very makeshift repair.

Next, the patch has to be cut. This is a fairly simple matter if the linoleum has a plain surface, but if patterned, care must be taken that the pattern on the patch fits in exactly with that of the rest of the linoleum. To make sure that the patch will fit perfectly, first cut a pattern out of thin cardboard. Lay the cardboard under the hole and draw the outline of it with a pencil. Trim the card a fraction larger than the penciled outline, Fig. 2, then see whether it makes a good fit.

If it does, use that as your pattern for cutting the linoleum patch.

The last stage of the repair is to fix the patch into position. Take a piece of thin but strong material—say heavy linen—considerably larger than the hole which is to be filled with the linoleum patch, and cover it with glue. Press the patch into the center of this glue-covered material and so leave a surplus all round Fig. 3. Work the patch into the hole from underneath the linoleum, and when exactly in position, press the overlapping sections of material against the underside of the linoleum to hold and anchor the patch permanently in position.

LOCK (Mortise) — Repair

Door locks should operate easily and silently, but of all the hardware fittings in the house, locks are usually the most neglected.

The general impression seems to be that there is some deep mystery connected with their working and that even to take off a lock and look at it will inevitably mean buying a new one.

This is not the case, and at least once every year all locks should be taken off and cleaned and oiled.

The only exception to this is the barrel section of the Yale type lock in which the key fits. This part must never be oiled.

The two types of locks in common use are called rim locks and mortise locks.

Rim locks screw onto the face of the door and mortise locks slide into a mortise cut in the edge of the door.

In each case first remove the small grub screw securing one of the handles, and remove this handle.

The other handle and the square spindle are then pulled out.

For a rim lock, merely unscrew it from the face of the door usually by removing three round-head screws.

For removing the mortise lock, take out the two countersunk head screws which pass through the face plate and then lever gently under this face plate with a screwdriver until the lock comes out of the mortise as in Fig. 1.

The lock is opened by removing the two or three small set screws holding on the cover plate and the mechanism is then revealed.

Fig. 2 shows the working parts of a typical mortise or rim lock together with the normal springs.

These may vary in some respects in different locks but they are all fairly simple.

Make a careful note of the way the various parts fit together, if necessary making a sketch, and then remove all the parts from the body of the lock.

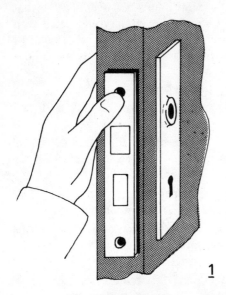

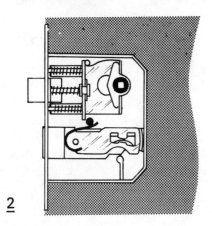

1

Doors and windows deserve the most attention, and it is surprising how many home-owners neglect to take even elementary protection against entry of thieves through these points.

On doors, efficient security can be had without spoiling the look of the door surfaces by fitting a special dead-latch which is extremely powerful and safe.

This fitting is actually intended as an auxiliary to an existing key-in-knob or other type of exterior door lock. Used in this way it provides maximum security at comparatively small cost.

The fitting of the locking device is done in much the same way as for a standard-type mortise lock as suggested in the illustration.

2

Clean them, applying a little lubricating oil, and then re-assemble.

If the springs are broken or seem at all weak, take the old springs to the local locksmith or hardware and get replacements.

LOCKS — Security

Whenever a home is being left vacant, and especially at holiday time, it is essential to make it secure against intruders.

A mortise is cut in the door edge for the casing, but only one hole—for a slim circular key—is drilled.

Note that this lock is placed slightly below the existing lock and all that is visible on the door face is the small escutcheon plate through which the key passes.

The keys are of unique design and are not easily duplicated.

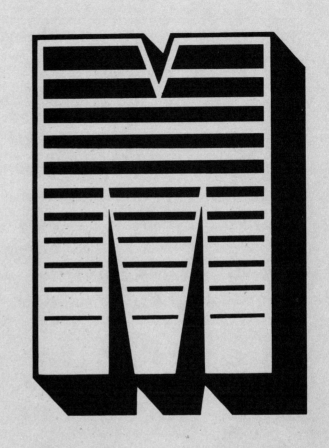

MARBLE	Cleaning
MATS (Floor)	Repair
METAL FITTINGS	Care
METRIC CONVERSION	Chart
MIRROR	Drill & Fix
MIRRORS	Arrangement
MITER JOINT	Details
MORTAR JOINTS	Restore
MORTAR	Mixing
MORTISE & TENON JOINT	To Make
MOVING	Useful Hints

MARBLE — Cleaning

How to keep marble clean and free from stains is a problem facing many people, so here are some cleaning hints.

If it's clean already keep it that way by wiping up spilled liquids immediately and giving it a periodic washing with warm water.

If it's dirty through long use, wet the surface with hot water, scrub with a mild, non-abrasive detergent, using a clean fiber brush, then rinse thoroughly to remove any traces of detergent. Dry immediately with a chamois or clean lintless cloth to avoid streaking.

If it's stained, here are the three main types to watch for:

1. Organic stains, caused by such things as tea, coffee, soft drinks, fruit juices, anything containing vinegar, iodine, ink and tobacco.
2. Rust stains, caused by lamp bases, ash trays, nails, bolts and any other metallic objects left in contact with the marble.
3. Oil stains, caused by hand creams, salad dressings, modeling clay, anything greasy, and milk products.

If it's organic, first wash with ammonia and rinse thoroughly. The remainder of the stain must be bleached out with a poultice made of hydrogen-peroxide hair bleach and some powdered whiting. Mix whiting and bleach to a thick paste, spread over stain, then add a few drops of ammonia to start the reaction. Keep damp by covering with plastic food wrapping for several hours.

If it's rust, you may be able to remove fresh stains by rubbing with a dry cloth. If not, use a special rust-reducing agent, available at chemical-supply houses and many tile and hardware stores. Apply as a poultice in whiting or according to the directions.

If it's oil, use a solvent of amyl acetate and acetone mixed together in equal parts. Apply as a poultice mixed with whiting, let stand until dry, then rinse off and repeat if necessary. If stain persists, bleach it out using the method described for organic stains.

MATS (Floor) — Repair

Mats and floor rugs may deteriorate in two ways as they get older—by developing bare or thin patches or by fraying at the edges.

Treatment depends on particular cases, but with modern latex-type adhesive, mats can be given a second life.

To put binding on a cut or frayed edge use comparatively coarsely woven carpet binding and apply the adhesive to both the binding and the mat.

Bring the two surfaces together immediately and thoroughly hammer the joint.

This drives the latex into all the spaces of the weaving and makes an extremely strong joint, see illustration, detail (A).

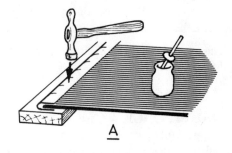

A

If a damaged part is to be cut out and the remaining parts joined up, cover the joint on the underside with a piece of burlap or old sacking.

Again coat both surfaces with adhesive and hammer together (B).

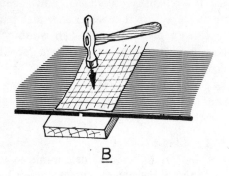

B

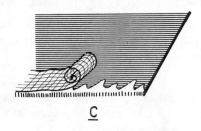

C

For a rug or piece of carpet use the binding on the under side to protect the edge.

Turn any loose strands and short ends under and stick them down before adding the binding as at (C).

If a mat shows a tendency to slip, coat the underside with some of the latex adhesive, either all over or only at the corners.

This provides a good resistance to sliding and does not mark the floor.

METAL FITTINGS — Care

An important part around the house is played by articles made of metal, from furniture fittings and decorative moldings to kitchen hardware.

Every handyman should know how to keep them in good order.

Some metals, like stainless steel and chromium plating, have a high resistance to corrosion, but even these need a certain amount of care.

Others need regular maintenance to prevent them tarnishing and deteriorating, and to preserve their appearance.

Here is a handy guide:

PLATED METALS, in wide use today, should not be polished too often. Frequent rubbing with metal polishes will eventually wear through the thin plating and expose the unpolished metal underneath.

Plated metals not subject to wear and tear, or to washing or heat, can be preserved almost indefinitely by giving them a coating of lacquer.

First clean off all tarnish and dirt by using a good quality of non-gritty metal polish. Use it sparingly, and rub only hard enough to clean and shine the surface. Then rinse thoroughly with methylated spirits to remove all residue left behind by the polishing.

Wipe dry with a clean lintless cloth, let the surface dry, then apply two thin coats of clear lacquer with a soft brush.

COPPER, BRASS, BRONZE all need much the same kind of maintenance. They tarnish rapidly unless protected by clear lacquer or other coating.

However, before any coating is applied, all dirt and tarnish must be removed with a good metal polish. Wash clean in hot soapy water, rinse thoroughly with water, and dry thoroughly with a soft cloth.

Then wipe off with a rag moistened in methylated spirits. Let the surface dry, then give two thin coats of clear lacquer.

To remove heavy tarnish or stains on articles of solid copper, brass, or bronze scrub with a non-gritty kitchen cleanser, then rub vigorously with a rag dipped in a solution of vinegar and salt. Keep rubbing until the surface is clean, then rinse with hot water, and finish with metal polish.

STAINLESS STEEL and CHROMIUM PLATING usually need only occasional washing with soap and water to keep them new looking and clean indefinitely.

However, some foods which contain salts or acids may pit these metals if left to dry on the surface, so spilled foods should always be wiped off promptly.

If a cloudy or sticky film forms and becomes difficult to remove, use a liquid metal polish diluted with water and rub on sparingly.

METRIC CONVERSION — Chart

The first essential in understanding the metric system of measurement is to know the various terms used:

Are: Is the unit of land or area measurement. For example, 1 hectare is equal to 2.7411 acres. Conversely, 1 acre equals 0.4047 hectare.

Centimeter: Is the hundredth part of a meter.

Decameter: (pronounced dekameter): Is a measure consisting of ten meters.

Decimeter: The tenth part of a meter.

Gram: The unit of weight. Strictly speaking, the weight of a cubic centimeter of water at 4° C.

Hectometer: A measure of 100 meters in length.

Kilogram: The weight of a liter of water at 4° C.

Kilometer: A measure 1,000 meters in length.

Liter: The unit of volume.

Meter: The French or metric unit of length. It is equal to approximately 39.3704 inches.

Millimeter: A thousandth part of a meter. A good comparison is the width of home movie film, e.g. 8 mm., 16 mm.

METRIC ABBREVIATIONS:

cm	=	centimeter
g	=	gram
kg	=	kilogram
km	=	kilometer
l	=	liter
m	=	meter
mm	=	millimeter
ml	=	milliliter

GENERAL CONVERSIONS:

1 ft = 0.30 m
3 ft = 0.91 m
6 ft = 1.83 m
12 ft = 3.66 m

1 meter = 3.28 ft

9 sq. ft = 0.84 sq. m
18 sq. ft = 1.67 sq. m
36 sq. ft = 3.34 sq. m

1 sq. in = 6.45 sq. cm
3 sq. in. = 19.40 sq. cm
144 sq. in. = 929 sq. cm

1 sq. yd = 0.84 sq. m
3 sq. yd = 2.51 sq. m
6 sq. yd = 5.02 sq. m

1 cm = 0.39 in.
3 cm = 1.18 in.
10 cm = 3.94 in.

1 gal. = 4.55 l
3 gal. = 13.60 l
6 gal. = 27.30 l

1 lb. = 0.045 kg
3 lb. = 1.4 kg
10 lb. = 4.5 kg

PAINT COVERING CAPACITY
100 sq. ft per gal. = 2.04 sq. m per l
150 sq. ft per gal. = 3.07 sq. m per l
200 sq. ft per gal. = 4.09 sq. m per l

MIRROR — Drill & Fix

There are several types of drilling jobs, and each calls for special care and possibly a particular type of drill.

For example rimless wall mirrors and glass splashbacks on wash basins can be fixed securely if drilled to take special decorative mirror screws of the type shown in the illustration at (A).

These screws are usually chromium plated, and are provided with detachable domed caps which hide the slotted heads of the screws once they are in position.

The first thing to do after buying the glass panel—or mirror—is to drill the necessary holes for fixing screws.

The glass may be taken to a glazier for drilling, or the home handyman can tackle the job himself if he has a suitable drill.

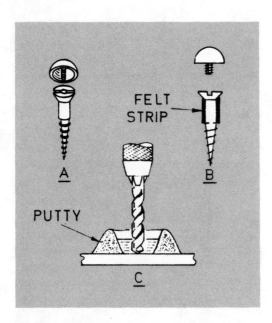

FELT STRIP

PUTTY

A   B   C

If doing the job yourself, make sure that the glass is held stable in a fixed position. It should be resting on a flat, reasonably soft surface. A table covered with felt or an old blanket is ideal.

An ordinary hand brace and special glass drill will do the job quite well. Scratch the glass where the center of the holes are to be with a sharp-pointed tool to prove a guide for the drill point.

Then make a small circle of putty or modeling clay around the hole center and fill with mineral turpentine as at (B). This will ensure that the drill is lubricated.

When drilling, use minimum pressure to avoid fracturing glass. Be especially careful when the drill is just about to emerge at the reverse side of the glass. If possible, drill from both sides to avoid splintering.

Where the screw will be supporting large glass panels or mirrors it is advisable to avoid having the glass rest directly on the shanks of the screws.

This may be done by wrapping small strips of felt around the screw shanks as shown in detail (C).

MIRRORS — Arrangement

Have you a problem room in your home? One that is badly proportioned, or hasn't enough windows, or has a window in the wrong place? Arranging furniture in such a room often presents real difficulties, either because the space seems too long and narrow or too small and overcrowded, or because whatever you do you're left with one long blank wall. Cleverly placed mirrors may be the answer. The illustrations on the next page show you how.

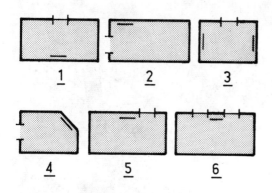

1   2   3

4   5   6

CUTTING. To ensure a frame that is strong and square the two pieces of a miter joint must be cut accurately. The best way to do this is with a miter box, and using a fairly fine saw as in Fig. 1.

When sawing, hold the piece of wood against the far side of the box, which should be held firmly, Fig. 2.

If you do not have a miter box, mark out the wood carefully with a miter-set-square, or by setting out as in Fig. 3. Make (B) equal to width of wood (A), and join the two ends to make a 45 degree angle.

Fig. 1. A narrow room with one window in the center of a long wall can be made to look wider by placing a mirror on the wall facing the window.

Fig. 2. Mirror placed at right angles to window in short wall of rectangular room will help make the room seem larger and better proportioned.

Fig. 3. To make a small room seem more spacious try placing mirrors to face each other on opposite walls. Reflection produced gives illusion of space.

Fig. 4. It's often difficult to arrange furniture in a room of this shape, but a mirror placed at an angle in a corner helps by giving added depth.

Fig. 5. A single window near the corner of a narrow room makes for lack of balance. A mirror next to the window restores harmony, giving the illusion of a double window.

Fig. 6. Two small windows divided by a section of wall can be made to look like one large window if a mirror is placed between them.

MITER JOINT—Details

The miter joint is one of the most common and practical joints in woodworking. Here are some of the basic rules for cutting and fitting.

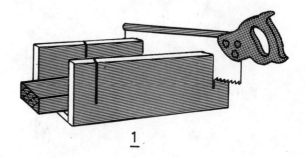

1

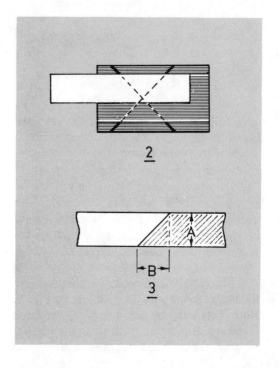

2

3

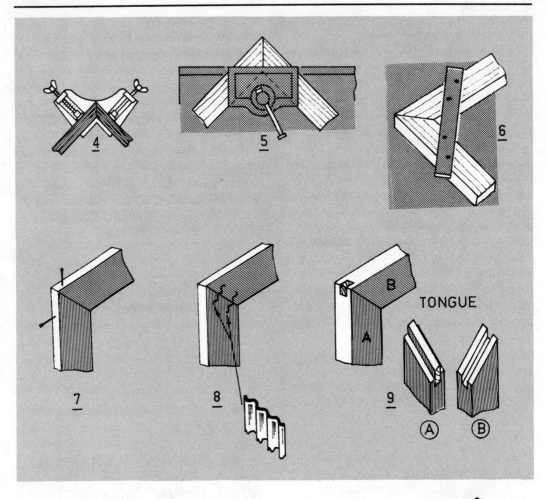

HOLDING. A firm hold on the two halves of the joint is essential. Most accurate way is with a miter clamp or vice as in Fig. 4. An ordinary vice can be used, as shown in Fig. 5. Make sure the two halves are at right-angles after assembly by testing with a try-square. If you have no vice, use a piece of plywood or hardboard, tacked across the angle with panel pins, Fig. 6.

FASTENING. Simplest method of fixing the joints is with nails, as in Fig. 7. Both parts must be held firmly. Corrugated fasteners, Fig. 8, are firm, though more noticeable. By cutting a slot in each piece, and

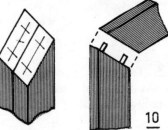

inserting a fillet, Fig. 9, a neat strong joint can be made, and with dowels, Fig. 10, the fastening is not visible. Mark the dowel positions as shown, to ensure an accurate fit. With all these fastenings, glue must be used.

MORTAR JOINTS — Restore

Mortar joints in brickwork deteriorate and fret away in exposed positions and should be repointed as soon as possible as they let dampness into the walls.

First rake out the old mortar to a depth of at least ¼ in. (possibly more if it is in very bad condition), then dampen wall thoroughly.

Mix a mortar consisting of fine sand (3 parts), Portland cement (2 parts), and 10 per cent hydrated lime. This will dry almost white, but vegetable black mixed with cement, before the sand and water, will turn it grey.

In the same way, red-oxide mixed first with the dry cement, will produce a red mortar. Apply the mortar to the open joints with a small pointing trowel, filling first the vertical joints, then the horizontal.

Finish the horizontal joints with a final stroke, pressing in more at the top than the bottom so that the layer of mortar is really leaning back.

MORTAR — Mixing

You need to know how to make mortar for simple maintenance jobs on brickwork, drains and paths.

There are two main kinds of mortar—made with cement and made with lime.

In between these two, a general purpose mortar for specific jobs can be produced by adding a little cement to the basic lime mortar to increase its strength, or adding lime to the cement mortar to make it work more easily. The cement and lime are the binding agents of the mortar in each case, and bulk is produced by adding sand. To use technical terms, the cement or lime is the matrix and the sand the aggregate.

For small jobs around the home where great strength and waterproofing is required, a cement mortar is used.

A mixture of three parts of sand to one part of Portland cement gives a strong mortar.

The cement and sand are mixed together thoroughly in the dry state first, after which the water is added to form a fairly stiff paste.

The mixing is done on a flat, even surface, preferably a wooden platform with vertical edging boards on two sides and at the back.

The sand, of course, must be free from stones and other rubbish, and it is a good idea to pass it through a sieve if there are any doubts.

If possible, also avoid using sand taken directly from the ocean beach, because of its salt content.

Sand obtained from a deposit some distance inland is ideal.

Especially in lime mortar, salt from the sand is likely to become damp in humid weather, and this accounts for many of those mysterious damp patches which often appear on interior plastered walls for no apparent reason.

Lime mortar is made up to the proportions of one part of lime to two parts of sand, and two kinds of lime can be used.

First there is hydrated lime, which is bought in bags and used in the same way as cement, and then there is ordinary rock lime which must be slaked first with water.

Slaking produces a putty or paste to which the sand is added, and it is best if you can leave this mixture for several days before using.

When about 10 per cent cement is added to the hydrated lime mortar, the strength is increased considerably.

MORTISE & TENON JOINT —To Make

No matter what the type of framing in which the mortise and tenon joint is to be used, the first thing to do with the stock is to plane the face side and edges of the wood true and square.

Plane the face side first, and mark it, then plane the best edge and place the edge mark (X) on it, as in Fig. 1.

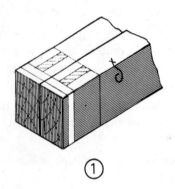

①

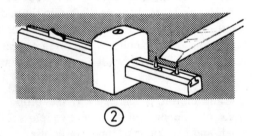

②

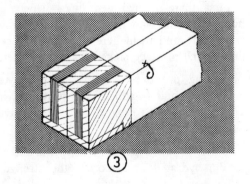

③

If the wood is too thick or wide, set a marking gauge to the desired width and thickness, mark the wood, gauging always from the face side and edge, and plane down to size.

Now set the two stiles with their face sides together, Fig. 1, and mark the length of the individual mortises with square and marking knife, carrying the marks across both pieces, so that they will be marked exactly alike.

The horn, or extra length at the end of the stiles, is important, because the excess wood here prevents the wood beyond the end of the mortise from being burst out when cutting or fitting the mortise.

Note that provision is made for haunching the tenon, and that lines denoting the length of the haunching are squared across the work.

Set a mortise gauge to the width of the chisel to be used for cutting the mortise, Fig. 2, and gauge the width of the mortises on the work, gauging from the face sides.

Mortises are usually cut one-third the thickness of the stock, so, when setting the gauge, the inner marking point is first set to one-third the thickness, then the outer joint is set to the chisel.

An ordinary marking gauge, of course, may be used, but it necessitates two settings and markings.

Then set the two rails together as shown in Fig. 3, and lay out the length and width of the tenons, the length and depth of the haunches, and lastly the thickness of the tenons, gauging marks for the latter down the ends of the rails as well as on the edges, and taking care always to use the gauge from the face side.

Next, take a rail, grip it in the vice as shown at (A), Fig. 4, and saw the cheeks

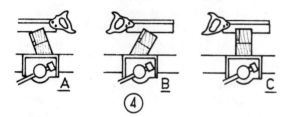

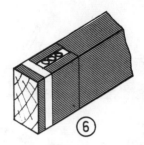

of the tenon down to the line marking its length, keeping the saw kerf in the waste.

Turn the rails around and saw down the opposite edge, as shown in the center sketch, (B), and finally set the rail upright in the vice and saw down straight, (C).

The saw kerfs first made will guide the saw and the amateur will find this method of sawing much easier than that of trying to saw straight down at once.

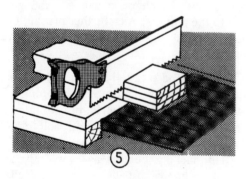

Cut along the line for the haunch in the same fashion. Lay the rail down on a bench hook, as shown in Fig. 5, and cut the shoulders, making a starting groove for the saw with a chisel. Finally, cut the shoulder on the haunch.

There are several methods of cutting mortises by hand, a popular one being shown in Fig. 6.

Select a drill bit, about ⅟₁₆ in. less in diameter than the width of the mortise, and drill out the waste as shown, taking care that the drill is kept square in both directions.

After most of the waste has been removed in this manner, the sides of the mortise and then the ends are pared with a sharp chisel.

The other two methods shown are similar in that the chisel alone is used to cut the mortise, but the method of using the chisel in each is different.

In either case, the work is gripped solidly in the vice, or clamped firmly to the bench.

Now take a chisel of the same width as the finished mortise is to be, and drive it in, slanting, as shown at (A), Fig. 7.

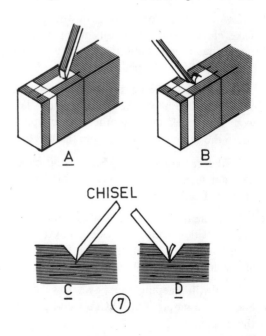

211

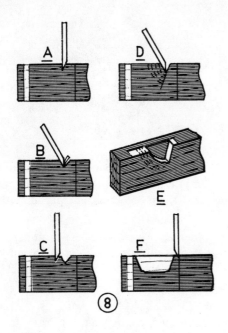

Pull the chisel out and drive it in as shown at (B), thus releasing a chip. Drive in again as at (C), remove, and release another chip, as at (D).

Use a mallet for driving in the chisel. Take chip after chip in this manner, until the cut has reached about the center of the mortise and is V-shaped.

The chisel is then held vertically to square up the mortise along the marked ends. The work is reversed and the other side chopped out in the same way to complete the mortise.

In the second method, Fig. 8, the chopping out of the mortise is started at the end instead of at the center.

Stand at one end of the work, and drive the chisel down into the wood, bevel away from you, about ¾₆ in. from the farther end of the mortise (A), Fig. 8.

Now still keeping the bevel toward the end, take a cut as shown at (B) and pry out the chip.

Take another cut as at (C) then a vertical cut along the line of the first one, and continue, prying out the chips and cutting, as indicated by the dotted lines in (D) and (E).

When half-way through the work take vertical cuts as at (F) to square up the ends of the mortise, then turn the work over and complete the mortise from the other side.

MOVING — Useful Hints

A few strong men and a truck can do a lot when it comes to moving, but the essential thing is to have a plan of campaign organized.

Before moving your furniture, make a rough sketch of the new floor plan, and decide where each piece will go, and give this to the movers. As a further precaution, have colored tags for each room and save confusion.

Curtains and rugs to be cleaned or altered should be sent away for attention before you move, and be merciless in discarding unnecessary bric-a-brac. Brooms, golf clubs, fishing tackle, and similar articles can be tied in one big bundle, as every separate parcel or bundle usually means extra cost.

As you pack, enter each item in a notebook. The system of list and label is invaluable in checking delivery, and a necessity when storing.

Gather all the cases and boxes you will need, and have plenty of newspaper (plain and shredded), cord, colored tags, labels, and thick colored crayon handy. Then, when all this is ready, pack room by room.

If rugs are to be stored, have them cleaned and mothproofed. Roll them on poles to prevent creasing or broken backing. When the rugs are to be relaid, see that they are loaded onto the van last, so that they can be unloaded first. The movers can then lay them before bringing in the large pieces of furniture.

Clothes may be left in wardrobes and drawers, but make sure all doors and drawers are locked and won't fly open.

Don't overload drawers, and remove anything that is likely to break or spill. It is a good idea to use the space inside wardrobes and cabinets for light linens, pillows, and blankets.

If you pack your own china and glassware, use wooden cases, never anything flexible like cardboard cartons or wicker baskets. Line the bottom of the case with shredded paper or old blankets. Wrap each piece in newspaper and bed in shredded newspaper with the heaviest pieces at bottom. Leave a little space at the top and always let the movers put the lids on. Be sure to mark the cases or crates "fragile" and indicate the right-side-up clearly with crayon.

NAIL BOX	To Make
NAILING	Points to Watch
NAILS	Cover Head
NOISE	In the Home
NUTS	Locking Devices

OIL-BASE PAINT	Advantages
OILSTONE	Make Case

NAIL BOX — To Make

The nail box shown in Fig. 1 is a piece of equipment that should be in every workshop. It measures 15 in. by 10 in. and is $2\frac{1}{2}$ in. deep inside. These sizes may be varied to make larger boxes for general work or smaller ones for screws.

The box is made entirely of plywood, and the various details as to size and number of parts needed are set out clearly in the sketches.

The sides are glued and screwed over the ends. Before fixing on the bottom, arrange for the partitions. The plan, Fig. 2, shows 10 compartments of different sizes, and these can be varied to suit individual needs. Note, however, that the short cross partitions are arranged so that they can be nailed —not housed—to the three main partitions. These are housed into the front and back sections, and the three short end partitions are also housed into the ends of the box frame.

It is easy to cut housings in plywood. Simply make two saw cuts the correct distance apart, then pare out one thickness of ply with a sharp chisel. The partitions are glued into the housings or grooves cut in this way. Fig. 3 shows how the partitions are assembled—they are housed at the sides, but merely nailed where they meet inside.

The bottom is allowed to protrude beyond the face of the box all round for a distance of $\frac{1}{4}$ in. and is secured with glue and with fine nails driven into the box sides and partitions.

The lid is cut to fit, and hinged with a pair of narrow butt hinges. A strong hook and eye catch or hasp and staple will complete the box, but a couple of side handles may also be added to facilitate carrying the box about.

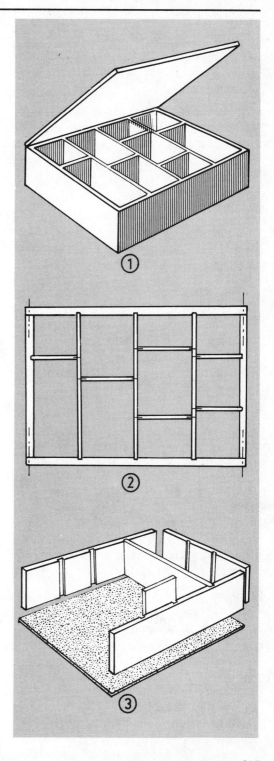

NAILING — Points to Watch

Many types of nails are available for wood-working jobs, but in all cases the following precautions should be observed.

For example, nails driven too close to the edges or ends of stock are likely to split the wood (A) and (B), Fig. 1: Also when edge-nailing, adverse grain may force the point of the nail sideways so that it breaks out on the face of the work (C) Fig. 1.

When starting nails under these conditions, be sure that each nail is centered or positioned accurately.

Two other suggestions which will minimise the risk of splitting are to drill pilot holes for the nails, and also to snip the sharp points off the nails before driving. Often it is necessary to drive a nail through a knot, and here a pilot hole is essential to avoid splitting (D), Fig. 1.

For maximum holding power on wood-to-wood joints it is a common rule that the nail length should be three times the thickness of the piece to be attached Fig. 2.

When joining two pieces of wood of equal width at right angles, take careful note of the direction of the grain. Then drive the nails so that no two of them are in the same grain line. This is called staggering the nails (A) and (B), Fig. 3.

When fixing uprights such as studs to a plate, the nails are driven at an angle as shown in detail (A) Fig. 4. This is called toenailing.

In detail (B) Fig. 4 the nails driven in at an angle provide a more secure grip than if driven in straight.

There is always a difference of opinion as to whether protruding nail points should

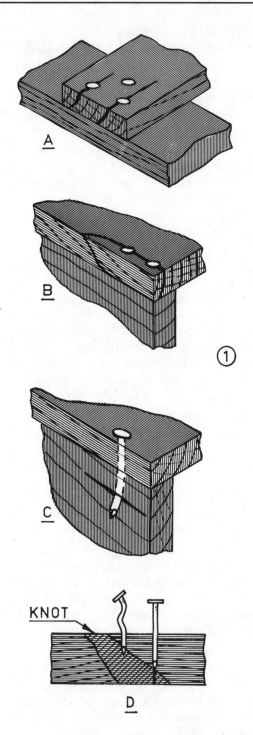

A

B

①

C

KNOT

D

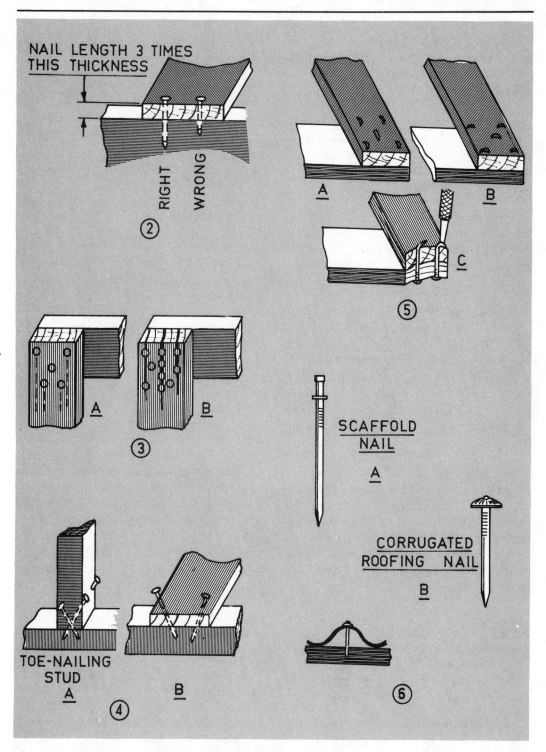

NAIL LENGTH 3 TIMES
THIS THICKNESS

RIGHT WRONG

②

A   B

C

⑤

A   B

③

SCAFFOLD
NAIL

A

CORRUGATED
ROOFING NAIL

B

TOE-NAILING
STUD
A   B

④

⑥

219

be clenched—that is, turned over—along the line of the grain or across. Usually it is easier to clench with the grain, but there is a risk of splitting the wood (A), (B) and (C) Fig. 5.

Apart from standard nails for woodwork there are special types used for scaffolding or concrete forming (A) Fig. 6, for use with asbestos sheets; and for securing corrugated roofing (B) Fig. 6.

The special scaffold nail has a double head. This allows it to be driven in securely, but at the same time provides for easy withdrawal when dismantling becomes necessary.

Asbestos sheet nails are usually galvanized to prevent rusting, and have a flat point. The reason for this is to minimize the risk of splitting the brittle sheets. If asbestos wall sheets have to be removed, the best procedure is to punch the nail heads through the sheets so that they can be lifted off the framework with little risk of breaking the sheets.

Corrugated roofing nails are usually referred to as springhead nails. They are always galvanized, and are driven into the crowns of the corrugations. It is always advisable to make holes for them in the iron with a special tool called a prick punch. Holes in corrugated asbestos or fiber glass should be drilled.

NAILS — Cover Head

You sometimes hear people say anyone can drive a nail. But simple as it seems, there are techniques that not only make work easier but result in a better job, too.

Here are several suggestions that may help:

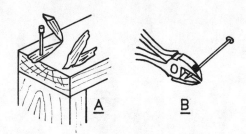

Occasionally a common nail must be used for maximum drawing power, but the head should not show.

Here the nail can be driven into a pocket as at (A). The pocket should be opened slightly larger than the head with a sharp, narrow wood chisel, parallel with the grain.

Drive in the nail until the head is approximately 1/32 in. above the surface of the wood, then sink it by using a larger nail, steel rod, or nail set.

Glue the flap of the pocket back into place, weight it down and sand-smooth when dry.

There are a number of ways you can keep wood from splitting when driving nails. Drilling a guide hole is one. Driving a hole with a smaller nail is another.

A third good dodge, which takes a little extra time, is to clip off the point of the nail that you are going to drive, as in (B). The sharp edges of the cut nail will cut the grain, whereas the point would act like a wedge, causing the wood to split.

An alternative to cutting the point is merely to dull or flatten the sharp point of the nail with a hammer. The effect is to produce a point which will punch a way through the wood fibers without spreading them to cause splitting.

NOISE — In the Home

Much of this noise comes from household fixtures and equipment, and can be eliminated by careful checking of likely trouble spots.

FAUCETS, TOILET TANKS. A new washer will often make a noisy faucet quiet. A toilet tank that won't stop running may need a new fiber washer in the outlet.

WINDOWS, DOORS. Make sure that sash cord pulleys on box frame windows are oiled regularly.

Paraffin wax rubbed in the grooves in which the window sashes slide also helps to prevent annoying squeaks, and anti-rattle fittings on the windows keep them quiet in windy weather.

Oiling and adjusting door catches, together with light oiling of the door hinges, should keep doors operating smoothly.

It is a good idea to fit a hydraulic hinge on a door which habitually bangs because of drafts.

MOTORS. If the electric motor in a unit such as a refrigerator becomes noisy, get an expert to check it. Rubber mountings on the motor may have deteriorated and need renewing.

A noisy electric fan may have one or more of its blades bent out of alignment, upsetting its balance.

The best way to reduce noise in a room is to line it with sound-absorbing material. Any absorbent sheet will reduce noise. Better still, you can get acoustic tiles for lining walls and ceilings.

One make of acoustic tile which comes in a variety of patterns, makes an attractive ceiling decoration. The makers say tests show that the tiles reduce noise by about 65 per cent.

Another manufacturer turns out a 24 in. square plaster tile, backed with a layer of sound-absorbing material, which can be painted.

NUTS — Locking Devices

Vibration, especially on fast-moving machinery, can play strange tricks. Nuts and bolts, which seem immovable when the machine was still, mysteriously appear to loosen.

Many devices have been employed to combat nut loosening. Probably the very oldest method of locking a nut on a bolt is the use of a check, or lock nut as shown at (A).

First a thin double chamfer nut is run onto the bolt and brought up against the item to be fastened. Another nut, usually double chamfered and of standard thickness, is tightened down on the thin nut. This is then held in position with a spanner, and, with a thin spanner, the thin nut is slightly slackened back onto the thick nut. Often the thick nut is applied first and the thin one on the top, because a thin spanner cannot be found. This is a friction locking device and is much used in engineering.

The locking arrangement shown at (B) uses a pinned nut. This is a very satisfactory method, but rather inconvenient for the amateur, as a hole must be drilled with the bolt in position. The nut is first drilled to take a tapered pin, then screwed into its final position. The bolt is drilled through the drilled hole in the nut. The tapered pin is then lightly tapped home.

The castle nut is available in a variety of designs (C) being one example. Again, the bolt must be drilled. A split pin is passed between a pair of opposite slots in the nut and through the hole in the bolt. The split pin ends are turned outwards in opposite directions. This method is often used in lighter, fast running machinery.

Detail (D) shows the "wiles" locking nut, sometimes called the sawn nut. A small set-screw passes vertically through one side of the nut, passing across a slot cut in the side.

After the nut has been tightened on its bolt, the set-screw is tightened. This slightly distorts nut and thread, locking the nut on the bolt.

An elementary method of securing a nut is to use it in conjunction with a spring-split washer as in detail (E).

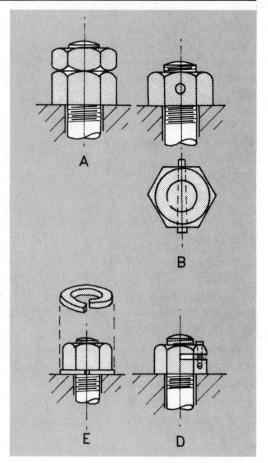

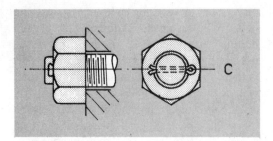

OIL-BASE PAINT—Advantages

Linseed oil paints, long considered the foundation of the paint industry, are still preferred by many professional and do-it-yourself painters.

In addition to a long history of satisfactory service, oil based paints have many other advantages.

One major advantage is excellent adhesion to a wide variety of surfaces. For example, linseed oil paints can be applied over a previously painted chalky surface with good results.

No primer is needed. The oil absorbs the chalk, and assures good adhesion to the previous coat of paint. On new wood, or in areas where the paint has worn thin, linseed oil penetrates the surface and serves as a preservative for the wood.

Slow drying—once considered a disadvantage—is now considered a plus factor, due to the excellent flow properties of oil paints. Lap marks and brush strokes are less apt to mar the finished job. This is especially true on hot, dry or windy days, when water-thinned paints have a tendency to dry too rapidly. Oil based paints flow on easily.

They cover better in one coat, because they contain practically 100 per cent solids —with a little volatile matter to evaporate. The latter is especially helpful to the do-it-yourself house painter. If the old paint is sound, one coat will give a gleaming new surface.

Oil paints have excellent hiding power, so there's less danger of applying too thick a coat in attempting to get the desired coverage.

Today's oil based paints are scientifically compounded to solve many painting problems. Mildew-resistant oil based paints discourage mildew discoloration in warm, humid climates.

Fume-resistant oil based paints are recommended for industrial areas where light coloured homes are subject to staining from fumes. And, while no one likes to think about repainting when they're buying paint, it's nice to know that the linseed oil based paint you apply this year will provide a dependable re-coating surface when the house needs repainting.

Primers are rarely necessary, except when new wood is painted or if the old paint is in very bad condition.

OILSTONE — Make Case

Oilstones should be protected from damage by keeping them in an enclosed case.

There are two ways of making such a case.

You can chop it out of a solid block, or make it of separate pieces dovetailed together.

The former is the usual method, and is probably the more satisfactory.

Maple is a good timber from which to make an oilstone case, and of course the size will depend on the size of the stone.

As an example, if the stone is 8 in. long, 2 in. wide, and 1 in. thick, the overall size of the case could be 9 in. by $2\frac{1}{2}$ in.

In this way $\frac{1}{4}$ in. thickness is allowed for the sides, and $\frac{1}{2}$ in. for the ends where end grain occurs.

It is, however, a good plan to allow an extra inch in length as there is less liability for the grain to split when the recess is being chopped.

The surplus length can be cut off afterwards.

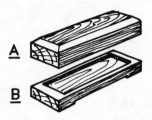

A

B

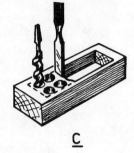

C

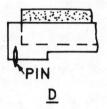

PIN

D

With a depth of 1 in. in the stone, ¼ in. might fit in the base and ¾ in. in the lid. The work of gouging out in both base and lid is similar, though the latter might have an easier fit.

The bulk of the waste can be removed by boring, and a depth gauge should be fixed so that all holes can be bored the same depth. See illustration (C).

Incidentally, this boring has to be taken into consideration when deciding the thickness of wood to be left after recessing, because the point of the bit projects beyond the depth it bores, and it would not do for this to project right through, leaving a series or holes.

A gouge is a useful tool with which to follow the boring for removing the waste timber and so form the recess.

This is followed by a chisel.

Start near one end and chop down across the grain.

The work will become easier once some of the waste is cleared away.

Finish off with a hand routing tool to get a perfectly flat base in the recess as it is important that the stone beds down level.

After recessing top and bottom sections chamfer the top edges of the lid (A) and shape the underside of the base as suggested at (B).

To prevent the case from moving about when in use, a nail should be driven into the underside at one end and be cut off leaving about ⅟₁₆ in. projection (D).

This is filed to a point so that it sticks into the bench.

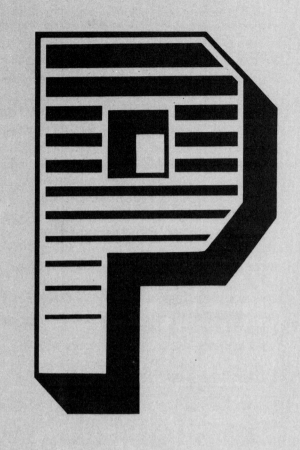

PAINT	Discoloration
PAINTING	Some Tips
PAINTING	With Spray Gun
PAINTWORK	Stripping
PALING FENCE	Care
PARAFFIN WAX	Lubricant
PATCHING PLASTER	Uses
PATHS	Slippery Cement
PINCH BAR	Improved
PIPES	Painting
PIPES	To Conceal
PLANING	And the Grain
PLANING	Procedure
PLASTER BOARD	Use
PLASTER	Smooth Finish
PLASTIC ROOFING	Corrugated
PLASTICS	Stick On
PLASTICS	Three Types
PLUMBING	Home Maintenance
POLYETHYLENE	Uses
POWER TOOLS	Basic Procedure
POWER TOOLS	Choice
PRIMERS	And Sealers

PAINT—Discoloration

Apart from the staining of newly applied paint films by diffusion from the underlying paint coating of a different color, commonly known as bleeding, the discoloration of a paint film can have a variety of causes.

Attack by mold growth is a very common cause of discoloration. By washing the surface with an antiseptic solution, the possibility of further attack is reduced; but for a permanent cure the source of the dampness on which the growth thrives should be found and eliminated.

Copper or brass fittings close to painted surfaces are always likely to cause discoloration. When the paint film contains lithopone the presence of the metal will bring about a chemical reaction which usually shows as small black spots.

The remedy is to wash the surface and apply a coat of aluminum sealer, followed by repainting with a paint based on zinc oxide, which is not so affected.

Lead paint is readily attacked by hydrogen sulphide, which is present in the air in areas containing chemical and gas works. The attack takes the form of dark streaks and patches. Here the surface should be washed down and repainted, using a zinc oxide or one of the leadless paints.

Hydrogen sulphide blackening can be distinguished from the discoloration caused by mold growth, etc., by rubbing the affected areas with a pad moistened with hydrogen peroxide, which will remove the hydrogen sulphide stains.

Hydrogen peroxide restores the color by changing the black sulphide to a white sulphate, and in slight attacks, this may be used as a cure. A coat of clear varnish prevents a further attack.

Iron particles entering paint will always discolor it, the discoloration being more noticeable when the paint is of a light color.

This danger is always intensified on new building operations where the painter is required to decorate while the other tradesmen, especially pipe fitters, are still operating.

Sometimes, too, small bits of metal will become bedded in cement or plaster, and show up later under water paint finishes as rust spots.

For this reason, it is not advisable to use steel wool for rubbing down wall or ceiling surfaces before painting, as small splinters of the wool may remain embedded in the surface.

PAINTING — Some Tips

Remove plates from light switches and wall outlets before painting.

Besides giving you a neater job, this will keep the paint from chipping away from the edges of the plates if they must be removed later to permit electrical repairs.

Take down picture hooks, fill the holes with patching plaster, and sand the patches smooth when dry.

With a new wall color, you may want to rearrange the pictures. It will be too late to fill in the old holes after you have painted.

When painting a kitchen, be sure to turn off the pilot burners in the range so the range can be safely protected with a drop cloth or newspaper.

A good safety rule; open the windows to ventilate any room while you are painting.

Punch four or five holes in the rim of each paint can that you use.

This will allow paint to drain back into the can after each brush-dipping.

When the lid is tapped back in place on the can, it will cover the holes and keep the can sealed.

When tapping lid on can, put the lid in place, then cover it with a cloth to keep any paint remaining in the groove from being spattered out with the hammer blows.

Wipe the can clean and dispose of the rag outside preferably by burning.

PAINTING — With Spray Gun

Spray painting with a gun isn't really difficult though the average home decorator often is afraid to try it.

Perhaps he thinks in terms of the expensive and complicated compressor plant used commercially.

But smaller units are made especially for the amateur. They are reasonable in price, and do good work.

Compressor plant used by the professional is designed to run for long periods under adverse conditions. The air supply can be varied at will to suit the materials in a pressure chamber connected to the gun.

The amateur who really needs a compressor plant can get a small portable unit at a reasonable cost. It will handle everything in the range of the home decorator.

It is more likely though, that the average handyman with only a comparatively small amount of work to do, will prefer to invest in one of the modern self-contained spray-units and vacuum cleaner attachment guns. These cost only a few dollars.

They rely on a constant stream of air supplied by a fan or something similar and have no pressure controls. It is therefore necessary to adjust the material used by thinning, though some manufacturers get over the difficulty by supplying different-size jets or gravity containers.

Practice on some scrap wood before you attempt your first job. It won't take long to

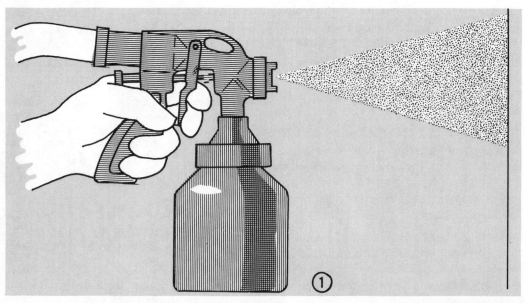

①

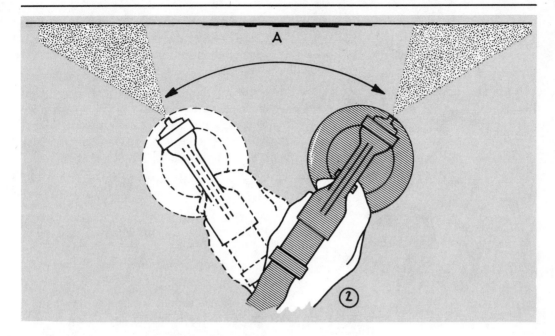

get the feel of the gun. Control of trigger movement is very necessary so that the spray action is started at the commencement of the stroke and cut off at the join-up with the previous application.

This should be done with a slight overlap not greater than half the spray pattern to ensure a perfect blending without any sign of join.

Hold the gun at right angles to the work, Fig. 1, and always keep it the same distance away. Don't swing it in a sweep from the elbow; this will give a patchy finish, for too much paint will be applied when the gun is nearest the work (A) Fig. 2.

As a good rule keep the gun about 6 to 8 in. from the work, Fig. 3. If it is too near, a lot of surplus paint will be deposited and you will have to increase the speed of movement to prevent sagging. If the gun is too far away you will get dry spray and excessive spray dust which in turn will cause a sandy finish, Fig. 4.

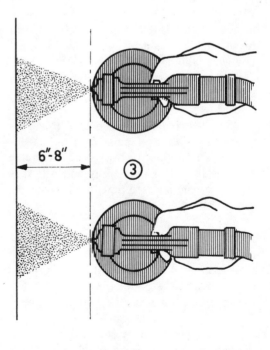

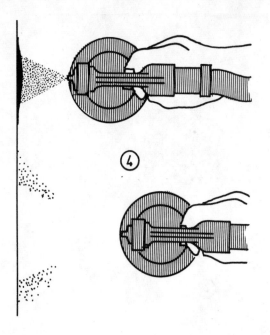

Move the gun evenly without jerky strokes. Aim for an even coating. Too slow a movement will lead to runs; too fast will mean that not enough paint is deposited and you will have to apply another coat. Jerky movement will produce an uneven coating.

When using a gun the center of the spray pattern receives more paint than the outside edges. This lighter spray at the extreme edges is known as over-spray and will vary with the material used and the distance the gun is held from the work.

Because of over-spray it is impossible to paint a sharp edge unless you shield the work with a piece of metal held over the surface not to be painted. Or you can use masking tape stuck on the work.

Window glass can be shielded with tape. A slight margin of ⅟₁₆ in. should be left between the tape and the wood to allow the

paint to lap on the glass and help prevent moisture seeping into the wood through condensation or after rain.

When spraying skirtings the walls and floors can be covered with newspaper held in place by tape. Run tape along the edge being sprayed to give a sharp edge. Masking need not be removed until all work has been completed and is quite dry.

A piece of metal 24 in. by 8 in. makes a useful shield. It will be found handy when spraying a wall where it meets the ceiling. In many cases it can be used instead of masking tape and will save a lot of time in the shielding preparation.

Woodwork consisting of molding with deep hollows should first be given a light mist coat by moving the gun slightly faster than normal and keeping it a little farther away. This will give better coverage in the hollows and avoid paint building up on the high spots and producing runs. A second application should be sufficient to give perfect coverage.

The sequence of working with a gun does not really differ from brush technique: for doors, spray moldings and panels followed by rails and stiles from the top down. Don't attempt too much at one time. The speed of spray work will allow ample time for an extra coat.

When working out of doors it is advisable to choose a day with little or no wind or the over-spray will be difficult to control even with a shield.

Preparation for work follows the same lines as when using a brush. Spray painting gives no short cuts as far as preparation is concerned. In fact, you should take extra care to fill all cracks and smooth down well. A sprayed coat is very even and will show skimped preparation more easily than brush work.

PAINTWORK — Stripping

When an old, painted surface is solid and in good condition, the usual procedure is to clean off any dirt or grime, rub down lightly with fine abrasive paper, and re-paint.

There are, however, times when there is no alternative to stripping off the old finish and starting again from the bare timber.

Chipped and blistered finishes cannot be made good, and, no matter how carefully one tries smoothing around the patches, painting over them will almost certainly cause ugly scars to show through.

Similarly, it is not satisfactory trying to strip an isolated area—the complete surface must be stripped.

Exterior woodwork may be stripped cleanly with a blowtorch and scraper. This job must be done with extreme care, first to avoid any fire risk, and second to avoid damage to the timber from scorching.

Modern butane gas torches are much cleaner and more convenient to use than the old paraffin type with its broad flame. The gas type allows adjustment of the flame to suit the work being done.

So far as the handyman is concerned, the most convenient way of stripping old paint or varnish is to use the viscous liquids available. They are merely brushed on and allowed to react on the old finish so that it can be scraped off.

The same sort of strippers are available in pressured spray packs and are merely sprayed on. Both types are convenient to use, but tend to be rather expensive if large areas are to be treated.

These strippers do not remove the actual color from, say, a stained and varnished surface as many homeworkers imagine they should. In other words, they are not a bleaching agent.

What they do is remove the surface finish of varnish or paint, although with paint they usually clean sufficiently to reveal the natural color of the timber.

Softening occurs almost as soon as the solution is applied, but it is a mistake to start scraping too soon. Wait a few minutes until the paint bubbles up, when the scraper should slide through easily, right down to the bare timber.

On a vertical surface scraping should start from the top, and where this is possible, in horizontal strokes. The scrapings should be caught on old newspaper and not left lying around.

Finally the exposed woodwork should be sponged down with water, preferably hot, and containing a little household detergent. Obviously, the wood must be allowed to dry out thoroughly before starting to repaint.

PALING FENCE — Care

Owing to the exposed position of the majority of dividing fences, a few months' lack of attention may lead to large-scale repairs.

A point not often considered, but which has considerable effect on the life of a paling fence, is the principle of attaching the palings to the exposed or windward side of the rails.

When palings are nailed on the leeward side, the continued action of the wind results in their breaking away because of the lack of support from the rails.

Flathead nails or clouts are essential for holding palings, and the use of galvanized metal strapping—sometimes called hoop-iron—nailed across the palings in line with the rails will provide effective reinforcing, particularly if the palings are weathered and splitting.

The most effective time to treat fence timbers is while fences are being erected. This allows all sections to be treated. Some parts will be inaccessible later, so here are a few points to note.

Joints in timbers, and sections where timbers lay face to face, harbor moisture for long periods and promote the rotting and general deterioration of the woodwork.

The sealing of all exposed end-grains and lapping faces will eliminate a good deal of this fault.

When timbers are cut to size and fitted, the joints and timber faces should be coated with red-lead primer. This will help to prevent water getting to the heart of the wood.

All timbers which are to go beneath the ground, including the base of the posts, struts and sole-plates should also be coated before the post is placed in position.

Creosote or bituminous paints are generally satisfactory for this work.

The most vulnerable part of a fence is at the surface of the soil. Here the timbers are subject to the continual wetting and drying processes which promote rotting.

Take note of the nature of the soil in which the fence is to be erected. Sandy soils are less helpful to fence durability than the heavier type.

Light soils tend to 'give' with the wind movement, and fences tend to sag and 'lay over'. Double strutting is helpful in these circumstances.

PARAFFIN WAX — Lubricant

Paraffin wax to most people is something used to seal off the tops of bottled jam, but it has many applications.

Many wood workers rub nails and screws on a bar of soap for easier driving but soap tends to rust the nail or screw in place, making it almost impossible to remove later, so try using paraffin wax.

Just rub the screw or nail over the flat surface of the paraffin wax cake a few times, or dip them in some of the wax which has been melted in a container.

When you make or buy a new wooden miter box, melt some paraffin wax with a hot soldering iron and allow it to run into the saw slots. When it hardens, draw the saw blade through the slots.

The hot wax will soak into the wood and lubricate the saw blades for as long as the miter box is used.

Paraffin wax is useful when curtain rings and drapery hooks refuse to slide on metal rods or poles. Take down the rod and rub the inner and top surfaces with a cake of paraffin until a thin film is evident. Place the hooks back on the rod and restore it to service.

Paraffin wax will also help a tight drawer in a cabinet to run freely. Remove a drawer which has a tendency to stick, turn it over and rub a cake of paraffin up and down the runner edges and also the sides.

Garden markers of the flat, white wood stick variety have an irritating way of becoming illegible. A dip in a pan of hot melted paraffin wax after the desired details have been printed with pen or pencil will preserve the writing for a considerable time.

Wooden porch and window boxes decay rapidly from within unless protected with a metal lining or other protective lining material.

The life of a less expensive planter box may be prolonged considerably if the inside surfaces are treated with paraffin wax when the timber is new and dry.

The paraffin should be melted in a convenient pan or can and brushed over the dry inner surfaces of the boxes before they are used.

Paraffin wax can be bought in blocks or cakes, but for most purposes, and especially for lubricating tools such as saws, an ordinary paraffin wax candle is the most convenient form.

PATCHING PLASTER — Uses

Patching plaster is available under several trade names. You can buy it in two forms —a powder which you mix with water or oil as required, and ready-mixed in putty form. Here are some suggestions for using.

CRACKS IN PLASTER OR CEMENT. Gouge out all loose plaster surrounding the cracks, and undercut them where possible to give the filling a key. Mix the patching plaster compound with water to a heavy putty (or use the ready-mixed kind).

Fill the cracks by pressing in and smoothing off with a broad knife. To give a uniform texture to cement-rendered surfaces, sand may be added. A small quantity of sand patted into the wet patching plaster after it is applied will match the wall texture. It's best to dampen the area surrounding the cracks before filling.

NAIL HOLES AND CRACKS IN TIMBER. Apply the patching plaster with a broad knife, after you've put on the first coat of paint.

You can use the water-mixed patching plaster, or Swedish putty. Swedish putty is made by mixing the powder to a heavy, dry paste with raw linseed oil, and reducing to working consistency with water. Sand the patching plaster smooth when dry.

Swedish putty is suitable for outside use. It is also preferred by many handymen for use as a wood filler.

SURFACING OPEN-GRAINED TIMBER, etc. Use either the water-mixed putty or Swedish putty, after the first coat of paint has been applied.

Use a broad knife, and fill the indentations slightly above the surface of the material. When dry, sand smooth before painting.

UNEVEN CEMENT-RENDERED WALLS. Mix with water to a thick paint consistency, slightly dampen the wall, and apply a full coat with a brush or trowel. Sand smooth when dry.

Patching plaster powder can be mixed with paint for better adhesion to a surface which has been oil-painted or sealed.

PATHS — Slippery Cement

A constant source of worry to many people, especially in wet weather, is a cement path or floor with a very smooth finish on the surface. It becomes very slippery and dangerous.

Such a surface has usually been finished with a steel trowel, and here are some suggestions for treating it to give a more secure foothold.

If care and patience are used a satisfactory job may be done by gently chipping the surface all over, with a chisel or small pick. The main thing is not to dig too deeply, and to make the chipped appearance as uniform as possible.

An easier way is first to wet the surface, then apply one or two coats of a hydrochloric acid solution. Dilute the acid in proportions of seven parts of water to one part of acid (by volume), and apply with an old brush or mop. As a precaution, wear rubber gloves when using the solution.

The acid has an etching action on the smooth cement surface sufficient to roughen it slightly.

When the job is finished don't forget to hose the path or floor thoroughly to remove all traces of the acid solution.

Incidentally, it is always best to finish the surfaces of paths and floors with a wooden float—not a steel trowel.

The wooden float gives just the amount of grip needed, and it a definite safety measure.

A comparatively recent development is the use of foam rubber or foam plastic sheet material over the face of a wooden float. This produces an especially even surface on the cement topping without making it slippery.

A third method of providing a safe foothold on a smooth cement path or floor surface is to apply a special type of non-slip paving paint. Available in a range of colors, this paint contains fine granular material, and is applied by brush.

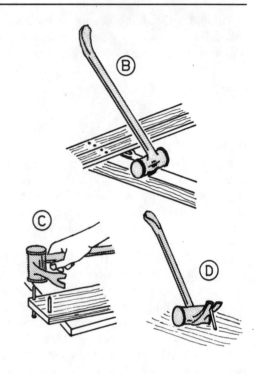

As shown at (B) it gives greater leverage when lifting, say, floor boards, and at (C) it is being used as a hammer to drive the nails through the board so that they can be withdrawn as at (D).

This latter feature is especially useful when large packing cases have to be broken up.

PINCH BAR — Improved

One of the most useful tools to have in the home tool kit is a pinch bar.

These bars usually are fitted with a claw hook at one end and a blunt chisel point at the other.

However, if a short thick bar is welded across the hook section as shown at (A) in the illustration, its efficiency is greatly increased.

PIPES — Painting

When decorating the interior of a house, disappointing results are often obtained on lead and copper pipes on various fittings.

There is a tendency for the paint to chip or scale off after a short while, and the only way to prevent this is to prepare the surfaces thoroughly before applying the paint.

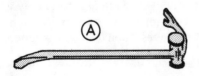

COPPER PIPES: Any exposed copper pipes to be painted should first be well washed with hot water and soap to remove all traces of dirt and grease. Follow by rubbing down with wet-and-dry abrasive paper, using mineral spirits as a lubricant.

This rubbing-down procedure prevents dust depositing on adjoining paintwork which can cause stains due to the formation of verdigris when the copper dust is attacked by the oil in the paint.

The rubbing down provides a key or "bite" for the paint, to make it adhere firmly. Finally, treat the surface with a mixture of one part acetone and two parts benzol. This could be rubbed on with a cloth.

When painting, flow the paint onto the surface of the pipes rather than use the usual brushing method. This produces a smooth finish, but don't overload the brush at this could result in unsightly 'runs' on the surface.

LEAD PIPES: Lead pipes should also be rubbed down to provide a key for the paint. It is very necessary in this case to use the mineral spirits to lubricate the wet-and-dry abrasive paper, as lead dust is injurious to health, and the liquid eliminates the dust. In all cases, use a fine grade abrasive paper to avoid scratches, and rub in the direction of the length of the pipes.

After rubbing down, give the pipes a priming coat of one part varnish and a half part mineral spirits or mineral turpentine.

A thin type of varnish, as used for exterior work, is best for this purpose, as it bonds well with the lead surface. After this base varnish is dry, the surface could be rubbed down lightly with the finest grade of abrasive paper, being careful not to cut through the varnish.

When applying the finishing paint, brush on several thin coats rather than one thick one, allowing ample drying time between each coat.

PIPES — To Conceal

In every home there must be plumbing pipes, but it is unfortunate that far too often they are left exposed on the walls of bathrooms, kitchens, and other rooms.

Besides being unsightly, unexposed pipes are bad dust collectors, and make painting and decorating awkward.

The solution to the problem of exposed pipes is to cover them, and the illustrated detail (A) shows how small-bore water pipes, which are not too far away from the wall can be easily concealed.

Two strips of timber are secured to the wall at the sides of the pipes. The thickness of the strips should be about ¾ in. and the width should be just sufficient to clear the front of the pipes.

Once this is done, fix a piece of hardboard or plywood on the face of the wood strips. This cover piece should be screwed in position—not nailed. This will enable it to be easily removed if access is required to the pipes at a later date.

A

If, however, the diameter of the pipes is quite large, or if they are positioned away from the wall, then the foregoing method is not very satisfactory, because the projection from the wall would be too great for the fastening screws.

The procedure to adopt here is to fasten two 1½ in. by 1 in. battens to the wall at the sides of the pipes so that the side members of the concealing box can be screwed to them as shown in detail (B).

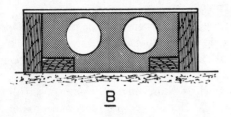

B

When this method is used, it is permissible to nail the hardboard or plywood facing in position because if access is required to the pipes, the whole box can be easily removed, leaving only the two battens on the wall.

PLANING — And the Grain

As direction of grain plays such an important part in woodwork, it is worthwhile giving some attention to the best method of using a plane in relation to the grain.

In a coarse-grained timber it is only too easy to tear the wood deeply with one stroke of a plane in the wrong direction, and if the wood has little thickness to spare, you may have to make it thinner than you intended to plane out these blemishes.

Fig. 1 shows a piece of timber which is to be planed on surface (A). Study the grain on the side (B). The grain indicates that planing should be in the direction of the arrow—that is, the direction in which the grain runs uphill.

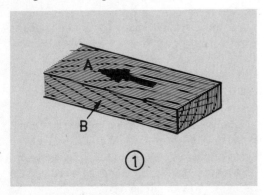

Enlarged detail of the grain, Fig. 2 shows how the cutter forces up the individual wood fibers if you choose the wrong direction.

The grain may, in fact, be likened to the hair on an animal's back. If stroked the right way, the hair feels smooth and tends to lie flat. If stroked the wrong way, it becomes roughened up.

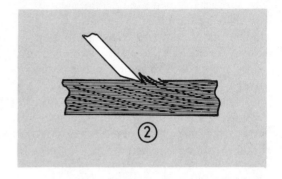

Sometimes the grain is interlocked, and, although sloping one way on surface (B) Fig. 1 at the end, it may slope the opposite way in the middle of the piece. This is known as cranky grained timber.

With wavy grain, also, the slope will often alternate throughout the length.

Where these conditions occur, the only method of finding the best direction is that of trial and error in planing.

Of course, don't forget to have the plane sharp and set finely.

Even then, you may tear out a certain amount of grain, but these patches can be eliminated by using a steel wood scraper after planing.

PLANING — Procedure

The most useful plane in the woodworker's tool kit is the steel smoothing plane.

One with a 2 in. blade gives the best results, and is just as effective on hardwood as on the softer timbers such as pine or fir.

For cabinet work where edges have to be planed accurately for jointing such items as table tops and bookshelves, a steel jack plane or steel trying plane is almost a necessity. Both these planes are much the same pattern as the smoothing plane, but much longer and with a wider blade.

The planing of timber is not a difficult job, but there are a number of points that must be remembered. To begin the planing operation, take an easy yet firm position directly behind the work. This postiion allows the worker to keep his eyes at a proper position or angle to sight the work and observe the results of each plane stroke.

For edge planing, hold the plane square with the face of the work. The right hand grips the handle; the left hand is held at the front, the fingers passing under the sole so that the tips just bear against the wood being planed. This helps in keeping the plane in a line with the wood.

It is really something of an art to plane the edge in such a way that it squares up with the face. Apart from proper holding, it is, of course, essential that the blade itself be adjusted for a thin, smooth shaving.

To assure a smooth, straight edge, the plane must be pushed with the grain. The expert woodworker may determine the direction readily by observing the grain on the surface.

Others may find it necessary to make a trial stroke of the plane. If the surface roughs or tears up, turn the board around, or reverse the stroke. In some cases, the grain may run both ways. The procedure then is to take an extremely fine shaving with the back iron set up very close to the cutting edge, and push the plane so that it takes a slightly shearing cut.

To keep the plane straight on the edge, press down with the left hand on the knob at the start of the stroke. Similarly, press down on the handle at the end of the stroke. Fig. 1 shows this clearly, and also indicates how the fibers of the wood give the direction of the grain.

The same rules about planing with the grain and having the back and cutting irons set finely for dressing cross-grained timber apply equally to surface planing. However, a mistake some workmen make is to use the wrong plane for the particular work on hand. For example, a smoothing plane is usually used for surface work, although it may also be used for edge planing on short stock.

Where long edges must be planed straight and true, a jack plane and, in extreme cases, a jointing plane, will be needed. Fig. 2 shows a trying plane in use. It bridges the low parts in an edge and does not take a shaving off them until all the high spots have been removed. A short plane will follow in the troughs or hollows, and thus cannot produce a true edge.

Planing of end grain always calls for a great deal of care. If the plane is pushed straight through, the corner is almost certain to split as indicated at Fig. 3. However, by making the cut halfway in each direction there is no risk of the corners splitting out.

Some workers place a waste strip against the edge, and plane against it; another method is to chisel a small corner section away down to the line and then carry the plane straight through.

To get good results from a steel plane, the sole must always be well lubricated. A wad of cotton well soaked in raw linseed oil can be kept handy and wiped occasionally over it. Alternatively, a short end of candle can be kept for the purpose, the candle being rubbed across the sole whenever the plane tends to cease working smoothly.

PLASTER BOARD — Use

For building or remodeling rooms and similar interior lining jobs, one of the most useful sheeting materials is that called plaster board or gypsum board.

Plaster board is made in sheets which have a plaster core, covered both sides with a facing material similar to heavy paper. It has a smooth finish which provides an excellent base for whatever decoration you fancy.

The joints between the sheets can be finished in two ways. The first method is to cover the joints completely to give the appearance of a single flat wall. The alternative is to use light cover strips, giving a paneled effect.

The sheets are $\frac{3}{8}$ in. thick, and are available in several widths and lengths—ranging from 3 ft to 4ft 5 in. wide, and from 6 ft to 16 ft long.

Two of the widest sheets—4 ft $5\frac{1}{2}$ in.—placed on their sides, will cover a 9 ft high wall from floor to ceiling, so that there is only one center horizontal joint to fill. The longest sheets will span the length of most rooms.

This range of sizes reduces to a minimum, cutting and waste in fitting the sheets. Where cutting is necessary, you merely score the surface with a sharp knife, snap the core, then cut the back paper.

To cut openings for windows or doors, use a sharp panel saw. A precaution to note when cutting is to do the work away from polished or carpeted floors to avoid having the fine plaster dust walked into the floor surface.

Invisible flush jointing of the sheets is done with the aid of a slight recess which is molded into the edge of the sheets.

The jointing process is first to fill the recess formed by adjoining boards with a jointing compound, using a trowel or broad knife.

Then embed a special reinforcing tape in the compound by brushing, and smooth off excess compound.

A steel plasterer's float is used to apply more of the compound to the joint, taking care to feather the edges so that the filled joint merges in flush with the main wall surface.

It is best to apply the compound in several thin coats to complete filling the recess. After each application, the compound should be allowed to dry before going on with the next.

After the final application has been troweled smooth and flush, sand the joint area lightly with fine abrasive paper for a perfect finish. The compound is also used to fill the holes created by punching the heads of the fixing clouts.

PLASTER — Smooth Finish

There are two main methods used for plastering a brick or concrete wall. These are referred to as cement rendering, and setting with putty plaster.

Cement rendering has the advantage of being very hard and durable, and the various textured effects that can be achieved are very attractive.

On the other hand, a surface finished with putty plaster is extremely smooth, and takes paint well. Unlike cement rendering, putty plastering is an interior finish only.

The actual work of applying the plaster is not difficult once you have tried it, and here are the proportions for the materials, and procedure details.

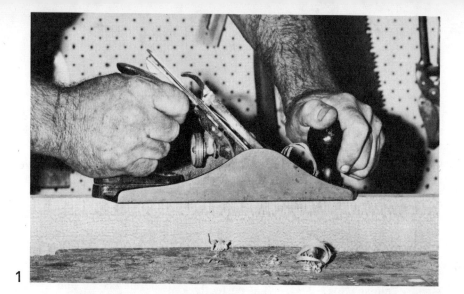

1

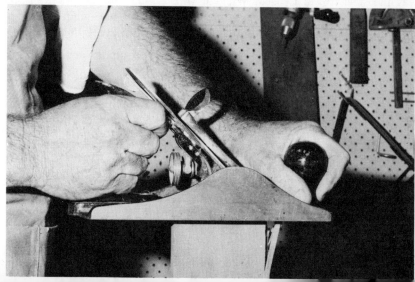

2

3

First apply a base coat of sand, cement, and lime mortar to a thickness of approximately ½ in. and finish off with a wooden float.

The putty coat that goes on top of this to form the fine finish is a mixture of dehydrated lime and hard plaster—in equal parts.

Mix with water to a putty-like consistency.

This mixture is inclined to finish with a slightly bluish tinge and, if a perfectly white putty coat is desired, the mixture could be varied to one part of dehydrated lime to half-part hard plaster and half-part superfine plaster. All these parts are by volume.

As the mixture sets fairly rapidly, no more than can be used immediately should be mixed at a time.

Before applying any putty plaster, dampen the base floating coat. Begin application on the top half of the wall, first applying a thin coat applied with a steel trowel the total thickness to be no more than ⅛ in.

Finish this half by stroking with a water soaked brush, followed immediately by the steel trowel, until the plaster putty becomes hard and smooth.

The secret of success in this work is in the way the steel trowel is used. Wield it with a long sweeping motion, keeping the leading edge slightly raised to avoid gouging a hole in the surface.

If an existing interior cement rendered wall is rough or uneven, it is possible to re-surface it effectively with the putty plaster.

PLASTIC ROOFING — Corrugated

Translucent corrugated plastic sheets, which can be bought in a large range of sizes, make lightweight yet strong roofs over patios and porches, and the colors are very attractive.

The material softens and breaks up the strong, direct rays of the sun without cutting out the light.

Fixing the sheets is not difficult, but there are certain precautions to be taken and points to be noted to produce a result which is strong, good-looking and leak-proof.

For the sake of economy order the material before erecting the frame. This way you can make the frame fit the available material exactly and avoid costly left-overs.

The colors most commonly used outside are blue, not green, or yellow. The usual dimensions for corrugated sheets—they could be either fiber glass or PVC—are 26 in. 33 in. or 40 in. wide and in lengths from 6 ft up to 12 ft.

The standard widths allow for an overlap at the sides to be made directly above rafters set on 2 ft 6 in. or 3 ft centers. By making these overlaps directly over rafters the overlaps can be hidden naturally and neatly.

When required, the ends of the material should overlap about 2 in. Give the roof a slight fall or pitch for drainage, and run the corrugations in the direction that you want the rain to flow. Mostly you can give the roof a pitch of 1 in. per foot—the desirable minimum for good drainage—and still have it look flat.

Lumber such as a good quality of fir is most often used for the roof frame. The dimension of the actual timber sections forming the roof frame is determined mainly by the sheet lengths and the span of roof.

Here is a useful guide for timber dimensions:

RAFTERS. Up to 5 ft length, 2 in. by 2 in.; up to 8 ft length, 3 in. by 2 in.; up to 12 ft length, 4 in. by 2 in.; over 12 ft length, 6 in. by 2 in.

CROSS-CORRUGATION BRACING. 2 in. by 2 in. every 4 ft on 26 in. wide plastic; 3 in. by 2 in. every 3 ft 6 in. on 33 in. wide plastic; 4 in. by 2 in. every 3 ft on 40 in. wide plastic sheet material.

Because all roof framework will be seen it is best to use dressed timber and to house the cross-members into the main rafters.

For this reason the ideal procedure is to assemble the roof frame on the ground and lift it into position as one unit.

PLASTICS — Stick On

You peel off the protective paper backing, press the sheet or tile into position, and there it stays.

Stick-on-plastics, in flexible sheets or tiles, are today's high-speed method of decorating.

These plastics materials are unaffected by stains, splashes, grease and dirt.

They can be repeatedly washed and make pretty and practical coverings for wall and furniture surfaces liable to specially hard wear.

Here are three practical ideas for using them:

1. The wall areas round the sink can be an awkward place to fit a conventional splash-back but flexible plastic sheeting can be cut with scissors to fit any wall space. Allow a slight margin for shrinkage. Smooth firmly into position, pressing out all air bubbles as you go.

2. The wall behind the hall table is another area liable to wear and tear, particularly if you have decorated the hall with delicate wallpaper. A row of contact adhesive plastic tiles, in a color that blends with your decorative scheme, will keep this corner permanently bright and clean. The tiles are 6 in. square, and can be cut with scissors.

3. If cigarette burns, stains and scratches have left their mark on your favorite coffee table, give it a face lift with a new top of gleaming plastic tiles. For decorative interest, you might choose tiles in two contrasting colors and set them in a checkerboard pattern.

PLASTICS — Three Types

There are probably as many kinds of plastic as there are kinds of wood, so it is no use regarding plastic as one kind of material with definite characteristics. Some plastics are soft and flexible, others are hard and rigid, while some soften and harden with differences in temperature. In many cases it is not necessary to know what an actual plastic article is made of, but there is an exception when the home worker wants to make something from transparent plastic.

Of the common transparent plastics there are three which may be confused. The oldest one is cellulose nitrate, which is generally known as celluloid. The non-inflammable form of this is cellulose acetate, often spoken of as acetate sheet. The third one is acrylic resin.

Although these three transparent plastics look the same, there are many jobs where it would be unsatisfactory to use any one. Celluloid is very inflammable and tends to yellow with age. Acetate has a greater resistance to burning and does not discolor so readily. Both suffer from a slight shrinkage with time. Acrylic resin is more glass-like and not as flexible as the other two. It does not shrink and remains clear. However, it is comparatively brittle and one of the others will last longer if the panel has to withstand flying stones.

If the edge of a sheet of acrylic resin is examined it will not show any color. Celluloid or acetate sheet may show a slight tinge of pink, green or blue as the edge is manipulated for the light to strike across it.

If a piece of acrylic resin is held up and tapped, it will give a ringing note. The note of the other two will be dull.

The only positive way to identify the three plastics is by trying to burn them. Celluloid will burn violently. Acetate will not ignite as easily and when it burns the flame will be smoky. The flame will not propagate downwards—if a burning piece is held with the flame upwards, the burning pieces will fall away and the flame will soon die out. There may be a slight smell of vinegar when the flame is extinguished. Acrylic resin burns more readily than acetate. The flame is clear and smokeless and will propagate downwards.

PLUMBING

Plumbers are expensive, but they are often necessary for alterations to the household plumbing system and for repairs that are beyond the ability and understanding of the handyman. However, between the high fee you pay the journeyman plumber and the complete passiveness of letting a leaky faucet drip and drip and drip, there are several things you can do yourself if you have some basic tools and information and reasonable skills.

THE PLUMBING SYSTEM. The plumbing system consists of two pipe-and-fixture systems—one to supply water and the other to carry away waste water and sewage.

Water supply plumbing is very simple. It can be considered as an extended hose with many branches to carry the water where it is to be used. The pipes can be small be-cause the water is under pressure and moves through them swiftly.

The waste drainage system consists of large pipes because the flow through them is slow. It depends on gravity, not pressure. For this reason, horizontal drainage pipes are laid with a continuous pitch of at least ¼ inch per foot, and the fittings used in assembling them allow for this pitch.

Horizontal drains are usually called waste pipes—or soil pipes if they carry toilet sewage. Large vertical drainpipes are called stacks. A stack that carries toilet waste is a soil stack.

The main drainage line from the house is called the house drain. It continues five to ten feet out through the foundation, and after that point it is known as the house sewer, which connects either to a septic tank or to a public sewer below street level.

The house drainage system is vented because it needs air to facilitate the flow of wastes and to allow sewer gases to escape from it. The vents also prevent waste water from coming back through traps in plumbing fixture drains. There is a vent near each fixture that may extend through the roof or may connect to a single large vent, which then extends through the roof.

The traps, or curved pipes, that are part of plumbing fixture drains act as seals against sewer gases by holding water in them at a certain level. Wastes pass freely through the pipes—unless they develop clogs—but the water level in the traps remains the same.

CLOGS. Perhaps the most common plumbing problem that comes within the handyman's reach—aside from the leaky faucet—is clearing clogged pipes, drains, and fixtures. For this operation, two simple, inexpensive tools are indispensable. One is the plumber's friend, force cup, or plunger. The other is the snake, a long flexible probe. Both are readily available at

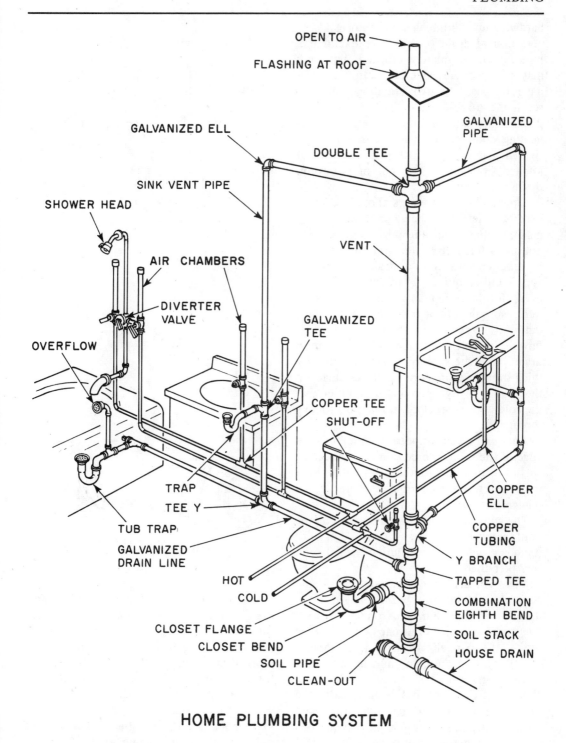

OPEN TO AIR

FLASHING AT ROOF

GALVANIZED PIPE

GALVANIZED ELL

DOUBLE TEE

SINK VENT PIPE

SHOWER HEAD

VENT

AIR CHAMBERS

DIVERTER VALVE

GALVANIZED TEE

OVERFLOW

COPPER TEE

SHUT-OFF

COPPER ELL

TRAP

TEE Y

TUB TRAP

GALVANIZED DRAIN LINE

COPPER TUBING

Y BRANCH

HOT

COLD

TAPPED TEE

COMBINATION EIGHTH BEND

CLOSET FLANGE

CLOSET BEND

SOIL STACK

HOUSE DRAIN

SOIL PIPE

CLEAN-OUT

HOME PLUMBING SYSTEM

hardware and plumbing supply stores.

Chemical drain openers are useful if a pipe is not completely clogged, but they may not provide effective action if they have to pass through standing water to reach the trouble spot. These harsh compounds are actually most useful in preventing complete clogging. Other preventive measures are to keep grease out of kitchen drains and hair out of bathroom drains.

Chemical drain openers should never be used in toilet bowls because the heat they generate may crack the porcelain. And do not use a force cup after you have poured these chemicals into a drain. They can splash and do quite a lot of damage to skin, eyes, clothing, and many other materials.

In using the plumber's friend, the important thing to remember is to close off overflow drains. If the problem is in the bathtub drain, block the shower extension either by tying shut the plunger or lever that turns on the shower or by removing it and blocking the hole with a wet cloth so that no air leaks through.

Applying a coat of petroleum jelly to the edge of the rubber force cup is an effective way to form a seal around it so that you get maximum force from a quick up-and-down plunger action.

The snake is simply eased through a pipe until the clogged matter is loosened or until it hooks onto an obstruction, which can then be pulled out.

You will also find clean-out plugs and caps throughout the plumbing system—usually on the drain traps under fixtures. There are also clean-out caps on the house drain. If your efforts with a plumber's friend or a snake fail, you may have to get a wrench and remove one of these caps. When you do it, have a bucket under the opening to catch water from the trap. And wear rubber gloves if you have poured a chemical drain opener into the drain.

CLEAN-OUT PLUG

CLEAN-OUT CAP

If you think the problem is in the house drain or beyond, it is probably time to call the plumber for diagnosis and treatment.

Clogs in the water supply system are a bit more difficult to handle, but still possible for the handyman. You know that a clogged faucet may be the problem if the flow of water is inordinately slow. But you should first check to see that the water shut-off valve on the pipe leading to the faucet is open—not as silly as it sounds when there are children in the household.

The second check to make is to compare the flow of water from the hot and cold faucets. A slower flow of hot water indicates that corrosion around the faucet valve may be the cause. Hot water pipes and fixtures corrode more rapidly than the cold water ones.

In faucets with aerators, a common and simply remedied clogging problem occurs in sections of the country where there is high mineral content in the water supply. Simply unscrew the aerator assembly and take the screens and washers apart, keeping them in order so that you can reassemble them after you have cleaned them. If the aerator is too badly corroded, replace it. Hardware and plumbing supply stores can easily help you if you take the aerator with you and remember the name of the faucet manufacturer.

A clogged aerator can produce some of the symptoms of a faucet needing repair. Water may ooze around the stem because the flow forces it to go somewhere when it cannot get through the normal outlet, and of course there is the matter of reduced flow.

FAUCET REPAIRS. Inevitably, there comes the time when you must face a faucet repair. A faucet that leaks, drips, or oozes can add several dollars a year to your water bill—besides creating a rusty stain on a fixture. And a faucet that makes a howling or chattering noise when it is turned on can be a real strain on the nerves.

Faucets are not all that difficult to fix. Most of the ones found in home water systems are similar in construction and operation. Turning a faucet handle screws the valve stem down into an opening called the valve seat. This closes the opening in the valve body and stops the flow of water through the pipe leading to the faucet.

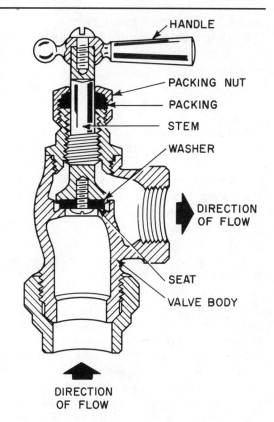

HANDLE
PACKING NUT
PACKING
STEM
WASHER
DIRECTION OF FLOW
SEAT
VALVE BODY
DIRECTION OF FLOW

A washer (in newer faucets, a seal) keeps this closure watertight, until the washer becomes worn. Then you have a leaky faucet or sometimes a noisy faucet. The valve seat can become worn, too. When this happens, replacing the washer will not stop the leak or drip, or if it does, the leak will soon be back. Refacing or replacing the valve seat is harder, but you will not need a plumber to handle it.

Another device to prevent leakage is the packing nut, found at the top of the valve stem. Under it may be rubber packing washers or graphite asbestos "twine." The purpose of the packing nut and the packing is to keep water from traveling up the stem and oozing around the handle. If the packing is worn, that is what to expect—water oozing around the handle when the faucet is on. Before you take the faucet apart, however, try tightening the packing nut a little with a pipe wrench. That may stop the oozing.

To replace a worn washer, follow these steps:

1. Turn *on* the faucet and turn *off* the supply valve under the fixture or the nearest valve that controls the flow of water to the faucet you will be working on.

2. When the water stops flowing from the faucet, loosen the hexagonal packing nut with a pipe wrench.

3. Begin turning the faucet handle in the "on" direction. You do not have to remove the handle unless you have to take off an escutcheon (shield) that covers the packing nut and other parts of the faucet. Keep turning until you can lift the handle, packing nut, and valve stem out of the valve body. Some modern faucets have escutcheons that cover the packing nut. In this case, remove the handle and the escutcheon, loosen the packing nut, and put the handle back on to help turn out the faucet parts, as described above. You may have to study your faucet a bit before you figure out how the handle comes off. The screw that holds on the handle may be hidden under a screw-in or snap-on button (often bearing the label H or C).

4. Remove the set screw from the bottom of the threaded valve stem and take off the old washer. (If the groove in the screw head has filled in with corrosion, make a new groove with a file or hacksaw or use a new screw—a brass one, not steel.)

5. Put on a new washer like the old one and replace the screw. To be sure that the new washer *is* like the old one, take the old one with you to the hardware store and buy one like it. As an alternative, you can use one of the new snap-in washers that have swivel stems. This feature keeps the washer from grinding against the valve

seat. The result is longer wear and fewer replacements. To use one of the new washers, you will have to file down the "lip" at the end of the stem—the rim that holds the old-style washer.

6. Turn the stem and handle assembly back into the valve seat, turning in the "off" direction. Tighten the packing nut with a pipe wrench.

7. Turn on the water supply valve to check your work.

To replace deteriorated packing materials, follow the first three steps above. Remove the old packing material. If it is twine, you may have to dig it out. Wrap new twine around the stem—in the "off" direction, the way you turn the handle when you turn off the water. Tighten the packing nut to be sure you do not have too much twine on the stem. Reassemble the faucet as directed in step 6 above.

If the packing material is a washer or ring, it is a good idea to take this and the faucet assembly with you to the hardware store to find a replacement.

Newer faucets that have a seal rather than a washer need less attention than older faucets, but the packing material may still wear out. Follow manufacturer's instructions (available through plumbing suppliers) in repairing these faucets. If you notice leakage around the stem, however, try tightening the packing nut a bit before going to the trouble of repacking it.

It is a bit more complicated to reface a worn and rough valve seat. You will need a seat dressing tool to handle this job. But find out first if the faucet has the type of valve seat that is part of a removable and replaceable sleeve. You may also be able to buy a complete valve assembly—an advisable move if the threads on the stem are worn. You can also buy snap-in valve seats to match the new snap-in washers.

If you have to reface the valve seat, begin with the first three directions given for washer replacement. Then insert the seat dresser into the faucet body and give it three or four turns. Remove the tool and examine the seat. If it is still grooved or rough, use the tool again. You should smooth and polish the valve seat to a shiny, regular surface. Flush out all metal shavings before you reassemble the faucet.

NOISY PIPES. Is there something wrong with your faucets when you hear a hammering in the water pipes just after shutting off the water? No, the problem is in the pipes. Usually the supply line to each faucet has an air chamber—an extension of pipe above the T-joint where water flows toward the fixture. The column of water in the pipe rushes into this chamber when the faucet is turned off, and the compression of air in the chamber absorbs some of the shock created when the water is stopped at the faucet.

The hammering noise you hear in your pipes may occur because there is no air chamber on the supply line leading to a particular faucet. If there is no air chamber, you can buy an anti-hammer device that can be installed without opening up the walls. Do not assume, however, that your plumbing does not have air chambers if you are hearing "water hammer." The pipes may simply need to be drained. Turn on the faucets and turn off the water supply valves until the water stops flowing. If there is not enough air in the chambers, this operation will replenish it.

Also likely is the possibility that a supply pipe lacks support at some point along its length and is knocking against another pipe, a wall stud, or a floor joist. Check all the exposed pipes in your basement, looking for loose mounting straps and places where the supply pipes give or sag. You may need to add new straps or devise other supports.

LEAKING PIPES. A sudden leak or rupture in a water pipe demands quick action because of the possibility of damage to the heating system, floors, walls, woodwork, and furniture. The first thing to do is to shut off the main water supply valve for the whole house or the supply valve that controls the flow of water to the leaking pipe. It is important to know where these valves are. If you did not find out when you took possession of your house, do it now.

Once the water is off, trace the source of the leak. If you can see the source, try taping it with aluminum-coated tape, waterproof pressure-sensitive tape, or friction tape. This can be considered a temporary repair only—until you can get a plumber to make a permanent repair. A leak can also be repaired with a rubber patch and a metal clamp, but this, too, should be considered temporary.

A leak at a threaded connection can often be stopped by turning off the fitting (use two pipe wrenches—one to hold the pipe, the other to turn off the fitting) and applying a pipe joint compound that will seal the joint when the fitting is tightened again. You can try doing this yourself, or you can call a plumber.

Vibration sometimes breaks solder joints in copper supply pipes. If a solder rupture has caused a leak, clean the joint and re-solder it. The pipes should be dry before you begin to work with the soldering iron. If the joint is not an easily accessible one, you will most likely need to call in a plumber.

INSULATING PIPES AND TANKS. Sweating pipes can scare you into looking for leaks. You should be relieved when you find out that condensation is causing the "leak." Wipe the pipes dry and wrap them with insulating strips or tape, or paint them with an insulating compound. These products are available at hardware and plumbing supply stores.

You can also buy molded fiber glass or rock wool to use for insulating pipes. The molded materials are more expensive, but they are worth considering, especially when you want to prevent heat loss from a hot water heating system.

Insulation slows down heat loss from water pipes, but if water stands in the plumbing system during long periods of below-freezing weather in an unheated house, insulation will not provide much protection against frozen pipes.

Under these conditions, the only sure protection is to drain the system.

One of the most "visible" areas in which insulation may be needed is the bathroom. A sweating toilet tank can be a great nuisance. A very simple solution to this problem is to use a colorful tank cover, which will absorb the condensed moisture on the tank. A more effective way to handle the problem is to install a styrofoam tank liner, which will buffer the tank walls against the cold water inside and reduce condensation. The most effective solution is to install a valve that allows some warm water to enter the toilet tank as it fills. In winter, when condensation is less of a problem, the valve can be turned off.

THAWING FROZEN PIPES. When water supply pipes become frozen, they should be promptly thawed to avoid possible bursting. In copper pipes, a bulge will disclose the location of the frozen area, but no such bulge will appear in other metals.

Some form of heat will be required to melt the ice in the pipes. The heat may be applied to the outside of a frozen pipe by electrical resistance, direct flame, or hot applications of water or steam. In thawing water supply pipes, it is best to start working near an open faucet. When thawing a waste pipe, start at the lower end and work upward, to allow the water to flow off as the ice is melted.

To heat frozen water supply pipes by electrical resistance, a source of low voltage, such as a welding generator, should be connected directly to the pipe with two electrical conductors clamped to the pipe to span the frozen section. As soon as a section has been thawed out, the conductors should be moved along the pipe to thaw another section. A welding shop or a plumber who has welding equipment and the necessary experience should be called to perform this work.

Caution: This method of thawing frozen pipe can be dangerous and should be done by an experienced person only. It cannot be used to thaw plastic tubing or other nonconducting pipe or tubing.

Direct flame can be applied to frozen pipes with a blowtorch, provided there is no danger of burning the adjoining woodwork. The flame should be played gradually along the pipe to spread the heat evenly. It would be slower but wiser, however, to use a hair dryer or a heat lamp.

Hot applications on a frozen pipe do not produce results as quickly as direct flame, but they are much safer because they lessen the danger of fire and the possibility of bursting the pipe. The pipe can be wrapped with cloths and saturated with boiling water, or the boiling water can be poured directly over the pipe. In both cases, a receptacle should be placed below the pipe to catch the water.

And do not overlook the possibility of using chemical drain openers to thaw frozen drainpipes near sinks or bathtubs. These compounds generate a great deal of heat. A pound of salt poured down a drain, followed by boiling water, can also thaw a sink or bathtub drain.

DRAINING THE PLUMBING. For minor repairs, such as replacing a washer in a faucet, shutting off the supply valve for a fixture is sufficient. Where extensive repairs such as pipe changes are proposed, the main water supply should be cut off and the pipes drained. And if a house is to be vacated, with no heat provided during cold weather, it is advisable to drain the entire water system. You may want to hire a reliable plumber to perform this service and to do whatever else is necessary to protect the piping and fixtures against freezing and possible damage.

To drain the pipes, first shut off the water. Then, starting at the top floor, open all faucets. When water stops running from the faucets, open the cap in the main valve or remove the plug to allow what little water that remains in the system to drain into a bucket or tub.

The water standing in the traps under sinks, toilets, tubs, lavatories, and showers should be removed by opening the traps and draining them, by forcing the water out with a force cup, or by drawing it out with a suction pump or a siphon hose.

Empty the toilet tanks by flushing them after the water has been turned off, and take out any surplus water with a sponge or cloth. Fill each trap with a half cup of auto antifreeze.

If a house is to be left unoccupied, the water heater should be emptied by opening the faucet at the bottom of the tank. All hot water faucets should be open while the tank is being drained. The gas pilot should be turned off.

If the house is heated by hot water or steam and is to be left unoccupied during the winter, the heating system should be drained. To drain the system, turn off the pilot, shut off the main water supply valve at the wall or curb, and draw off the water from the boiler by opening the draw-off cock at the lowest point in the heating system. The water supply valve to the boiler should be opened so that no water will remain trapped above it. After that, in any hot water system, open the air valves on all radiators as the water lowers; begin at the highest radiators. In a one-pipe steam system, open every radiator valve to release the water or condensation. After a heating system has been drained, never start a fire under the boiler until it has been properly refilled.

If a house is to be left vacant in the summer, it is not necessary to drain the water supply pipes, but the water should be shut off as a precaution against waste from a dripping faucet or damage from a leak.

TOILET MALFUNCTIONS AND REPAIRS. Most of the common malfunctions of toilets are easy to repair. If you have been suffering the inconveniences of a toilet that won't flush unless you hold down the handle, that won't stop running unless you tap the handle, or that makes strange noises as it fills, suffer no more.

The illustration accompanying this article will acquaint you with the flushing mechanism and the terms that describe it. Although the general designs and the flushing mechanisms of toilets vary, they are enough alike that you should be able to apply the general repair instructions.

Before trying to make any repairs, however, take the tank lid off and set it in a place where it will not get bumped. Flush the toilet and watch carefully as the mechanism functions. Careful observation should pinpoint the source of trouble. When you have it figured out, close the cut-off valve and flush the toilet again to empty the tank. If your toilet does not have a cut-off, flush it and lift up the float rod immediately. Work quickly but gently to avoid bending the rod. Support the float with a wire coat hanger, bent to fit over the front and back edges of the tank and under the float rod.

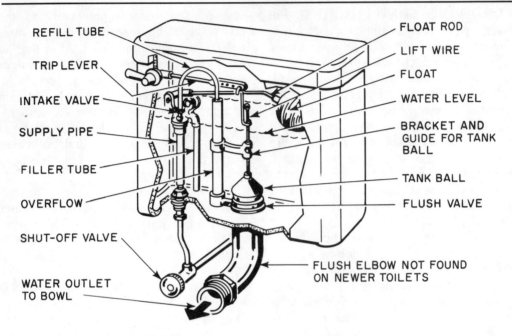

REFILL TUBE

TRIP LEVER

INTAKE VALVE

SUPPLY PIPE

FILLER TUBE

OVERFLOW

SHUT-OFF VALVE

WATER OUTLET
TO BOWL

FLOAT ROD

LIFT WIRE

FLOAT

WATER LEVEL

BRACKET AND
GUIDE FOR TANK
BALL

TANK BALL

FLUSH VALVE

FLUSH ELBOW NOT FOUND
ON NEWER TOILETS

COMMON FLUSHING MECHANISM

The parts that usually require repairs are the flush valve, the intake valve and the float.

The tank ball, which closes the flush valve, is made of rubber in older toilets. The rubber may soften and lose its shape, and the wire and guide that lift and lower the ball may malfunction. If the ball and valve do not form a perfect seal, water will trickle into the toilet bowl after flushing. If the lift wire does not lower the ball onto the valve seat, water will continue to run into the bowl after flushing, and the tank will not fill. If the lift wire does not lift the ball high enough, the toilet may not flush unless you hold the handle down.

When the ball is the source of a flush valve problem, unscrew it from the lift wire and install a new one. When the trip lever or lift wire are malfunctioning, clean off any corrosion or replace the parts, as necessary.

If a hardware or plumbing dealer tries to sell you a new flushing mechanism, consider it. Many of the newer types are virtually trouble-free.

The float shuts off the flow of water through the intake valve when the tank refills after flushing. If the valve does not close fully after the tank has filled, the water will keep running and trickle down the overflow pipe. Lift the float (by the rod, please) to see if you can stop the flow of water. If you can stop it, then the float does not rise high enough during normal operation of the mechanism. It may have water in it, or the rod may simply need to be bent down a little so that the float rides higher in the tank. In the latter case, grip the rod firmly in two places and bend—slowly and gradually. Don't exert pressure on the float itself because you could easily cause a leak in it.

A waterlogged or leaky float is easy to diagnose. It will feel a bit too heavy, and you will hear water sloshing around in it. Screw it off the rod and replace it—preferably with a leak-proof plastic one.

Lifting the float will not close the intake valve if a worn washer is responsible for the leakage. This valve is a simple faucet. To get to the washer, remove the two thumb-screws that hold the float rod levers and push out the levers. Lift out the valve stem, and check the washer. Replace it and any corroded brass parts, or buy a new valve assembly. Examine the valve seat and reface it if necessary.

In some cases the intake valve may not be responsible for that trickle of water after the tank has filled. The overflow tube may be rotted away at the base in an old toilet. If it is, it will allow water to trickle into the toilet bowl, too. Check this possibility and replace the tube if necessary.

Common sources of noise when the tank is filling are the intake valve and the filler tube.

You will hear a whine or gurgle when the tank refills if the flow adjustment on the intake valve lets too little water through.

A noisy cascade of water when the tank refills should prompt you to look for a leaking or broken filler tube.

An obstruction in the toilet trap or leakage around the bottom of the bowl may require removal of the toilet. Follow this procedure:

1. Shut off the water.
2. Empty the tank by flushing it, empty the bowl by siphoning or sponging out the water.
3. Disconnect the water supply pipes to the tank.
4. Disconnect the tank from the bowl if

the toilet is a two-piece unit. Set the tank where it cannot be damaged. Handle tank and bowl carefully; they are made of vitreous china or porcelain and are easily chipped or broken.

5. Remove the seat and cover from the bowl.
6. Carefully pry loose the bolt covers, and remove the bolts holding the bowl to the floor flange.
7. Jar the bowl enough to break the seal at the bottom. Set the bowl upside down on something that will not chip or break it.
8. Remove the obstruction from the discharge opening.
9. Place a new wax seal around the closet horn and press it in place. A wax seal or gasket may be obtained from hardware or plumbing supply stores.
10. Set the bowl in place and press it down firmly. Install the bolts that hold it to the floor flange. Draw the bolts up snugly, but not too tight because the bowl may break. The bowl must be level. Keep a carpenter's level on it while drawing up the bolts. If the house has settled, causing the

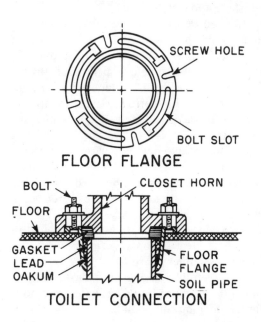

FLOOR FLANGE

TOILET CONNECTION

floor to slope, it may be necessary to use shims to make the bowl sit level. Replace the bolt covers.

11. Install the tank, and connect the water supply pipes to it. Be sure to replace all gaskets—after cleaning the surfaces thoroughly.

12. Test for leaks by flushing a few times.

13. Install the seat cover.

INSTALLING FIXTURES. A careful workman protects bathroom fixtures from blows, scratches, falls, and other mishaps during delivery, room finishing, and installation. He sees that fixtures are well covered with suitable materials and that plaster, paints, and acids do not get on them.

The damaged surface of a porcelain fixture cannot be restored. Special fiber glass repair materials are available for fiber glass fixtures. When competently applied, they restore the damaged areas to new condition.

Here are some tips on fixture care during finishing and installation:

1. Uncrate fixtures carefully. Leave protective wrappings on.

2. If fixtures are delivered uncovered, cover them with several layers of strong wrapping paper held in place with tape or cover them with corrugated cardboard or with materials available from plumbing suppliers.

3. Do not use newspaper or dyed paper next to enamel; they may leave permanent stains. Newspapers can be used for added protection if a fixture is first covered with unprinted paper or plastic.

4. Keep fixtures and roughed-in plumbing clear of tools, scrap lumber, wet paper, and other debris.

5. Carefully remove any plaster or cement on a fixture by using water or a nongritty cleaning compound.

6. Soften paint drips with the recommended solvent and remove them carefully.

You should get expert advice in planning the installation of bathroom fixtures. Some points to consider are selection of materials, clearance between fixtures and adjacent or facing walls, access to pipes for repairs, and ability of floors and walls to support fixtures.

Bathroom fixtures are available at different price levels. The price depends on the material of which the fixture is made, the size, the styling, and the color.

Vitreous china is always used for toilets, and can be used for lavatories. Porcelain enameled cast iron and pressed steel are used for tubs and lavatories. All china and porcelain enameled fixtures now on the market are acid resisting.

In recent years, fiber glass fixtures of good quality have become available. The gloss and color of the gel coat finish is similar in appearance to that of enameled or china fixtures and is resistant to ordinary household chemicals. Tub-shower units and shower stalls that are made in one unit with the surrounding wall area have the advantage of leakproof construction.

The matter of clearance is perhaps most crucial when it comes to installing a toilet. Allow a minimum of 18 in. clearance at the front and 15 in. at the side. To determine the front clearance, measure from the front edge of the bowl to the wall. To determine the side clearance, measure from the center of the bowl to the wall. If you are planning to install a new toilet on an existing floor flange, measure the distance from the back wall to the center of the flange; toilets are built with differing back clearances.

Planning for access to the bathroom plumbing for repairs can save much struggle and expense later on—especially with bathtub plumbing. Try to arrange for an access panel behind the bathroom wall. It is ideal if this panel can be put in a closet, but it can also be hidden behind a door or decorative panel in an adjoining room.

In a bathroom remodeling project, have floor joists and wall studs checked by an experienced builder to make sure they will support the planned installation. Porcelain enameled cast iron and steel sinks and tubs are heavy. Fiber glass fixtures are comparatively lightweight and therefore lend themselves to remodeling projects where the structure may not support heavier fixtures.

POLYETHYLENE—Uses

Polyethylene film or sheeting is one of the most practical modern developments, and is now being used in almost every phase of our commercial and industrial activities.

Polyethylene film has a wide and varied role in the building industry. It can also be of great assistance to the handyman in his work around the home.

The sheeting is manufactured in various widths and lengths and in thicknesses ranging from .0015 to .010. The thicknesses mainly used in building work is from .002 to .010. It is made in natural and black.

You can use the sheeting as a waterproof membrane under concrete floors to prevent the penetration of moisture through the concrete to the surface. It can be used as sarking under roof sheeting, or behind the external wall sheeting.

When it is used as sarking the thickness can be .002 or .004. A heavier sheeting, such as .006 can be used as the membrane under concrete floors.

Black polyethylene sheeting .010 in thickness and of suitable widths can be the dampproof course in brickwork and as flashing around door and window openings.

You can use it as a temporary weather barrier over door and window openings while waiting for these items to arrive on the job. When employed for this purpose it has the advantage of allowing plenty of light in, while excluding wind and rain.

Polyethylene is also extensively used to protect valuable building materials from rain and dust.

POWER TOOLS — Basic Procedure

Here are some details of using power tools to the best advantage.

GENERAL USAGE:

1. When using a power tool, try to keep your hands from covering the air vents, which serve to keep the motor cool.

2. If, through heavy usage, the power tool does become over-heated, don't switch off at once. Disengage it from the work and leave the motor running for about thirty seconds. This will draw cool air through the motor.

3. Store the power tool in a dry atmosphere. If it is kept in a garden shed, the motor could get damp and short-circuit. If any excessive sparking occurs when the motor is running, switch off at once and have the power tool examined—a precaution that could save an expensive repair.

4. Always ensure that the ground wire is connected unless you have a double insulated power tool, which is marked accordingly.

5. Wherever possible material to be worked on should be securely fastened. Generally clamps or a vice will be sufficient, but sometimes entire areas need to be clear—when sanding, for instance. One possibility when the work is too big to be gripped securely is to pin down to the bench through waste edges, areas to be hidden by joints, etc. Another useful method is to drive nails at intervals around the piece

of work, so that it cannot slide about. The security and stability gained is worth the **little extra work.**

6. When sharpening on a grinding wheel, avoid excessive heat build-up in the tool being sharpened, which should be dipped frequently in cold water.

7. To keep the power supply cable clear of the work in hand, wind a length of cable round an arm, leaving most of the spare cable behind the body, and the shortest practical length between the hand and the tool.

8. When fitting a power tool attachment, tighten up on all three holes in the chuck. Using just one could cause the attachment to slip.

9. For better workmanship and a longer life for the power tool, operate it at speeds appropriate to the work being done. High speed operations are: sawing, planing, orbital and rotary sanding, small diameter drilling, hedge trimming and floor polishing. Low and medium-speed operations are: paint stripping, paint stirring, turning, metal polishing, furniture polishing, large diameter drilling.

DRILLING:

10. When drilling, keep to the maximum sizes of twist drills and wood boring bits recommended for the power tool. Larger capacity drills with shanks ground down to fit a smaller chuck will throw undue strain on the motor.

11. Ordinary twist drills are suitable for drilling soft metals, but for anything harder than mild steel, high speed drills (marked HS on the shank) are necessary. When drilling in wood, use wood-boring bits in preference to twist drills. A wood bit gives a greater speed in drilling and throws less strain on the motor.

12. A masonry drill should be used at a low speed, to keep the tungsten tip cool and

to safeguard it from chipping. If you haven't got a variable-speed drill or speed-reducing chuck, apply the drill to the work for a few seconds at a time. Switch off after each operation, and cool the tungsten tip in water.

13. A rough and ready depth gauge can be made for drilling by wrapping a strip of adhesive tape round the bit at the required depth.

14. When using a wood-boring bit, allow the drill to stop spinning before withdrawing the bit from the hole. This is to prevent the flank of the drill head from tearing the wood around the entry of the hole.

15. **In drilling metal, first use a center-**punch to make a start for the drill. If you don't the drill will wander and produce inaccurate drilling.

16. For stirring paint in small cans (up to quart size) secure a meat skewer in the chuck. Switch off before removing the skewer from the paint.

SANDING:

17. For all sanding operations, select a sanding sheet one or two grades finer than you think you need. The speed of a power tool makes it a fast waste remover, even when a fine grain paper is used, and the finer the grain, the greater the degree of control.

18. Keep the face of a sanding disc at an angle of about 15 degrees to the work, so that between 1 and $1\frac{1}{2}$ in. of disc surface is in contact. This gives a fine control over the disc and avoids the erratic motion that throws a power tool out of control when a disc is applied flat. A wire brush should be applied in a similar manner.

19. Take great care when using a sanding disc for finishing work, because its edge will tend to dig in and produce ridges in a flat surface. Keep the disc moving, and apply it lightly. An orbital sander will pro-

duce a vastly superior finish. For a glass-like finish, first work through coarse, medium and fine-grade papers with the orbital sander. Then wet the surface of the wood to raise the grain, and sand down again with the worn fine paper used earlier.

SAWING:

20. When sawing, switch on so that the blade is running before it bites into the work. If the teeth are engaged when the motor is switched on, the blade may jam, causing rapid and heavy overload of the motor.

21. Make sure that wood is well supported before sawing. Any sag or other distortion in the work could clench the blade, causing an overload.

22. Never assume a saw attachment is square. Check before cutting by holding a try-square against sole-plate and blade.

23. Use a spare piece of wood as a push stick when feeding the last few inches of a board into a bench saw.

24. Place plastic laminates face downwards if cutting with a power saw. The cut must go into the finished side on plastic laminates, and a circular saw blade cuts upwards. A jig saw can be used for rough cutting, but is not recommended for precision trimming of plastic laminates.

25. For smooth, professional results with a jigsaw, clamp the work firmly. The aim is to eliminate as much vibration as possible.

POWER TOOLS — Choice

Electrically operated power tools make do-it-yourself easier, but many handymen find it difficult to decide which type to buy from the wide range available.

Power tools can be divided roughly into two types—portable tools and bench tools. Bench tools are the ones mounted on some fixed support.

The first question that faces the man who has decided to buy a power tool is whether to get individual tools, each doing a specific job, or a combination tool that can be adapted to do a variety of jobs.

This is a matter not only of expense, but also of the kind and amount of work he plans to do, and also of the workshop space available.

For most handymen, the portable combination tool kit will do all they want, and it is much less expensive than the more elaborate bench tools.

Such a portable kit is essentially an electric drill fitted with many kinds of attachments, which enable it to be used also for sawing, sanding, buffing, grinding, and so on.

The drill is naturally the most important unit in any power tool kit, and the dual-speed type with a chuck capacity of $\frac{3}{8}$ in. is ideal.

A comprehensive kit may contain as many as twenty-four separate items, all packed into a sturdy metal carrying case.

Such a kit will do the work of a saw, grooving plane, grindstone, power polisher for small floors and other jobs, shaper, and wood, metal or masonry drill.

For the handyman who wants a bigger job, and is prepared to pay more, there are many types of circular-saw benches.

The modern sawbench—essentially a circular saw with attachments—will rip, cross-cut, miter, cut compound angles, grooves and moldings.

With it can be made windows, screens, picture frames, flower boxes, and furniture of all types—in fact, almost any job that involves straight-line cutting.

For general use, a sawbench with an 8 in. diameter saw blade operated by a $\frac{3}{4}$ h.p. motor is the most suitable for a home workshop.

Three basic blades will be needed for use with such a unit. They are the rip, cross-cut, and novelty blades. The latter is slightly hollow-ground, and has no set on the teeth. It makes an extremely smooth cut without splintering, and is ideal for cutting plywood and other processed boards.

PRIMERS — And Sealers

The terms sealer and primer are very much in the handyman's vocabulary, but many questions are asked about their exact meaning and the difference between them.

In certain circumstances, they mean much the same thing, but a primer is nearly always used to precede a coat of paint, whereas a sealer might be used as a final coat. To take a very simple example: New wood should be primed before painting with undercoat and finishing coats. In this case the primer is a thin red-lead base paint that soaks some way into the wood and makes it less absorbent.

A prepared "pink primer" sold by all paint stores is perhaps the most convenient type for general use. If a primer were not used, there would be a risk that the paint would soak in and leave little more than the pigment on the surface.

That would soon flake off, and the wood would suffer. These points naturally refer specifically to oil paint application on exterior woodwork or other exposed surfaces.

A good example of a sealer is the plastic fluid that can be applied to, say, a stained floor. It protects the surface by sealing the pores of the wood. But when we come to sealers for hardboard for example, they are hard to separate from primers. Such sealers serve the same purpose as does the usual pink primer on new woodwork.

A spirit varnish like shellac works very well, and so does metallic aluminum paint. They both seal the surface so that it is uniformly porous. The sealing prevents that patchy appearance of which many complain when they paint hardboard without applying sealer or primer first.

And then there are wall sealers—or primers. Size is used before painting with non-washable waterpaint or before paperhanging. This prevents too much waterpaint or paste being soaked up by the plaster, and ensures that the wall surface is equally porous all over.

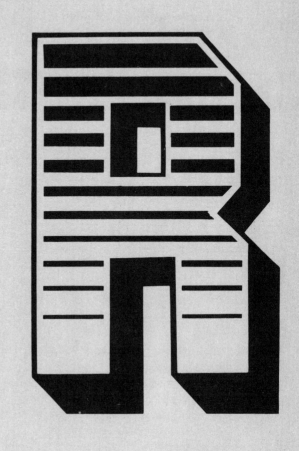

RASP-PLANE TOOL	Uses
REPAIR PLATES	Uses
RIVETS	To Use
ROLLER BLINDS	Adjust
ROLLER PAINTING	Advantages
ROOF	Gutter Care
RUBBER	Needs Care

RASP-PLANE TOOL — Uses

In any minimum kit of tools that could be suggested for the homeworker there are three that are included automatically.

These are a plane, rasp, and a flat file of some kind. All are designed for finishing either the face or edge of timber.

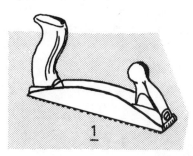

A tool of the type shown in Fig. 1 combines the features of all these, together with others peculiar to itself. It is available in either the plane or file type, Fig. 2.

The tool is basically a cutting strip held in a rigid frame. This cutting strip is made up of hundreds of extremely sharp cutting edges which give a controlled depth of cut, and may be replaced when necesasry.

The main advantage of this tool is that it can be used on wood, rubber, leather, fiber, plastic sheets, and non-ferrous metals.

Unlike a solid file, the cutting face of this tool is unlikely to clog as the waste passes through the pattern of fine openings formed by the extruded cutting edges on the surface.

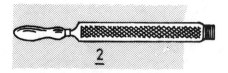

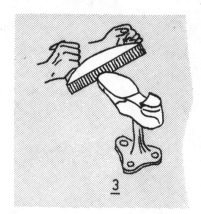

A typical use for the plane-type version of the tool is shown in Fig. 3 where the sole of a shoe is being trimmed to a smooth finish after repairs.

REPAIR PLATES — Uses

In many households today, when "make-do-and-mend" is the rule, there are some simple repair jobs to furniture, and other articles, which can be cheaply and effectively carried out by the use of repair plates. These plates, which are made of sheet brass or iron, are obtainable in various sizes and shapes, as shown in the accompanying illustrations, and are provided with countersunk holes for fixing screws.

LOOSE JOINTS: A loose joint between the seat rail and leg of a chair can be made firm again by screwing an angle plate in the corner, as in Fig. 1, after applying a little glue to the joint.

Picture frames sometimes become loose at the corner joints owing to a fall. In such cases it is a simple matter to screw on a thin brass L-shaped plate, as in Fig. 2, after gluing the joint.

Loose joints are a common source of trouble with front garden gates, a broken tenon often being the cause. This can be

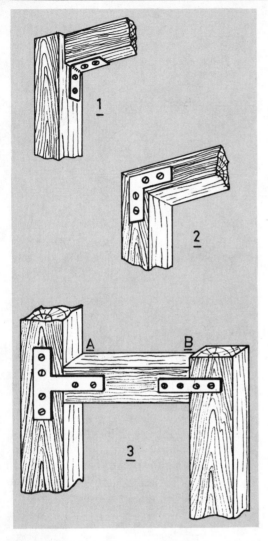

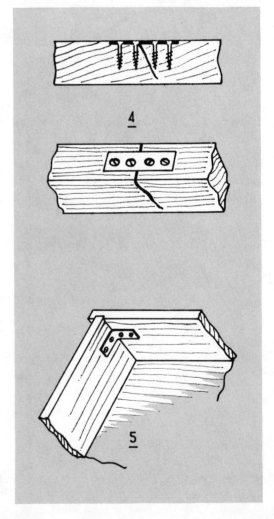

FRACTURES: Where an upright, or leg of a piece of furniture becomes fractured, it can be made good by fixing a repair plate, as shown in Fig. 4.

The wood should be recessed with a chisel so that the plate can be screwed in place flush with the surface of the wood. It would be as well to apply a little hot glue to the cracked part before finally fixing the plate.

Repair plates can also be used for strengthening the corners of boxes, and drawers, as shown in Fig. 5.

remedied by means of an iron T-shaped repair plate, as at (A) Fig. 3. When a top rail joint of a gate works loose it can be strengthened in the same way by a repair plate, either of angle pattern, or straight, as at B (Fig. 3).

If the repair plates are fixed on the inside of the gate, with the correct size screws, so that the heads of the screws come flush with the surface of the plates, and are painted over the same color as the gate, they will hardly be noticeable.

DECK CHAIR REPAIR. The weak parts of the framework of a folding deck chair are usually the notched parts of the sloping members which take the horizontal struts of adjusting the position of the seat. These members sometimes fracture at one of the notched portions, as indicated at Fig. 6.

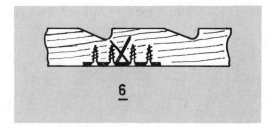

6

In such cases a strong repair can be effected by the use of a stout brass repair plate. If the faulty member is completely severed, apply some waterproof glue to the two fractured surfaces, and fix the joint with one or two panel pins to hold the parts together while the glue is setting. Cut a recess on the underside of the member to take the repair plate, and fix it in place with four countersunk screws, as indicated in the sketch.

RIVETS — To Use

The rivet is one of the most effective and practical ways of joining two or more metal surfaces together.

Other types of rivet are used extensively for leatherwork, and the planks of small boats are generally fixed together with copper rivets.

In many repair jobs around the home rivets can be used instead of solder.

Rivets are not advisable for every type of joint, and care should be exercised in choosing the right kind for the job.

The round or snap-head and the countersunk are, perhaps, used more than any other type. These are clearly shown in Fig. 1.

The top row of Fig. 1 shows various rivets before use, and the bottom row as they appear when finished off.

Before describing the various rivets in detail, let us first consider a few practical hints which will apply in general to most of them.

The size of the rivet—that is, the diameter of its shank—should not be greater than three times the thickness of the sheet.

The rivet hole should be only slightly larger than the rivet shank—the clearance need not be more than about 5 per cent of the diameter.

When working in sheet metal the distance between rivets should never be less than three times the diameter of the rivet, or greater than eight times, if a strong job is wanted.

Rivets should not be placed too near the edge of sheet metal—twice the diameter of the rivet is the very closest—otherwise the

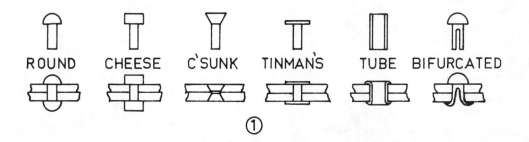

ROUND   CHEESE   C'SUNK   TINMAN'S   TUBE   BIFURCATED

①

joint will be weakened. Any burrs made in drilling or punching the holes should be filed flat so that the edges are clean and flush.

Failure to do this will result in a bad joint, and if it is on a utensil for holding a liquid there is bound to be a leakage.

The amount that the shank of a rivet projects beyond the sheets to be joined is important. A safe rule is to allow about one and a half times the diameter of the rivet.

All rivets should be comparatively soft so that a well-shaped and evenly spread head will be formed during the hammering.

When the rivet is not made of the same metal as the job, then the rivet should be the softer of the two.

Even when both metals are alike the rivet should be annealed.

The round-head, or snap rivet as it is sometimes called, is used more than other types, and for hand-riveting it is best. To form a neat, round head is quite an art and requires a certain amount of practice.

After passing the rivet through the sheets to be joined, don't hit directly on the end with a heavy hammer, as this may cause it to fracture and probably bulge badly in the the center.

A series of light taps is much better, and these should be started round the edge of the projecting shank and gradually worked toward the center.

Round-head rivets, and also their companion, the cheese-head type, Fig. 1, can be bought quite cheaply in a large variety of sizes and of various metals such as copper and aluminum.

In some jobs it is necessary that the head of the rivet should not project above the surface, and here the countersunk rivet may be used.

The ordinary countersunk rivet, however, can be used only on medium and thick material. It is not satisfactory for sheet metal thinner than 20 gauge because of the need to recess the hole to accommodate the countersunk head.

Thin metal sheets are usually held together by a tinman's flat-head rivet, Fig. 1, the head of which covers quite a large area and helps to keep the thin sheets in close contact.

For small work, where there is very little strain, a tubular rivet is sometimes used, and a good example of this type is the eyelet of a shoe.

Special punches are necessary to make a satisfactory job. Fig. 2 shows a pair of such punches ready to close over the ends of a tubular rivet.

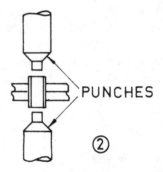

Another very useful rivet is the bifurcated type.

Chiefly used in leather and fiber work, it is only necessary to place it in the holes and clinch over the projecting ends.

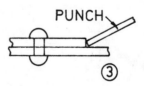

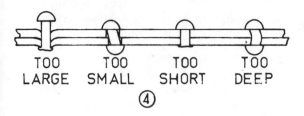

TOO LARGE   TOO SMALL   TOO SHORT   TOO DEEP

④

To draw two riveted plates together to form a watertight joint, a process called caulking is sometime adopted.

This can be done only when thick plates are used. It consists of hammering along the edge of one of the plates with a punch as shown in Fig. 3 to force the edge of the metal into close contact with the other plate.

A few of the main mistakes to avoid when using rivets are shown clearly in Fig. 4.

ROLLER BLINDS — Adjust

Temperamental spring roller blinds which jerk back suddenly, hang limp, jump off the brackets, or develop other faults, are not difficult to adjust.

When a shade will not wind up properly, pull it all the way down to the window sill. Then remove the roller holding the fully extended shade or blind material from its brackets and roll the shade up by hand.

Replace the roller on the brackets, and test the shade for winding tension. If the tension is still too weak, repeat the process.

Each time you wind the shade by hand in this way it serves to wind the spring tighter.

If the spring tension in a roller blind is too great, making it snap or jerk up too rapidly, reverse the winding procedure outlined for the limp shade fault.

Raise the shade to the top of the window and remove the roller from the brackets as before. Then unroll the shade about half-way by hand, and replace the roller on the brackets. This unwinds the spring to reduce tension.

Occasionally a roller blind will fall from a window because the space between the supporting brackets is too wide. If these brackets are on the outside of the window frame it is a simple matter to move one of the brackets in slightly.

Move it until there is just enough clearance—about the thickness of a quarter—to allow the roller to turn without binding.

Pry off the metal cap that fits over the end of the roller at what is known as the dead end and fit a thick cardboard or plywood spacing disc which is the same diameter as the roller.

Then push the cap back on, crimp it to the roller, and replace the roller on the brackets.

In most cases the adjustment needed to make the distance between the brackets correct is very slight. Where it is not possible to alter the position of one bracket as suggested, the roller itself may be lengthened.

When shades roll up or down unevenly in a jerking fashion, there are three possible causes of trouble—a broken spring, a warped roller, or a bent or corroded pin on the dead end of the roller.

There is little you can do about the first two, except to buy a new roller.

A pair of pliers should straighten a bent pin and a piece of emery cloth or some steel wool will clean any rust off the pin and allow it to run freely.

A roller blind that won't stay put can usually be fixed easily.

Take the blind down and look at the spring end of the roller. You'll see a little recess with two small pieces of metal—the pawls or tumblers—which are pivoted so that they can move up and down by gravity.

When working properly, the pawls should move freely and should drop into the gap in the shaft as the blind is rotated. This provides the locking action which stops the blind.

But dust, rust, fluff or other foreign matter sometimes gets in the little recess and prevents the pawls moving freely.

Using a pin or metal skewer, clean out the recess. Then use a tiny brush dipped in kerosene to complete the cleaning, and wipe dry with a piece of soft rag on the end of a matchstick.

If there is any rust, the kerosene will help to remove it, so that the pawls can move freely again.

Oil must not be used on the pawls, however, because it will gather dust and make them stick again, although you can use a little talc or French chalk, which acts as a lubricant.

ROLLER PAINTING — Advantages

In the sphere of home decoration, there is often discussion about the comparable merits of brush and roller painting.

There is nothing new in the idea of applying paint and color by rolling it on. The printing trade has rolled on ink for hundreds of years, and despite antagonism and conservatism, there appears to be a strong case for the inclusion of a paint roller in the kit of every painter.

However, it is obvious that the roller will never supersede the brush as a painting tool. It should be used in conjunction with the brush.

For example, the brush will always be used for cutting-in at sharp corners, and the brush, too, is naturally supreme on highly irregular surfaces, such as the old-style highly ornate plaster ceilings, and on window frames.

On the other hand, the roller is claimed to be much superior to the brush on surfaces with a rough or textured finish.

Brush wear is severe on rough surfaces, and a lot of work is necessary to get effective coverage with a brush, but with a roller, both time and labor is cut considerably.

Tests have proved that the time taken to paint, say, a cement rendered wall or a porous wallboard surface with a 7 in. roller is half that taken to do the same job with a 5 in. wide brush and using the same paint.

It is simple enough to go further and experiment on a textured concrete or plaster surface. One stroke of a brush, even when heavily loaded with paint, will only skim the surface, showing a lot of holes and sections untouched. But one stroke of the roller will press paint into every minute crack and crevice.

It is sometimes said that paint applied by roller does not have good adhesion. The fact is that the paint applied to a rough surface with a brush, unless it is forcibly stippled in, tends to be merely dragged over the surface, whereas the action of a woven-fabric roller especially is to force the paint into the surface under pressure.

There is scarcely anything which the paint roller cannot paint easily and swiftly. Paint may be rolled right over wallpaper, plaster, wallboard, brick, concrete, and other surfaces.

Oil, rubber base, and water base paints can be used with equal success with rollers. These include flat, gloss, and semi-gloss, enamels, varnish, aluminum paint, and shellac. Most of these can be used just as they come from the can.

To begin painting, the roller tray, which can be placed conveniently on the floor or table, or attached to the ladder top or rung, should be filled about half way up its slanted surface. Lining the tray with heavy paper or aluminum foil will save cleaning and permit quick changes of color.

Before actually painting the main wall surfaces of a room with a roller, a small trim roller or brush should be used progressively to cut in along the cornice or ceiling edge, and around architraves and skirtings. Do not do this trimming on more than one wall at a time.

A 7 in. roller is suitable for most general home jobs, and after being dipped into the paint tray, is rolled back and forth on the ribbed base of the tray to remove excess.

Paint is applied to the surface with an easy back and forth rolling motion in any direction. Some workers recommend a criss-cross starting stroke.

Be sure to keep the roller on the wall without spinning at the end of the stroke, and progress slowly and carefully into the previously trimmed edge, to within an inch or two of windows, corners, and edges.

Painting ceilings, one of the most tiring jobs, can be done easily with a long-handled roller. There are three important points to note for success in ceiling painting.
1. The roller should be worked easily back and forth across the narrowest dimension.
2. Care should be taken not to lift the roller from the surface nor to spin it.
3. Work should not be stopped until the entire ceiling is completed.

This will prevent the appearance of distinct lap marks. There is no more bending, stooping, or tedious kneeling associated with floor painting when a long-handled roller, or a regular roller attached to an extension handle, is used. Floors of concrete, wood, or linoleum can be covered with equal success.

Apart from the standard paint rollers for walls and ceilings, there are others designed for special purposes. There are those molded or shaped to suit the corrugations in sheet roofing, and also a range of design rollers. These permit you to roll a wallpaper pattern on the wall surface.

ROOF — Gutter Care

Because the inside of a roof gutter is not seen from the ground, it very rarely receives any attention in the way of protection from rust and corrosion.

It is only when a leak develops, or the downpipe becomes blocked and causes the gutter to overflow, that something is done about putting things right.

In all cases, the first precaution necessary to prevent the gutter becoming a chronic trouble spot around the home is to see that it is lined up properly with sufficient fall towards the downpipe openings.

This is something that should be done when the house is built, and sufficient downpipes to carry off the volume of water from the roof must also be provided.

A frequent cause of damaged gutters is the resting of ladders against them carelessly when it becomes necessary to climb on to the roof, or when painting work is being done.

Here, too, the edge of the gutter is often used as a stepping stone from roof to ladder, with the result that the gutter is distorted and a depression is formed.

This in turn means that rain water will collect in pools which may lie stagnant for days.

Even if all the precautions mentioned are observed, there still remains the problem of keeping the inside of the gutter and downpipes clear of leaves and other rubbish which could block the free flow of the water.

This should be listed as a regular maintenance job to be carried out every three or four months, and, in addition, the inside of the gutter should be painted occasionally with a bituminous roof paint as protection against rust.

However, this painting should only be done when the metal has been cleaned thoroughly and is dry.

A clip-on mesh has been developed to keep leaves and other debris out of gutters. Illustration (A) shows the general application of the mesh, with a close-up view at (B).

The mesh allows water to flow freely through it, but the grid is small enough to keep leaves and twigs on top of it, for the wind to blow away.

It is embedded at one edge in a continuous plastic extrusion designed to grip the gutter edging.

The home handyman needs only a ladder and a pair of tinsnips to fit the mesh himself.

Apart from the fact that the installation of such material will help to prevent the risk of damage to the gutter, it also minimizes the hazard of fire which is always present when leaves accumulate in gutters during the hot summer months.

(A)

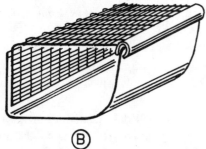

(B)

RUBBER — Needs Care

Household articles of rubber need care to preserve their resilience and usefulness.

When putting them away, do not shut rubber articles in a closed box or drawer. They need air to breathe in order to maintain their strength. Also choose a dark place in which to store rubber things, as they have a tendency to dry out in too much light. Therefore, if you keep them in a place that is not dark, first wrap the rubber objects in something like newspaper to prevent light penetration.

Folding a rubber apron or bed protection pad is not good practice, as it may crack on the folds. To prevent this, sprinkle a little cornstarch or talcum powder on the rubber articles before folding. Better than that, make a roll out of a few thicknesses of paper, or use a corrugated mailing tube, or an old broomstick, and roll the rubber article over it, avoiding wrinkling.

Rubber gloves worn for household chores must be handled with care. After your work is done, wash them carefully with warm water and soap while the gloves are still being worn. Rinse in clear water. Take the gloves off, sprinkle cornstarch or talcum powder inside them before putting them away.

Save old rubber rings from your preserve jars. Glue them to the bottom of book ends. lamp bases, ash trays, or other articles which might scratch the surface of a table top or desk. They are also useful to sew into the four corners on the underside of a small scatter rug to make the rug skid-proof.

A little known but very important fact worth noting is that rubber in any form should not be in contact with silverware. Even the simple act of wrapping silverware for storage in paper, and securing the paper wrapping with rubber bands has resulted in unsightly corrosion marks on the silver.

SALT	Many Uses
SAWDUST	Is Useful
SAW HORSE	For Large Work
SAW HORSE TRESTLE	To Make
SAWING	Methods
SAWS	Sharpening
SAWS	Tooth Details
SCISSORS	Keep Sharp
SCREEN DOORS	To Fit
SCREWDRIVERS	Types and Use
SCREW HEADS	Covering
SCREWS	Keep Secure
SCREWS	Selection
SEALERS	Some Uses
SHARPENING	Keep Angle
SHEET METAL	To Flatten
SHELLAC	Many Uses
SILVER	Care
SMALL TOOL	Using
SOLDERING	Main Points
SPOKESHAVE	Details
SQUARE	Roofing
SQUARE	Sliding
STAIRS	Stop Creaks
STEPS (Worn)	Repair
STONEWORK	Cut and Shape
STRAIGHT EDGE	Testing

SALT — Many Uses

In addition to seasoning food, common table salt has many other uses. Silver spoons tarnished by eggs are easily cleaned by rubbing them with damp salt.

Deep vases may be cleaned by allowing a solution of salt and vinegar to stand in them for an hour. Shake well, then wash and rinse.

If salt is used in the bottom part of a double boiler, the cooking time will be shortened.

Cracked eggs can be boiled without the whites running from them when a tablespoon of salt is added to the water.

When milk has been accidentally scorched, place the pan in cold water and add a pinch of salt to remove the scorched taste.

To be assured of whole nut kernels for special recipes, soak the nuts in salt water for twelve hours before cracking them.

A salt water bath will ease the itching caused by mosquito and other insect bites.

Fruit stains are removed from the hands by rubbing lemon juice and salt on the stains followed by a clear-water rinse.

A pinch of salt slowly swallowed will often stop an annoying tickling in the throat.

Salt eaten before taking bitter tasting medicine will render it tasteless and in a similar way, if a little salt is sprinkled over fresh pineapple before eating, it prevents the stinging of the tongue which usually occurs.

Salt can be used for removing mildew from linen. Mix salt, starch and lemon juice into a paste and apply to both sides of the fabric. Then lay it out in the sun until the stain disappears and wash in the usual way.

Perspiration stains are more easily removed from cotton clothing if soaked in salt water a few hours before washing.

To brighten the colors in an old carpet or rug, sprinkle it lightly with salt before sweeping or using the vacuum cleaner.

However, be very careful to pick up all the salt used in this way, as any left could absorb dampness and possibly show as a stain.

SAWDUST — Is Useful

Many home workers, especially those who own power woodworking machines, accumulate a lot of sawdust, which is generally swept away.

Sawdust, however, is a very useful by-product, and a sackful will have plenty of uses about the workshop and house.

As is well known, sawdust damped with disinfectant is useful for keeping down dust when sweeping.

Not so well known is the fact that if sawdust is scattered freely on the floor while some messy job, such as wallpapering, etc., is being done, subsequent cleaning up is made easy.

Lathe belts which have become oily and greasy may be cleaned by having fine sawdust rubbed into them with a stiff brush. When it is scraped off again most of the grease comes with it.

A rough finish may be given to certain wooden novelties by sprinkling them with sawdust which has first been sifted to remove hard lumps. Small objects may first be painted, and then, while the paint is still wet, sprinkled with the sawdust.

When dry the object is lightly brushed to remove loose particles and then given another thick coat of paint. For larger articles, especially those intended for outdoor use, the paint and sawdust can be mixed and then applied thickly.

Model-makers might bear the above in mind when trying to represent grass. If some sawdust is dyed green and sprinkled on a wet-glued surface it gives a realistic impression of a lawn.

SAW HORSE — For Large Work

A sawing horse of the type shown in the illustration will be found very useful around the home for numerous timber-sawing jobs, especially where the shape is irregular.

Perhaps the best timber for the legs is 3 in. by 2 in. hardwood. All other pieces are 3 in. by 1 in. hardwood. No fine carpentry is called for, and only one joint must be cut.

The setting out of the legs is done by crossing the two pieces on the workshop floor and positioning them to the dimensions given.

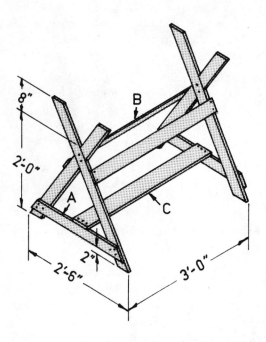

It is then easy to mark off the joint where the two cross. This joint is halved and screwed. Two sets of identical legs are required.

When both legs have been completed, they are strengthened and joined, the overall length of the horse being 3 ft. Piece (A) is first screwed in place, and as indicated in sketch, this is located 2 in. from the leg ends.

The two upper rails at (B) are next added to join the two sets of legs together. These pieces are positioned 1 in. from the cross of the legs on the lower side.

The bottom stretcher rail (C) is then secured to prevent spreading at the base of the legs. It is screwed directly to the center of the cross rails (A) at each end.

In use, make the saw-cut on any timber outside the frame to avoid sawing through the rails (B). Lower very large pieces of timber or logs gently into place, and, if necessary, add a bolt at each of the cross-joints to reinforce the screws.

SAW HORSE TRESTLE — To Make

Pair of trestles or saw horses made to the design in the illustration have the advantage of being very light in weight yet strong and sturdy.

The top at (A) is made first from a piece of softwood such as fir, measuring 4 in. wide, 2 in. thick, and 2 ft 6 in. long. When notching the recesses for the legs (B), note that they are beveled so as to give the bottom of the legs an overall spread of 1 ft 6 in.

The four legs (B) are cut from 1 in. thick fir or similar softwood to the size and shape shown. The tapered edges face inwards and the width between the outside edges of the

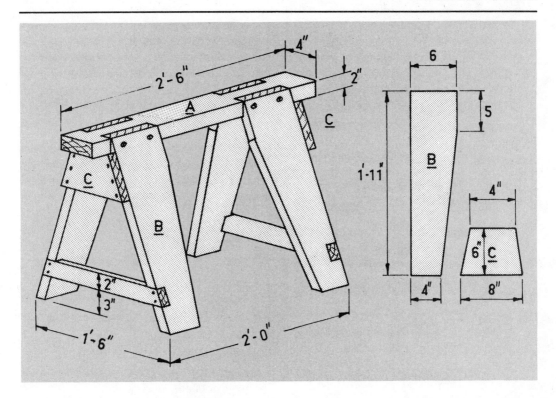

legs is 2 ft which means that the top overhangs the legs by 3 in. at each end. The depth of the beveled recesses in the top section should be sufficient to allow the legs to finish flush with the edges of the top; they are screwed with two countersunk head screws.

The bottom stretcher rails are housed into the bottom outside edges of the legs, and screwed into position. The small beveled pieces (C) which are used to strengthen the legs immediately under the top piece are not housed into the legs as are the stretcher rails; they are simply screwed on.

SAWING — Methods

If using a handsaw is just plain hard work and the results are never as good as you expect them to be, here are some things you will want to know.

Accurate sawing depends on:
1. Having a good sharp saw that is filed and set correctly.
2. Using the right saw for the job.
3. Applying the proper technique.

Quality saws have taper-ground blades that are thinner at the back than at the toothed edge. This makes sawing easier and minimizes binding of the blade in the cut or kerf.

Hand saws are made in two types—crosscut and rip. While they are interchangeable for short cuts, crosscut saws should be used for cutting across the grain in wood and rip saws for sawing with the grain.

The basic difference between crosscut and rip saws is in the shape of the teeth. The teeth of a crosscut saw are shaped like sharp pointed knives, whereas rip saw teeth are filed straight across to cut like a series of tiny chisels.

273

At all times the teeth in both crosscut and rip saws must be of equal height. The upper half of each tooth is bent or "set" in the direction of its flat side. Thus alternate teeth are set in opposite directions.

The set determines the width of the kerf, and its purpose is to allow the blade to move freely. As a general rule crosscut saws need more set than rip saws.

The number of tooth points of crosscut saws varies from seven to twelve points per inch, while an average rip saw would have five and a half points per inch. Coarse-tooth crosscut saws cut faster but leave a rougher surface than fine-tooth saws.

A coarse saw with considerable set is best for cutting green or wet wood, while a fine one is best for dry, seasoned timber.

Crosscut blades are made 20, 22, 24 and 26 in. long. Those shorter than 24 in. are called panel saws. Rip saws are usually 26 in. long.

The exact position of a saw cut should be marked off on the work. For a cut at right-angles to a straight edge use a square, and for other angles an adjustable bevel. Make the line either with a marking knife or sharp hard pencil.

Guide lines for ripping can be made with a marking gauge if the cut runs parallel to a straight edge. The saw kerf or cut should always be made in the waste portion of the stock outside the marked line. If the edge of a rip sawed board is to be planed to the line, make allowance for this when ripping.

When sawing bring your eye above the saw blade to observe if the blade is being held perpendicular to the work surface. If in doubt check with a try square as in Fig. 1. Grasp the saw handle comfortably and easily with the index finger pointing toward the saw tip, Fig. 2 to help in guiding the blade.

Whether crosscutting or ripping start a cut by setting the heel of the blade alongside the mark, then pulling the saw back slowly, guiding the blade with the thumb of your left hand about an inch above the teeth as in Fig. 3. The palm of the hand rests firmly on the work.

The correct sawing angles, 45 degrees for crosscutting and 60 degrees for ripping, should be maintained throughout cutting.

The starting stroke should be almost half the length of the blade, without any excessive pressure. The weight of a saw is enough to start a kerf if the blade is sharp.

Never start with a down stroke; you may apply too much pressure, splintering the wood or causing the saw to jump.

After the first back-stroke, push the saw forward without increasing the pressure and continue with short strokes until the kerf is deep enough to retain the blade.

When a saw drifts away from the marked line, apply a slight twist on the handle to bring it back, as in Fig. 4. Don't twist the blade forcibly, as this may kink it.

A saw that has a constant tendency to run off toward one side is not filed or set correctly, or the blade may be bent out of true.

Vibration of the saw blade on upstrokes usually indicates that it is being held at too steep an angle with the work. When the timber being cut pinches the blade, sawing becomes difficult and kinking of the blade may result.

When crosscutting you may be able to open the kerf slightly by exerting pressure on the waste portion with your hand. Or you can use a wedge above the saw position as in the rip sawing operation in Fig. 5.

1

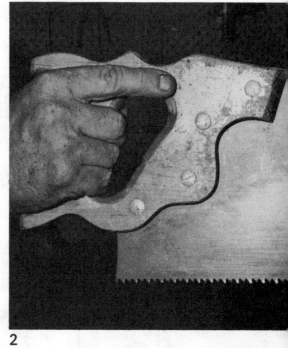

2

3

4

5

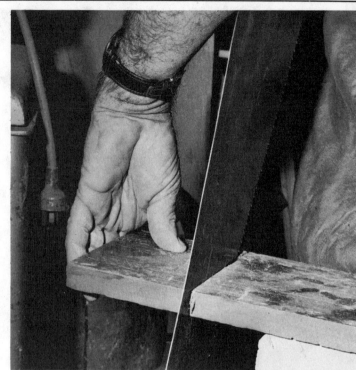

6

7

Sometimes binding occurs when cross-cutting a length of timber supported on stools. The remedy here is to move the off-cut section so that it projects, then hold with left hand while cut is made with right hand as in Fig. 6.

To avoid splintering when ripping a small section from a board hold it as in Fig. 7, until the full length of the cut has been completed.

SAWS — Sharpening

Every person who uses a saw, and especially those who plan to sharpen and set their own, should know that the complete job involves five steps, but all may not be necessary on all occasions.

1. JOINTING. The points of the teeth must be in line if each tooth is to do its share of cutting. A poor filing job, sawing into a nail, dropping the saw, or careless handling may result in some of the teeth being shorter than others. In such cases, a flint file is run lengthwise over the tops of the teeth until they are all even. This is called jointing, it is necessary only when some teeth are low.

2. RE-SHAPING TEETH. This step is necessary only after the jointing. Re-shaping is done by filing at right-angles to the blade. The gullets are filed to equal depths, the fronts and backs of the teeth to the proper angles, and the teeth to uniform size.

If the teeth are of unequal size, the file should be pressed against the sides of the larger ones until half of the flat tops are filed away. The tooth is filed to a point by filing in the next gullet. Cross-cut saw teeth are not beveled at this stage. Figs. 1 and 2 illustrate these details.

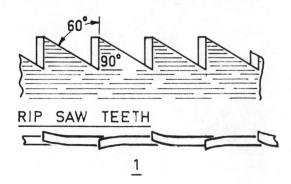

RIP SAW TEETH

1

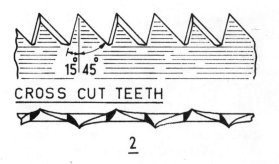

CROSS CUT TEETH

2

3. SETTING. The process of setting the teeth is discussed in Saws-Tooth Details. If it has been found necessary to joint and re-shape the teeth, resetting of the teeth will probably be necessary, too. A well tempered saw does not require resetting each time the teeth are touched up or sharpened.

4. FILING THE TEETH. When the teeth have the proper shape and set, sharp cutting edges are filed on the teeth. This step is very similar to shaping the teeth, except that in the case of cross-cut saws the file is held at an angle. Fig. 3 shows the position of the file and the correct shape of the teeth.

A fine flat file passed lightly over the tops of the teeth will leave a small bright point on each tooth, and this bright spot is a useful guide for finishing the filing of the teeth.

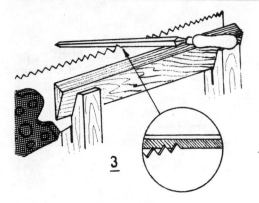

3

Rip saws are filed in the same way, except that here the teeth are filed straight across. Fig. 5 shows the different tooth shapes for cross-cut and rip saws.

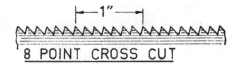

8 POINT CROSS CUT

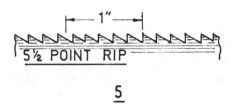

5½ POINT RIP

5

As the saw is in the vise, the teeth which are set away from the person sharpening the saw are filed first. Start in the gullet to the left of the first tooth, hold the file level, and push it across the saw.

If the saw is a cross-cut, the file should make an angle of about 45 to 60 degrees, and the work proceeds from the point of the saw towards the handle, Fig. 4.

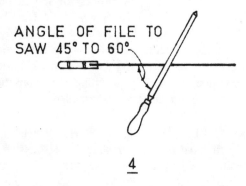

ANGLE OF FILE TO
SAW 45° TO 60°

4

Leave just a trifle of the shine on the point of the teeth when filing the first side, as this can be removed when the other side of the teeth is filed. Repeat this process in every second gullet throughout the length of the saw. The saw is then reversed and the alternate teeth filed in the same manner, starting again at the point and working towards the handle.

5. SIDE JOINTING. Side jointing of a saw that has been sharpened and set is often omitted, but an oilstone passed lightly along the sides of the teeth to remove any burr caused by the filing will result in a finer cutting saw.

SAWS — Tooth Details

Saws of various kinds are used in woodworking, but very few tradesmen or handymen know exactly how a saw cuts, so here are some details.

Wood consists of a mass of closely packed fibers running in one direction, called the way of the grain. Whenever a saw-cut is made in a piece of wood, either along or across the grain, these fibers must be severed by the saw teeth.

The important point as far as buying handsaws is concerned is that there are two basic types—the cross-cut saw and the rip saw. Taking the cross-cut saw first, see Fig. 1. When a knife is used to make two cuts about ⅟₁₆ in. apart across the grain of a piece of wood (A) Fig. 1 the fibers left between the cuts are very short and crumble away as the cuts are deepened.

The teeth of a cross-cut saw, specially designed for cutting across the grain of wood, are so arranged they do much the same thing to produce the kerf or sawcut shown at (B) Fig. 1. In effect, the saw teeth act like a series of knives as shown in (A) and (B) Fig. 2.

When a saw-cut is made along the grain of wood, a rip saw is needed, and here the cutting action is different.

To sever the fibers the teeth of the saw must now make cuts at right-angles to the blade, like chisels, as in Fig. 3. The saw teeth in a rip saw are thus formed into a series of chisels, one behind the other.

Details (A) and (B) Fig. 4 show this clearly.

To prevent the saw from jamming or binding in the saw-cut, the orthodox procedure is to set the teeth. Alternate teeth are bent outwards to make a kerf just wide enough to clear the blade of the saw. This is done with a special tool called a saw-set.

It is important to note that slightly more set is required on cross-cut saw teeth than on rip-saw teeth, and the cross-sectional views in Fig. 5 show clearly both the shape and set of both teeth.

To improve this clearance, and also produce a much cleaner and sharper cut, best quality saws are taper-ground.

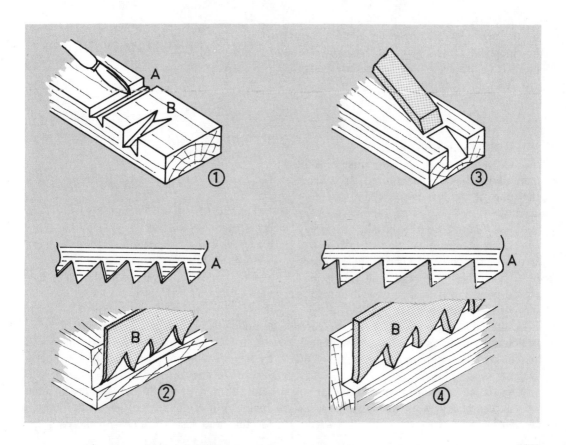

KNIFE POINTS
CUT FIBRES

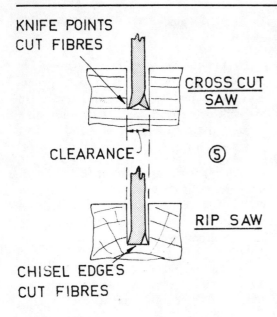

CROSS CUT
SAW

CLEARANCE ⑤

RIP SAW

CHISEL EDGES
CUT FIBRES

The blade is of uniform thickness along the toothed edge and near the handle, but the thickness of the blade is gradually reduced from the teeth toward the back edge and from the handle to the point of the blade.

SCISSORS — Keep Sharp

Like all cutting tools, scissors must be kept sharp if good work is required. It is most annoying trying to use a pair of blunt scissors.

Again, like all tools, you can buy cheap scissors, made from inferior metal, so soft that it is impossible to keep a sharp cutting edge. It is cheaper in the long run to buy a good-quality article that is well tempered and correctly designed.

In the illustration at (A) is shown a section through a scissors blade; as indicated, the cutting edge is ground at an angle of 60 degrees.

A fine emery wheel can be used to sharpen the blades, but if it is unavailable a flat file can be used.

Take care to grind or file the blades evenly and to the correct angle.

During this sharpening process a burr is formed on the inside of the cutting edge. Remove the burr on an oilstone. Place each blade flat on the oilstone and rub very gently to remove the burr without reducing the inside surface of the blade (B).

Although the sharpening is very important, of equal importance is the pitch of the blades.

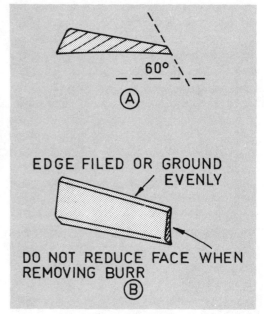

60°

Ⓐ

EDGE FILED OR GROUND
EVENLY

DO NOT REDUCE FACE WHEN
REMOVING BURR
Ⓑ

The rivet holding the blades together can be adjusted in such a way as to keep the blades as close as possible without making them hard to work.

This adjustment is illustrated at (C) and (D). If this adjustment is slack, the material being cut will jam between the blades instead of being cut.

Scissors are correctly set and sharpened by the manufacturers, and all that is necessary when they are to be resharpened is to remove the rivet to allow the blades to come apart. When sharpened, place the blades together and fasten firmly with the rivet.

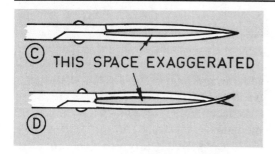

THIS SPACE EXAGGERATED

If you look at a long pair of scissors in the closed position they will appear as at (C) with the points together as shown and a space between the blades along most of the distance between points and rivet.

Now if you partly open them as at (D) the point of contact will move back to where the edges cross each other. You can see from this that the cutting edges are bearing on each other along the length of the blades. This produces the cutting action.

If the inner faces of blades were flat, straight and parallel, then materials would wedge between them, especially near the points of long scissors, which would spring apart sufficiently to let the materials through.

Cutting a piece of fine sandpaper several times is sufficient to sharpen a pair of scissors that has the cutting edges only slightly dulled.

SCREEN DOORS — To Fit

Selection and fitting of flyscreen doors deserves very careful consideration.

The three main points to note are:

(1) The position in which the door will swing.
(2) The correct opening size.
(3) Ordering the best type of door for this opening.

Most home doors open inwards. Thus the screen door will swing outwards, and it should be hinged on the side least likely to obstruct access to the building.

The ideal position is to have it swing flat against a wall when open.

Standard house doors measure 6 ft 8 in. long by 2 ft 8 in. wide. They are fitted inside the rabbets of the door frame as shown in the illustration at (A).

This means that a screen door may be fitted in either one of two positions.

First position (B) is between door jambs where opening width is reduced by depth of two side rabbets and the height is reduced by the rebate depth on top.

On standard door frame this gives an opening size of approximately 6 ft 7½ in. by 2 ft 7 in. but of course each door should be measured accurately for any variations.

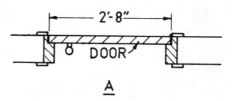

2'-8"

DOOR

A

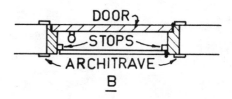

DOOR

STOPS

ARCHITRAVE

B

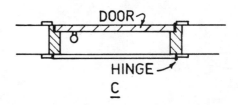

DOOR

HINGE

C

In second position (C) the door is swung on the outside of the frame. Here it may be possible to hinge to the architrave if the latter has a square edge.

On the other hand special square stock of the same thickness as screen door frame can be substituted for architraves to make hinging possible.

In the case of the first position (B) square closing stops for the screen door are fixed to door jambs with light panel pins. These stops could be ¾ in. square.

The outside of the jamb itself acts as the stop when the screen frame is fitted to outside of the main door as in (C).

SCREWDRIVERS — Types and Use

A good screwdriver is a basic essential in any kit of tools, but there are dozens of different kinds and sizes. Only four are necessary for do-it-yourself jobs.

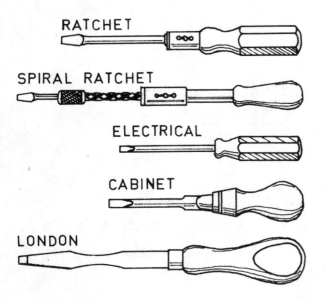

RATCHET

SPIRAL RATCHET

ELECTRICAL

CABINET

LONDON

RATCHET (see illustration). Originally developed for hanging doors. A preselector gear in the ferrule can be set to forward or reverse drive, or to fix the blade. Makes a good general-purpose tool. Is produced with blade lengths ranging from 2 in. to 8 in. Choose one with a 5 in. blade—the most useful size for common screws. If you do a lot of screwdriving, invest in a spiral-ratchet screwdriver. A spiral-ratchet driver can be set to drive or remove screws simply by pushing the handle.

ELECTRICIAN'S PATTERN. Next in order of usefulness, fitted with an insulated handle. Used mainly for moving fuse screws; is ideal for turning any small screws. Choose one with a 3 in. blade.

CABINET PATTERN. All the screwdrivers are shown in the drawing. Made in blade-sizes from 3 in. to 12 in. Choose a 4 in.

LONDON PATTERN. The strongest type of screwdriver. Buy only if you frequently encounter tough screws. Produced in 3 in. to 14 in. blade lengths; buy one with a 6 in. blade to complete your outfit.

Consider these four, in their listed order, as basic essentials. You can add other sizes if necessary; the basic four give you blade lengths of 3 in., 4 in., 5 in. and 6 in., to deal with every screwdriving job you are likely to encounter.

HOW DO YOU SCREW. Take a screwdriver in your hand and go through the motions before checking your skill with this driving test.

1. Press handle firmly into palm of driving hand. Point forefinger and thumb down to grasp handle, as near ferrule as possible. Curl the remaining three fingers round top of handle.

2. Place screw in prepared hole, and hold with tips of forefinger and thumb of free hand for first turn or two. Then crook index finger of free hand round lower end of blade to prevent driver wandering.

3. Hold tip square in slot. If leaning, it's almost certain to skid.

4. Grip tool while turning and press into slot as firmly as possible without pushing screw out of center.

5. Use the longest screwdriver, for the size of screw, for the most powerful action.

6. Use a driver of the correct width. Never wider than head of screw; never less than two-thirds of slot.

7. The tip of the tool should always be flat and level. If beveled at sides it will ride out of slot; if rounded at corners it will slip out of slot.

Finish your driving test by examining the top of your screwdriver. You can keep it in perfect shape with a file.

SCREW HEADS — Covering

When screws are used in the assembly of furniture it is often a problem to cover the screw heads so that they won't be seen.

The solution will depend to a large extent on the kind of finish to be used, and where the articles will be placed.

For a painted finish, it is sufficient to countersink the screw heads slightly below the surface and fill the recesses with plastic wood.

Build up the plastic wood a little above the surface to allow for shrinkage, iet it dry thoroughly, then sand level and smooth with glasspaper. When painted over, the fillings won't be noticed.

On the other hand, if a natural color or a lightly stained clear finish is called for, a better idea is to hide the screw heads with wooden plugs.

Before driving the screws in, bore a hole the same size as the diameter of the screw head, so that the screw sinks well below the surface. This is called counter-boring, and should be done with a clean-cutting bit.

The obvious and easiest method of plugging is to cut off a short length of dowel rod the same size as the diameter of the counter-bored hole, and glue it in place.

The disadvantage here is that the end of the dowel will show distinctive end-grained markings when stained and polished.

A much better procedure is to make wooden plugs from the same timber as that used in making the furniture. This way they will match in both grain and color.

These plugs can be made with a special tool called a plug-cutter, which can be bought in a range of sizes. It is really a hollow bit which is used in a power drill or brace.

An improvized plug-cutter can be made from a length of metal tubing with one end filed to form teeth. The inside diameter of the tubing should be equal to the diameter of the holes to be plugged.

Glue the plugs into the holes above the screw heads, making sure that the grain in the plug-ends runs in the same direction as that in the furniture.

Use a colorless woodworking glue that won't stain. Sand smooth when the glue has set, and the plugs will be practically invisible.

SCREWS — Keep Secure

Although a well fitted wood screw should remain secure and tight, this is not always the case.

If it is fitted into something which is subject to much vibration or shock, in time it may work loose.

Unless you want the trouble of having to tighten it up quite often, a locking device is needed.

There are several ways in which this can be provided.

Screws that have to be taken out occasionally will receive different treatment to those which are permanent fixtures.

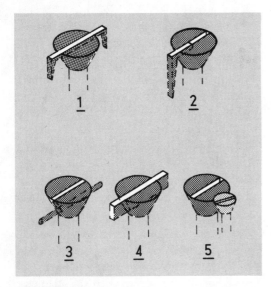

The simplest way to fix the permanent type is to drive a staple or bent wire across the slot as shown in Fig. 1.

A brad driven in at one end and bent over into the screw slot as in Fig. 2 is a variation of this method.

When the screw is recessed below the surface of the wood a slot can be cut and a piece of wire laid across the slot and soldered in.

This method is especially useful if you do not want to puncture the wood with the points of a staple.

A sectional view of the wire in place for this method is shown in Fig. 3.

A very neat and secure job is made by cutting a circular or square recess a little larger than the countersink recess and gluing in a plug, Fig. 4.

When neatly done with the same kind of wood it will be practically impossible to detect the insert.

When the screw has to be withdrawn occasionally a slightly different technique must be adopted.

File a small semi-circular section from the side of screwhead and insert a very small locking screw as in Fig. 5.

SCREWS — Selection

The efficiency of screws depends on the kind we use and the way we use them. So it's worth knowing something about them.

There are three principal kinds of screws shown in the illustration—being respectively, the countersunk head, the oval head and the round head.

Notice that the length in each case is measured from a different place on the head; the gauge of the screw is determined by the diameter of its shank.

Thus a $\frac{3}{4}$ in. by 6 gauge screw would measure $\frac{3}{4}$ in. length, and its shank would have a diameter of $\frac{9}{64}$ in.

Gauge numbers are: 1—$\frac{5}{64}$ in; 2 and 3—$\frac{3}{32}$ in; 4—$\frac{7}{64}$ in.; 5—$\frac{1}{8}$ in.; 6—$\frac{9}{64}$ in.; 7—$\frac{5}{32}$ in; 8 and 9—$\frac{11}{64}$ in; 10—$\frac{3}{16}$ in.; 12—$\frac{7}{32}$ in; and 14—$\frac{15}{64}$ in.

You can get most sizes and types in brass, chromium plate, stainless steel and Japanned black finishes. You can get a slotted head screw, or a Phillips head which needs a special screwdriver. Both of these are shown in the illustration.

There's an art in driving a screw properly, and it is correct pre-boring which ensures easy, effective screwdriving. If you look at the illustration you will see that two holes are needed—the clearance hole for the shank to pass through, and the thread hole into which the screw threads are driven.

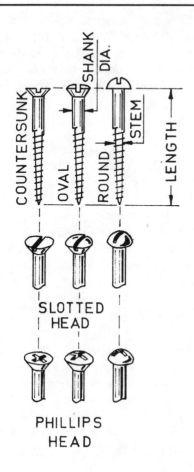

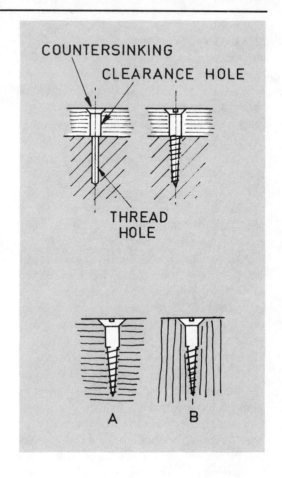

It follows, then, that the shank hole should be a trifle bigger in diameter than the screw shank, and the thread hole should be the same diameter as the stem. Make the thread hole the full length of the screw if you are boring in hardwood; it need only be half the length, however, in softwood. It is essential to do this pre-boring when using brass screws.

The last operation is to work the countersink which takes the heads of the screws, and you'll need a proper countersinking bit for this.

The important thing to remember is that brute force should never be used—it does not increase the holding properties of the screw, and indicates that the pre-boring is incorrect.

It is a good idea to smear a little wax, grease or soap onto the threads of the screw to eliminate the risk of shearing the screw heads, and it helps to stop the threads rusting in the wood and making removal difficult.

Details (A) and (B) show the correct and incorrect way to insert screws.

In (A) the screw threads grip across the grain and make for a strong fastening, while in (B) they enter the grain longitudinally and the strength is considerably less.

SEALERS — Some Uses

In painting, decorating and polishing reference is frequently made to the use of surface sealers and priming coats. It is important that the correct type is used for each job.

The function of a sealer or primer is usually to provide a base so that the following coat of paint won't soak into the surface too much.

However, some modern paints can be applied directly to masonry or plaster, so check the directions for use before starting a job.

As a general rule, if you don't use a sealer or primer under oil paints and enamels, so much of the liquid part of the paint may soak in that it leaves little more than the pigment on the surface, so preventing formation of a proper protective paint skin. Flaking or chalking of the paint surface will result.

New wood on exterior jobs, such as on the outside of a house, is usually given a coat of red-lead primer or "pink primer." This makes a suitable base for the undercoat and helps to make the finishing coats weather-resistant. On interior jobs the primer can be omitted on new wood.

When painting brickwork, plaster and cement rendering or asbestos cement sheets it is advisable to apply a coat of special cement sealer first. This is available in either clear or pigmented form. The pigmented sealer has the advantage of providing a color base in addition to sealing the surface.

On new plaster walls, an alkali-resistant sealer should be used to prevent any lime in the plaster reacting on the paint.

Because it is porous, hardboard will soak up paint quickly and produce a patchy appearance unless a sealer is used. Hardboard sheets may be bought already primed and sealed. This saves considerable time in painting.

Sealers of a different kind are used to treat new wooden floors. They're called floor sealers, but the object is the same—to fill the pores of the wood and provide a good base for finishing coats of floor varnish or plastic.

SHARPENING — Keep Angle

The sharpening process for edge-cutting tools such as plane iron and chisels is first to grind the edge to shape and then produce a keen cutting edge on an oilstone.

This latter operation is called honing, and it is here that extreme care is needed.

When the tools are first bought, the blades are ground to the correct shape, but they must be honed or sharpened to a keen cutting edge before use.

The important point is to retain this angle, and this means holding the edge firmly on the face of the oilstone, and moving the blade backwards and forwards with a steady action.

There is a tendency with most workers to rock the blade in an undulating motion, and this in turn results in the cutting angle being rounded over.

To overcome this problem, a tool called a honing guide, Fig. 1, can be used. These are made in various patterns, and Fig. 2 shows one in operation.

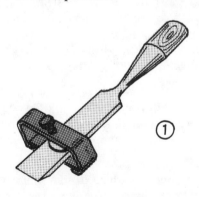

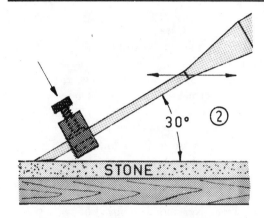

The simple but effective principle of the tool allows the blade being sharpened to be adjusted quickly to the required angle and held there during the honing operation.

A ball bearing travel or roller on the underside of the guide maintains balance and ensures that the blade moves freely to cover the full surface of the oilstone.

SHEET METAL — To Flatten

Flattening a piece of sheet metal which is badly buckled is not as easy as it looks. By following a few simple instructions, however, there should be no difficulty.

Let us first consider a metal sheet badly buckled in the center, and see why it has buckled. The center portion contains a larger surface area than is needed to create a flat surface or, in other words, this part has been stretched and has, therefore caused it to buckle.

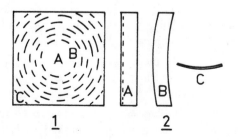

It is obvious that hammering it in the center will further stretch it, and therefore increase the buckle. It is the surrounding area which must be stretched in order to equalize the greater stress at the center.

Place the sheet on a smooth surface such as an old flat-iron, and start by hammering round the buckle at (A) Fig. 1. Go round in circles as shown by the dotted lines, making the second hammering at (B), and gradually increase the distance from (A), to finish off on the outside at (C).

The strength of the taps, too, will vary as the work proceeds, starting gently and increasing the force of the blow gradually as the outside is reached. This increase should not be excessive, otherwise the sheet may be buckled in other places.

The best type of hammer to use is one with a slightly rounded face, and it should strike the metal squarely so as to avoid making ugly marks.

This process of hammering a metal to stretch it in certain places can be very useful for shaping various articles.

A metal strip as in (A), Fig. 2, will assume quite a curve (B) when hammered along the edge, indicated by the dotted line.

When doing this, however, the strip is inclined to curl upwards (C) especially if it is at all thin. This can be corrected by turning it over and gently hammering the other side.

SHELLAC — Many Uses

It's a good idea to keep some shellac on hand, for it has a dozen uses around the home.

French polishing furniture is, of course, done with shellac. It can often be used to repair a marred finish.

Application to knots in wood before any paint is applied ensures that resin from them will not subsequently bleed through the coatings. It is also useful at other times as a sealer, and sometimes is an effective filler or stopping.

Cracks in woodware, such as a fruit or salad bowl, can be repaired by cleaning as far as possible and filling them with shellac. Wipe off excess so that the shellac is left flush with the surface of the wood.

Metalware, such as brass that has been polished, will not tarnish if it is coated twice with thin shellac. If removal of the shellac is subsequently necessary, methylated spirit can be used.

If you haven't a scrap of the same linoleum to repair a hole, use a paste consisting of cork powder and shellac. When the paste has hardened, smooth it with fine abrasive paper and paint it to match the linoleum.

If you haven't any parchment, a lampshade can be rejuvenated by replacing the covering with decorative paper, which can be made more durable with two thin coats of shellac.

Coating the silvering on the rear of a bathroom mirror helps to protect it from moisture.

Seed rows in the garden can be given labels that will last for a season by cutting the names from the empty seed packets and attaching them to stakes, afterwards coating the paper with shellac.

Brightly colored autumn leaves that are not dry and brittle can be preserved for decoration by coating them with shellac. Lay the leaves as flat as possible on newspaper and coat one side, including stems. When the shellac is dry, turn the leaves over and coat the other side.

SILVER — Care

Silver is ranked, next to gold, among the precious metals, though other metals are rarer and more expensive than either.

The term sterling silver is one we hear frequently, and means that the metal contains a certain amount of copper.

The purpose of this addition is to harden the pure silver which would be too soft for normal use.

Perhaps the most important rule is that sterling silver should be used daily.

Constant use gives it the deep mellow tone or patina that is really a network of very fine scratches.

Wash your silver promptly after each use, using hot suds and a soft cloth.

Rinse it in hot water and dry immediately.

By following this procedure, you will not have to polish it often.

There are two methods of cleaning tarnished silver.

The first is hand rubbing with a prepared polish—liquid, paste, or powder—and the second method is to use the electrolytic process.

The latter is quick and easy, but it has a tendency to leave the surface dull and without luster.

Hand rubbing, on the other hand, gives a depth of luster that is beautiful, and at the same time highlights any decorations.

When you polish silver, take time to do it carefully. Wash first in soapsuds, then apply a reliable polish with a soft cloth sponge or chamois.

Rub each piece briskly, but not hard, using even, straight strokes. Do not rub silver crosswise or with a rotary motion.

A special silver brush is useful for cleaning hard-to-reach crevices, chased surfaces and beaded edgings.

Last of all, wash each piece again carefully in hot suds to remove every trace of polish.

The brush will come in handy here, too, to insure that no powder is left clinging to raised patterns.

Polish left on silver causes it to tarnish again quickly.

Silver does not need to be polished each time it is cleaned. Often it is only necessary to wipe off the tarnish with your silver preparation.

Gold linings in articles such as jugs, cups, bowls, and salt cellars must be treated very carefully.

Keep your polish away from these delicate finishes as the gold is soft, the lining thin, and it will vanish with constant rubbing.

Of course gold linings can be restored by a jeweler at a fairly reasonable cost.

The electrolytic method of cleaning silver calls for an old aluminum pan, or a porcelain pan in which a piece of aluminum —or zinc—has been placed, also a quantity of salt and baking soda.

Place in an aluminum pan one teaspoon of bicarbonate of soda and one teaspoon of salt for each quart of water required.

Bring the water to the boil, then put in the silver, making sure that it is covered completely.

Boil two or three minutes, or until the tarnish has disappeared.

If you use a porcelain pan, make sure that some of the silver is in contact with the piece of aluminum used, and that all of the pieces of silver touch each other.

Remove the silver, wash it in hot suds, rinse and dry with a soft cloth.

This method of silver cleaning involves an electro-chemical reaction by which the tarnish is removed from the silver and deposited on the aluminum.

Note that this method of cleaning should not be used on table silver with hollow handles that may be fastened with cement, or on antique silver.

SMALL TOOL — Using

To give it its full title, the tool illustrated is a plasterer's small tool.

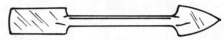

It is used for all types of plaster repair work, and could be classed as an essential item in the home-repair tool kit.

With such a tool it is important to buy the best quality, as the pointed trowel-end and flat spatula must be flexible. Only high-grade steel ensures this.

For home use, buy a small tool that is at least 10 in. long. When it is not likely to be used for some time, smear with a little petroleum jelly to protect the metal against rust.

In addition to applying patching plaster, a small tool is ideal for re-pointing brickwork, applying roofing compound to holes or cracks in a gutter or around faulty flashing, and for all types of molding jobs where plaster, cement or other plastic materials or compounds are used.

SOLDERING — Main Points

When you do a soldering job, watch these three main points of preparation and selection of materials.

1. The soldering iron should be properly tinned and heated to the right temperature.
2. Select and use the right flux for a particular job.
3. Make sure that the articles to be soldered are clean.

Tinning the iron means putting a thin coat

of solder on the four facets of the tip. It should be re-tinned frequently when in use.

A soldering iron—or more accurately a copper bit—that is not properly tinned won't "take" the solder and transfer it to the joint.

To tin the iron, heat it until the flame shows a bright green color, and then clean it with a wire brush until the copper shines. If the point is badly coated with oxide, use a coarse file to expose the bright metal.

Rub the tip on a block of sal ammoniac, or apply a little resin flux to it, then flow on solder until the whole tip is covered. Finally, wipe with a damp cloth with a twisting motion to spread the solder uniformly.

Don't overheat the iron. This is a common fault and results in the tinning on the point being burnt off.

When the flame in which the iron is heated begins to show a bright green color, it is hot enough. A gas flame is the best for heating the iron.

The flux to use on a job depends on the metal that is to be soldered. Zinc chloride is a good all-purpose flux for soldering iron, steel, copper, brass, bronze.

Zinc chloride is made by dissolving scraps of zinc in hydrochloric acid until it will take up no more. Do the dissolving in a glass or earthenware container.

For galvanized iron, use hydrochloric acid or a partly saturated zinc chloride solution. For lead, use resin or tallow.

The various paste fluxes available are usually suitable for most ordinary soldering jobs with metals other than iron or steel. Resin-core solder is useful for light jobs.

Cleaning the work to be soldered is done with sandpaper, or emery cloth, steel wool, files, or a wire brush. A final wipe with methylated spirits is always a good plan as it removes any oil or grime which would prevent the solder adhering properly.

SPOKESHAVE — Details

A spokeshave is used mostly nowadays for trimming the shaped edges of wood, making shaped legs, etc.

Made in both wood and metal and choice is largely one of personal preference. Wood types are apt to wear quickly, particularly at the mouth, and some have a brass mouth plate to prevent this.

Usually the cutter is held by its tangs in holes in the stock, but some have screw fastenings which simplify adjustment.

The cutter is sharpened on the narrow edge of an oilstone or with an oilstone slip. Cutters are from $1\frac{1}{2}$ in. up to 3 in. and the stock is of beech or boxwood.

Metal spokeshaves are usually 10 in. long with $1\frac{3}{4}$ in. or $2\frac{1}{8}$ in. cutters, and have either round or flat face. Cutters are sometimes adjustable.

SQUARE — Roofing

Alternatively known as a steel square, rafter, or framing square, this tool is used to obtain the various bevels, or cuts as they are called, also used to enable the length of rafters to be ascertained. Different makes vary as to the tables and markings, but the method of marking angles is much the same in all. The long blade is 24 in. and the other, or tongue, 16 in.

On one side both blade and tongue are divided into sixteenths at the outer edge, and into eighths at the inner edge. On the reverse side the outer edges are marked in twelfths, the inner edge of the blade into thirty-seconds, and the inner edge of the tongue into tenths.

Scales are marked on the center. It functions on the principle of the right-angle triangle.

SQUARE — Sliding

A square of some kind is essential in the woodworker's kit.

The ordinary try square is suitable for most jobs, but a sliding square of the type shown in Fig. 1 has additional advantages. In effect, it is a combination of several tools.

In a sliding square the blade is separate from the stock, and is free to slide and give any required amount of projection. It is fixed in any desired position by means of a small thumbscrew.

Every practical man knows that, whereas the 12 in. square is necessary for larger work, the 6 in. size is handier for general bench work.

Thus, in the ordinary way, the sliding square is used in the position indicated in Fig. 1. When wanted for larger jobs, it is merely a matter of sliding the blade along.

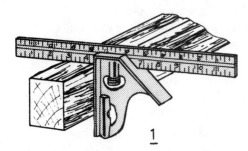

1

The sliding square can be used equally well for marking miters, as shown in Fig. 2.

Apart from its general bench handiness, however, it can be used for purposes for which the ordinary square would be useless.

Suppose you have to test the rabbet in a door frame or similar recess to see that it is square.

The ordinary square could not be used because the blade projects too far. By giving the blade of the sliding square a projection slightly less than the rabbet width, it can be used to test as shown in Fig. 3.

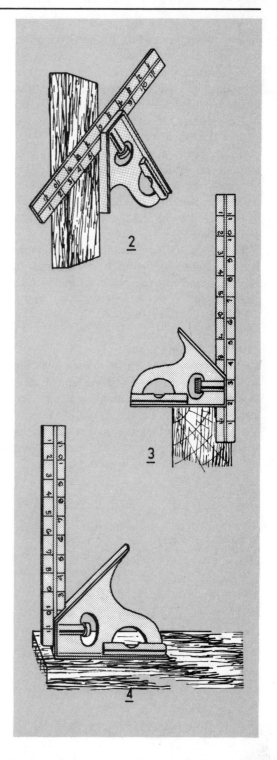

2

3

4

As the blade of the square is marked clearly in inches and fractions, it may be used as a rule or gauge.

When used as a gauge it is simply a matter of setting the blade projection to the desired width and holding a pencil against the end of the blade as the stock is drawn along the edge of the timber being marked.

Sliding squares can be obtained with or without a spirit level in the stock.

Fig. 4 shows how a square fitted with a level is used to test a horizontal surface. The blade may be pushed back out of line of the stock edge.

For testing a post or frame to see whether it is vertical have the stock in the center of the blade and rest the blade on the surface being tested.

STAIRS — Stop Creaks

Creaking wooden stairs are most annoying and the cause can usually be traced to a loosening of the wedges used to tighten the stair treads to the risers.

If you can get at the underside of the staircase to reach these dove-tailed wedges, see illustration at (A), it should be possible

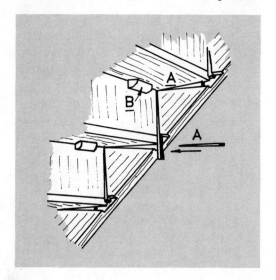

to remove any loose wedges and drive in new ones, gluing and pinning them in position.

The glue blocks (B) in the angles between the treads and the risers occasionally work loose and these can be removed and reglued, or additional glue blocks stuck in position.

If the inside of the staircase is inaccessible, a creaking stair can sometimes be cured by drilling and countersinking the edge of the tread and screwing down into the riser.

It may also be possible to drive in wedges above the end of the tread where it fits into the housing or recess in the side stringer of the staircase.

Any gap left at this point after driving in a wedge can be filled with plastic wood.

STEPS (Worn) — Repair

After a few years' use, concrete, stone, and brick steps tend to wear in the center where most traffic occurs.

On the other hand, the front edges of steps may become chipped and broken, and when either of these faults develop, there is a risk of accidents.

The illustrations refer specifically to the repair of worn steps, but much the same procedure is adopted when the front edges are chipped and broken.

To start, the step should be marked to form a rectangle or square at least 1 in. greater in length than the worn area, Fig. 1.

Then with a hammer and cold chisel, carefully chip out a recess to the shape suggested in Fig. 2.

Preferably, have the sides of this recess undercut or sloping in slightly to provide a "key" for the patching material.

Next place a board along the face of the step with the edge flush with step top.

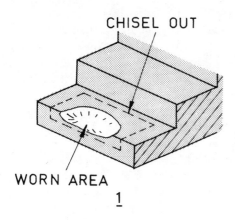

CHISEL OUT

WORN AREA

1

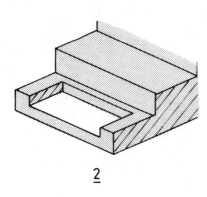

2

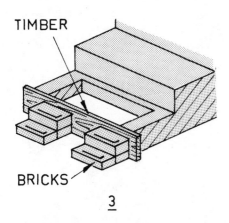

TIMBER

BRICKS

3

This board could be held in place with pegs, or secured firmly by a number of bricks arranged as in Fig. 3.

The patching mixture is a mortar consisting of one part cement to two parts of sand. The addition of a PVA bonding agent to the mixture ensures a firm grip.

Mix this thoroughly and then dampen the step to prevent excessive suction when the patching mortar is placed in position.

With the recess filled with the mortar, smooth off with a trowel and apply about one ounce of carborundum powder to the wet surface and cover with a damp cloth for about four hours.

After this time, remove the cloth and the timber facing, and by means of a block of timber about 3 in. long, $2\frac{1}{2}$ in. wide, and 1 in. thick dipped in water, rub gently over the whole of the step for about a minute.

The step should be covered over for about two hours, then remove the covering and rub over again, wash the step with cold clean water and cover for forty-eight hours.

After this time the step may be uncovered, but as a precaution place a temporary covering board over the front edge for several days to guard against rough usage.

The application of carborundum powder will make the step non-slip, and the repeated rubbing will enable the patched surface to take on a uniform coloring.

STONEWORK — Cut and Shape

Stonework, properly laid, has a pleasing appearance and blends perfectly with the surroundings of many homes.

In many areas it is possible to use local stone which splits easily, and here are some details of the procedure and tools needed.

Steel gads are first on the list. They are not unlike cold chisels, except that the edges as well as the back and front are beveled to assist in splitting. A heavy hammer for driving the gads should weigh at least 4 lb.

A bolster in the illustration at (A) is a wide-cutting blade on a shank and is used for cutting sections of the split stone to shape. The bolster is a standard bricklaying tool.

The scutch or comb hammer shown at (B) resembles a hatchet and the combs which do the cutting are replaceable. It is used for trimming the stone to shape after cutting, and it is also possible to produce a textured surface on the stone with this tool.

In addition to these tools, trowels for laying will be required—especially a small pointing trowel for the joints. Also needed will be a level and a chalk line.

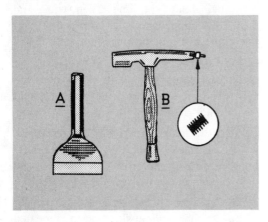

Splitting the stone is not really difficult, but a few pieces are bound to be ruined before the knack is acquired. Select the line of grain nearest to where the cut is wanted and drive the first gad in a short distance. Don't drive too hard or too far, but follow with others two or three inches apart, all around the edge of the piece.

Before long the stone should begin to split along the line of grain as the gads are driven in, and if the stone is comparatively soft, it may part after only three or four gads have been used.

STRAIGHT EDGE — Testing

A straight-edge is needed in many jobs, but to be effective the edge must be really straight and true.

If you need only a short straight-edge—say 18 in. long—the simplest method of ensuring that the edge is straight is to prepare two pieces of wood and plane them in the form of a joint.

Use a steel jack or trying plane set very fine. Plane one piece at the center without touching the ends until the plane will remove no more shavings, then take a couple of shavings right through.

Do the same with the other piece, and try them together.

If your plane is true, the two should make a perfect joint, and both should be straight because they have had the same treatment.

Note that the true fitting of two edges does not necessarily prove them to be straight. One might be hollow and the other slightly round, and so they would complement each other as in the illustration at (A).

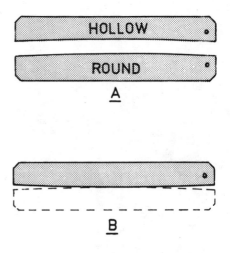

This, however, would not happen if you try to make both edges hollow by planing the center only, then shaving it right through.

The edges will be straight for carpentry accuracy if they make a good joint. It depends how accurately you handle the plane.

For long straight-edges the method of checking to see that the edge is perfectly straight is illustrated clearly at (B).

First plane the edge as true as possible to judge by eye, then lay it on its side on a flat clean board or sheet of plywood and draw a fine line along it with a sharp pencil or sharp scriber.

When the straight-edge is reversed, and laid against the first line, any inaccuracy of the nature indicated by the dotted outline at (B) becomes apparent.

Correct it as far as you can judge with the plane, and repeat the test, marking in a new line. A third test may be needed before the two lines coincide as the straight-edge is reversed against itself.

A straight-edge should be made preferably from a dry piece of soft durable timber —cedar or straight-grain fir.

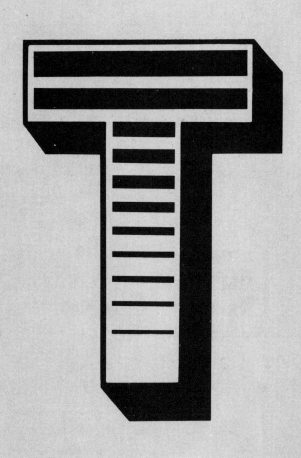

TABLE TOPS	To Secure
TABLE	To Square
TAPE	Cellulose
TILES (Ceramic)	Cutting
TILES	Restore Joints
TIMBER	Faults
TIMBER	Selection
TIMBER	Shapes
TIMBER	Surface Finish
TIMBER	Surface Repairs
TIMBER	To Order
TINSNIPS	Using
TOY MAKING	In Workshop

TABLE TOPS — To Secure

When buying furniture, look at the hidden parts—the sides and bottoms of drawers, the undersides of tables, the backs and tops of cabinets.

One such point to watch carefully is the method used to secure table and other furniture tops to side rails.

The details in the illustration and text will act not only as a guide when buying but for those who make their own furniture.

There are two general methods, each with variations, for such fastenings. One allows for expansion and contraction of the wood; the other keeps the top stationary.

The stationary fastener is usually employed where the top is of frame construction or made of laminated materials.

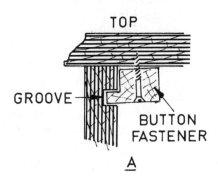

TOP

GROOVE

BUTTON
FASTENER

<u>A</u>

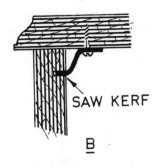

SAW KERF

<u>B</u>

A good example of the free-moving fastening is the button fastener shown at (A). The insides of the rails are grooved near the top before they are glued into place.

Then wooden blocks are rabbeted on one end so that the tongues fit into the rail grooves and the other ends fasten to the top at intervals. Care must be taken when making the rabbet to allow for a slight gap between the block and the top.

Thus, when the screws are driven in, the block will be pulled up to get a tight hold on the rail, yet will be free to move when shrinkage occurs.

A modification of the button fastener is a small piece of flat iron bent to the off-set shape shown at (B) and drilled at one end for a screw.

One end fits into a saw kerf made on the inside of the rail and the other is fastened to the underside of the table top. Space such fasteners at approximately 12 in. intervals around the table.

TABLE — To Square

When gluing up tables, chairs, cabinets, or boxes, it is very important that the work be checked for squareness before the glue has been allowed to set.

One of the best methods used for checking the work is by measuring the diagonals from corner to corner. These distances should be identical if the work is square.

The use of single-gauge rods will check the diagonals, and a set similar to those in the illustration not only checks the diagonals but may be left in the work to brace it while the glue is given time to set.

The exact diagonals of the piece to be glued must be determined. If on measuring the work before it is glued it is found that the diagonals do not check, it means that there is something wrong with the work.

If eight pieces are made in lengths of 24 in., 12 in. and 6 in., they may be interchanged in a set of rods that will take any diagonal from a fraction over 6 in. to almost 36 in.

Two 24 in. pieces, two 12 in. pieces and four 6 in. pieces are required. One leg of the rod has a ¾ in. wide by ⅛ in. deep groove cut in it, while the other leg is rabbeted to fit this groove. A slot is cut in both pieces, as illustrated, to take a carriage bolt and wing nut. The outer ends of each leg are pointed so as to fit into the corners of the work that is to be checked.

TAPE — Cellulose

There are many uses for cellulose tape in the home and workshop besides securing parcels and repairing books.

For instance, artists or students who use a wooden ruler or scale can keep the calibration marks and figures clean and legible by covering the scale with a strip of the clear tape before use.

When using a hand drill to bore a number of holes to the same depth or a single blind hole to a predetermined depth, cellulose tape comes in handy as a depth guide.

Take a small strip of the tape and wrap it around the bit or drill so that the lower edge of the tape is the desired distance from the top of the bit. Without removing the bit frequently for inspection, you can now drill safely until the edge of the tape is flush with the surface of the work, thus eliminating guesswork.

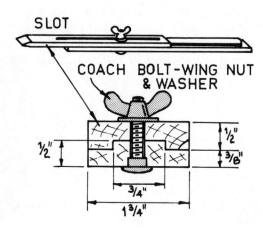

SLOT

COACH BOLT-WING NUT & WASHER

½" ½" ⅜" ¾" 1¾"

When the diagonals have been obtained, the rods are set for the correct measurement, then put in place. The rods are made of 1¾ in. by ½ in. timber. The length, of course, will vary.

Naturally, a set of rods that have been made for use on checking tables could not be used for chairs or smaller pieces. For this reason it may be advisable to make the rods in three different sizes so that a complete set will be available for future work.

In places where screws cannot be held in a starting position with the fingers, they can be started easily if taped to the tip of the screwdriver. With the tip in the slotted head of the screw, a small piece of cellulose tape is wrapped around both the head of the screw and the head of the screwdriver.

The greater width of the tape should be stuck to the screwdriver blade so that when the latter is pulled from the screw the tape will come away with it.

Still on the subject of screws, it is easy to find a screw of the right size if you keep them in rolls of suitable cellulose tape. Take the box of miscellaneous screws that you have on hand and sort them in lots of the same size and gauge. Lay each lot in a row on a strip of tape with the sticky side up and roll them up.

When you want any particular screw, just peel it off the roll.

Cellulose tape provides a quick and effective gluing clamp for model work and other jobs where it is necessary to keep small or intricate parts together as in repairing broken china or glassware. Small parts of almost any shape can be held together and the tape removed easily without damage to the work.

Finally, removal of decals or transfers is made extremely easy if cellulose tape is applied to the unwanted decal, pressed on firmly and peeled off. The design will usually adhere and come off with the cellulose tape.

TILES (Ceramic) — Cutting

Whether it is a complete re-tiling job or merely replacing a few loose tiles, the chances are that one or two tiles will have to be cut or trimmed.

Cutting of glazed ceramic tiles is best done with a glass cutter. Run the cutter over the face of the tile as with a sheet of glass, guiding it against a straightedge.

If the section of tile required is very narrow, it is best broken away with a pair of wide-mouth pliers. For a normal break near the center, the method shown in Fig. 1 is good. Here a small-diameter dowel has been placed below the line of the cut, and

when both sides are pressed down firmly, the tile should break cleanly along the line.

To cut holes for fitting the tiles around water pipes or other fixtures, each tile is gradually clipped away with pincers as shown in Fig. 2. Don't attempt to remove too much at a time, or the tile will possibly fracture. The comparatively rough edges of these shaped tiles will be hidden by flanges or decorative plates.

If it is necessary to have a vertical row of cut tiles to fit the wall, keep these at the ends or in the most inconspicuous position possible. Behind a door, for instance, would be a good spot. In any case, equalize any cut tiles on a wall so that they are approximately the same size at each end.

TILES — Restore Joints

Joints between wall tiles that become stained and darkened or where the grouting has fallen out can be repaired with white grouting compound from a hardware store. Here's the method:

Scrape away the loose or soiled cement with the point of a knife (be careful you don't loosen the tiles).

Mix some of the dry compound with water to the consistency of whipped cream, and smear it over the joints with a piece of cardboard, so it fills them.

Remove surplus cement from the tiles before it dries by wiping with a clean damp sponge. Wipe over the joints, too, to remove surplus cement there.

Any spots in the joints where the cement hasn't filled completely can be filled up by putting a small dab of cement on your finger and running it along the joints. Then wipe again.

Finally, polish the tiles with a clean, dry cloth after the cement has dried.

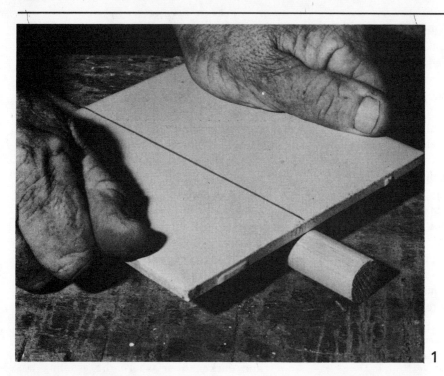

1

2

TIMBER — Faults

All flaws in timber do not necessarily mean the piece of timber is weak.

For instance, there are two kinds of knots. First, there are "sound" or solid knots which are so interwoven with the grain that they are not detrimental. From the point of view of strength, timber containing these can be accepted safely.

On the other hand, loose knots often look sound, but there is a risk they will drop out when the timber dries.

Hollow knots have a small hole about ¼ in. in diameter in the middle and also are liable to drop out.

Fractures in timber are sometimes called shakes. In the illustration detail (A) shows a heart shake which is caused by old age. At (B) is a star shake which comes from incorrect or forced seasoning. As a matter of interest, there is also the cup shake (C) and the through shake (D).

Provided all the affected timber is cut away, the strength or quality of the main bulk of the timber is not affected by any of these shakes.

However, certain timbers have thunder shakes, which are cross fractures of the grain. They cannot be seen from the outside, and only reveal their presence as the timber is being cut or planed. Timber with thunder shakes may fall apart.

A check is a split or crack along the grain and is usually confined to the surface. Although unsightly, it is a minor fault.

Detail (E) shows a board with end splits. These, too, do not lessen the value of the board.

"Waney-edged" is the term applied to a board with an edge as shown at (F). It is the result of the edge of the plank being cut too near the outer circumference of the log so that the surface breaks through here and there. It has no effect on the quality of the board.

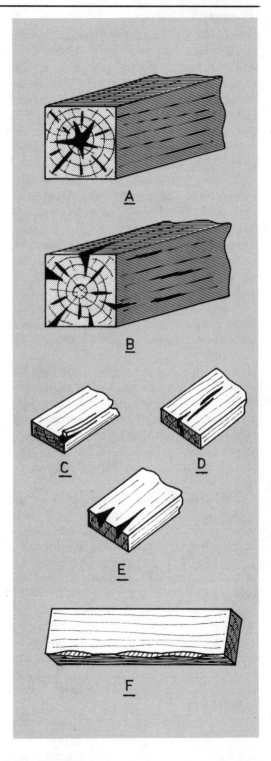

TIMBER — Selection

One of the early problems confronting the handyman is the choice of the most suitable available timber for the job in hand, for though there is generally a fairly wide range of suitable timbers, particularly for cabinet-making, one will probably be better than the others.

There are two kinds of wood, according to *biological* classifications—softwood and hardwood. Softwoods come from needle-bearing trees like pine and fir. Hardwoods come from broad-leaved trees like oak and ash.

These terms cause great confusion in selecting wood for projects. Some softwoods are actually harder than some hardwoods, and many softwoods are much more difficult to work than some hardwoods. For home projects, you will deal mostly with softwoods: Douglas fir, pine, spruce, cedar and so on.

Maple and oak are hardwoods; they are often used for floors and stair treads. Generally, hardwoods are used in flooring, cabinet work, millwork and in making containers. When working with hardwood, you should pre-bore your holes if you think there is any danger of splitting the wood.

GRADING. Due to the nature of the woods and the way they are used, softwoods and hardwoods are cut and graded differently. Quality grading is done according to rules that cover characteristics of wood species in performance and appearance.

Select grades of softwoods are best. Wood graded "select" is used for finishing purposes and is classified into subgrades, which are usually designated by letter. The two highest subgrades of select, A and B, are usually combined and sold as B and better select.

Select grades are clear, or practically clear, wood. B and better select (B & btr) is stamped on the highest quality of interior and exterior finish, trim, moldings, paneling, flooring, ceiling, partition, beveled siding, and drop siding. C and D select grades can be used where lower cost is considered more important than perfect appearance. All select grades, including C and D, take natural finishes well.

Next step down are the common grades. These woods are used for utility and construction purposes. Common grades are subgraded 1 to 5 or 1 to 3. Use No. 2 common pine or No. 2 common cedar if you are interested in letting the knots show for informal effect in a paneled wall. A good common grade of some species of softwood will give you a very satisfactory surface for paint.

As a matter of fact, the best thing to do is to use the lowest grade possible for the job you have in mind. Many times you can get twice as much lumber for the price. Your lumber dealer can give you practical advice here. Just tell him how you are going to use the wood, how it is to be finished, what tools you have, and your own special preferences.

For joists, studding and bracing, you will look for yet another grade—dimension timber. Dimension timber is graded by natural characteristics that affect its strength, stiffness and general suitability. Usual subgrades are 1, 2, 3 and sometimes 4. The top grades carry more load, but all grades are suitable for most light construction projects you might undertake.

In industrial grades of hardwood, "dimension" includes interior trim and molding, hardwood stair treads and risers and solid hardwood wall paneling.

WORKABILITY. Every kind of wood has its own reaction to cutting tools. Don't assume that softwood will be easy to work or that hardwood makes for a hard job. A lot of softwoods are murder to work, and a lot of hardwoods are a dream. You can turn to your lumber dealer for practical advice on the workability of woods, but the following paragraphs will give you some initial guidance.

HARDWOODS. Among the commonly available hardwoods, maple is one of the easiest to work. It is light reddish brown and is used for flooring and other planing mill products, interior finish, furniture, handles, vehicle parts and athletic equipment.

Gum is fair to work. Ranging in color from light grey to reddish brown, it is moderately heavy, fine and uniformly textured. It is used for furniture, interior finish, millwork, shipping containers and novelties.

Walnut, also fair to work, ranges from light to chocolate brown and is heavy and moderately hard. It develops beautiful finishes and is often used in cabinet work, interior finish, paneling, furniture, flooring, gun stocks and caskets.

Beech and oak are among the hard-to-work hardwoods. Beech ranges from white to reddish brown and is heavy, hard and strong. It is used in furniture, flooring, interior finish, handles, woodenware and containers.

Oak ranges from brown to reddish brown and is also a heavy, hard and strong wood. It is used for flooring, interior finish, furniture, cabinet work, planing mill products, vehicle parts, timbers, handles and agricultural implements.

SOFTWOODS. The easy-to-work softwoods include cedar, various pines and white fir.

Cedar is an aromatic red wood with broad grain. It is soft but resists decay very well. Common uses for it include siding, shingles, light construction, paneling, poles, posts, boxes and crates. A type of cedar called incense cedar is used for sid-

ing, finish, framing, boards, panel work, pencils, posts, cedar chests and closet linings. Cedar has good gluing properties, and it takes paints and stains well. It can be left unfinished, too, so that it "weathers" naturally.

Lodgepole pine, Norway pine, Ponderosa pine and white pine (including Idaho, northern white and sugar pine) are soft and easy to work.

Lodgepole ranges from yellow to brown and is used for siding, framing, boards, paneling, ties, poles and mining timbers.

Norway ranges from light red to reddish brown. It is moderately heavy and moderately soft and is used for light construction, poles, boxes and crates.

Ponderosa ranges from creamy white to reddish brown. It is moderately heavy and moderately soft and is used for light building construction, boxes, crates and paneling.

White pines range from creamy white to light brown and are soft, light, easily worked and stable under moisture changes. The woods are used for millwork, patterns, sheathing, subflooring, boxes and crates.

Among these four kinds of pine, the Ponderosa and white are the easiest of all to work with.

White fir is oyster white, lightweight, soft and straight-grained. It is used for framing and sheathing, millwork and boxes. Because it is relatively nonresinous, it will take paint and other finishes well.

Softwoods that are fair to work include cypress, rangewood and spruce.

Cypress ranges from yellowish brown to dark reddish brown and is moderately light, strong and decay-resistant. It is used for siding, millwork, finish, greenhouse construction, tanks, boxes and boat work. Because it is durable in moist conditions, it can be used in the ground as well.

Rangewood is creamy white to dark brown in color and is moderately light and strong. It resists rot and decay and is used for general construction, millwork, shingles and outdoor furniture.

Spruce ranges from yellow to brown and is moderately light, strong, stiff and tough. It is used in millwork, siding, light framing and some cabinet work.

Hard-to-work softwoods are Douglas fir and yellow or Southern pine.

Douglas fir ranges from yellow to red and is heavy and strong. It is used for all types of building and general construction, siding, flooring, millwork, doors, plywood, boxes and crates. It is not suitable for unusually damp conditions, however, because it is susceptible to decay with constant exposure to high moisture.

Southern pine ranges from yellow to reddish brown. It is moderately dense, strong and stiff, but it splits and warps. It is used for all types of building and construction, siding, flooring, planing products, millwork, doors, boxes and crates.

TIMBER — Shapes

Much time and labor can often be saved by making use of the varied ready-milled timbers available. However, before this can be done effectively, it is necessary to know something about the names or terms used to distinguish one type from another.

For example, square-edged stuff is that which, in cross section, presents a uniform rectangle, see illustration at (A). It may be square or it may be wider than it is thick. The term applies when all corners are right-angles—that is, square.

Splayed, beveled, and chamfered are three terms that cause quite a lot of confusion, because they produce a similar effect.

In splaying, one side only is beveled off to the full width or thickness of the piece (B).

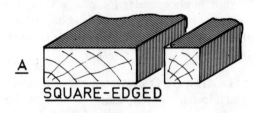

A SQUARE-EDGED

B SPLAYED

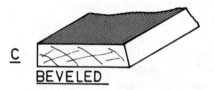

C BEVELED

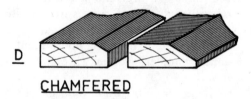

D CHAMFERED

E

A window sill, for example, is splayed to carry off water, although here it is modified slightly with a rabbet or flat section on the back edge for a bead.

The beveled edge (C) usually applies to the thickness, and as a rule the joiner or cabinetmaker will run his own level according to the angle required.

A chamfer (D) is distinct from a bevel by being restricted to one edge or corner. Thus a chamfered board will show the top edge beveled and the under edge square.

When an upright standard or post of square section (E) is chamfered on all four corners it looks thinner from an angle.

TIMBER — Surface Finish

The procedure for producing a really fine finish on timber before painting or polishing is first to dress the surface with a sharp, finely set steel smoothing plane, follow up with a steel scraper, then finish off with medium and fine grade sandpaper.

On occasions, however, the nature of certain timbers upsets even this careful preparation. A case in point is when the grain fibers show a tendency to lift up during and after planing.

Two examples of this trouble are shown in the illustration. At (A) grain splinters have lifted on the face of dressed timber.

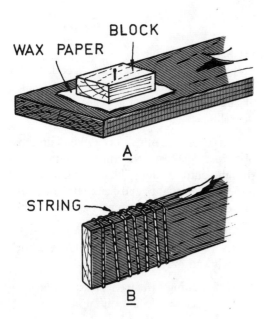

The remedy is to apply some clear glue, place a sheet of wax paper over the top, then tack a light block down until the glue sets. The wax paper is to prevent the block sticking to the timber.

At (B) a close series of splinters is best treated by applying the glue, then binding closely with string until the glue hardens.

Then both the string and any surplus glue can be scraped and sandpapered down smooth.

If any sections of the grain break out completely, try to glue them back in place immediately. Failing this, fill the gap or hole with plastic wood, allow to harden, then rub down smooth.

Always allow a slight surplus of plastic wood to stand above the surface to counteract any slight tendency for this material to shrink in drying.

TIMBER — Surface Repairs

Sometimes an otherwise satisfactory timber surface has one or two unavoidable blemishes. These could be a knot-hole or a hole left by a screw or bolt.

The best repair procedure is to cut around or bore out around each blemish and fill with a plug of sound wood of the same kind as the ground-work.

The simplest plugs are known as pellets, as in the illustration at (A), and may be turned on a lathe or cut with a special tool known as a plug-cutter.

They merely require a hole to be bored in the wood, the pellet being glued, tapped in, and leveled. Note that it is essential that the grain runs crosswise in the pellet so that when in position it runs in the same direction as that of the groundwork. A dowel is unsuitable because the grain runs lengthwise and would remain standing up in the event of the wood of the groundwork shrinking.

DIRECTION OF GRAIN

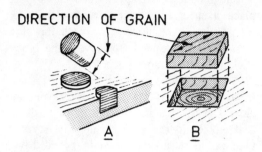

A   B

Large blemishes can be filled with flat plugs, as at (B). Cut a plug large enough to cover the knot, making a slight taper downwards, and place in position. Mark around with a pricker and chop out with a chisel. The fit should be close but make sure that the plug beds down hard at the bottom. Otherwise the position may show up later as a slight depression. This applies also to the pellet filling. In any case allow the plug to stand up slightly above the surface, and level after the glue has set thoroughly.

Small holes left by nails and screws can be filled with plastic wood. This is best applied in several layers, with a little surplus left standing above surface to allow for shrinkage in drying.

TIMBER — To Order

Those who plan to build their own home in their spare time should find these details about ordering and buying timber useful.

Most timber used in building work, with the exception of moldings, battens, etc., is sold at so much per board foot. A board foot of wood is a piece of rough, green unfinished wood 1 in. thick by 1 ft wide by 1 ft long, or an equivalent amount.

The number of board feet is calculated by multiplying the thickness in inches by the width in feet by the length in feet.

To see how this formula works out, suppose fourteen lengths of timber, each 10 ft long by 3 in. wide and 2 in. thick, are needed for building a small shed.

The number of board feet of timber required would be 2 (thickness in inches) x $\frac{3}{12}$ (width in feet) x 140 (14 x 10, the total length in feet). This equals 70 board feet.

Another important point to remember is that dressed timber—that is, planed on four sides—is always less than the ordered width and thickness.

If you want the planed timber exactly to ordered size, you'll have to pay for having wider, thicker stock planed to your finish size. Since this will greatly increase your costs, always try to plan your work to use standard timber sizes.

Remember, too, that width affects the price of timber. The wider the boards, the higher the rate per board foot, so don't order wide boards with the idea of cutting them into strips or battens. This will prove expensive.

TINSNIPS — Using

Properly used and cared for, a good pair of sheet-metal cutting snips—commonly called tinsnips—should last for years in the home workshop.

For general use there are three main types of snips. They are the regular pattern, for straight cutting only; the combination pattern, for straight and curved cuts; and curved-blade snips for cutting curves only.

Always cut with the handles at right-angles to the metal. Slanting makes cutting difficult and may spring the blades.

While cutting, use even pressure and take short strokes, especially on curves.

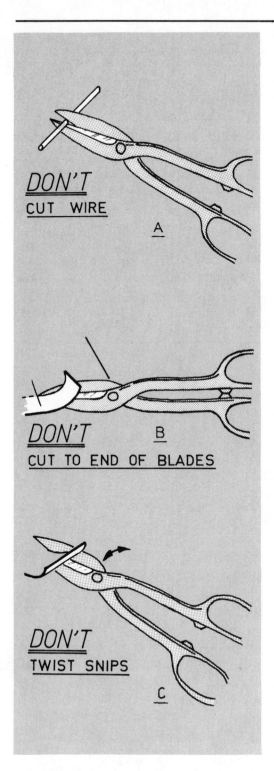

DON'T
CUT WIRE
A

DON'T
CUT TO END OF BLADES
B

DON'T
TWIST SNIPS
C

When very strong leverage is required, rest the snips on the bench and bear down on the upper handle. Never force the cut by hammering the handles.

It is especially important to keep snip blades free from rust.

Illustrated are three practices that must be avoided at all times:

Cutting wire (A) will gap the blades; carrying a cut right through to the ends of the blades may crack the metal (B); twisting the snips to clear a way through metal may spring the blades (C).

TOY MAKING — In Workshop

Toymaking is always a popular home workshop activity not only around Christmas but for birthdays and other special occasions. In practically all cases scrap ends of material can be put to good use, and here are some suggestions.

Don't overlook cardboard for making indoor toys. Properly assembled with plenty of corner braces set in edgeways, cardboard toys are every bit as strong as those made from plywood or hardboard.

Use pins, rivet-like, along seams and cover the pin heads with glued-on paper to prevent them working out. Set at a slight angle, the pins interlock with each other.

When wood has to slide over cardboard or wood over wood, smooth running can be obtained by rubbing the contacting surfaces with candle wax or with graphite. Don't use oil.

On wheeled toys, round-head steel screws make good axles and, to ensure free rotation of the wheels, slip a free running washer over the screw shank on both sides of each wheel.

It goes without saying that finished wooden toys should be sandpapered thoroughly to remove any rough edges or splinters. Always make toys as realistic as possible.

Children are far more observant and critical than might be imagined. This point applies not only to the actual design of the article but also to the selection of authentic colors.

With toys or nursery equipment intended for very young children, great care must be taken in selecting the type of paint or other finish. Many items can be left unpainted, or finished with two coats of French polish which is shellac dissolved in methylated spirits.

For painted toys, use only a lead-free enamel or lacquer—never ordinary house paint. This precaution is extremely important because most young children have the habit of sucking or chewing playthings.

A lightweight tack hammer and a pair of light pincers are two essential tools in the toymaker's kit. Also have a good supply of fine-gauge panel pins, cup hooks, round head screws, small washers, and upholstery tacks.

Glue-painting is an effective finish for forts and the bases of such things as signals on model railway layouts and windmills.

Have some powdered stone or fine sand handy. Then paint the surface with a medium-strength glue and when still tacky, throw the powder at the surface.

Glue-painting gives a good copy of concrete, rough stone, trampled-in cinders, and similar surfaces.

UNDERLAY	Using
VENEERING	Method
VENTILATION	Below Floor
VISE	Hinged
VISES	Saw Sharpening
VISES	Types
VINEGAR	Using

UNDERLAY—Using

Hardboard underlay makes vinyl, linoleum, rubber and cork floor coverings look better and last longer because, unlike timber floorboards, the joints rarely show through.

The hardboard underlay is .215 in. thick and comes in sheets measuring 4 ft by 3 ft

This is how it should be laid on a timber floor:

Depending on its condition, the floor is machine-sanded and then hand-sanded or planed to remove high spots.

The hardboard sheets are laid smooth-side up, in ashlar pattern to stagger joints, leaving ⅛ in. space at wall edges and ¹⁄₆₄ in. between sheets.

Hardboard sheets are cut to size by a fine tooth saw or by scoring with curved linoleum knife or trimming knife and then breaking along the scored line. The knife cut edges face the wall when the underlay is laid.

The sheets may be secured to the floor in three ways. By compressed air stapler, impact stapler, or hammer and nails.

Fix at 3 in. centers along edges (⅜ in. from edge) and at 6 in. centers over rest of the area. The joints are then sanded level.

After it has been swept carefully, the sanded area is sealed with a solution of shellac and methylated spirits.

Final floor covering is laid, taking care to keep underlay joints free of adhesive. Overlay and underlay joints should not coincide.

VENEERING — Method

Although veneering work is not done as extensively now as in the past, there are still occasions when the process can be used to advantage, and of course there are numerous repair jobs where veneering is essential.

Basically veneering is the covering of plain-grained, sound wood or built-up panels of plywood or laminated board with a thin sheet of choice wood. The latter may be in a single piece or consist of a built-up pattern such as a halved or quartered design.

There are three main methods of application. These are referred to as the hammer, caul, and press methods respectively.

For the first, animal glue is used, the veneer being pressed down and the surplus glue squeezed out by the zig-zag movement of a veneering hammer.

The caul is a flat board or zinc-covered board which is heated and clamped down over the veneer for the same purpose.

A veneer press may be either manually operated by large wing nuts fitted over screws or be hydraulically controlled.

The base or groundwork must be sound and free from defects, and in best quality work both sides are veneered to avoid uneven tension which could cause the groundwork to become distorted.

A toothing plane is used to roughen the surface of the solid base or groundwork to provide a key or grip for the glue.

VENTILATION — Below Floor

Dampness under the house can threaten the house footings and floors with decay, and every householder should be on the lookout to guard against it.

Ventilators in external walls, it's estimated, should provide a clear airway of at least 1½ sq. in. for each foot in length of the wall. And it's preferable to have as much as 4 sq. in. per foot.

Internal partition walls should have a greater proportion of openings.

Ventilators and openings should be located so they ventilate all parts of the space below the floor. There should be a ventilator not more than 3 ft from each corner, to avoid dead-air pockets.

The ventilators should not be blocked by earth underneath the house.

The clear airway of some types of terra-cotta and concrete ventilators is less than 10 per cent of their overall size. The woven-wire type of ventilator, with open mesh, is better in this respect, as it gives up to 50 per cent of clean air space and is at the same time vermin-proof.

To avoid decay and other faults in floors it is essential to have adequate ventilation below the floor, so that excess dampness can't build up, building experts say.

Ventilation openings are provided in the walls, of a house for this purpose, so that air can enter and circulate freely under the floor, but in some cases they may not be adequate.

The amount of ventilation needed depends on a number of things, such as the height of the floor above the ground, the dampness and slope of the site, the positions of nearby buildings and fences, and even the direction of the prevailing winds.

Where there is dampness under a house and it's difficult to provide enough ventilation, the amount of moisture given out by the soil can be greatly reduced by covering it with waterproof material such as roofing felt or polyethylene sheet.

This material should be lapped at least 2 in. where it joins.

VISE—Hinged

The metal-worker's vise fitted on top of the home workshop bench can be a nuisance when you're using the bench for planing timber or assembling furniture.

See the illustration at (A) for a practical solution to the problem.

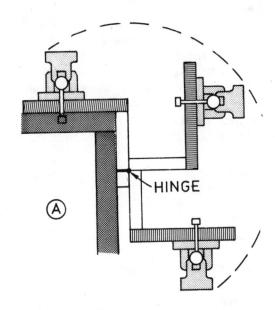

HINGE

(A)

Attach the vise to a hinged angle plate, which in turn is fitted to the end of the bench to allow the vise to be swung down out of the way when not required.

This is indicated clearly by the direction of the arrow.

Only hand tools are needed to do the job, and the materials needed are a short end of angle iron to suit the size of the vise, a 4 in. narrow butt hinge and screws, three bolts and six countersunk machine-thread bolts for attaching the hinge.

The size of the angle iron could be 6 in. by 6 in. by 9 in. long by ⅝ in. thick for a large vise, or smaller as required.

Cut a strip from one side of the angle with a hacksaw and drill and tap both strip and main angle section to accommodate the hinge, which is held by two countersunk belts across the two pieces as at (B).

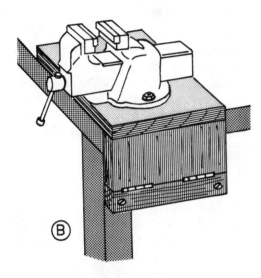

The vise can be mounted directly on the other outside face of the angle iron by means of short bolts and nuts.

Alternatively, a circular base of heavy plywood or coreboard can be cut to form a turntable, which is mounted on the angle iron with a center pivot bolt.

The vise is bolted to this timber circular base.

The advantage of this arrangement is that the vise will swivel to any desired position.

The assembled unit is now bolted or screwed to the side of the bench with two bolts or screws through the ends of the lower strip as shown at (B).

VISES—Saw Sharpening

When sharpening a saw, it is necessary to have some kind of vise for holding the blade firmly while it is being filed.

For the home use the wooden saw sharpening vise shown in Fig. 1 is ideal. When sharpening a saw, it is essential to place the vise where the light strikes upon the top of the teeth. This will enable the handyman to see clearly when the teeth have been filed to the required angle and shape. This saw vise can be leaned against the side of the bench and the armrests closed down, or it may be used near a window or wall with equal success. In the latter case, the short armrests (E) Fig. 2 are turned out to keep the vise free from the wall.

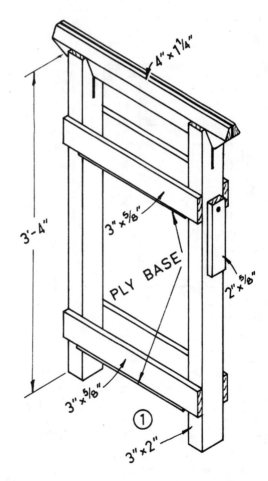

A softwood like pine could be used and the two legs (A) Figs. 2 and 3 are held in position by cross rails (B) which are nailed or screwed to the legs. The top of each leg is cut to a V-shape to receive a pair of tapered jaws (C). The saw is inserted between the jaws which are then tapped down lightly with a hammer or file end to grip the blade firmly. Under each pair of rails, a plywood bottom (D) is nailed to form a tray for holding files and other small items of tools. The short arms (E) are screwed to the frame as indicated in Figs. 2 and 3, they act as distance pieces if sharpening with the vise against a wall or window.

The jaws are cut from timber 4 in. wide, 1¼ in. thick, and 2 ft 2 in. long. They are tapered to match the V cut in the legs, and the top edges of both jaws are beveled as shown. In addition, the bottom corner of each jaw piece is splayed to make room for the saw handle.

The positions of the four cross rails are indicated clearly in Fig. 3 and the short arm pieces (E) are placed about level with the top cross rails. Fasten each arm with one screw, and tighten the screws just sufficiently to allow the arms to be moved with pressure. It will then be found that they will stay in a set position automatically.

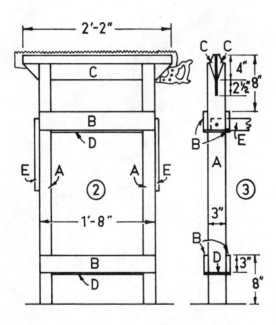

The V cut in the legs extends 3 in. from the top of the leg, and is 2½ in. at its widest part. One leg is sawn vertically from the bottom of the V for a further 2½ in. down the leg, and this is shown clearly in the sectional view provided in Fig. 3. The wide end of the saw blade sinks down into this cut, and the teeth are brought level until they are slightly above the top of the vise jaws.

VISES—Types

Every handyman must have at least one bench vise to hold wood or metal while he shapes it.

The type shown in Fig. 1 gives the best results and is intended for all work where timber is to be gripped firmly.

Such vises come in two styles, one with standard action and one with a more elaborate quick-action release.

The latter is worth the extra cost for the time it saves.

A good size for this type of vise is one with 7 in. long jaws.

It should be noted that after fitting a vise such as this it will be necessary to fix protective wooden blocks to the two inside metal faces of the jaws as a protection against bruising work held in the vise.

A precaution with a woodworking vise is to avoid using it for metalwork of any kind.

What is needed for such work is the engineer's vise shown in Fig. 3.

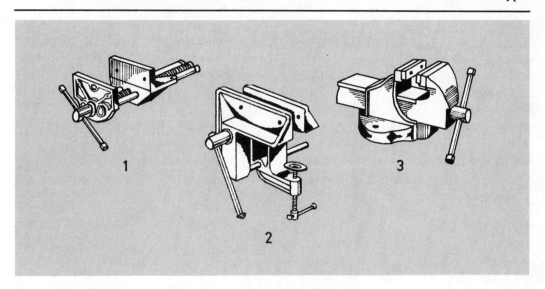

1

2

3

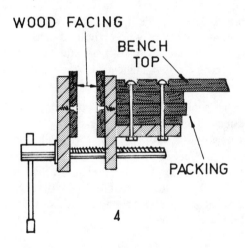

WOOD FACING

BENCH TOP

PACKING

4

Sizes vary, but a good size for general work is 4 in.

This refers to the length from side to side of the jaws, and not the width that the jaws will open.

As a general rule, the engineer's vise is not fixed permanently to the woodworking bench, but adapted so that it can be removed or set up as required.

The small vise shown in Fig. 2 is most useful for jobs away from a bench. It may be clamped to a stool.

Fig. 4 shows how the woodworker's vise, Fig. 1, is fitted to a bench.

If the bench has an apron, remove this and cut a gap to take the vise. Position it about a foot from the left end if possible, but position of the bench in the workshop may prevent this.

Usually a packing piece is necessary between the underside of the bench top and the fastening plate of the vise. The illustration shows how to make up and secure a packing piece and bolt in the vise.

It is advisable to have timber facings on the vise jaws. These are best cut from dry hardwood with a thickness of about ½ in.

Arrange the facings so that the top edges are just clear of the metal jaws and the sides about 1 in. wider.

When delicate articles or highly polished surfaces must be clamped in a steel vise, fiber grips will prevent damage.

Or, you can sheath the jaws in lead, copper or brass—whichever is most suitable for the material to be placed in the vise —formed as illustrated.

When bending metal in a steel vise, always make the bend against the rear jaw, not against the movable jaw.

If the metal is bent over the movable jaw, heavy hammer blows required for the bending may damage the vise screw.

VINEGAR — Using

Vinegar is a familiar commodity that is not used enough in the home. Add a little vinegar to the water to improve the color and flavor of vegetables.

Meat suspected of being tough should be well rubbed with vinegar before cooking. A few drops added while boiling fish will keep the flesh firm and white. It will also prevent egg shells cracking and the white running, when boiling.

A little in the washing-up water helps to clean greasy dishes. Stains in glass vases, decanters and so on can be removed by soaking in hot water containing vinegar and salt. Added to the rinsing water, it will give glassware a luster.

To brighten the colors and revive a shabby carpet, brush it well and then rub it with a mixture of one part vinegar and two parts warm water. Add it to the water when washing linoleum to freshen the colors and make it shine.

To prevent the color of material running in the washtub, soak it in cold water and vinegar before washing, using one tablespoonful to a gallon.

Dull brass can be quickly cleaned by rubbing with a rag dipped in a mixture of vinegar and salt. Steelwork too will clean much more easily if it's first wiped over with vinegar. Windows will shine brighter washed with water containing a little vinegar, and polished.

Slimy sponges should have an overnight soak in a mixture of one-third vinegar, two-thirds water. Afterwards rinse them well in hot water.

A few drops sprinkled onto a shovel and waved about a sick room for a few minutes makes an excellent and refreshing deodorant. A cup of vinegar poured into a hot bath will take away stiffness after strenuous exercise. It is beneficial to the skin, too, making it soft and white.

To relieve pain and bruising on a knocked elbow or knee, make a paste of vinegar and oatmeal and spread it thickly over the bruise, then bandage and keep on for an hour or two or overnight. The pain and discoloration will almost disappear. This is an excellent remedy and deserves to be better known.

WALLPAPER	Cleaning
WALLPAPER	Lining
WALLPAPER	Pastes
WALLPAPER	Removing
WALL	Sloping
WALLS	Resurface
WASTE PIPES	Cleaning
WATER PIPES	First Aid
WEATHERBOARDS	Care
WHITE ANTS (Termites)	Details
WINDING STRIPS	Their Use
WINDOWS	Frosted
WINDOWS	Paint to Plan
WINDOWS	Reglazing
WINDOWS	Replace Cords
WOODSAWS	Types

ZINC	Is Durable

WALLPAPER — Cleaning

Wallpaper will collect dust and dirt and needs periodic cleaning to keep it bright and fresh.

The more expensive textured papers are harder to keep clean than plain surfaces, and great care must be taken when cleaning so as to avoid damage to the pattern.

The procedure is first to brush the wallpapered surface down to remove surface dirt. For this, use a wall brush, a soft cloth, or the brush attachment on the vacuum cleaner.

The aim should be to flick the paper. Hard rubbing merely presses the dirt into the surface.

In severe cases, the paper may have to be sponged lightly.

Wet first with clean water, then rub gently with soft cloth or sponge dipped in water containing detergent.

Start at an upper corner and wash out and down, covering about 10 sq. ft at a time.

The main precaution is not to make the paper too wet, as this could possibly cause it to lose its grip on the wall.

For grease spots, one method is to moisten a clean rag with mineral spirits or cleaning fluid, dab it into Fuller's earth, then brush it over the area.

Let this dry, then repeat, and finally brush off the Fuller's earth remaining on the surface.

The spirit loosens the grease, and the Fuller's earth absorbs it.

It is common for children to scribble over wallpaper with crayons, and here the first step in removal is to scrape off any excess in one direction with a knife.

Then cover the marks with a mixture of Fuller's earth and mineral spirits, overlapping the marks a few inches. Let this dry overnight and then brush it off.

Don't try to clean crayon marks off with cleaning fluid alone, as it may spread them over a greater area and make complete removal difficult.

WALLPAPER — Lining

The use of a lining paper under wallpaper is something the average home decorator may be a little doubtful about.

On occasion it is essential for lining paper to be used to achieve a satisfactory result, and here is a summary of such occasions.

1. When a paper has a surface that reflects light, such as a varnished, waxed, satin or satinette, then a defect on the plaster, or any unevenness, will be accentuated when hung. The lining will level this surface.

2. All heavy embossed papers, when pasted, have a tendency to stretch as the fibers absorb the paste and shrink on drying. This often causes the joints to open, due to the paper losing its grip on the plaster surface. Lining paper will stop this.

3. When delicate types of paper are used on which the colors are lightly bound, the paste is liable to soak into the paper causing stains to appear as it dries. The lining in this case acts as a sheet of blotting paper and takes up the excess paste.

4. When the surface to be prepared is smoothly troweled plaster, with very little absorption, once again the paste will be absorbed into the wallpaper quicker than into the wall. Also paper tends to open at the joints as it dries because the smoothness

321

and hardness provides a weak key to receive the wallpaper.

5. Previously painted surfaces, especially the glossy type, have a poor surface for receiving wallpaper and promote condensation which will eventually cause (through damping up) the paper to loosen.

6. When relief decorations are to be hung. Because they are heavy, lining papers greatly assist in holding them to the ceiling or walls.

The advantage of lining walls before paper-hanging is that it provides a ground of uniform absorption and a key for the wallpaper to attach itself.

The hanging of lining paper follows the same practice as applied to wallpaper, except, unless the edges are damaged, it does not require trimming.

Strips should be hung horizontally to the walls, being right-angled to that of the wallpaper. This creates good bonding.

WALLPAPER — Pastes

One of the greatest concerns of the home paperhanger is to avoid marking the surface of the paper.

Without great care at every stage—in pasting, handling, and smoothing out—some paste blotches can reach the front surface of the paper.

The risk of staining depends to some extent on the type of paste used, and in this regard cellulose paste is less likely to stain than other types.

Nevertheless, the home decorator especially should be warned that even a cellulose adhesive may cause a blemish in another direction.

The high water content which in most cases reduces the chance of leaving a surface mark will have more tendency to disturb the pattern of some loosely bound pigmented papers.

Always avoid brushing across the face of such papers with a wet brush, and any paste blots should be left to dry naturally.

Another ill-effect of an ultra high water content wallpaper paste can be through excessive penetration from the back.

Embossing may be softened and lost, and on some papers there is a possibility of a bloom or watermark effect. In such cases a paste containing less water is needed.

Although the cellulose-type wallpaper adhesive has various advantages, it is worth remembering that the well-known and proven cold water paste powders also have considerable merit.

For example, such pastes having a much greater solids content, are less likely to disturb the pattern of loosely bound pigmented papers and have less tendency to strike through from the back of the paper.

Cellulose adhesives have been successfully used to hang a very wide range of papers, including quite heavy weights. The water content should be reduced when hanging the heavier weights of paper, and double pasting is recommended.

Any failure to hold, or of bubbles appearing, or peeling occurring are usually due to insufficient or patchy pasting.

It is important to make sure that the paper is completely covered with a good layer of paste. Unless this is done it is possible that a patch of paper may have been brushed over once with a thin film of adhesive which, although appearing at the time to have been well covered, will quickly soak away or dry out, leaving insufficient paste on the surface to grip the wall.

Again, it should be remembered that the old-fashioned flour paste have first-class properties of immediate grip and good slide for adjustment, and may be made suitable for certain papers or jobs.

For the homeworker, these comments will underline the importance of using the most suitable paste for the particular paper selected. It is always a good idea to ask the advice of the wallpaper firm on this matter when buying the paper.

WALLPAPER — Removing

To strip off old wallpaper before redecorating a room, you should wet it thoroughly first.

This softens the old paste and enables you to scrape the paper off more easily.

The simplest way to wet the paper is with a large brush.

You let the water soak in for a few minutes before getting to work with the stripper blade.

If the paper is very firmly stuck and especially if there are several layers, try using wallpaper paste instead of water to moisten the paper.

Mix the paste rather thinner than you would for pasting and brush it evenly over the whole wall. Let it almost dry out, then thoroughly wet the wall with hot water, treating small areas at a time, and the paper should peel away more easily.

The paste prevents the water evaporating and ensures that it soaks into the paper.

It also avoids water running down the wall and making puddles on the floor.

WALL — Sloping

Small garden retaining walls offer greater resistance to pressure from built-up garden beds if they are on a slight slope or rake.

However, to look attractive, small walls must have a uniform slope throughout their length.

It is a comparatively simple matter to ensure this by using an easily made plumb-bob which does away with guesswork. Just build up a light framework from 2 in. wide by 1 in. thick battens.

As shown in the illustration it is a back upright and two horizontal rails, the top rail being longer than the bottom one. Set the upright at the desired angle, with the top and bottom rails square and parallel to each other.

Drill a hole through the top rail for the plumb line and mark a cross on the upper face of the bottom rail in exact alignment with this hole. Then mount the plumb-bob in the frame so that it swings free of the bottom cross rail.

To use, hold the sloping upright against the wall as shown, and note the position of the plumb-bob in relation to the cross mark. When the point of the plumb-bob is directly over the cross the wall will be at the same angle to the ground as the upright member of the wooden frame.

When such walls are built permanently with mortar joints the plumb-bob frame is used to check slope as work proceeds.

WALLS — Resurface

Brickwork is bound to get shabby in time, especially in cities or industrial areas. Attempts to make the brickwork look new by painting over and picking out the mortar joints in color are usually disappointing, and need fairly frequent renewal.

More permanent results can be obtained from colored cement finishes, especially those based on renderings applied over the brickwork, which are then given a subsequent finish of decorative material.

Modern improvements in technique have greatly widened the choice both as to color and texture.

One of the big advances has been the introduction of the hand-cranked projector called a Tyrolean applicator, which has greatly simplified the application of the decorative finishes. Normally, the best results are obtained when the final finish is applied on top of a coat of rendering but it is in fact possible to build up a satisfactory thickness by direct application on top of unrendered brickwork.

Most people will have seen pebble-dashings and similar finishes applied by hand—the operator uses a wooden scoop to fling the material forcibly against the rendering while still soft—and enough clings to the wall to form the surface.

With the projector method the material is applied mechanically, the granules being propelled forward by paddles attached to a hand crank.

The projector also has the advantage of being able to apply semi-liquid mixes which form attractive surfaces on the wall, and which could hardly be applied in any other way.

However, even without a projector, some attractive decorative finishes can be produced, and no special skill is required. Some use can be made of brushes for stippling, for example, or of wire combs for giving an uneven surface of considerable depth.

Some of the modern cement paints give a solid surface and dry with a granulated effect. Suitable surfaces for decoration in this way include old and new concrete, existing rendered walls, bare bricks or block walls, even cement-asbestos sheeting.

WASTE PIPES — Cleaning

Even when the greatest care is exercised, the waste pipes serving kitchen sinks and bathroom basins are sure to require cleaning sooner or later.

Naturally the kitchen sink is the unit most likely to give trouble, and every effort should be made to prevent rubbish finding its way into the waste pipe.

When trouble does occur it is usually found in the trap immediately underneath the sink.

The purpose of this trap is to form a seal against the offensive odors contained in the drain and prevent them rising and entering the kitchen via the sink waste pipe.

To enable the grease and other rubbish which accumulates in the trap to be released, a plug or cleanout cap is put on the bottom of the trap as shown in the illustration.

Sometimes plugs are round, with two projections on the surface. Place a flat tool between these two spurs and, holding the trap firmly with the free hand, unscrew the cap.

However, before doing this, place a bucket beneath the trap, so that when the cleanout cap or plug is removed, much of the waste will immediately drop out and be caught in the bucket.

Use a piece of stout wire to rake any stubborn pieces of rubbish out of the trap, and flush out with warm water run into the sink above.

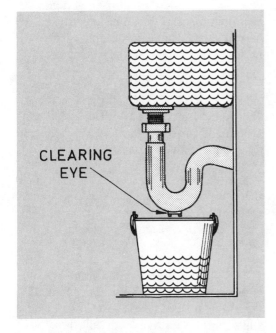

CLEARING EYE

Examine the cleanout cap to make sure that the washer or sealing gasket is intact, then replace it, screwing it back as tight as possible with the fingers. Flush more water through waste pipe, and if it runs freely, tighten the cap fully—but don't over-tighten.

WATER PIPES — First Aid

A water pipe has cracked and you want to make a repair. What can you do?

If the water is not under much pressure, force stiff bituminous roofing compound into the crack. Then wrap several layers of adhesive tape around the pipe over the repair.

This should hold until you can get a permanent repair made.

If the water is under considerable pressure, use this method: Brighten the metal around the crack with emery cloth, then wrap a piece of clean copper wire around the pipe over the crack and smear with soldering flux.

Next flow solder over the wire so that it adheres to the pipe. This repair should last a long time if properly done. You must first turn off the water at the main before starting on this job.

WEATHERBOARDS — Care

The appearance of a weatherboard house depends mainly on the condition of the weatherboards themselves, and regular maintenance work is necessary.

Rotting or damaged boards should be cut out and replaced carefully with boards of the same size and pattern. It is advisable to paint the new sections all over before nailing. Use good quality exterior oil paint.

Cracks, holes, etc., in otherwise sound boards should be filled with linseed oil putty. However, paint these blemishes first with priming or undercoat, so that the putty will adhere properly. Joints between the boards should also be puttied after undercoating, if necessary.

When painting, pay particular attention to exposed ends of weatherboards where moisture can enter through the end grain and cause rotting of the wood.

If you have to do fairly extensive replacement of weatherboards or on new work, the following suggestions will be useful:

Work on the principle that all joints are unsightly, and avoid grouping joints together. You must also keep the boards straight especially where the lines can catch the eye.

This means picking out the straightest boards for those places which come most directly under notice, also choosing the boards to suit the wall-length wherever possible.

First sort the weatherboards into their different lengths. Where possible use long boards without joints for better appearance.

Always stagger the joints—that is, never join two successive rows of boards on the same wall stud. It is always best to have at least two continuous boards between any joints directly above each other.

Never make joints directly above or below the sides of windows or doors, and keep them away from openings.

When a joint can't be avoided, leave the end of the first board free, then slide the other board behind it and mark with a pencil to give the cutting line. This will ensure a well-fitting joint.

To avoid the risk of splitting, the ends of boards at all joints should be drilled for the nails. Afterwards all nail heads are punched slightly below the surface. The holes are filled with putty after the surface has been primed.

When fitting boards against a window or door frame, and the joint is to be covered with an architrave, there is no need to worry about a perfect fit.

WHITE ANTS (Termites) — Details

In the task of controlling and eradicating white ants, it must be realized that house foundations which are well off the ground are less liable to attack, because they allow a greater amount of light to penetrate, and there is also a better circulation of air.

In addition, high foundations allow periodical inspections to be made with greater ease and effectiveness. That last point is perhaps the most important, because if the termites can be prevented from making their tunnels or runs from the ground, they cannot do any damage to the building.

Of course, it is not sufficient merely to destroy the runs along which the white ants operate. If possible, the nest or colony in the ground should be destroyed, too.

All the preparations used for exterminating work are poisonous, and should be used with extreme care, and preferably under the supervision of an expert in their application.

The placing of galvanized iron caps over all piers and walls in the foundation is a very necesary precaution in the fight against white ants, but even with all these safeguards, periodical inspections are essential.

WINDING STRIPS — Their Use

When narrow surfaces such as the edges of boards are planed, a true planed surface, free from twist, must be obtained, especially when the edges are to be glued or otherwise joined together.

Providing the face side is free from twist and perfectly planed, the try square could be used to test the squareness of the edge, and also to show whether or not there was any twist in the edge.

On a narrow ledge, however, it is not always easy to detect small errors or variations in the surface.

On this account, winding strips, as shown in the illustration are particularly useful.

Two straight edges, or parallel strips of some fairly soft, dry timber, are made to any convenient size—say 12 to 15 in. long and 2 in. wide.

These are then laid on the edges or face to be tested. They are placed towards opposite ends and with long boards a third strip in the center is an advantage.

A sight is taken across the top of the strips from behind in the manner shown. Any twist in the planed edge can be immediately detected.

The sketch here clearly shows that the edge of the wood being tested has a slight wind or twist. The two winding strips, instead of being parallel, tilt in opposite directions.

It can be seen from this that winding sticks are particularly useful for testing narrow edges. Larger winding sticks can be used for detecting the twist or warp in the face of a wide board or even in a complete frame.

WINDOWS — Frosted

The correct method of getting a frosted effect on glass is by means of etching with an acid, or sand blasting the surface.

But it is possible to produce a satisfactory frosted or matt effect on plain glass windows by methods that are well within the scope of the handyman.

Perhaps the simplest and cheapest method is to employ ordinary flat white paint, such as that sold as a white undercoating. This dries with a matt surface.

When used for frosting windows, it should be applied with a short-bristle, flat-ended brush, known as a stipple brush.

The smallest possible quantity of paint should be taken up on the brush, any surplus being removed by dabbing the bristles on a piece of board or paper.

Having charged the brush satisfactorily, apply the paint to the glass in a series of consecutive dabbing movements, tapping the glass once in each position, then moving the brush to one side before giving another tap. Of course, the paint should be applied to the inside of the window pane.

Another method is to mix lead acetate crystals with some hard, clear varnish to a thin, creamlike consistency.

This is also applied with a stipple brush in the same way as the flat undercoat.

A good mixture for greenhouses, etc.,— and one that can be removed fairly easily if necesary—is made by dissolving woodworker's glue to a fairly thin consistency and mixing it with whiting to form a paint which can be applied with an ordinary paint brush.

For those people who wish to look out of a window but prevent anyone looking in, a special tinted glass can be used.

However, a better alternative would be strip mirror sheet, the outside surface of which is made up of alternative plain glass and mirror strips.

WINDOWS — Paint to Plan

Of all the painting jobs around the house, window sashes and the main window frames can be the most difficult unless the working procedure is planned.

The correct method of painting a window depends on its type, and the various forms that you are likely to encounter are as follows:

The double-hung, or box frame window is made of wood in most existing homes and consists of two sections. These are the top or outer sash, and the bottom or inner sash.

The sashes are pushed up or down to open, and counterbalanced with weights or springs which hold the sashes in any position. The window is secured by a catch which locks the two sashes together.

Casement windows can be of wood or metal, and hinged at the top, bottom, or sides.

They may open either outwards or inwards, and a stay is usually fitted to control the amount of opening. A separate catch keeps the window closed.

Pivoted windows may be hung to swing either vertically or horizontally so that the outside can be cleaned from within the room. Like casements, they may be of wood or metal.

The correct painting procedure is first to pry off the staff or stop beads, clean them down with fine sandpaper and prime or undercoat.

Then, when the frame and sashes have been prepared and undercoated, the staff beads can be replaced before the final coat is applied.

This avoids the possibility of windows jamming because of paint build-up on the beads; it also means that if the beads have to be removed later in order to renew a broken sash cord, they will come away cleanly without leaving a ragged paint edge on the frame.

All window fittings such as handles and catches should be removed to make for easier painting.

Catches should be cleaned and oiled; if you intend to paint them, remove the old paint to ensure free movement.

Where the window sash or sashes have a number of small panes fitted in glazing bars, Fig. 1, these bars should be painted first.

To do this neatly calls for careful cutting-in. The tradesman painter achieves this by skilful work with a sash brush held at a

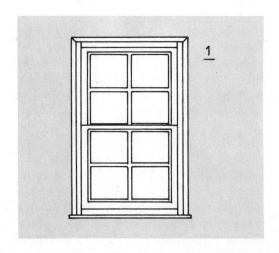

45 degree angle, but the amateur may find it easier to use a light metal shield to protect the glass from streaks of paint as painting proceeds.

Alternatively, he can mask the panes with tape before painting, or paint slightly on to the glass and remove the surplus with a razor blade scraper when the paint is dry.

Never scrape off surplus paint until it is absolutely dry. If the paint is still tacky on the underside, it may stick to the finished surface and spoil it.

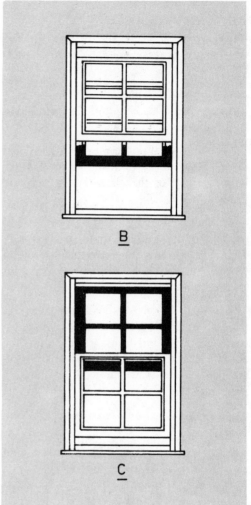

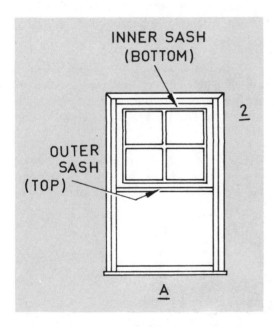

The correct sequence of painting for a box-frame window is shown clearly in Fig. 2.

Push the inner (bottom) sash up as far as it will go (A), and pull the outer (top), sash down until about half of it is visible below the bottom edge of the inner sash.

Then paint the visible part of the outer sash (B) and pull the inner sash down again to within a few inches of its closed position, and push the outer sash up to a similar position as shown in detail (C).

You can now complete the painting of both sashes. Remember, however, that the top and bottom edges of the outer sash are painted the same color as the outside of the window frame. The top and bottom edges of the inner sash are painted to match the inside of the frame.

There must be no build-up of excess paint on the top edge of the outer sash, or on the bottom edge of the inner sash, and these two surfaces must be allowed to dry thoroughly before the window is closed.

WINDOWS — Reglazing

Replacing a badly cracked or broken window-pane is an essential job for the householder.

Three tools are needed, a putty-knife, a hammer, and a hacking-knife; an old chisel is also useful.

First remove all loose pieces of glass that can be pulled away from the frame and dislodge the rest of the glass that is still held firmly.

This can be done by chipping away the old putty with the hacking knife and hammer as in Fig. 1. This must be done carefully to avoid damaging the rabbet by cutting into the wood.

When all the broken glass has been removed, continue to chip away the putty all round the window-frame, and, with the chisel, scrape the rabbet clean, after removing the brads which held the the old pane in place.

The next step is to take the measurements for the new piece of glass. This must be done carefully, preferably with a 2 ft rule, and the length and width of the new pane should be $\frac{1}{8}$ in. smaller than the opening between the rebates.

Your supplier will cut glass to the required size and will also supply the putty.

Before you place the glass in the rabbet, a thin bed of putty has to be formed all round for the edges of the glass to rest against; but before doing this, give the rabbet a coating of paint and allow to dry before applying putty.

To form the bedding take a piece of well-kneaded putty in the hand and proceed to apply a layer round the rabbet by pressing it in place with the thumb as shown in Fig. 2.

Carefully place the new pane in position, bottom edge first, and gently press it along the four edges so that it squeezes some of

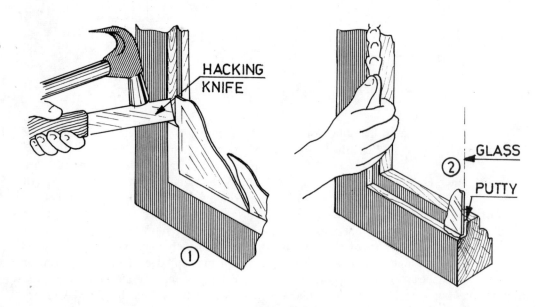

HACKING KNIFE

① ② GLASS PUTTY

the putty out at the back, as in Fig. 2. This superfluous putty is afterwards removed with a knife.

Now hammer in two or three small brads along the side of the glass to hold it temporarily in place, as in Fig. 3.

When tapping these brads in place, keep the hammer-head flat against the glass to avoid breaking it. These brads are finally covered with facing putty and left in.

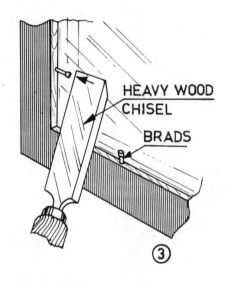

HEAVY WOOD CHISEL

BRADS

③

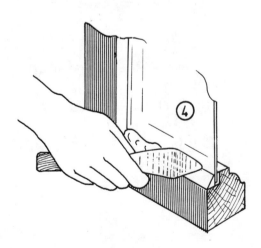

④

Now, with the thumb, work some putty well into the corners of the window-frame and glass, putting it on as evenly as possible.

With the putty-knife smooth the putty to a neat bevel all round the window-frame, as in Fig. 4. Hold the knife flat and firmly on the putty, drawing it along from corner to corner.

Finally, trim off the surplus putty at the back of the glass. The top edge of the bevel at the front should be level with the top edge of the rabbet on the inside of the window-frame.

The window should be left for twenty-four hours before the glass is cleaned, in order to give the putty time to harden. It can then be painted to match the rest of the window frame.

In some types of window the glass is held in position on the outside of the frame with narrow wood beading instead of putty. The glass is first bedded in putty in the back of the rabbet, pressed in place and the strips of beading, mitered at the corners, are fixed with fine nails.

In this case brads will not be required for holding the glass.

WINDOWS — Replace Cords

The box frame type of window in which the two vertically sliding sashes operate on cords and weights, has demonstrated its efficiency over many years.

An occasional broken cord is about all that can go wrong with them and this can be replaced quite easily.

The two weights, one on each side, which serve each sash are together approximately as heavy as the sash—which means that when you open the window it stays put and does not move down to the bottom.

When the cord breaks, the weight to which it is attached becomes disconnected, and it is important to renew sash cords immediately.

You will have to take the sashes out in any case, so you may just as well make one job of it, particularly as paintwork is liable to become chipped in the process. It is always well to examine cords and replace them if necessary before you start repainting a room.

Buy only the best waxed cord from your ironmonger. This will last much longer than unwaxed and will obviate the need for replacement at frequent intervals. It is sold in hanks measuring about 12 yds sufficient for between three and six windows, according to size.

Follow the instructions here and you will not only save time but use the new cord without waste. Working from the inside of the house, lower the top sash and cut the four cords where shown in Fig. 1.

Lift the cut end of each cord up to the pulley before letting it go.

Loosen the two vertical staff beads, one on each side, by inserting a blunt chisel between them and the frame, about half-way up. Then grasp each bead and spring it out with your hand. The beads are generally attached by three nails and can be released without trouble, Fig. 2.

But if, when you are springing them out, the top and bottom nails are not exposed sufficiently for removal without snapping the bead, you will have to cut them, with wire snips or a hacksaw. As a rule, there is no need to remove top and bottom horizontal beads.

With the vertical beads removed you can take out the lower sash. Now pry off the parting beads and take out the upper sash.

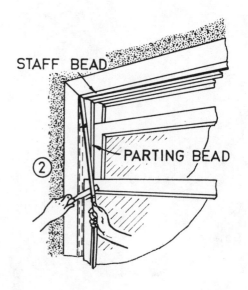

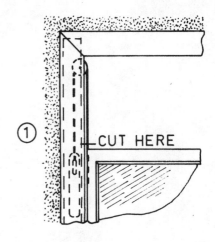

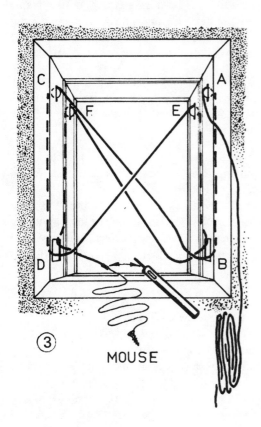

③ MOUSE

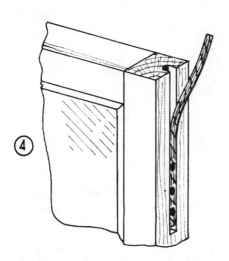

④

With a blunt chisel remove the pocket covering sash boxes. You will find them near the foot of each pulley stile at (B) and (D), Fig. 3. Put your hand inside the apertures and take out the two weights. Inside you may find loosely fitting dividing laths. Pull these on one side and take out the other two weights. Remove the old cut cords from weights and window sashes.

Tie one end of a length of thread to a "mouse." The mouse can be a screw or nut small enough to ride over the pulley wheels. Tie the other end of the thread to one end of the new hank of sash cord and pass the mouse over pulley (A), Fig. 3, until it drops sufficiently low for you to put your hand into sash box (B) and pull it out, dragging the heavier cord in its wake.

Don't cut the cord at this stage, but pass the mouse over pulley (C) and drag it, with the sash cord attached, out of box (D).

Unfasten the sash cord from the thread and attach it to one of the weights by inserting it through the hole at the top and tying a couple of retaining knots. Hammer the knots into the counter-sunk part of the hole so that ends do not stick out and interfere with the passage of the weight up and down in the sash box.

Place the weight in box (D) on the far side of the dividing lath. Pull on the cord where it passes over pulley (F) so that the weight is brought to the top and then pull again, this time extra hard, to stretch it to the utmost and tighten the knot.

Measure three-quarters of the height of the window opening from the top. Cut the cord at that point and keep it in position by lightly nailing it into the groove where the dividing bead has been, Fig. 5.

Tie the cut end of the cord to another weight and place in box (B), again on the far side of the lath. Pull hard on the cord passing over pulley (E), cut at three-quarters way down and lightly nail to the other dividing-bead rabbet on that side.

Repeat the process over pulley (C), placing the weight this time on the near side of the dividing lath. Repeat again over pulley (A), with the weight in box (B), again on the near side of the dividing lath.

Pull out the nail temporarily holding the cord which passes over pulley (F), and attach the cord to the left-hand side of the upper sash, nailing it firmly in the groove provided with three clout nails, Fig. 4. Do the nailing near the bottom of the groove not at the top or you will find the sash will not close properly.

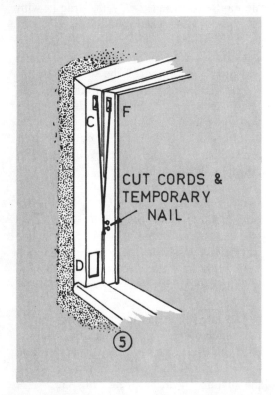

CUT CORDS & TEMPORARY NAIL

Pull out the nail holding cord passing over pulley (E) and attach with three clout nails to the right-hand groove of the upper sash.

Place the upper sash in frame; replace pocket piece and parting bead. Test the sash to see that it rides up and down properly.

Pull out the temporary nails holding cords passing over pulleys (C) and (A), and clout nails to the left and right-hand grooves of the bottom sash. Place bottom sash in frame. Nail on the staff beads, punching the heads below the surface, and level up with putty or other filler—and the job is done.

WOODSAWS — Types

Wood saws can be sub-divided into three main classes: saws with long, flexible blades, generally called handsaws; those with shorter blades stiffened along the top edge, called backsaws; and those where the blade is very narrow and can be fitted into a suitable frame, called bow saws. These classifications are somewhat arbitrary since there are a number of variations possible. See illustration.

The main handsaws are those used for the preliminary cutting of timber, and sometimes for the cutting of large joints.

Teeth forms vary according to the requirement of the saw, for example, a large set for cutting across the grain, smaller teeth for fine cutting.

Ripsaws for cutting with the grain differ from other handsaws in that their teeth are sharpened on the vertical edge only and so cut only on the forward stroke. Crosscut saws cut on both strokes and can also be used for ripping.

A panel saw is used for finer work, having smaller teeth—that is more points per inch. A crosscut saw and a panel saw are minimum requirements for the woodworker. A ripsaw is optional.

The padsaw or keyhole saw is a specialized handsaw with a narrow, flexible blade used for small curved work. Skillfully used, it can take the place of a bow saw for much curved cutting, although it is most easily handled when cutting thin stock.

The blade of a keyhole saw is very liable to buckle if forced too hard and so, as a general rule, the shortest length of blade possible is used, consistent with cutting requirements.

The coping saw frame is usually made of round metal rod and slotted to hold special blades which may be looped on the ends or fitted with pins.

Backsaws—commonly called tenonsaws, are widely used for all kinds of bench work —general duty saws, in fact, since the stiff blade is capable of withstanding quite an amount of rough treatment. Tenon saws are made in a wide variety of blade lengths and widths.

The depth of cut possible is, of course, governed by the free width of the blade. Like handsaws, the handle is shaped in the form of a convenient grip, either closed, as in the sketches, or open ended. Strictly speaking a backsaw is designed for cutting tenons and similar work.

The dovetail saw is essentially similar, except that the teeth are much finer, thus making it suitable for fine, light work. The dovetail saw is a favorite of the model maker.

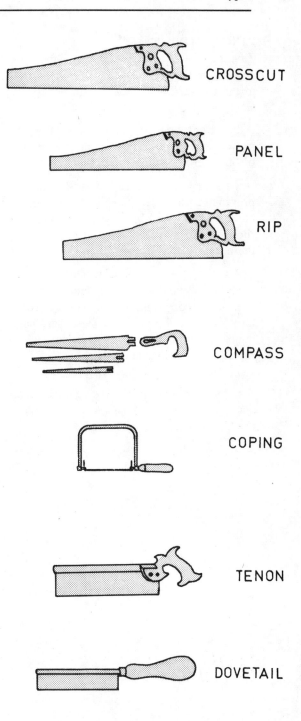

CROSSCUT

PANEL

RIP

COMPASS

COPING

TENON

DOVETAIL

ZINC — Is Durable

Zinc has been used for roofing since the 1830s, particularly on the Continent and in the United Kingdom although not extensively in the United States.

In recent times science has greatly improved zinc by blending small percentages of titanium and copper with the base metal.

This new alloy gives an all-round improvement in properties, including much greater rigidity and hardness, increased tensile strength, resistance to heat and reduced thermal expansion.

Zinc is a pure metal, which does not rust, is comparatively light, and extremely resistant to corrosion. This makes it particularly valuable in industrial and salt-laden atmospheres. However, it will deteriorate rapidly if brought into direct contact with some acids.

It forms its own protective coating which does not flake off under temperature changes, even up to 120 degrees F.

This coating process takes from three to six months to occur after which oxidation is uniform over the entire surface.

While zinc does not need to be painted for protective purposes, painting will further increase the service life of the metal.

The corrosion film once formed provides a good surface for painting.

In the case of bright new zinc the surface should be prepared or roughened before painting.

Hard zinc is best for roofing gutters, down-pipes, and valleys. Half-hard zinc can be used for easier working on flashing, roofing, and thick downpipes.

It can be easily worked on the site, making it ideal for roofing construction, particularly roll-cap.

A zinc roof properly laid and of suitable gauge metal should last at least 50 years—and would need no maintenance at all.

PROJECT IDEAS

GARDEN FURNITURE

As garden furniture has to withstand extremes of temperature and weather conditions it is necessary to pay special attention to the selection of timbers. Western red cedar and California redwood are highly durable and take clear finishes well. Others such as fir and hardwood are best painted—using first a primer undercoat and finishing with a top grade exterior oil paint.

A pleasing rustic effect has been created with old hardwood railroad ties used here as a retaining wall and for steps.

Variations in garden and patio settings made preferably from redwood or western red cedar. They take clear finishes well. Suggested size of framework is 2 in. by 4 in., minimum thickness of table and seat tops is 1½ in.

These slatted seat and back garden chairs are assembled with bolts and screws, preferably galvanized or brass.

Sturdy seat or form with precast concrete base legs. The seat is made from 2 in. by 4 in. hardwood and is bolted onto the cleat and stand. The timbers are approximately 1" apart. Note that the top of the seat is chamfered.

DRIVEWAYS

Concrete driveway is finished with roughened surface to provide good foothold. Note especially the divisions between slabs as a precaution against cracking. Colored gravel or crushed brick can be laid between the two strips. See Concrete Paving for full details concerning projects such as these.

Attractive concrete sweep. A driveway suitable for a deep frontage.

This pebbled path hugging
the line of the house has
been greatly enhanced
by the addition of an
attractive rock garden.
Note retaining edge strip is
flush with lawn to allow
for easy mowing.

Cacti has been planted
in the pockets of a
natural outcrop of rock.

Redwood or western red
cedar T & G boards
are most suitable for this
gate. Especially milled
matchboards provide the
distinctive V-joints.
Aperture for wrought iron
or cast aluminum insert
should be allowed
during the making of
the gate rather than cut
out afterwards.

GATES

*Gates can be decorative as well as functional, but like
all exterior woodwork it pays to keep them well
painted.*

Clinker brick makes a
complementary
material to this otherwise
severe grill gate.

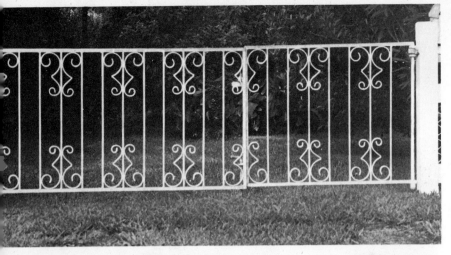

Wrought iron gates should always be galvanized to prevent rusting. However ungalvanized gates can be removed, sandblasted and galvanized for permanent protection. An alternative is to remove the rust by wire brushing and then to apply a rust inhibitor before finishing with paint.

Neat double picket gate.
Note provision of cross
braces in the frames
to ensure rigidity.

Old railroad tie is
used as an upright,
horizontal rails are bolted
inside the channel and
galvanized coach bolts
provide a studded look
to the exterior.

Rose pergola is made from
4 in. by 4 in. hardwood
posts and 2 in. by 8 in.
back and front bearer
plates with 2 in. by 4 in.
joists jointed by 1 in. by 2
in. battens. Sawn timber is
suitable for this job.

FENCES

The fabrics of the house and the environment should dictate the choice of domestic fence, and if painted, unobtrusive colors should be chosen. It should, in fact, blend with its surroundings.

Woven or basket-weave fence provides privacy. Thin, wide timber slats or strips of tempered hardboard may be used for the fabrication.

Scallop
arrangement of
pickets suits
conservative
architectural
styles.

Dwarf picket
fence blends well
with the natural
sandstone.

Wood and brick is in keeping with the character of the house. The line of the retaining garden strip softens the expanse of the fence.

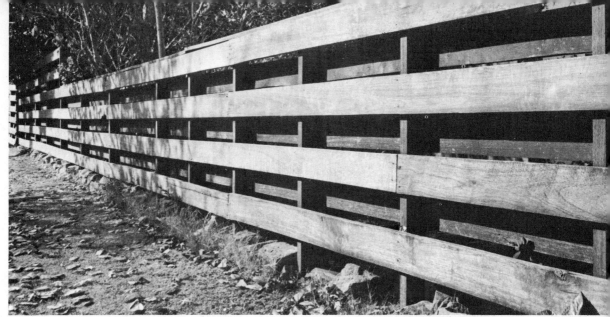

Two different but simple fences. It is sufficient merely to butt joint the horizontal rails on the corner posts. Galvanized nails should be used in all outside woodwork.

Hardwood 1 in. by 6 in. is most suitable for this ranch style fence. Joints should be staggered to provide maximum strength. A capping piece on top of the fence while being attractive, also helps shed water.

The extra high horizontal fence provides minimum but effective privacy while not "closing in" the area.

Lattice may be easily fabricated or bought in compact units ready for expansion and fixing. If making your own lattice it is advisable to prepaint all slats before assembly. Standing lattice is best painted with a spray gun.

Natural stone whether laid geometrically or stacked gives a sturdy appearance and more importantly requires little if any, maintenance.

This is the answer when minimal demarcation or privacy is required.

Transformation of an otherwise unattractive entrance.

WALLS

Screen walls have grown from being purely functional to decorative and imaginative, which is evidence of the vastness of the materials and techniques now available. In many cases walls have taken the place of fences, especially where it means an enlargement to the living area.

There are limitless possibilities for extending living areas outside the house, most particularly in rural settings.

Discarded railroad ties bonded into position serve as effective retaining walls on sloping sites. They should be battened for greater stability.

There are occasions when natural boulders can be used to advantage to form a dry, rubble wall. Drainage presents no problem with such walls.

The mass production of
a vast range of concrete
masonry blocks in
modular sizes has made
easy the construction
of attractive walls
of endless variation.

The introduction of concrete masonry blocks has proved a great boon to home workers because of the comparative ease of laying, which can be done by using standard cement mortar or epoxy cements.

The fashionable application of wrought iron and textured bricks in a wide range of colors provide unlimited possibilities.

A basalt spall type retaining wall gives great strength and excellent drainage.

Pleasing variation on standard brick wall. Clinker and common bricks and brick bats have been combined here.

New designs of concrete masonry blocks are continuously launched onto the market. Brick screen walls can be made individual according to the pattern in which they are laid.

This rough textured rendering is achieved with a trowel. Old or imperfect bricks are most suitable for this wall as they are less costly and give a secure base for the cement rendering.

Wooden formers necessary for the construction of a brick arch are easily made by the home handyman.

To get the best result when painting brick walls white it is advisable to take the trouble of first sealing the surface with a cement sealer especially if oil paint is to be used. Alternatively use a wall paint which has been especially formulated and contains sealing properties.

A stepped wall is usual when building on a sloping site. Such a wall should be buttressed at 8 ft intervals.

Thin slabs of multicolored sandstone arranged in a random pattern are extremely attractive and effective as retaining walls. Provision must be made for weep holes in the surface to carry off soakage.

KITCHEN FURNITURE

As in every area of home construction, kitchens have undergone a revolution in layout. New materials and a greater awareness of work patterns are two contributing influences. The kitchen is one room where color can be startling and wild and right. A well-planned room is essential—you will be reminded of an ill-arranged one at least three times a day.

These cupboards are made of double-faced laminated composition board.

Much can be done with cupboard doors by the application of provincial molding which can be purchased ready for use.

These easy-to-make composition board shelves inside the walk-in pantry are cut in one piece from thick large sheets. Planed and careful cutting of the sheets can mean considerable saving. Small metal brackets or light wooden cleats hold the shelves in place.

Scrap ends of plywood have been used here to form compartments for practical kitchen storage. They are housed in grooves at the inside of the draw front and draw back.

A revolving corner cupboard, sometimes called a lazy susan, uses otherwise wasted space. The most effective method of operation is a ball-race base assembly.

Western red cedar can be used effectively for vertical planking on interior walls. This may be finished in either gloss or eggshell flat clear plastic. The use of small mosaic tiles as sink and bench splashback make an interesting variation from the large ceramic tiles.

For the most efficient operation of a pull-out work shelf it should be fitted with a ball bearing runner. It is not difficult to alter existing cupboards to fit this useful accessory.

Two uprights and a cross rail above this refrigerator is all that is needed to form a compartment and so utilize what is normally waste space.

CUPBOARDS

Trends in cupboard construction are influenced greatly by the range and variety of pre-packaged units. Many of these are in whitewood which permits a staining to suit practically any type of interior. A considerable choice of grain and color is now available due to the amount of imported woods used in these pre-packaged units.

Cocktail bars in most cases are of a simple box construction, consisting of two ends with a top and center shelf and bottom, housed into the ends. This one below and on the next page has a top finished in a cloth vinyl with a padded strip around the front and ends. Suitable timber for this project would be maple or cypress pine.

Wood gives warmth and atmosphere to a room. This top slatted section over shelves is an effective room divider.

A useful bank of shelves can be formed from light battens with cross rails. Each upright is formed by two battens with cross rails fitting between them. The assembly is held together by dowel rods running the full length. All main assembly of parts is by means of studs or bolts.

Interior arrangement of a very practical cupboard construction which can be either fixed or free standing. Solid timber boards or processed panels are used throughout. Note the stopped housing of shelves into uprights and the draw runner detail.

Knotty grain pine either left in its natural state or finished with a clear plastic is most suitable for occasional tables, cupboards, and other practical items of furniture. This table and shelf unit can be made by cutting the four legs to the desired height and the top and shelf to size, then it is only necessary to attach the shelf to the four legs by means of a half-lap joint and screw the top to the four legs. The outer top edges of the legs are rounded over. Timber 1¼ in. would be suitable.

Cypress pine flooring has been used to create a most unique cupboard. Prior to assembly of the front and ends the upright boards have been chamfered on the face edges to create a V-joint effect. On the front edge of the top neither the tongue nor groove have been planed off. The base assembly also of cypress pine could be made of timber 3 in. wide by 1½ in. thick.

In recent years the use of framed louvers as doors for cupboards has become very popular mainly because these units have become available at a reasonable cost and in a wide range of sizes. The inside of this cupboard is comparatively shallow but can be adapted quite easily as a writing desk. Only 6 in. deep and 7 ft high it can be fitted into a very small space while providing maximum storage particularly for small items.

Apart from windows, doors are the points most frequently requiring maintenance in the home. Front doors need special attention due to weather and the need for extra security in the way of locks and catches. It is also possible to add character to an otherwise undistinguished building by highlighting the front entrance and door.

The two separate frames forming this Dutch door are assembled by means of mortise and tenon joints. The bottom section which is usually solid has a flush cross brace. Both sections are fitted with butt hinges.

Maple, redwood or cedar would be suitable timber for this framed ledge door with its front facing vertical boards.

This beautiful wooden door is an example of fine craftsmanship not often seen. Made of solid timber it could be finished in a variety of clear varnishes or even French polished.

A rather ordinary door has been dressed with eight panels to harmonize with the solid character of this house.

A dramatic door created by adding carved relief panels. This treatment however should be used with caution as it can be overpowering.

Conservative stately atmosphere has been accomplished with this door by the simple addition of provincial or bolection molding.

Handsome double doors
with colored leadlight
insets and carved bolection
molding, which can be
purchased ready made.

LETTER BOXES

Right
A rather ordinary
ready-made letterbox and
bread and milk container
have been tastefully set
among ivy.

A way to utilize cypress
pine weatherboard offcuts.
The cap or top is
covered with a sheet of
flat metal as protection
against weather conditions.

A letterbox is an essential adjunct to a house and demands more attention than is usually given it. The selection shown here gives many useful and attractive ideas. The most logical place for a house number is near or on the letterbox.

Two simple but
functional uses of timber
offcuts to form
combination letterbox
and house number.

Unusual letterbox which can be made extremely cheaply by using offcuts from rafters and joists of a building. The timber used here is fir and has been left unpainted.

Formed from cypress pine weatherboard with mitered corners, this box is fixed to the fence by a central bolt through base.

The unusual design of this tasteful wooden letterbox minimizes deterioration through weather.

A decorative cypress
weatherboard letterbox.
Welded rods support
box and give balance to
upright pipe.

Woodturners would be
delighted to tackle
this letterbox and
house number panel.

Gable-type letterbox made
from shiplap boarding
supported on a metal
chain which has
been welded to form a
rigid upright support.

Both metal letterbox and
house name are attached
to a 3 in. by 3 in. upright.

GARAGE DOORS

There are three basic types of garage doors—hinge, tilting and roller. Each has distinctive advantages and choice will depend on space available, location, cost, and character of the house.

Marine plywood, with its weather-resisting qualities, is a suitable timber for garage doors such as these. Unpainted wooden doors should be sealed with at least two coats of a clear plastic finish.

Two attractive examples
of hinge foldback doors.
Such doors usually
require a wider opening
to allow for doors
when folded.

The panels on this tilting door are formed with the application of bolection or other molding.

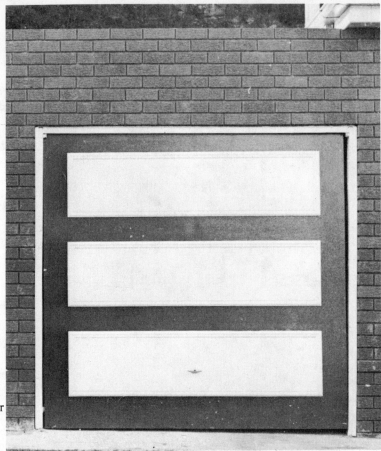

A good example of a pair of framed ledged garage doors fitted with large scotch tee hinges.

WINDOWS

Hopper windows provide maximum ventilation and are easily fitted.

Left bottom
Tall, narrow box frame windows in Colonial setting. The ledge is trimmed with wrought iron—painted to match the stain of the wooden frame.

These floor-to-ceiling, double hung, box frame windows provide maximum light.

Box frame windows are by far the most popular choice of window for homes in the United States. They are easy to make and look attractive no matter what their size. They are probably the most versatile of all window designs. A representative selection of box frames as well as casement, sliding, hopper and fixed windows are shown on the following pages.

Much extra space and ventilation can be obtained by the provision of dormer windows. Given that the roof design is suitable it is a less expensive operation to add a room through the roof than to add laterally. It is important that dormer windows be in character with the architecture of the existing house.

Where the primary
consideration is to provide
extra light and ventilation
these illustrations show
two ways these can
be achieved.

Shutters can form additional security against intruders.

Variation on French doors and windows. Note the combination of box frame with lower fixed panels.

These decorative and functional shutters on a small apartment building are hung from an overhanging box panel Their sliding action makes for ease of operation.

BARBECUES

Left
Hammered copper canopy
and flue is readily
available and easy to
install. It is combined
here with a cradle grate
and a slab hearth,
made from quarry tiles.

Outside barbecues can be
simple or highly elaborate.
These pictures show a
simple grill set into a rock
garden, one built from
comparatively cheap,
concrete masonry blocks
with grate and upper
hot plate, and a third in
quite costly natural
sandstone with built-in
fuel bunkers. Note
masonry blocks are laid
dry whereas the sandstone
is laid in mortar in
the normal way.

Left
The potential and
application of wood is
graphically shown
opposite.

Top left.
Excellent example of
unique grain figure
in cypress pine which
has been milled into
shiplap planks.

Top right.
Unique effect is produced
by shotblasting the
surface of Douglas fir.
The wood can
then be highlighted by the
application of a clear
sealing preparation.

Below left.
Very attractive effects can
be gained by using
western red cedar shiplap
planks, just as they
come from the saw.

Below right.
The use of random-width
shiplapped boards form
attractive feature walls.

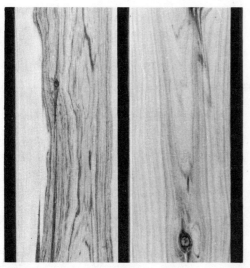

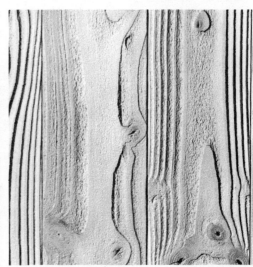

Parquetry flooring can be
laid with little effort
by the home handyman.
It is normally supplied in
panels of contrasting
woods and fixed with
special adhesives to a solid
base.

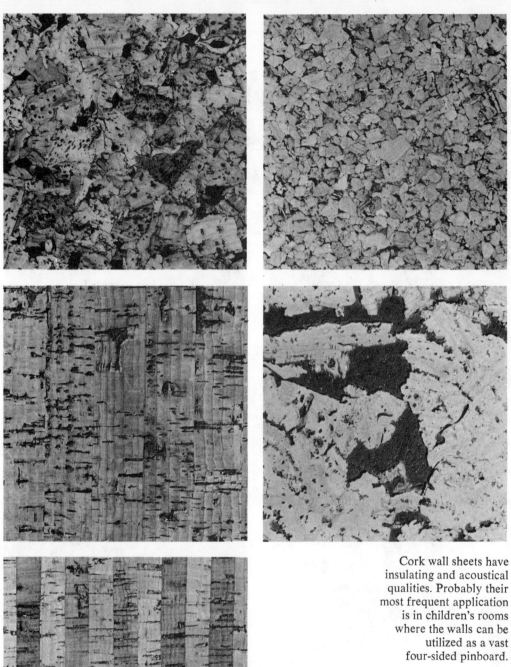

Cork wall sheets have
insulating and acoustical
qualities. Probably their
most frequent application
is in children's rooms
where the walls can be
utilized as a vast
four-sided pinboard.

Adjustable aluminum louvers may be built and used to fill the opening between a balcony handrail and the roof eaves as is shown here, to give privacy and shade. This unit is secured with bolts to the handrail and to the fascia board by means of hanger plates.

There are few problems associated with adding a balcony. Rough hardwood is an ideal material and common structural supports are 2 in. diameter galvanized waterpipes. Suggested finish for all woodwork is a colored stain. The decking is laid with gaps of approximately ½ in. Remove arris from all timbers to avoid splinters.

GLOSSARY

INTRODUCTION

To do any kind of job successfully, it is essential to have a reasonable knowledge of the terms and expressions connected with the work.

This is especially so in building work where so many trades are covered. For the craftsman, such knowledge is gained through experience over many years, and it becomes second nature for him to use the correct term.

Even so, this glossary of building terms should still be of benefit to him while serving at the same time as a guide for the student and amateur builder.

In compiling the glossary, every effort has been made to cover the terms and materials in common use, and these have been arranged in strict alphabetical order, irrespective of hyphenation or whether two or more words comprise a term.

The entries are not confined to brief definitions. Where necessary for greater clarity these are expanded, and in some cases grouped together under a general heading. An example of this is the entry headed Electrical Terms.

ACCESS

Broadly applied to mean entry to an area or room. In building construction it denotes points at which concealed services—such as water, gas—can be reached for inspection and repair.

ACCESS ROAD

Describes a short length of road which provides a right of way.

ACETYLENE

Is a gas produced commercially from carbide of calcium by means of water. It is used in conjunction with oxygen to produce a hot flame for welding or lead burning.

ACOUSTIC BOARD

Refers to a wall or ceiling covering sheet or panel made in a wide range of sizes. It is so compounded that it absorbs a certain amount of sound and thus prevents excessive reverberation or echo.

Some types have a cellular structure and others are of soft pulpboard with a perforated surface. Acoustic board is used widely in theaters, radio and television studios, and office buildings. It also has uses in the home for reducing noise from recreation rooms or workshops and in restoring ceilings.

AERATOR

A fitting that screws into a faucet nozzle. It mixes the water with air.

AGGREGATE

This term is applied to that part of a concrete mixture which is bound together by the Portland cement content after the addition of water. As a general rule, the crushed screened metal or gravel in the mixture is referred to as the coarse aggregate and the sand as fine aggregate.

What is called all-in aggregate refers to aggregate containing a proportion of material of all sizes, as obtained from a pit or river bed.

AGRICULTURAL DRAIN

Is a channel or conduit for drawing water off the land and away from foundations or gardens. This can be done in a number of ways. A simple method is to use trenches filled with stones and other hard rubble.

An improvement on this method is to lay special earthenware pipes in the bottom of the trench first. These pipes have no end flanges and merely butt end-to-end loosely. This allows soakage water to percolate through the joints between the pipe ends.

Recently introduced is a perforated plastic drainage tube in a continuous length which speeds up the work and conforms freely to the land contour.

AIR BRICK

Is a specially perforated brick which provides ventilation to a cavity wall or directly into a building particularly the under floor space.

AIR DRYING

This description is applied to the process which permits finishes such as enamel, varnish and lacquer to dry and harden on exposure to the air, as opposed to those which dry by artificial heat such as baking in a kiln or oven.

AIR LOCK

Generally refers to two layers of water or liquid in a pipe or tube which are separated by a pocket of air which prevents circulation. It could also be air imprisoned in a radiator, impeding the circulation of steam or hot water. The trouble can usually be overcome by the provision of a vent pipe or valve.

ALKYD RESIN

Synthetic resin produced by heating together glycerine and phthalic acid—or similar acids—and used extensively in the manufacture of paints and synthetic finishes.

Alkyd resin paints are considered extremely tough and less likely to fade than say oil-base paints. Furthermore, alkyd resin-base paints dry fairly rapidly and do not have the disagreeable odor characteristic of many of the oil-base paints.

ALLEN SCREW

Setscrews or cap screws which have a hexagonal socket in the head are called allen screws. They are adjusted by means of a special allen key.

GLOSSARY

ALLEN WRENCH OR KEY

Designed for use with allen screws which are more like a bolt than a screw, the wrenches or keys come in various sizes to fit individual allen screws.

They are usually off-set at one end and straight at the other. It is an advantage to buy a range of these tools in a bunch which makes selection of the required size easy. The allen screws are commonly used to keep metal or machinery parts together as in the holding of blades in a jigsaw or the sliding arm of a saw fence or guard.

ALLIGATOR CLIPS

These serrated-edge clips come in a number of designs and sizes. They are used with radio and television wires for temporary hook-ups, and also for testing battery wiring to bells, toy train sets and similar appliances.

ALLIGATORING

Is the term used to describe the appearance of a painted surface which develops a crazy pattern of lines and cracks resembling an alligator skin. This is caused by the top application of paint being applied before the under surface is thoroughly hard and dry. It could result from an extremely hard finish being applied over a comparatively soft undercoat which would have a tendency to move. Sand or scrape surface smooth before repainting.

ALUMINUM FOIL

Flat aluminum sheets of wafer thickness used for thermal insulation in both the home and industry. This type of material is effective because bright metal surfaces are good reflectors and poor radiators of heat. It is also light and easy to handle. Aluminum foil is available mounted on kraft paper and used in this form for insulating the roof of a house or other building.

ANAGLYPTA

This is the name given to range of heavyweight embossed paper patterns which are used to provide relief decoration on ceilings and walls. These patterns are available in a wide selection and are attached with an adhesive. Also available in the same material is a ribbed cover strip designed to be fixed over wall boards or panel joints which have a tendency to expand and contract.

ANGLE IRON

A bar of metal, usually mild steel, which has been rolled into an L-section. Such bars have many uses, including that of an arch bar over a fireplace or door opening to support a mantel or lintel.

This term is also used to describe one type of metal fastener which is used to reinforce and repair wood joints. They come with pre-drilled holes to take countersunk-head screws.

ANILINE COLORS

Is the term generally used to indicate coal-tar dyes or derivatives. They are used in making timber stains.

ANT CAPS

Flanged plates of galvanized iron that rest upon the tops of piers under wooden floors in buildings. Their function is to impede and therefore prevent the passage of termites (white ants) from the soil to the timbers of the house or other building.

ANTI-CORROSIVE PAINT

Is a paint designed to inhibit corrosion and protect metals. This is applied directly to the bare metal and is usually followed by special paint or enamel. Around the home, such paint could be used to advantage on gutters, downpipes, wrought iron railings and gates, in fact, all ungalvanized metal parts.

ANVIL

Although an anvil is mostly associated with the old conception of the village blacksmith, such a tool has many practical uses in the workshop. It provides a solid base for many clinching and riveting jobs in sheet metal.

Many bench vices are made with an anvil block as part of the vice. A very useful anvil can be made from a short length of H-shaped steel girder.

APRON

This describes a timber strip or molding which has several applications. The most common is as the molding or casing used under the window sill inside the home. Its purpose is to conceal any opening between the sill of the window and the building frame. The front board of a workbench to which the bench vice is usually fixed is also called an apron.

ARBOR

This term has two distinctly different meanings and applications. Firstly there is the garden structure which should be strong enough to carry the weight of flowers and foliage which train over the framework.

On the other hand, the term describes the shaft upon which a circular saw blade, grinding wheel, or other rotary tool is mounted.

ARCHITRAVE

Is the ornamental molding fixed at the sides and tops of doors, windows, and other openings. Its purpose is decorative, and it also serves to cover the joints between the wall lining and adjacent woodwork. It is customary to mount electric light switches on the vertical architraves of doorways adjacent to the door handles.

Apart from timber, architraves can also be formed in cement rendering, or in hard fibrous plasters.

ARRIS EDGE

Is the sharp edge formed by two adjacent plane surfaces. It is usual to remove the sharpness by taking off a shaving with a finely set plane, or lightly rubbing with sandpaper. This is called taking off the arris.

ARRIS RAIL

Is a triangular rail in a wooden fence to which the boards of palings are nailed. Such a rail is formed by ripping a square section along its diagonal length. The main advantage of such rails is that they shed rain easily and so reduce the risk of rot and timber decay setting in.

Another version of the arris rail fence is sometimes found around parks and ovals. The tops of the posts are cut to a V-shape after which square top rails are dropped into the cuts and secured with hoop-iron straps over the top of each post.

ASBESTOS

Is an incombustible fibrous mineral which is used in various forms as an insulating material. A typical example is the use of asbestos tape or strips wrapped around hot water pipes and other sections to retain heat. (See LAGGING.)

ASBESTOS CEMENT

Is a combination of fibrous asbestos and Portland cement highly compressed in manufacture. It is not affected by exposure and does not require painting except to provide decoration; continues to harden with time and is very durable though rather brittle. Asbestos cement is widely used for flats and corrugated sheets, decorative wall and ceiling linings, rainwater gutters and down pipes, and many molded goods.

It may be drilled and sawn to size and shape although straight cutting of flat sheets is best done with special shears.

ASHLAR

Is interesting because it is a term used only to describe a perfectly constructed stone wall. It refers to the building of walls with uniformly dressed blocks of stone, laid in courses with fine joints.

ASPHALT

Asphalt is a versatile material of many uses. It is used in paving driveways, and also as a waterproofing agent in damp cellars and basements. Asphalt is also processed into floor tiles and sheets.

ASTRAGAL

Is a small semicircular molding which can be used to cover the joint between adjoining wall sheets. It does this neatly because of a double rabbet on the underside. Astragal molding is used extensively when making decorative garage doors from plywood panels.

GLOSSARY

AUGER

This tool is sometimes called a snake and is used to clear blocked pipes. It is in the kit of every plumber, and electricians also need it at times. There are numerous types available, but the two most commonly used consist of a flexible flat spring steel coil or a spiral-wound cable of heavy steel wire. Both are fitted at the leading end with a screw or twisted hook which serves to break or dislodge obstructions.

AWL

There are two main versions of this useful little tool. One with a pointed end is used mainly by workers in leather, whereas the other has a flat point which is not unlike a small screwdriver. This type is called a bradawl, and is used to form pilot holes for small screws and nails.

AXLE PULLEY

An axle pulley is the fitting recessed into the pulley stile of a box-frame or double-hung window frame. The cords which operate the sashes and weights in such windows run over these pulleys which are housed in a metal case. For trouble-free running of axle pulleys lubricate them occasionally with a few drops of oil.

BACK FILL

Is the rubble or soil packed or placed behind a retaining wall. It could also refer to rough masonry built behind a wall of face bricks or the filling between the two faces of a hollow wall.

BACK-FLAP HINGE

A hinge in which the plates are wide and short instead of long and narrow, as with a butt hinge. It is used to connect two flat surfaces which are hinged in such a way that they may be flush when the hinge is opened out.

BACK IRON

A part of the cutting arrangement of a plane which is fixed to the cutter with a screw. The purpose of a back iron is to break the shavings and prevent the grain tearing out.
German jack planes designed for rough planing work do not have back irons, nor do block planes which are mainly used for planing end grain.

BACK PUTTY

Layer of putty pressed into a rabbet of sash before glass is placed in position. Back putty forms a bed or cushion for the glass and helps to prevent fracturing if the sash is subjected to heavy use.

BACK SAW

This is another name for a tenon saw. It derives the name back saw from the fact that there is a stiffening strip of metal—often brass —fixed to the back edge of the blade.

BADGER PLANE

A plane useful for making wide rabbets. Its shape is similar to a jack plane, but the cutter extends across the full width of the plane base.

BAKED FINISHES

Enamels or finishes applied in an oven, under infra-red lamps, or by induction heating. The article so coated must necessarily be able to withstand the temperature required for the proper baking of the finish. This finish is usually used on refrigerators and other metal objects.

GLOSSARY

BALANCER VENEER

Veneer to opposite sides of a panel to reduce warping and distortion. The same principle applies when making flush-panel doors. Plywood fixed to both sides of the inner frame reduces risk of the door twisting. Also, when using laminated plastic sheets on say a table top, fixing a balancing panel underneath to prevent distortion in the solid table top.

BALK

Timber roughly squared from one log. Such pieces are used on heavy jobs such as bridges and wharves.

BALL PEEN HAMMER

The ball peen type hammer is sometimes called the engineer's or mechanic's hammer. It is used with cold chisels for metal chipping work, for flattening and shaping metal, and for all types of work with rivets.

BALL VALVE OR BALL COCK

Device employed in a toilet tank to regulate the flow of water. It consists of a copper or plastic ball of thin gauge attached by a lever to the body of the valve by a pivot pin.
In the body of the valve there is a plug which is moved by the floating ball according to the level of the water in the tank.
When the level reaches a pre-determined limit the plug, at one end of which is a rubber washer, is forced against the seating and shuts off the water.

BALUSTERS

These are vertical pillars supporting a rail or capping. Their most common use is to support the handrail on a stairway.

BAREFACED TENON

A tenon flush with one side of the rail as in a door, with a shoulder on the other side. It is used where the rail is thinner than the stile and where it is desirable to have the mortise near the center.

BARGE BOARD

Board fixed along the incline of a gable to cover the projection of the roof. Traditional types are often highly ornamental. Modern types are plain.

BATTENS

Are light sawn strips of timber used for numerous purposes. For example tile battens to hold roof tiles or cover battens fixed over open joints.

BATTER BOARD

A temporary framework used to assist in determining the slope of the surface formed by excavation.

BAY WINDOW

Is a window projecting beyond the general wall face of a building. It may be square, circular or any desired shape.

BEADS

A molding of semicircular section with or without one or two quirks. COCK BEAD: Bead inserted between two parts of a flush surface and projecting above the surface. STOP BEAD: Used to retain sash within the main window frame; sash stop of beaded section. PARTING BEAD: Bead fixed to the pulley stile of a box frame to separate one sash from another.

BEARING WALL

This type of wall is designed to support a load in addition to its own weight. The exterior walls of a building to which the roof plates are secured are always load-bearing walls.

BEAUMONTAGE

A wax stopping used for filling small cracks, nail holes, etc. It is made up in little sticks or kept in a tin. Make your own with little lumps of beeswax in an empty shoe polish tin, adding about an equal quantity of resin, a few flakes of shellac, and some coloring pigment such as burnt sienna or Venetian red for mahogany; burnt umber for oak, or lamp-black for ebony. Uncolored beaumontage is suitable for natural oak and similar light-colored woods.

When melted, the stopping is applied with a matchstick, or by holding a stick of it against a hot pointed iron. It sets almost at once, any excess being removed by paring with a chisel, followed by sandpapering.

BENCH HOLDFAST

Is a special type of vertical clamp which fits into a hole bored in the bench top. It can be adjusted to hold work securely on the bench for easy sawing or chiseling.

BENCH HOOK

A device used when cutting off short lengths of wood or for shouldering tenons, etc., at the bench. It allows the work to be cut through without damaging the bench.

BENCH SCREW

The screw fitted to the bench vise. Formerly of wood, it is now invariably steel.

BENCH STOP

A bench stop is essential when doing woodwork in the workshop. In its simplest form it is a strip tacked to the bench top to hold timber which is being planed. However, a more satisfactory idea is to fit a special metal type which can be adjusted up or down or recessed slightly below the bench top.

BENZENE

(Sometimes called benzol.) A very powerful solvent for many finishing materials, a fire hazard, and highly toxic. It should not be confused with benzine.

BENZINE

Highly volatile petroleum product used as a lacquer diluent. It is a fire hazard both in shipping and storage and when used by inexperienced people in the home.

BEVEL

An edge which is at any angle other than a right angle.

BEVEL-EDGED CHISEL

A chisel having the edges beveled. Available in all normal widths and with both tang and socket attachment.

BEVEL, SLIDING

Tool used for marking out or testing odd angles. The blade is adjustable and is fixed by a small bolt and winged nut.

BICHROMATE OF POTASH

Obtainable in crystals for staining mahogany and sometimes oak. They are steeped in water which assumes a clear orange color. This, however, bears no relation to the color produced on the wood. The action of the stain is chemical and the result depends upon the amount of tannin in the wood. Some varieties of mahogany are more affected than others. It is usual to make up a concentrated solution and dilute it as required. A slight dust deposit is left on surfaces when it dries and this should be brushed off.

BIFURCATED

Split into two branches. The most common example is a bifurcated rivet.

BILL HOOK

Is a concave-edge lopping tool for pruning twigs and light branches. Attached to a long handle it is ideal for cutting back overgrown vines and bushes.

BINDER

The non-volatile part of the paint which serves to bind or cement the pigment particles together to form a solid surface covering. These may be oils, varnishes, proteins, or other process developments.

BINDING

Term generally applied to hinges in which part of the wood fits too tightly against another causing rubbing or preventing closing or opening.

BIRD'S EYE

A figuring found in maple. It is due to conical formations in the grain which, when sliced through either by rotary cutting or plain sawing, produce a series of circular markings dotted at random over the surface.

BIRD'S MOUTH JOINT

Is basically a notch cut in a piece of wood. It is used widely in roofing work and structural framings. Rafters are generally birds-mouth jointed to the wall-plate. In cabinet work the joint is often used for the diagonal ribs of barred doors, the notched end of the rib fitting on the corner of a square or oblong frame.

BISMARCK BROWN

An aniline dye of fiery red color. Should be used with caution as it is powerful.

BITUMINOUS FELT

Fibrous material impregnated with bitumen and rolled into sheets for roofing and flexible damp-proof courses. It is waterproof and durable but must be protected from mechanical damage. A reinforced bituminous felt is made for use where high resistance to tearing is required.

BITUMINOUS MASTIC

A waterproof material of a soft plastic nature used in making water-tight joints, painting and repair work. It retains some ductility for a long time and does not shrink.

BLACKBOARD COATING

Ready-made preparation can be obtained. Alternatively, give coat of black priming paint. Rub down when dry and give second coat to which about two tablespoons of fine pumice powder to the pint have been added.

BLEEDING

Migration or working of a dye or stain from the wood or an undercoat into successive coverings. Usually this is caused by the vehicle of the top coat working on the undercoat to make it soluble. This is prevented by sealing the under surface or wood by an intermediate coat of shellac, aluminum paint or emulsion paint.

BLIND BOLT

A bolt which is let flush into the edge or back of a door.

BLOCKBOARD

Composite board having a core made up of strips of wood each not more than 1 in. wide, otherwise it is as battenboard.

BLOCK PLANE

A small metal plane, generally with screw adjustment for regulating the depth of cut. Sizes range from 3½ in. to 7 in. with cutter widths of 10 in. to 1⅜ in. Block planes are invaluable for trimming small work and end grain. There is no back iron to the cutter which is used with the bevel upper-most. Some types are double-ended, the cutter being reversed for use as a bull-nose plane when necessary. General model has pitch of 20 degrees. Special low angle block plane has a 12 degrees pitch.

BLOOMING

The formation on the dried surface of varnish and polish of a dull film something like the "bloom" often seen on black grapes. Lacquer which is sprayed in wet or humid weather will also bloom unless work is done in a specially prepared booth.

BODYING

Process in French polish which consists of building up a full, flat surface of polish by continuing the skimming process. It is done by rubbing a small amount of linseed oil over the surface with a specially-prepared rubber.

BOILED OIL

Drying oil made by adding driers, used to shorten the drying time of paints.

BOLECTION MOLDING

A molding rabbeted at one edge to enable it to fit over a framework. The molding thus stands out from the face of the work.

BOND

The overlapping of bricks or blocks in an orderly arrangement designed for strength and appearance. ENGLISH BOND has one course of stretchers to one course of headers, alternating. FLEMISH BOND has alternate stretcher and header in each course. ENGLISH GARDEN WALL BOND, sometimes called Three-and-one Bond, has one course of headers to three courses of stretchers. HEADER BOND consists of all headers in every course with a 2¼ in. side lap. STRETCHER BOND consists of all stretchers in every course with a 4½ in. overlap.

GLOSSARY

BONING ROD

A batten with cross-piece on top, used between fixed sighting rails to check level of bottom of trenches, fall of pipes, etc.

BOSS

A decorative block used over the intersection of two timbers generally in ceilings. It is usually carved, but sometimes turned.

BOX-FRAME WINDOW

Sometimes called double-hung window, in which two sashes are balanced either by cords and weights or a spring fitting and slide vertically past each other. Name derives from box framework in which weights rise and fall. Various spring fittings do not require the box cavity and so provide a greater glass area.

BOX GUTTER

A square gutter usually formed between a parapet wall and the roof timbers behind. It may be lined with sheet lead or galvanized sheet metal.

BRAD

Is a type of finishing nail or pin of light gauge. The head is small so that it may be punched below the surface neatly.

BRADAWL

Used mostly for making nail or screw holes. Blade sizes range from about $\frac{1}{32}$ in. to $\frac{1}{8}$ in. or so in diameter. The lengths are from 2 in. to 3 in. The tang of the blade fits into a hardwood handle. The cutting edge must be kept sharp by filing and honing on an oilstone. The edge of the blade should be across the grain, not with it. When screwing, the bradawl is used for making the hole for the thread of the screw. The brace and bit are used for making the larger shank hole.

BRAZING

A form of soldering in which a higher temperature than that used for ordinary hard soldering is required. Brazing spelter is used instead of solder. Brazing is particularly suitable for jointing steelwork.

BREEZE BLOCK

A term applied colloquially to rectangular slabs of concrete composed of Portland cement and coke breeze or other appropriate aggregate the usual proportions being four parts of coke to one part cement. Breeze concrete slabs from 2 to 4 in. in thickness to 12 in. wide, or up to 6 ft. in length can be purchased ready prepared. They are light in weight, hygienic, and fire-resistant. Surface of the block is porous and must be faced with an impervious material.

BRICK-ON-EDGE COURSES

Bricks laid on the 3 in. edge so that the end is exposed in an upright position, the course being 4½ in. high. Widely used over heads of doors and windows, for coping and projecting ornamental courses.

BRICKS

Standard brick size is 9 in. x 4½ in. x 3 in. Bricks are also made in various grades, shapes, sizes, etc., for special purposes. Some of the names applied to bricks are; common, face, squint, single, bullnose, and double bullnose. The last is often used as top course on fences, veranda rails, etc. Textured bricks and the smaller textured brickettes are used extensively on feature work such as fireplaces.

BRICK VENEER

Is a method of construction in which an inner frame of timber is covered by a single exterior brick wall to give the appearance of a solid brick building. The inner frame is secured to the brick work with metal frame-ties.

BRIDGING

Pieces fitted in pairs from the bottom of one floor joist to the top of adjacent joists and crossed to distribute the floor load, sometimes pieces of width equal to the joist and fitted neatly between them.

BRUISE

An indentation on a wood surface caused by a blow. Can usually be raised in solid wood by applying a hot iron over a damp rag.

GLOSSARY

BUILDING LINE

Is the term used to describe the one of the outside face of a building wall.
It also refers to the line on a block of ground beyond which the law forbids that a building be erected.

BUILT-UP

Refers to construction when two or more pieces of timber are glued together to give the required width or thickness. Frequently the building-up is local only to save the wastage involved in using large timber, much of which would be cut away as waste.

BULL-NOSE PLANE

A small metal plane, resembling a shoulder plane but with shortened nose which enables the tool to be worked-up fairly close to corners of stopped rabbets, chamfer, etc. The nose, in some cases, is adjustable or detachable, enabling the plane to work right into a corner.

BUNSEN BURNER

A burner giving a powerful gas flame, used for heating up soldering bits, and for hardening small tools, etc.

BURNT SIENNA

A warm red-brown pigment used in making stains, stoppings, etc.

BURNT UMBER

A gold-brown pigment used in making stains, stoppings, etc.

BUTTERFLY ROOF

Could be described as an inverted gable or a double lean-to in which both sections sweep up from a center box gutter.

BUTTERING

This term describes the act of placing mortar on a brick or masonry block before it is laid. The mortar is usually applied with a standard bricklayer's trowel.

BUTT HINGE

The simplest form of hinge used for hanging doors, etc. It consists of two flaps moving on a pivot.

BUTT JOINT

The most common joint met with in home carpentry, where one member is fastened securely at right angles to another.

BUZZ SAW

This is the name which is often applied to the standard type of circular saw mounted in a bench or table.

CAM

Projection on the side of a wheel to impart movement to other parts. Power driven jig saws usually operate on a crankshaft principle.

CAMEL-HAIR MOP

Brush used for applying stains, French polish, cellulose lacquers, and enamels. The mop is a bunch of hair mounted into a quill which is bound with wire. Sometimes a handle is fitted into the quill. They are sold in sizes which are numbered according to the quantity of hair in the quill. The flat brushes are from $\frac{1}{2}$ to 3 in. wide, and the thickness of hair is from $\frac{1}{8}$ to $\frac{1}{4}$ in.

CANTILEVER

A structural member which projects beyond the face of a building and supports a load.

CAPILLARY JOINT

Method of joining copper pipes by drawing solder into the space between them by capillary attraction. For an effective joint the clearance between pipe and socket should be as small as possible.

CARBON TETRACHLORIDE

Is a liquid solvent for oil and grease so is used widely as a cleaning agent.
Use only where there is good ventilation as its vapors are poisonous.

CARCASS

A term referring mainly to furniture construction, and more specifically to the box-like frame of the article before doors, drawers, shelves, and other interior fittings are added.

CARRIAGE BOLTS

Sometimes called coach bolts these bolts are black, round-headed, square-shouldered, partly threaded and have square nuts.
They have many uses in woodwork.
They are obtainable from 1 in. long by $\frac{3}{16}$ in. thick up to 16 in. by $\frac{1}{2}$ in. thick.
The latter is a special size used under the rungs of ladders.
A special feature is that the head shouldering prevents the bolt shank from turning when tightening or removing the nuts.

In softwood the shouldering makes a bed for itself, but in hardwood it may be necessary to chisel out a recess for the shoulder.

CASEMENT WINDOW

The term casement in connection with domestic architecture refers to the cottage type of window where the opening light or casement is hinged like a door. The frame can be either of metal or wood; both types of frames are built into the wall as in the case of an outside door.

CASTELLATED NUT

This nut is designed for maximum security. The top is slotted and resembles a castle. A cotter-pin is inserted through the slots and a hole in the bolt to keep the nut from loosening.

CAULKING COMPOUND

Plastic material used to seal joints or fill crevices around windows, chimneys, doors. It comes in thinner solution for use in caulking gun, or in ribbon or paste type for application with knife.

CAVITY WALL

A form of wall construction used in many houses. It consists of an inner and outer wall with an air space between, the purpose being to ensure a warm dry building. The usual width is 11 in. each wall being $4\frac{1}{2}$ in. thick. The two walls are united by galvanized iron ties about 10 in. long so designed that water cannot creep across from the outer to inner walls. Properly constructed, a cavity wall is damp-proof.

CEMENT

In general, a cement is any substance which, by hardening, causes objects, between which it is applied, to adhere firmly. In building work, standard Portland cement is used with sand or other aggregates and water to form mortar or concrete.

CEMENT MORTAR

Mortar prepared with Portland cement and sand, usually in the proportion of one part cement to three parts sand, (by volume).

CEMENT RENDER

Means to cover a brick, concrete, or other suitable wall surface with a facing of cement mortar. This mortar is mixed in the proportions of approximately 3 parts sand to 1 part cement and is applied with either a special steel trowel or wooden float.

CENTER BIT

A useful tool for boring large holes. It consists of a piece of steel shaped to fulfill three requirements: (a) a center, (b) a circle-cutter, and (c) a chisel to remove the core of the hole.

CENTERING

A temporary timber erection to support the bricks of other components of an arch while being built.

CENTER PUNCH

When drilling a hole in metal the position should be first popped with a center punch to prevent the drill moving out of position. It is also needed for wood when a morse drill is used.

CERAMIC TILES

These are a baked clay tile with a glazed finish which is easy to keep clean.
They may be laid with a cement mortar or special epoxy cement.
Such tiles may be cut with a glass cutter or special tile cutting tool.

CHAIN MORTISER

A machine with an endless chain of cutting teeth. It speeds up the cutting of mortises in joinery and furniture making.

CHALKING

Decomposition of the surface paint film to a dry powdery dust. This washes off to leave an unprotected surface. Vigorous brushing or sanding to remove this dust is necessary before the surface is repainted.

CHALK LINE

A line against a wall or surface by means of flicking a piece of string which has been chalked, so that it hits against the wall and leaves a line of chalk. The chalk line is used for ensuring that shelves, etc., are fixed straight.

CHAMFER

An angle planed at an edge. Its purpose is chiefly to lighten the appearance and to reduce weight. Frequently the chamfer is stopped at one or both ends, the stop being fashioned in various decorative ways. A distinction sometimes made between bevel and chamfer is that the latter is a small flat surface worked at an edge, whereas a bevel is a sloping edge running across the entire thickness of the wood.

CHAMFER BIT

Is a bell-shaped tool used in a brace. It's job is to trim the ends of dowels so that they will enter the dowel holes easily. It operates something like a pencil sharpener.

CHASES

Grooves cut in brick or concrete walls to house conduit, pipes, wires, etc., before the surface is plastered.

CHATTER

Term applied to the digging-in action of a plane, usually caused by the cutter being ground at too low an angle, by its being at too high a pitch, or by not bedding properly on the frog. The cutting edge is bent back and downwards, flies up again, and so on, resulting in a series of unsightly marks across the wood. In a circular saw it refers to the noise set up when a piece of bent wood is being sawn hollow-side downwards.

CHECKING

Narrow cracks which form in the paint film. Some of the patterns of these cracks resemble small squares or the print of a bird's foot.

CHEEK

A term applied to the sides of a tenon, or to the pieces sawn away in cutting the tenon, sometimes also for the sides of a mortise.

CHEVAL MIRROR

A tall mirror giving a full-length view and supported on a frame. It is usually hinged in the center for easy adjustment.

CHROMIUM OXIDE Is a green pigment, commonly called cement green. It is used with Portland cement to produce a green surface on cement paths, floors and cement rendered walls.

CHUCK Is that part of a drill or brace which holds the drill bit or other attachment fitted with a shaft. Some chucks are tightened by hand, but the type which is adjusted with a special key is more secure.

CISSING A defect in varnishing when the varnish runs together in globules such as water does on a greasy surface. Rubbing the surface lightly with wet-and-dry abrasive paper will overcome cissing.

CISTERN Vessel, usually of material suitably protected against or resistant to, rust for storing water or other liquid. In the case of a water tank, the level in the tank may be controlled by a ballcock fixed on the supply main. The term is obsolescent except for small-capacity vessels such as flushing cisterns for toilets, larger storage containers being more generally called tanks.

CLEAT A strip of wood, usually grooved and glued, so fixed as to cover end grain, as at the ends of drawing boards.

CLENCHING Sometimes called clinching. Hammering over the points of nails projecting through work.

CLOSERS Sometimes called bats. They are small pieces of bricks nominally one-fourth the length of a brick, and used to preserve the bond or proper arrangement of the bricks.

COLLAR TIES Timbers fixed horizontally to pairs of rafters to strengthen and stiffen the roof structure further.

COLOR-IN-OIL

Paste formed by mixing a color pigment in linseed or other vegetable oils used for tinting or staining.

COLUMN

Any part of a construction which will support or transmit loading by its resistance to compression in the direction of its length. The terms pillar and column are used somewhat loosely in a design sense as meaning a member in compression. In a constructional sense it is customary to refer to members of this type as columns where they consist of circular sections, and as stanchions when constructed from steel joists and channel sections or built-up sections consisting of rolled steel joists and plates.

COMBINATION PLANE

By using different cutters this tool will do the work of several different individual planes. For example it can be used for beading, rabbeting, and cutting tongues and grooves.

COMBINATION PLIERS

As the name suggests, these pliers can be used for various jobs of loosening and gripping odd shapes. Most of them have a slip-joint which permits easy adjustment.

CONCRETE

Hard-setting mixture of cement, sand and water, combined with an aggregate such as broken stone or shingle, the proportions varying according to the purpose intended. Two mixtures in general use are three parts metal screenings ($\frac{3}{4}$ in.): two parts sand: one part cement; or four parts screenings: two and a half parts sand: one part cement. The first mixture is ideal for driveways and the second for house paths, piers, etc.

CONDITIONING

Adjustment of the moisture content of timber or other materials to the conditions and purposes for which it is to be used—by leaving timber in the room for several days; or by scrubbing water into the back of hardboard.

GLOSSARY

CONDUIT

Pipe of suitable material into which insulated cables or wires may be drawn.

CORBEL

A bracket projecting from the face of a wall. It is also the name given to two or three courses of bricks to provide a support for a wall plate.

CORNICE

The horizontal molded projection at the top of a building or of a component part of a building, usually under the eaves. An ornamental molding running round the walls of a room close to the ceiling. Also a slight wooden molding running round the walls of a room at a convenient height for the support of pictures by hooks. Also a frame or molding often gilded, covering the rods and hooks used for hanging curtains. The latter has come to be called a pelmet.

CORRUGATED FASTENER

Sometimes called wiggle nails, corrugated fasteners are used for fastening joints in timber. There are two types available. One has ridges or corrugations running parallel, the other with the ridges running at a slight angle to one another. The latter type has a tendency to tighten a joint.

COTTER PIN

Is the name of pin which is used to secure a nut on a bolt or fittings on a shaft.

COURSE (BRICKWORK)

One complete layer of bricks laid on the same bed.

COVE

Curved junction between wall and floor or wall and ceiling. A plaster cove is often used to provide an ornamental line where the wall joins the ceiling. A coved skirting is often fixed at the base of the wall, especially in floor and wall tiling.

CRAZY PAVING

A form of path construction consisting of random pieces of flat stone laid on cement to form a more or less attractive pattern.

CREOSOTE

A wood preserving liquid. Can be used on fence posts and floor timbers of building to prevent growth of fungus and deter termite attack.

CURING

Treatment of concrete to prevent the surface drying before the cement sets. A concrete surface covered with sheet plastic or damp burlap will cure correctly.

CURTAIN WALL

A wall carrying no roof and used merely as a screen or division.

CUTTING-IN

The process of finishing off the edges in painting. For example, when a wall has been painted, the edge that adjoins the fixed woodwork is cut-in with a small brush, so as to avoid any paint going on the woodwork.

DADO

The term used to describe the part of the wall from the skirting up to a height of about 2 ft. 9 in. to 3 ft. This space, if covered with paneling, fulfills the double purpose of protecting the lower part of the wall and adding to the decorative effect of a room.

DAIS

A raised platform to hold a chair or table and chairs to accommodate a person of authority or importance.

DAMP-PROOF COURSE

A layer of impervious material built into a wall to prevent damp rising or descending through it. Damp-proof courses are also laid to parapets, chimneys, and under concrete floors to prevent damp passing through. Sheet lead or bitumen based sheeting is especially suitable for latter purpose.

DATUM

Base line from which distances are measured.

DEAD-BOLT LOCK

A lock which can be actuated only by the key, as distinct from one with beveled bolt which will catch as the door is closed. May be of the screw-on type with box staple, or mortise type to be let into the door.

DEAD WHITE

Describes white paint which is without gloss, that is a matt finish.

DEADWOOD

Commercially inferior timber which comes from over-matured trees. The term, however, applies generally to withered branches which have dropped and have been left to decay, and trees which are dead before being felled.

DIE

A hardened block of steel having teeth with which to cut male screw threads on a metal object, such as a bolt.

DISHED

A surface with the center lower than at the outside. Thus it is similar in form to a dish or plate.

DISTANCE PIECE

A length of wood used to hold two members the right distance apart. It is usually a temporary item removed after the members are fixed.

DISTEMPER

Term often encountered in overseas technical magazines referring to group of water paint finishes such as whitewash and calcimine.

DIVIDERS

Used for transferring measurements from a rule to the work in hand, dividing spaces, and scribing circles, etc. Type with close adjustment screw is preferable.

DOG

A wrought iron U-shaped connector with sharp ends used to hold two pieces of timber together.

DOOR CHAIN

A special fitting attached to a door jamb and fitting into a slotted bar. It is designed to allow a door to be opened slightly so that caller may be checked before admitting.

DORMER

Upright window in a sloping roof. They provide head room and also provide proper ventilation and light.

DOUBLE GLAZING

Provides for two panes of glass instead of one so that there is a confined space between the panes. It serves to provide both sound and heat insulation.

DOUBLE-HUNG SASHES

This is another name for the well known box-frame or push up type window in which the sashes slide vertically and are balanced by weights and cords.

DOUBLE NAILING

Mainly refers to the laying and nailing of floor boards. Two nails are driven and punched at all points where the boards cross the floor joists.

DOUGLAS FIR

The timber of one of the most noble of British Columbian trees widely used for heavy constructional work, bridges, masts, agricultural implements, interior woodwork, etc. For long it has been known under alternative names such as British Columbian pine, Oregon pine, red pine, yellow fir, and red fir.

DOVETAILS

A dovetail joint may be defined as a joint made with tenons shaped like a dove's spread tail. It is the strongest and one of the best methods of joining two pieces of timber, end to end, at right angles to each other. There are three chief types of dovetail joints, the plain through joint, as used for boxes, etc.; the stopped joint, as used for drawer fronts; and the secret, or miter, joint.

DOWELING JIG

A tool enabling holes to be bored accurately in exact positions. Specially useful for doweling door frames, miters, and similar work. There are metal sleeves, varying in size, supplied with the jig enabling various bits to be used.

DOWN DRAFT

A prevalent cause of smoky chimneys, due to the pressure of air in the flue preventing the upward flow of the heated air and smoke from the fire. In the case of new houses, it may be caused by the air in the flue remaining damp.

DRAWER LOCK CHISEL

A cranked chisel for cutting recesses to house locks in drawers. Made with $\frac{3}{8}$ in. and $\frac{5}{8}$ in. wide cutters, the edges of which are at right angles to each other. It can be used in a confined space where it would be impossible to use an ordinary chisel. It is tapped into the wood with a hammer.

DRAWER PULL

Is the name of the handle fixed to the front of a drawer.

DRESSER

Although this term could describe a piece of bedroom furniture, it is also the name of a wooden tool used by plumbers to shape sheet lead.

DRIER

An ingredient of paint added to help the paint to dry in a reasonable time. There are two forms of drier, the liquid and the paste, the former being the more powerful.

DRIVE NAIL

Drive nails make driving in masonry walls simple. First a hole for a shield is drilled and is then tapped into place. The driving action of the nail into the shield secures the anchorage.

DRUNKEN SAW

Mounted upon the circular saw on a special arbor fitted with tapered collars. The saw is held at a slope, the angle of which can be varied by altering the position of the collars. Thus grooves of varying width can be cut. The bottom of the groove is necessarily slightly hollow, but this is so slight as not generally to matter.

DRY-MIX

This term could apply to either a cement-sand mortar or concrete mixture in which the water content is low. A typical job is the mixture of sand and cement used for making cement masonry building blocks or cement garden ornaments. Here the mixture is rammed firmly into a mold resting on a pallet. The mold is removed immediately after the ramming is finished and the article placed on one side to cure and harden.

DUNNAGE

Dunnage could be offcuts of timber of uniform thickness used in stacking timber. Mainly refers to loose timber laid in the hold of a ship to keep cargo clear of bilge water and to prevent movement.

DUST BOARD

In chests thin boards fitted between drawers to protect the contents from dust. They fit into grooves plowed in the inner edges of bearer rail and drawer runners.

EASEMENT

Is a type of right-of-way or privilege enjoyed by an owner of land over or in, that of another. It could refer to some specified right such as drainage, and is something that should be checked carefully with local government or other authorities when buying land.

EASING

The act of removing a little surface material from such items as doors and drawers. For example, planing a little from door edges, or the runners of drawers will produce a better fit or more efficient operation. An alternative is to spray or rub the moving parts with a dry lubricant.

EAVES

A projecting finish to a pitched roof with a gutter into which rainwater is drained. Boxed eaves consist of a soffit board underneath and a fascia gutter is secured to the fascia board with brackets.

EDGE MARK

A V-shaped mark on the face edge of timber denoting that it is straight and is square with the face side which has been previously trued by planing. All subsequent marking or testing is from either the face side or face edge.

EFFLORESCENCE

White soluble salts deposited on the surface of a wall or solid floor. The salts are present in Portland cement and certain brick clays. They are drawn to the surface as dampness evaporates, and crystallize in a white deposit which can be scraped off, though further dampness and evaporation may cause the trouble to recur.
On brick walls the white deposit may be treated by brushing on a diluted solution of muriatic acid and afterwards hosing down with clean water.
The proportions of the solution are: muriatic acid, one part; water, six to eight parts. All parts are by volume. Mix the solution in a glass or earthenware container, and apply to bricks with a stiff fiber brush.

EGGSHELL FINISH

Is the term used to describe the dull or semi-gloss finish given to a painted or enameled surface.

ELASTICITY

The property of a material to regain its original shape and size after being stretched or compressed. Also refers to this quality in a caulking compound which permits it to expand and contract under extreme conditions of heat and cold without breaking a seal or bond between two adjoining surfaces.

ELBOW

A pipe fitting used for joining lengths of pipe at right angles.

ELECTRICAL TERMS

Although the homeworker is not likely to do much in the way of electrical installation, it is useful to know something about the more common electrical terms in use. Here are some of the more important, together with their meaning.

A.C.—Alternating current is the type of power used in most home power systems.

Ampere—This is a unit of measure of the rate of flow of electricity, in much the same way as gallons-per-minute in a water measuring system.

Circuit—The complete flow of electricity is traced through what is technically called a circuit; it is the flow of current through a wire from the source of supply to one or more outlets and then back to the source of supply through another wire.

Circuit-Breaker—It performs the same function as a fuse in opening or breaking the circuit when there is an overload of current, but needs only to be reset.

Conduit—This metal or plastic tubing through which wires are run. It is used frequently when running wires underground or in areas where exposed wires are in danger of being frayed, broken, or cut.

D.C.—Means direct current as opposed to alternating current (A.C.). It is not in general use, but a good example is the current flow from batteries where one wire is always positive, or live, and the other always negative, or ground.

Fuse—A safety device which breaks the flow of current or electricity whenever a circuit is overloaded.

Grounding—The connection of the electrical system to the earth, a precaution necessary to prevent damage from lighting and to minimize the danger from shocks.

Insulation—A protective sheathing used over wires to prevent contact with electricity.

Junction Box—A box, either square or octagonal, in which wires from different circuits are joined.

Outlet Box—A unit in which an outlet, or to which a fixture such as a ceiling light, is secured and joined to the wiring system.

Overload—Terms used to describe an electrical condition in which too much current is flowing through the line for the fuse controlling that particular line.

Short Circuit—Popularly called a short, it is an improper connection between live wires or between a hot wire and a neutral wire.

Switch—A device for opening and closing the flow of current.

Switch Box—A metal unit, usually a rectangle but can be square, in which a switch or switches are connected to the circuit.

Volt—This is a unit used in measuring electrical pressure, like pounds in a water system.

Voltage Drop—This term is used to indicate the loss of voltage due to over-loading or when the current has to travel a great distance through a long extension lead.

Watt—This unit shows the current drain taking into account both voltage and amperage. For example, one watt is equal to one ampere at one volt, or seventy-five watts on a bulb indicates that the bulb consumes about .64 (slightly more than %10) of an ampere at 115 volts.

Watt Hour—One watt used for one hour one watt hour; 1,000 watt hours equals one kilowatt hour (Kwh), which is the unit by which electricity is metered.

ELEVATION

Is a drawing of the front or vertical face of a building. The other views normally shown are Plan—General layout—and Side Elevation.

EMERY CLOTH

Is available in sheets or strips. It is made up of powdered emery glued to a thin cloth. Emery cloth is used for removing file marks on metal and for polishing metallic surfaces.

ESCUTCHEON

Is the term applied to the plate around a keyhole and the shield around a faucet.

EXPANDED METAL

Metal sheeting cut and expanded by machinery to produce a grid-type of fabric used extensively as a lathing or base for plaster or cement rendering. The material, in aluminum, is used extensively for grilles and other decorative finishes.

EXPANSION BOLT

Is a masonry bolt or anchor.
The brick or concrete is drilled to take a metal casing fitted with a wedge-shaped nut. As the fixing bolt is screwed into the casing it expands and grips the side of the hole.

EXPANSION JOINT

Expansion joints are necessary when laying concrete slabs in a path or floor.
Asphalt strips can be laid between the sections so that when expansion and contraction occurs there will be less risk of cracking.

GLOSSARY

EXPANSION PIPE

A pipe leading from a water heater and either taken right through the roof or curved over the cold tank. Its purpose is to relieve pressure which would cause the hot-water system to explode. In effect, it is a safety valve.

EYE BOLT

An eye bolt has an eye or loop at one end instead of the usual head.
The other end is threaded for the nut in the usual way. Such bolts are used to receive ropes or hooks.

FACADE

Is the front elevation or view of a building.

FACE & EDGE MARK

The pencil mark put on the face side or edge of a piece of timber.
The face edge is the better edge of a piece of timber. It is planed straight and square with the face side and marked with a pencil. All subsequent marking and testing are from this or the face side.

FACE PLATE

A metal plate to be attached to a lathe mandrel in place of the usual chuck, and having a series of screw holes in it to enable the wood to be fixed to it. It is needed for turning flat items such as platters, small circular table tops, bowls, etc.

FANLIGHT

Is the glazed sash fitted over a door or window. It is usually pivoted in the center and is designed for ventilation and the admission of light.

FASCIA BOARD

A board fixed to the lower end of roof rafters. Its top edge sometimes projects upwards and acts as a tilting fillet for the bottom row of tiles. The gutter is generally fixed to it. Also used to describe flat portion above shop window.

FAT EDGE

Is a painting term and refers to to an accumulation of paint on an external angle such as a door edge or window sash.
Such faults can prevent the efficient operation of doors, windows, and other moving parts.

FERRULE

A metal collar fitted around a tool handle to prevent splitting. Also used for the metal fitting fixed to some peg legs.

FIBER BOARD

General term used for many building and wall boards made from wood pulp, cane, straw, and so on.

FIBROUS PLASTER

Fibrous plaster is best known in the form of sheets for lining interior walls and ceilings. It takes paint well and is fireproof.

GLOSSARY

FIDDLE-BACK FIGURE

Attractive ripple grain with light and dark pattern running across the grain. Found in some varieties of mahogany, sycamore and maple. Often used on the backs of violins, hence the term.

FIGURE

Ornamental markings seen on cut surfaces of timber formed by structural features of the wood.

FILE CARD

Is a small wire brush which is used to clear the cutting face of a file or rasp.
The material of the brush is fabric and is glued to a shaped wooden handle.

FILLER

Special composition used to fill the pores of wood before applying paint, varnish or polish.

FILLET

A narrow strip of wood. Cover fillet: strip used to cover a joint in joinery or between joinery and adjoining work. Glazing fillet: a small strip of wood used to retain glass in a rabbet.

FINIAL

A projecting ornament at top of newel post, church pew end, apex of gable on a roof, etc.

FIREBRICK

A special heat-resisting brick used as a backing for parts in a stove or fireplace exposed to the direct flames of a fire.

FIRMER CHISEL

This is the standard bench chisel. It is stronger than the beveled chisel and is used largely for chopping. Both tang and socket types are available. Normal chisels range from about 4 in. to 5 in. in blade length, but extra long paring chisels can also be obtained in the larger sizes. Firmer chisels are made from $\frac{1}{8}$ in. full up to 2 in. wide, with ash, beech, or box handles

FISH PLATES

Plates of metal or wood used to join wood beam, etc., in length. They are bolted or screwed at each side.

FITCH

A brush used for painting. It is the smallest size of sash tool.

FLAGSTONE

Large, flat paving stone. Could be either natural stone or cast concrete.

FLANCHING

The cement rendering of the top of a chimney stack to seal against the entry of dampness.

FLASHING

A strip of lead, zinc, or copper used to cover the abutment of a roof, canopy, cornice, etc., against a wall or chimney. The top of the flashing is bent at right angles so that the edge can be turned into a bed joint in the wall and then wedged and pointed. Flashing trays must also be fitted under window sills and above the heads of exterior window and door frames.

FLAT ROOF

A flat roof is one having an incline or pitch of not more than 20 degrees.

FLATTING AGENT

An ingredient used to reduce the gloss of lacquer or varnish. Some are metallic soap, calcium, aluminium or zinc stearate.

FLIGHT HOLE

Small round holes in timber attacked by the furniture beetle. They are the holes from which the beetle emerges.

FLOAT

Is the tool used for finishing off the surface of a concrete path or floor. It is a flat piece of dry timber with a handle attached to back.
In a toilet tank, the float is the hollow ball that rises with the water level and closes the intake valve to shut off the flow of water when the tank is full.

FLOORING CLAMP

A special device of which there are many varieties. All work on much the same principle, the purpose of which is to enable floor boards to be pressed tightly together when being nailed down. The pressure is produced by virtue of a strong grip obtained on the joists.

FLOUR SANDPAPER

The finest grade of sandpaper, also known as No. 00. Used for fine finishing, wood which has no definite grain direction, and in the polishing process.

FLUSH

Term denoting that two surfaces are level.

FLUSH DOOR

One in which the surfaces are plane across. There are various forms of construction, and it also varies with size. Small cabinet doors may be in multi-ply or laminated board which is veneered both sides, or made up of a framework with thin plywood panels glued each side. Larger room doors are usually of this latter construction with cross rails and various fillings to prevent local sinking of the panels.

FLUX

A preparation used to assist the flowing of solder to prevent the surface of the clean metal from oxidizing when it is heated by the soldering bit. The three fluxes for most soldering jobs are zinc chloride, resin, and tallow.

FOUNDATION

The terms foundation and footings are often confusing. The foundation is the natural material on which the house is built. It may be rock, shale, clay, sand, loam, gravel or a combination of some of these.
The footings are the base materials of the building which are put directly on the foundation, and may be concrete, reinforced concrete or brick.

FRENCH CURVE

An appliance for drawing, nowadays mostly in plastic material, but formerly in wood. The curves are largely elliptical, and the purpose is to enable shapes to be drawn quickly. By reversing the curve the exact opposite sweep is obtained.

FRENCH DOORS

A pair of fully glazed doors giving access from a room into a garden or patio.

FRETSAW BLADES

Obtainable for fine, medium, and coarse cutting, the standard length being 5 in. There are two kinds of fretsaw blades available, one for cutting wood and the other for metal and plastic materials.

FROG

A depression formed in the broad flat surface of a brick, reducing the weight of the brick and affording a grip, or key for the mortar.

FULL

More than the dimensions described.

FUR

Name given to the lime deposit that forms on the inside of kettles and boilers, especially in the districts where the water is hard.

GABLE

In architecture the triangular part of the end of a building from eaves to ridge. In woodwork the end parts (solid or framed) of such a carcass as a wardrobe, bookcase, cabinet, or sideboard. In building construction the term "gable roof" is applied to a roof which finishes with a gable.

GAD

Small wedge for splitting soft stone. It is used with a heavy hammer.

GAIN

The shallow notch or recess made in the frame of a door jamb or the door itself to receive the wing of a hinge.

GALLETING

The term applied when small fragments of stone, or pebbles, are pressed into the mortar of large joints.

GANTRY

A timber or metal staging over pavements, etc., as a landing stage for building materials, or as a platform from which materials from an excavation or mine are loaded into trucks. A gantry is often screened by a protective hoarding.

GASKET

Made of paper, metal, rubber or special composition fiber. It performs a function similar to a hose washer. Set between two flanges—usually metal to prevent leaking at joint. The material used as a gasket must be sufficiently pliable to mold itself to the contours of the two surfaces which are to be joined under pressure.

GAUGE BOX

Square box frame without a bottom for measuring the dry volume of the ingredients to be mixed together to form concrete which is being mixed by hand. For small jobs a box 12 in. square, and 12 in. deep, interior measurements, is ideal as it holds one cubic foot of material. In use it is placed on the mixing platform and filled with the required number of parts. After filling, it is merely lifted up.

GAVEL

Small wood mallet, usually turned, on a wood-turning lathe.

GERMAN SILVER

Is an alloy of copper, zinc and nickel. It is used in handicraft work and also as a solder to join certain metal together.

GESSO

A material made from whiting, linseed oil, and glue. It is thickly applied as a decorative coating to other materials, when set, it can be carved, and gilded or painted.

GIMP

Narrow strip of leather or material in decorative pattern used at the edges of upholstery to conceal raw edges and fixing tacks.

GIMP PIN

Made in two forms, cut and wire. The former has the advantage of being sharper and therefore staying in position with pressure from the fingers before the hammer is used.

GIRDER

Heavy beam, usually built up of rolled-steel sections and plates.

GIRTH

The measurement around the circumference of a log. In a tapering log it is generally taken at the central position to obtain the average.

GIVE

A member or part of one which will accommodate itself to stress without breaking is said to have give. Thus, sometimes in assembling, a member may have to be bent to enable it to be sprung into position, and thus gives sufficiently for the purpose.

GLAZED DOOR

Any door having a glass panel or series of panes. It may vary from the simplest of doors with a single pane fitting in a rabbet to an elaborate design with molded bars.

GLAZED WHEEL

A grinding wheel which has lost its cut owing to the pores having become clogged. It should be corrected with a dresser which has a group of alternate ring and star wheels which are free to revolve. It is brought into close contact with the revolving grinding wheel, when the star wheels dig out the pores between the granules.

GLAZIER'S POINTS

Are small, flat, triangular metal pieces which are used in addition to putty to hold the glass panes in window sashes. Light panel pins may be used in place of the points.

GLAZING

This term has two applications. (A) Application of a thin wash of color, usually over graining and marbling, to secure additional depth, richness and transparency. (B) Fixing of glass in a prepared sash or frame. In a wooden sash, the glass is held in position by points or panel pins and is bedded in putty composed of raw linseed oil and powdered whiting. The rabbet for the glass should be coated with paint to prevent the wood from absorbing the oil from the putty. For internal glazing, thin strips of wood, known as glazing beads, are used. The glazing of metal sashes is executed with metallic putty composed of whiting, raw linseed oil and red and white lead. Metal sashes usually have special glazing clips to hold the glass.

GLAZING BAR

The metal or wooden members in a window unit which form the framework of individual panes.

GLIDERS

Polished steel fittings of domed shape with projecting spikes. They are knocked into the bottoms of furniture legs, enabling the item to be drawn easily over the floor.

GLUE BLOCKS

Small blocks of wood planed square and with a fairly broad chamfer at the outer corner. The inner sharp corner is also taken off to ensure that the surfaces bed right down. The blocks are glued and rubbed back and forth once or twice. They serve to strengthen the joint. When added to joints in which the grain runs crosswise several short glue blocks should be used with a slight gap between rather than one long one as in this way shrinkage is not impeded and danger of splitting is avoided.

GLUE SIZE

Melted glue diluted with water to form a weak jelly when cold. It is used to lessen surface porosity before hanging wallpaper.

GOLD LEAF

Thin sheets of beaten gold used in gilding and in quality sign writing work.
Obtainable in books of 25 leaves, 3¼ in. square, and in both loose leaf and transfer form. The former is free and is interleaved between tissue paper, whereas transfer gold is attached,to the tissue paper with a film of wax.

GRAINING

A method of decorating the surface of wood by painting it to resemble the grain of figured timber. First apply a base color, then, when this is dry, a coat of another color. Before this second coat is dry, remove part of it with special graining combs, rollers, sponges, or brushes to obtain the desired timber-grain effect.

GRAPHITE

Can be used as a lubricant.

GREEN

A term used for unseasoned timber which is full of moisture.

GROMMET

Sometimes spelled grummet, is a twisted end of rope or rubber to provide a loop or ring for fastening. They are also metal fittings used to reinforce holes in fabric such as awnings and tents.

GROUND COAT

Surface coating material applied before the paint, lacquer, varnish, or other material.

GROUNDS

Rough wood framing fixed in or to a brick wall to which building sheets, panels, etc. are fixed. Also called furring.

GLOSSARY

GROUT

A mortar, liquid enough to be poured. Used as a filler for open brickwork joints or as a bonding agent for paths laid by penetration method.

GRUB SCREW

Headless, metal thread often used to hold a pulley on shaft.

GULLEY

Is the opening to receive waste from baths, sinks, and wash basins before passing through to the drains. The term is often meant to include the trap which is placed beneath the opening to prevent the escape of foul gases into the atmosphere.

GUM

Secretion found in some species of timber. Also called resin, and pitch.

GUSSET

Steel packing cases used to connect and reinforce the sections of a truss roof.
Gussets of plywood are also used in furniture construction to give added strength and rigidity.

GUTTER

Shallow trough fixed along the eaves of a roof, behind a parapet wall, or between two sloping roofs, for carrying off rain water.

GUTTER BRACKET

A metal support shaped to hold a gutter and which can be fixed to the fascia board or the ends of rafters.

HACKING OFF
The action of chipping or cutting the surface of brick or stone to remove old plaster.

HAFT
The handle of a hammer, axe, or mallet.

HALVED JOINT
A joint formed by two members, the end of each being sunk to half its depth; when joined at right angles, the projection on one member fits into the sinking on the other.

HAND. (of Door)
This term or expression is used to denote the direction in which a door swings, or which side of a door or window sash frame is hinged as seen from the face on which the knuckle of the hinge is seen.
The door or sash is said to be either left or right-hand hung. The term is also applied to locks. As an example, if the door should open away from the user while the lock is on the left and the latch bevel is facing, the lock and furniture are said to be left-handed.

HANDRAIL BOLT
Special bolt threaded at each end for a square nut and castellated or slotted nut respectively.
It is used mainly for connecting continuous lengths of staircase rails.

HANDSAW
General term applied to a cross-cut, rip, or panel hand operated saw.

HAND VISE
Small vise, 4 in. to 5 in. long, enabling small pieces of metal, plastic material, etc., to be cut, filed or drilled, the jaws being tightened by a winged nut and opening by spring action as the nut is slackened. Often used by the cabinet maker, especially the furniture repairer, when making small metal fittings such as escutcheon plates. The hand vise simplifies filing and fitting, being more convenient than a steel bench vise or a metal sash clamp.

HANGER BOLT

This is the special type of bolt used for attaching legs to tables and other furniture assembly jobs. On one end is a machine bolt thread and on the other is a coarse wood screw thread.

It is commonly found in the end of a leg which is screwed into a metal plate under the table top.

HANGING

Is the general term used to describe the fixing of doors or casement window sashes by means of hinges so that they can be swung open or closed. The term also refers to a cabinet to hang on the wall rather than to stand on the floor, and sometimes to a wardrobe in which clothes are hung.

HANGING STILE

Is the post or upright jamb to which a door, a sash frame or gate is hinged.

HARDBOARD

Available in various sizes of panels and in several thicknesses such as $\frac{1}{8}$ in. and $\frac{3}{16}$ in. A specially compressed and impregnated type also is made, suitable for outdoor work. Perforated board with small holes at regular intervals is used for display stands, etc. Embossed patterns of various designs are produced for decorative effects.

HARDENER

Used in resin glues to cause setting. In some makes the powdered glue contains the hardener, and setting begins when water is added. In others the hardener is a separate liquid, and no setting begins until it is brought into contact with the glue. The usual method is to apply the glue to the one part and the hardener to the other. Hardeners of varying speeds can be obtained.

HAUNCH

The small piece left on the tenon of a haunched tenon and mortise joint to give added strength and prevent the rail from twisting. It is always used where the joint is at the end of a stile, as in door and window sashes.

HAWK

This is a plastering tool. It is a small, square board with a handle underneath. Plaster or mortar is placed on the surface of the board.

The hawk is held in one hand and the plaster or mortar is taken from the top of the board and applied with a trowel held in the other hand.

HEAD

The topmost horizontal member of a door or window frame.

HEADER

A brick laid in a course so that its end forms part of the wall surface.

HEADROOM

The clear space between the floor and ceiling or underside of the roof to allow for free walking and access without the risk of striking the head. For example, a standard door opening is 6 ft. 8 in. high, which provides ample headroom for even unusually tall people. Provision of adequate headroom above a staircase is especially important.

HEWN

Timber which has been squared or roughly shaped with an axe or adze. Timber which is hewn tends to be more resistant to rot and decay than sawn timber.

HIDING POWER

The capacity of the surface coat to hide the wood or previous finish applied beneath.

HIGH SPOTS

This term is used in most trades. It refers to points to be removed by grinding, scraping, or planing in order to obtain a perfectly plane or flat surface.

GLOSSARY

HINGE BOUND

This term denotes the fault which occurs when a door or sash frame is difficult to close because it fits too closely into the rabbet of the frame. The fault can usually be overcome by a slight adjustment of the hinges to throw the door outwards.

HIPPED ROOF

A roof which, instead of a gable, has the eaves continued across the end of the building, and the roof is sloped up from these eaves, so that a triangular surface of roof is formed, terminating at the ridge and with the sides of the triangle meeting the two main slopes of the roof. On a plain rectangular roof all four sides slope and there are four hips. A hip rafter is fixed at each external angle and jack rafters are beveled against it.

HOD

Although not now in general use because of the introduction of mechanical conveying methods on building sites, the hod is a tool or device by which a laborer carries bricks and mortar. It should be made of a dry, durable timber such as cedar, and consist of two sides at right angles and filled in at one end. It is approximately 16 in. long, and the sides are 8 in. wide and 1 in. thick.

A handle similar to a stout broom handle is attached to the bottom of the frame with a metal angle. In use the hod is balanced on the shoulder of the worker. A good hod carrier—called a hoddie—can climb or scale ladders very quickly with a full load of bricks or mortar.

HONING

Means the sharpening of tools on an oilstone. In particular it refers to the fine finish on the edge of a razor.

HOPPER WINDOWS

Sometimes called hospital windows, they are used extensively in tropical areas.

Hopper windows are hinged to open outwards from the top and provide maximum ventilation.

HOUSE INSPECTION

There are many trouble spots around the house that should be checked regularly and here are some suggestions:

Exterior

1 Mortar joints which may require repointing.
2 Painted surfaces to see if blistering, cracking or peeling has started, and if painting is necessary.
3 Window sills which require added protection from paint because of exposed position.
4 Holes or cracks around window frames to see if caulking or repair is needed.
5 Windows which may require re-glazing to replace broken panes of glass.
6 Replace any damaged putty around glass in windows.
7 Remove and check condition of fly screens, blinds, and shutters for repair or painting.
8 Tile or slate roofing for cracked or broken tiles or slates.
9 Metal or roll roofing for cracks or open joints.
10 Flashing around chimney stack or any other part where sheet lead or any other sheet flashing material is used.
11 Need for replacement of chimney caps or pots.
12 Roof gutters which may require cleaning of accumulated leaves and other rubbish. Regular painting of the inside of gutters is a basic maintenance job.
13 Posts and rails on outside fences and garden fixtures for possible rot and decay. Pay particular attention to the point around ground level.
14 Under the floors to see that there is adequate ventilation. Also check for dry rot and termite attack.
15 Repair damaged steps which could possibly cause accidents.
16 Concrete paths which may have subsided or become cracked or stained.
17 Basements which may be damp and require water-proofing.

18 Removal of weeds or built-up gardens around foundation walls.

19 Check drains, waste pipes, etc., and clean where necessary.

20 The need to fit new washers on water taps. Water pipes may need renewal, and existing galvanized water pipes are best replaced with copper pipes.

Interior

21 See whether re-wiring of electric light and power installation is needed. Here consult a qualified electrician.

22 See that electrical appliance cords are in good condition.

23 Examine doors and windows to see if adjustment or re-fitting is needed.

24 Locks, catches, etc., to be checked with view to replacing with more secure types.

25 Window cords to see if they should be renewed.

26 The repair of damaged plaster on walls and ceilings.

27 Check ceilings for any sign of sagging.

28 Floors or stairs which creak when walked upon.

29 Advisability of laying new flooring over old.

30 Prevent draughts by checking entry points around door and window frames.

31 Replace loose floor and wall tiles.

HOUSING

A recess cut into one member to receive the end of another to form a secure joint. The housed joint is used for securing studs to wall plates and fixing shelving to uprights.

IMPREGNATION

The forcing of a substance into the cells of wood. It may be a preservative or a resin and may be carried out by heat or compression. Repeated brushing will eventually cause a preservative such as creosote to be absorbed.

INDENT

Space left in course of brickwork to take a projecting brick of another wall at a junction to create a firm bond between the two.

INDIGENOUS

Term used to describe woods native to a particular country.

INITIAL SET

Is the hardening action of cement and plaster which occurs 30 to 60 minutes after mixing with water. For this reason, concrete should be placed in its final position as soon as possible after mixing.

INLAY

A form of decoration in which shallow channels are made in solid wood, and then filled in with pieces of contrasting colored wood or other material. The strips are glued in place. They stand slightly above the surface and are sanded down flush. This procedure is also called intarsia.

INNER BEAD

Bead planted round the inner edge of sash frame.

IN SITU

Or to give the full expression, "cast in situ" refers to concrete poured into the position it will occupy when set. The alternate method is to use pre-cast blocks or slabs.

INSULATION

The use, in a building, of a material or method that will obstruct the passage of sound, light, heat, or vibration from one surface to another.

IRON

Applied to the cutting blade in a plane or spokeshave. In fact it is of high grade tool steel. Also as in soldering iron, which is really a copper bit.

ISOSCELES

Refers to a triangle which has two sides of equal dimension and two of the angles equal.

JACK PLANE

The most useful general purpose woodworking plane is the steel jack plane.
It is usually about 14 in. long and 2½ in. wide. It is especially useful for reducing wood approximately to size before finishing off exactly with the steel smoothing plane.

JAMB LINING

Is the wood lining at the sides and head of a door or window opening. It is usual to make the prepared lining material into a frame before securing inside the opening.

JIG

A jig is any device which acts as a guide for handwork or machining.
It enables a job to be done more accurately and in less time. There are many jigs that can be made as required for a particular job, and others which should be part of a standard tool kit.
In the latter group are a doweling jig and a drill-bit grinding jig which ensures that the drill-bit point is always ground to the correct angle.

JIG SAW

A reciprocating machine saw for cutting internal shapes which the bandsaw could not reach. For the small workshop the bench model is used in which the throat distance is the limit the saw can operate from the edge of the work. Larger trade machines are of the floor-to-ceiling type in which there is no throat restriction. Some machines have spring plunger control of the saw; others the cross-bow type spring.
Another form of jig saw has the saber saw in which a short, stiff blade is used. Portable jig saws have this arrangement. For woodwork, jig saws operate at about 1,000 to 1,400 strokes per minute.

JOGGLE

A projection or horn left on the stile of a vertically sliding sash so that the mortise is not too close to the end where it would be liable to split. It is usually given an ornamental shaping.

JOINER

Refers to tradesmen whose main work is the preparation and making of such fitments as windows, doors, and paneling. It is usual to find that many carpenters are also joiners because the two trades are so closely connected.

JOISTS

Basically, joists in a building fall into two groups. First, there are the floor joists which rest on edge or bearers and at right angles to them. They are securely nailed to these bearers and usually spaced at 18 in. centers. The floor boards are nailed to these joists which are generally of 4 in. by 2 in. hardwood. Ceiling joists are also 4 in. wide by 2 in. thick but are usually of fir.

They span a room and rest on the wall plates. Like the floor joists, ceiling joists are also spaced at 18 in. centers. It is usual to fix a wide beam on edge across the tops of the ceiling joists at intervals and at right angles to them. This serves to keep them rigid and support the sheet ceiling material.

JUMP

Refers to a rise or step in a concrete or brick footing. It serves to adjust to a sloping site.

JUMPER

The portion of the faucet to which the washer is attached. It prevents the rotation of the washer when the faucet is turned on. If the washer were to rotate with the faucet stem, it would soon wear out on the valve seat. In most faucets, when the stem is removed, the jumper will remain in the cavity and must be lifted out.

KAOLIN

Is a mineral white pigment used as an extender for paint.

KERF

This is the term used to describe the width of the cut made by the teeth in a saw blade.

Most woodsaws have the teeth alternately set to right and left so as to provide clearance for the blade in the kerf. The extent of this setting will determine the width of the saw kerf.

KEY

One application of this term denotes the roughening of a smooth surface to provide a bond or grip for an adhesive or cement.

On the other hand there are numerous devices called keys which serve to hold parts securely together. For instance, these square-section and tapered steel keys are used to hold wheels, gears, and pulleys on shafts and arbors. Then of course there are the lock keys which need no description.

KEYED JOINT

This joint is often seen in Colonial furniture designs. It normally provides for a mortise and tenon joint to be made in the normal way with the exception that the tenon protrudes for some distance. A small mortise is cut through this protruding tenon close to the frame and a slightly tapered key set through the tenon.

KEYHOLE SAW

As the name suggests, this tool is designed for cutting keyholes and other sharp-curve circular shapes. The blade is tapered and it is advisable to buy the type of tool which has a cluster of interchangeable blades. These blades are usually designed for wood, metal, and ceramic cutting jobs respectively.

KEYSTONE

Is the topmost stone at the crown of an arch or dome. It really locks the unit in place.

KICK PLATE

Is a metal plate—usually sheet brass—screwed to the lower portion of a door. Its purpose is to protect the finish from being ruined, by feet kicking against the bottom of the door.

KILN DRIED

Describes the procedure for seasoning or drying timber. It is done basically by heat and air circulation, and results in a considerable saving of time over the old natural method of stacking timber to dry for a long period after cutting.

KNIVES

There are various types of knives used in woodwork and painting.

First there is a marking knife and scriber used with a square for fine setting-out.

Then there is a draw knife for cutting circular shapes. In painting work, there is the essential putty knife which is used with putty for window glazing and stopping holes and cracks in surfaces to be painted.

KNOT

Is a defect in a piece of timber which may weaken the timber from a constructional point of view and is bad when in a tenon or mortise. A knot is really a portion of a branch enclosed in the timber by natural growth of the tree. Knots take several forms and here are some details.

Dead Knot: Knot whose fibers are intergrown with those of the surrounding wood to an extent less than one-quarter of the cross sectional perimeter. Enclosed Knot: One that does not appear on the surface of the timber. Loose Knot: One not held firmly in place. Sound Knot: A live knot, free from decay, solid across its face, and at least as hard as the surrounding wood.

KNOTTING

Is a type of spirit varnish similar in some ways to French polish which is used to seal the surface of knots in new timber.

It serves to prevent resin from around the knots bleeding through the paint film. It also seals the surface of the knot to make it less porous. This in turn ensures a uniform absorption of paint over the entire surface.

KNURL

This is a type of finish on tools which permits a more secure grip.

The surface is slightly roughened, as for example on a punch or thumb screw so that they are easier to hold.

LAGGING

Lagging is the process of heat insulation, especially when employed on pipes, hot water vessels, or cold water cisterns. The term is also used as a noun to describe the actual materials used for these purposes. Most lagging materials are in granular or fibrous form, and owe their efficiency to the air pockets which they contain.

LAGGINGS

Are battens or laths of wood secured to the top edge of the wood framed center support of an arch. The strips may also be used to form a protective frame around columns or other parts during building operations.

LAID DRY

Term used to describe the laying of stone garden or retaining walls without mortar. Such a method retains a natural look and permits soakage water to drain away freely.

LAMINATED PLASTICS

The best known examples of this material are the hard sheets under various trade names used to cover table and cupboard tops. They are made up of layers of paper or fabric impregnated with synthetic resin, and bonded together under heat and pressure. They are desirable because of their high resistance to heat and stains and because of the wide range of patterns and colors in which they are available. They imitate wood grain so well that they are being used extensively to replace wood veneers in furniture manufacture.

LAMP BLACK

A fine pigment powder used for making black stain or polish. A binding agent should be added for staining.

LARRY

Is a tool mainly used by bricklayers and plasterers for mixing mortar. It consists of a long handle to which is fixed a semi-circular flat steel head with part of the center removed. It is not unlike a garden hoe in appearance. In use, the larry is drawn through a heap of mortar in a jerking motion to mix it thoroughly.

LATHING (Metal)

Sometimes called expanded lathing or expanded metal, it is used as a base for cement rendering over a frame wall.

The sheets of expanded metal are fixed to the timber studs or uprights with galvanized clouts or nails.

LEADED LIGHTS

Sash window or door panels built up of small pieces of glass, usually of different colors and to a pattern.

These glass sections are held in grooved lead strips called cames.

LEAD HOLE

Sometimes called a pilot hole, the principle involved has numerous applications.

For example, if boring large holes at an angle, it is a good idea to drill small diameter lead holes first. This way any necessary adjustments can be made before drilling the main holes.

Also, when drilling large holes in metal, by drilling small lead holes first, then replacing the small drill with a larger one, less effort is required to complete the drilling, and the result is extremely clean-cut holes.

LEDGED DOOR

A door made up of a series of battens or tongue and groove matched boards. They are held together to form the door by three crossrails called ledges. Diagonal braces between these ledges ensures that the door does not sag. It is known as a ledged and braced door.

LEFT-HAND THREAD

There are parts of machinery where the threads on screwed sections are cut in the opposite direction from that normally used so that it is necessary to turn the nut in a counter-clockwise direction to tighten. This is referred to as a left-hand thread. An application of a left-hand thread is when a circular saw blade rotates in a clockwise direction. The arbor may have a left-hand thread to avoid risk of the blade working loose as it revolves.

LIGHT

Describes a window or other construction for the admission of light to a room or enclosed space within a building. The term also denotes the sections into which a window sash is subdivided by sash bars to make say a two-light, or four-light window.

LIME-CEMENT MORTAR

Made with a mixture of hydrated lime, Portland cement, and fine sand. It is not quite as strong as straight cement-sand mortar, but works easily off the trowel and has little shrinkage.

LIMEWASH

Is a mixture of freshly slaked lime and water to make a solution which can be used for coating interior or exterior brick or stone walls. It may also be used on rough exterior woodwork. For exterior work, add tallow or other fatty substance to serve as a binding agent.
A useful recipe for limewash is to set a quantity of lump or rock lime, slake it with boiling water, and then thin to working consistency with skimmed milk. One ounce of alum, dissolved in water, should be added to each gallon of the mixture.

LINING PAPER

Is a thin plain wallpaper designed to be used over certain types of wall surface as a base for the main wallpapers.
It helps to even out the suction of porous walls and cover minor blemishes in a wall. It is hung horizontally with standard wallpaper paste.

LINSEED OIL

Principal drying oil used in oil paint. It is also combined with whiting to make glazing putty.
The oil is obtained from the flax plant and the main types are raw and boiled linseed oil respectively. Boiled linseed oil, to which a drier is added during the heating process is often used as an exterior coating over brickwork to seal and impart a gloss to the surface. Linseed oil is also used in the manufacture of linoleum.

LINTEL

A beam placed across the top of a window or door opening and of sufficient strength to carry the weight of the wall above and that part of the roof which bears upon it.

The most common form of lintel is a precast beam set in place and built into the wall as the work proceeds. Another plan is to use a piece of stout steel angle or channel across the opening.

LIPPING

Strip of wood, veneer, or other material, applied to the edge of a flush door or around the edge of a table top.

LOCK-RAIL

Is the center rail in a framed door. It is usually wide enough to permit the fitting of a lock.

LOCK WASHER

This washer is split and the ends are slightly raised. It serves as a compression spring. That is, it holds the part or parts firmly, even where there may be vibration.

LUG

Small projection on any frame or member to permit a unit to be fixed in position by screwing or nailing.

LUMBER

Is a term to describe timber which has been converted by sawing.

MACADAM

Road or driveway surfacing material named after its originator John McAdam.
It is basically hard gravel spread in layers, rolled, and bound together by tar bitumen.

MACHINED

Timber having a surface of a dimension that has been subject to machine operation after initial conversion from the log. That is, it may have been planed or shaped to become a molded section such as architrave or quadrant molding.

MADE-UP GROUND

New ground generally achieved by filling in depressions, swamps, or other areas previously of little use. Care should be taken about building on made-up ground to avoid the risk of excessive settling.

MAKING GOOD

Repairing and putting into good condition any part of a building or piece of furniture which is damaged or has fallen into a state of disrepair.

MALLET

This is a hammer-like tool made in a number of designs and from various materials. These include wood, rawhide, plastic, or rubber and will not damage surfaces in the way a steel hammer might do.
A wooden mallet is a woodworking tool used mainly for driving a chisel when cutting a mortise or similar work.

MANDREL

Chiefly a plumber's tool used as a former or mold for shaping the inside of cylindrical objects.

MANSARD ROOF

A roof with a double pitch, the lower part of the slope being steeper than the upper section. This design provides more room inside, and is used widely in Europe. The name derives from a French architect Francois Mansard.

MASKING

The term used to describe the protection or covering of a surface while painting or spraying adjoining sections or areas.
Special masking tape is available for the purpose.

MASONRY

Blocks of stone laid in walling to overlap or bond, usually in mortar, but sometimes dry, together with stone moldings, cornices, steps, sills, arches, lintels, and other features.

MATCHBOARD

A board that has a tongue on one side and a corresponding groove on the other. The face edges are usually slightly chamfered so that when the boards are fitted together, a V-joint is achieved. Matchboards are used for making wall panels and partitions, also for ledged doors and window shutters.

MEETING RAIL

The bottom rail of the top sash and the top rail of the bottom sash of a double-hung or boxed frame window.
In the closed position, the two rails meet flush, to be secured with a special meeting-rail catch.

MEMBER

In framed work, especially furniture and joinery, each piece making up the frame is a member. They also have special names. In a framed door, the upright members are stiles, and the horizontal members rails.

MEZZANINE

Describes a low room, or an intermediate floor or story between high principal rooms.

METAL NIBBLER

Is a tool which cuts sheet metal quickly and to practically any shape.
There are various types of hand operated nibblers, also a nibbling attachment to be used with a portable electric drill.

MODULE

Is a standard or unit for measurement. It is a term used in prefabricated and sectional construction for the basic unit on which dimensions of rooms and parts are based.

Many products have taken 4 in. as a basic measurement. A good example of this is concrete masonry blocks which are based on multiples of 4 in. when allowance is made for mortar joints.

MONKEY

Is the weight used as a hammer or ram in a pile driver.

MORTAR

A prepared substance used to bed and joint brickwork. It distributes the pressure evenly throughout the brickwork, it holds the bricks in place and prevents the transmission of moisture, sound, and heat from one face of the wall to another.

Mortar is composed of two ingredients, one called the aggregate and the other the matrix, the strength of the mortar depending on the proportion of these ingredients. Portland cement or lime is usually the matrix, sand, the aggregate.

MOUTH

Opening in the sole of a plane to allow shavings to pass through. Also refers to a hardwood piece recessed into the sole of a wooden plane to reduce the mouth width when the latter has become too wide—the result of repeated truing.

Some metal planes have adjustable mouths. The term is used for the opening in any tool through which shavings, chips, or dust must pass.

MULLION

The upright division between the lights of a window or other opening.

MULTI-PLY

Means plywood to a thickness of over a quarter of an inch by more than three layers or plys. These plys or layers are laminated in odd number groupings—such as 3 ply, 5 ply— so as to have the grain direction the same on back and front surfaces.

MUNTIN

The vertical division in a framed door contained between horizontal rails. Also applied to the rail running from back to front in the bottom of a large drawer to avoid sagging.

NAIL SET

Also called a nail punch, it is a small tool used to sink nail heads below the surface of timber. A good nail set should have the point slightly cupped or hollow so as to get a good seat on the nail head. They are available in a range of sizes to suit various nail gauges. The common name for this tool is a nail punch.

NATURAL OIL STONE

One which is quarried and prepared to shape as distinct from an artificial or manufactured one. As with all types of such stones, this one should be kept in a protective case.

NEAT'S FOOT OIL

Pale yellow oil which is suitable for use with an oilstone or as a leather dressing. It is made by boiling the feet and shin bones of "neat cattle," a British term for common cattle.

NECK

The narrow part at the top of a column or of a turning joining two wider parts.

NEWEL

A post used in stair construction. There is a newel at the foot of the stairs and another at the head on the open side. The balustrade is fixed between these newel posts.

NICHE

Recess in the thickness of a wall for a vase or statue.

NOGGING

Short piece of wood fixed between studs or uprights of a timber framed building or partition wall. They are fitted to a line and serve as a support for the horizontal edges of wall sheets and also stiffen the frame.

NOMINAL SIZE

Is the size of sawn timber before being planed or dressed. Thus a piece of timber which is nominally one inch thick may finish a bare $\frac{7}{8}$ in. thick after planing.

GLOSSARY

NOSING

Describes a circular saw blade having a group of cross-cutting teeth followed by a large fillet. Sometimes a raker tooth is included, this being square-topped and of slightly less projection than the other teeth. Its purpose is to clear the kerf. Sometimes known as the planer saw, it produces a very smooth cut with little splintering on the underside of the cut.
Novelty saws are intended for both ripping and cross-cutting.

NOVELTY SAW

Mainly refers to the rounded edge on such parts as stair treads and narrow ledges attached to window sills inside a room.

OBTUSE

Applied to an angle which is greater than 90 degrees. An acute angle is less than 90 degrees.

OFFCUT

The falling, or wasted piece of timber left after sawing to a specified dimension.

At all times it is desirable to order and mark out work so as to avoid excessive off-cuts which could be wasteful.

Alternatively, plan work so that off-cuts can be used to advantage on smaller projects.

OPACITY

Is the quality of being opaque. That is, a paint film of good opacity will completely obliterate the color of the undercoating. Such a paint is said to have a good hiding power.

ORBITAL SANDER

An electric portable sander in which the individual abrasive granules move in a small circular path. It is specially useful for surfaces with joists and for work with no definite direction to the grain, as in burr walnut. The pad over which the abrasive paper is fixed retains its direction but, instead of moving back and forth as in a reciprocating sander, it has a circular movement.

OREGON PINE

Alternative name for Douglas fir. It is an ideal timber for construction work, being light and easy to cut, plane, and nail.

OVER-ALL SIZE

Dimension of an item which includes all projections such as moldings, edge strips, etc.

OVERFLOW PIPE

A pipe fitted in a toilet tank to carry away excess water should the ball valve be out of order.

OXALIC ACID

A poisonous acid used chiefly in woodwork as a mild bleach. The crystals are dissolved in water and applied with a rag, several applications being given if necessary. When dry it is neutralized by wiping over the surface with an alkali such as borax, otherwise it may attack any finish subsequently applied.

PAIRED

Refers to the right hand and left hand members of a frame or unit of furniture which is being assembled. In other words, it denotes two of the same item, one left hand, and one right hand.

PARGETING

Lining the inside of a flue or chimney with lime mortar to give a smooth airtight finish. It acts as a fire deterrent.

PARLIAMENT HINGE

A window hinge with very long flaps, which swing the window, when open, away from the frame, leaving sufficient space to admit the passage of the arm for cleaning the exterior. Such hinges may also be used on doors.

PARQUETRY

Refers mainly to treatment of floor surfaces overlaid with blocks of different colored woods to form geometrical patterns.

PARTING BEAD

The thin beaded slip which separates the sliding sashes of a window. The term "parting slip" is applied to the bead which keeps the weights apart.

PARTY FENCE WALL

Walls separating the land of different owners, when built partly on the land of one owner and partly on the land of the other are called party fence walls. They are the mutual property of the two adjoining owners and are maintainable at the joint expense of the two owners.

PATINA

The gloss acquired on woodwork through years of polishing.

PEBBLEDASH

A method of finishing the outside walls of a house. It consists of throwing small washed pebbles onto a coat of cement.

PEDIMENT

A triangular or otherwise shaped frontal head feature to a doorway, clockcase, or a tall piece of furniture such as a wardrobe or bookcase. Now rarely seen, these pediments were a feature of furniture in the late 18th and early to mid 19th centuries.

PEGGED JOINTS

Method of locking a joint by passing a peg through both mortise sides and tenons so that the latter cannot be withdrawn. Dowels of ¼ in. or ⅜ in. diameter are mostly used today, but originally the pegs were roughly shaped squares sometimes with the corners taken off, and tapered.

PEENING

The beating over or smoothing over of a metallic object, such as a rivet, with the peen end of a ball peen hammer.

PELMET

Covering at the head of a window to hide curtain fittings. It may be of soft material (valance) or of plywood, hardboard, etc.

PENCIL BRUSH

Small round pointed brush used by the polisher to touch up small blemishes such as filled-in nail holes, discolored parts, etc.

PENCIL, CARPENTER'S

Oval pencil with side, large lead. Used to mark out carpentry work. The large lead is long wearing and needs resharpening infrequently.

PENETRATION

Is the ability of one substance to enter another and usually refers to the porosity of wood. In particular it is used in connection with veneers and their liability to penetration by glue; also to solid wood in connection with preservative liquids.

PIANO HINGE

Is really a very long butt hinge as seen on piano lids. It is ideal for use on say a table leaf where there will be considerable strain.

PICTURE RAIL

This usually marks the junction line between lower wall and frieze. Milled molding material for the purpose is supplied in widths from 1 in. to 3 in. The moldings are rounded on top to engage the picture hooks. In recent years picture rails have gone out of fashion, most people preferring plain wall surfaces.

GLOSSARY

PIERS

Columns of concrete or masonry to carry a structural load. They may be incorporated in a wall or stand independently. When in a wall, they are known as engaged piers.

PIGMENT

Is the solid constituent of paint which provides the color and hiding power. Most pigments are obtained from earth, vegetable and mineral substances, or they may be manufactured products.
Earth colors include the ochres, siennas and umbers. They are in the form of powder and are ground in oils to form the pigment paste.

PIPING

Narrow pipe-like detail used in upholstery in joining material at the edges. It consists of cord covered with material.

PISÉ DE TERRE

Wall construction of natural earth and clay. A formwork as for concrete is built and the earth and clay rammed in firmly.

PITCH

In building, is the term which refers to the slope of a roof or stair.

PLATE

In a timber-framed building there is a top and bottom plate between which are fitted the upright studs forming the wall frame.

PLINTH

Describes the framework or base secured to the underside of cabinets, wardrobes, etc., to keep them clear of the floor. In effect a plinth replaces legs.

PLUG

Piece of suitable material inserted in wall to enable a nail or screw to be driven into it. Old type plug is merely a piece of wood wedged into a wall joint. Patent fiber, metal and composition plugs are now widely used for screw fixings.

PLUGGING CHISEL

One entirely of steel with deep but narrow blade, intended for chopping holes in the joints of brickwork to receive wood plugs.

PLUMB

Means to be truly vertical. Plumb rule has line with brass or lead plumb bob which hangs in a recess down the side of the rule. It is used for testing surfaces for the true vertical.

POCKET

Opening in the pulley-stile of a box-frame window to enable the weights to be withdrawn and replaced. Both ends are notched, the top being cut at an angle so that it is retained in position. The bottom may be screwed but is frequently just tapped into position.

POKERWORK

A type of surface decoration where the outline of the design is burnt into the surface of the work with a red-hot needle. The design is then colored with stains or poster colors, which are fixed with shellac or varnish. Pokerwork is suitable for trays, boxes, vases, bookends, etc.

POLYURETHANE FOAM

Form of interior for upholstery. The foam may be in bulk to cut to shape, or in specially molded shape.

POLYVINYL ACETATE GLUE

One of later adhesives, generally known as P.V.A. A white glue used cold and with many advantages. It is at its best in close-fitting joints as it is not normally regarded as a joint filler. It does not become brittle hard and is therefore not hard on cleaning up tools. The glue has great tensile strength, but under the sheer test has a lower reading than some other glues. It does not cause staining, but some makes turn brown on setting or on contact with iron.

PRE-CAST CONCRETE PRODUCTS

Products such as steps, sills, blocks and slabs made by casting in molds. Now widely made in specially equipped factories, the wet concrete being vibrated in the mold to ensure maximum density and expel air bubbles. Many products are reinforced to prevent fracture and cracking.

PRIMERS, PRIMING

Priming is the name given to the operation of applying primer paints. It is the act of applying the primary coat—that is, the first coat of paint on new or unpainted surfaces. It is clearly incorrect to refer to two priming coats. A better expression, if it is ever desirable to apply two coats of priming paint, would be "two coats of primer."

PURLINS

The wooden beams supporting the rafters. They must be of sufficient strength to perform their duty to prevent sagging in themselves. They are supported by struts, and in some cases by walls also. Their size and number depends on the area of roofing carried and supported by them.

QUADRANT

Is quarter of the circumference of area of a circle. It also refers to a molding which fits into a corner and is sometimes called quarter-round moldings.

QUANTITIES

The amounts of various materials and of labor to be used in the construction of a building, from which an estimate of the cost is calculated.

QUARRY TILES

Hard baked tiles which are mainly used on exterior patio and veranda floors.
They are unglazed in a range of colors, and are laid in a cement mortar.

QUIRK

A small groove in, beside, or between moldings or beads; also a molding or bead having a groove on one or both edges.

QUOIN

The external corner of brickwork.

RABBET

A recessed edge, much used in joinery, as in door and window frames.

RABBET PLANE

Sometimes called a rebate plane, it is a specialized tool used to cut a recess or rabbet along the edge of a board.

RAFTERS

The members that support the roofing material. They are usually supported at their ends by walls, ridges, hips, etc. and intermediately by purlins and other members.

RAG BOLT

A fixing or anchor bolt with ribbed or barbed shank. It is used to provide a secure hold in concrete.

RAIL

Horizontal member of a sash, door or other such piece of framing.

RANDOM WIDTH

Is the term used to describe boards cut in varying widths. They are often used in making wall panels which show off the grain and texture of the timber.

RASP

Resembles a file in appearance. A wood rasp is a very useful tool for removing timber where it is not possible to use a plane or saw and also for smoothing circular edges.

REDUCING SOCKET

A socket reduced at one end and having threads to fit two different sized pipes.

REINFORCED CONCRETE

Portland cement concrete in which has been incorporated by design a series of steel reinforcing rods, or steel reinforcing fabric. By this means the maximum strength under load is given to the concrete. The design of reinforced concrete is of the greatest importance in civil engineering and is given special attention throughout the profession.

RENDERED

It used to be the custom to coat brick walls internally with plaster, composed of lime and sand, and to use two or three coats. The finish was very smooth, but the material was soft and easily chipped.

Rendered walls have now almost completely replaced such plastered walls.

The rendering is done in one coat with cement and sand, and the resulting surface is much harder.

It can be steel troweled to finish smooth or you can have a sanded, or wood float, finish. The wood float finish gives a fine texture and a very interesting surface, without the high spots which are usually inevitable with a steel trowel job.

RIDGE

This is the topmost member of a roof structure. It runs at right angles to rafters for full length of roof section and the shaped ends of rafters are fixed to it.

RISER

The vertical board between two treads of a flight of stairs.

RISING-BUTT HINGE

This type of hinge has one specific purpose. When a pair is fitted to a door, it allows the latter to rise above a high carpet or other floor covering as it is opened and to drop back gradually to the closed position. Such hinges are very effective on exterior doors as they eliminate a large gap between the bottom of the door and the door sill which would probably be necessary with standard butt hinges on a door swinging over a high carpet.

RIVERSIDE DOOR

A riverside door is a glass door, with the glass divided into panels by means of narrow strips of wood called glazing bars.

RIVING KNIFE

Curved blade fitted behind a circular saw blade to keep the cut open and prevent any jamming or binding.

ROTTENSTONE

An abrasive of brown siliceous stone; softer than pumice stone, but similar in nature and use.

ROUTER, ELECTRIC

This machine may be the large floor type with wide machine table and central pin, or it may be the portable type. Both are high-speed machines, with anything up to about 27,000 r.p.m. It is rotary in its cutting action, and a wide range of bits is available for various operations. Typical uses for the machines are molding, grooving, rabbeting, chamfering, recessing; and it works equally well around a curve as along a straight line. Depending upon the job the machine can be fitted with a fence, or it can be guided by the pilot pin of the cutter itself. All types are adjustable in cutter projection, some having micro-adjustment for close accuracy.

RUBBER-BASED ADHESIVES

Also known as contact adhesives. Generally used for fixing a plastic panel to a timber base. Both surfaces are coated and left for a time which varies with the make. When the two are brought together the hold is immediate, and the position of the one in relation to the other cannot be altered. Sometimes used for small veneered parts and for repair work over which it is difficult to apply cramps.

RUNG

Commonly a stave of a ladder, but in cabinet work a turned tie-rail between the legs of a chair is frequently referred to as a rung.

RUNS AND SAGS

These are related painting terms, but not meaning quite the same thing. A run is a definite drip of paint, as from a door molding on to a panel. A sagging effect is seen where the paint has clearly been applied too heavily. Though laid-off well, it is still unable to support itself during setting and it slumps or "curtains" down the surface.

SABER SAW

Reciprocating saw of the jigsaw type. It is gripped in the lower jaw of the machine only and is heavier and wider than the normal jigsaw blade. It is usually used for curves which are not too severe. A saber saw is also used on the portable jigsaw. The teeth are pointed towards the body of the tool so that it draws the wood towards its sole on the power stroke.

SADDLE

Device used by electricians and plumbers to hold conduit and pipes.
They are fixed to joists and uprights with clouts or screws.

SAFE-EDGED

A file having a plain edge free from serrations.

SAND BLASTING

Technique sometimes applied to Oregon pine plywood which has the effect of removing the softer parts, leaving the figuring in relief. Also a method of decorating glass and also for scouring metal to remove rust by means of sand driven by a blast of air or steam.

SANDING BELT

Continuous abrasive belt of cloth or paper used in a belt sanding machine. Can be obtained in various sizes and grades of abrasive.

SANDPAPER

A term that is not really appropriate since sand is not used as an abrasive. The abrasive compound most often used in making sandpaper is silicon carbide.

SANDWICH

Term used for work which is built up in layers. Thus in blockboard the center core is sandwiched between the face veneers. Some roof trusses are also sandwiched, the sloping and horizontal beams having upright and diagonal members contained between them.

SARKING

Is a term in general use describing the installation of building paper over roof rafters before fixing roofing tiles, corrugated iron, etc. Main purpose of sarking is to insulate but also prevents entry of rain leaks and dust.

SASH

Any casement, fan light or other framed structure, normally glazed, hung or fixed in an opening in a frame.

SASH CORD

Is the cord which holds the weights in a double-hung or boxed-frame window. It runs over a sash pulley and because of friction needs renewing occasionally.

SAW DOCTOR

Common description of person who specializes in the sharpening and repair of all types of saws.

SAW PIT

Used years ago before the days of power saws for the conversion of logs into usable sizes. It consisted of an oblong-shaped hole in the ground across which the log was laid. Two men used a pit saw, one standing on the log and the other down in the pit. Still occasionally used in districts where no power is available.

SAW SET

Is a special tool designed to set the teeth of a saw by bending the tips of the teeth alternately to right and left. This provides clearance in the cut or kerf so that the blade runs freely.

SCANT

Term used for material which is of bare measure.

SCRATCH COAT

Is a thin rough coat of plaster or cement mortar over walls, etc. before the main coat is applied. Its purpose is to provide a good key or grip for the finishing coat.

SCREED

Narrow strips of plaster or thin battens fixed to a wall or laid on a floor which is to be plastered or cement-rendered, as guides to obtain an even or true surface, are called screeds. They are placed a few feet apart and when the wet mix of plaster or cement mortar is spread between them, a straight-edge—or screeding rule—is passed over the screeds to produce a true surface.

GLOSSARY

SCREW GAUGE

Is a measuring tool designed to determine the gauge of a screw.
The head of the screw is slipped into a tapered slot until the gauge is noted from a scale on the side.

SCRIBE

To shape the abutting end of one member to the profile of another. To cut a member to fit an adjacent surface. The shaped surface formed by above work.

SCRIM

As used by decorators, a kind of canvas made of hemp or jute.

SCUTCH

Bricklayer's tool similar to small pick with chisel-like points. It is used for dressing and leveling rough brick and sandstone surfaces.

SEALER

Coat of paint or other material applied to a surface to seal pores and prepare for further finishing processes.

SET (On Saw)

This is obtained by bending (springing) the points of the teeth outwards alternately in opposite directions, to ensure that the saw kerf is wider than the thickness of the blade.

SETTLEMENT

The sinking or subsidence of a building as the result of faulty foundations. This often happens on made up ground or in soil with high clay content.

SHELLAC

Is a type of resin found in trees in various parts of the world as a result of the action of the lac insect. When dissolved in methylated spirits it becomes French polish.

SHIM

Is a thin piece of metal, wood, or other material used to pack or build up articles or sections that may have to be aligned or leveled.

SHIPLAP

Shiplap is used to describe the edge treatment of boards which interlock. These boards are rabbeted on both edges. They are used for covering partition walls and similar jobs.

SHORING

Temporary supports for buildings which are considered to be unsafe on account of damage, decay or adjacent building operations. The supports should be of adequate strength and arranged for easy dismantling when rebuilding is complete.

SHUTTERING

Is an alternative name for formwork built to hold concrete which is poured in position on the site.

SIDE AXE

One which has its bevel on one side only. Used largely by coopers in fashioning the staves of a barrel; also used by wheelwrights.

SILL

Horizontal bottom member of a window frame. Sometimes also applied to the bottom member of a door opening which is more accurately termed a threshold.

SILVER PLATE

Or E.P.N.S.—Electroplated nickel silver, to give it is full name. It is an alloy of nickel, copper and zinc covered with a skin of silver. The thickness of this skin determines the quality of the plate. It is interesting to know that each article is placed in a special solution with plates of pure silver. An electric current passing through this bath makes the silver dissolve and then adhere to the base metal. Many reliable firms make silver plate which will last, with care, for a lifetime.

SKARSTEN SCRAPER

A scraper made in various patterns used for cleaning up wood surfaces. Blades are replaceable and are sharpened with a fine file. There is also a toothed pattern for breaking up a tough surface which has been painted. For floor work a long-handled tool is available.

SKEW NAILING

Driving nails at an angle instead of square on. Sometimes needed when nailing in a corner, or to clear a detail.

SKILLION

Term applied to the single sloping roof of a shed or greenhouse. Also called a lean-to roof.

SKIN

Tough layer of pigment formed on the surface of paint or varnish caused by exposure to the air. Cut around this skin and remove before stirring the paint.

SKIRTING BOARD

A wooden board generally with the top edge rounded or chamfered. It is placed at the bottom of a wall, resting on the floorboards. Its purpose is to protect the bottom of the wall, and also to provide a decorative finish.

SKYLIGHT

Glazed roof light parallel to the roof surface and sometimes made to open.

SLEEPER WALL

A low wall under a ground floor which provides intermediate support for the floor joists. It should be honeycombed with narrow openings to allow cross ventilation.

SLURRY

Generally applied to a liquid mixture of water and neat Portland cement. Such a solution is often brushed onto the bottom of a wooden post which goes into the ground as a protection against rot and decay.
It may also be poured from a watering can or bucket onto broken bricks or stones forming a path. The cement slurry finds its way between the pieces to bond them together, after which the top is finished off with a cement-sand mortar.

SNAKE

A flexible cable or coiled wire used to clear clogs from drains and plumbing fixtures.

SOFFIT

Is the underside of the eaves projection on a roof, or the ceiling to a bay window. If the eaves are boxed in, the covering panel is called a soffit board.

SOFT SOLDERING

A method of uniting metals by means of an alloy composed of tin and lead. The process is suitable only when the joint area is large or where a joint of low mechanical strength is sufficient. The following metals are all readily united with ordinary tinman's solder: Copper, brass, tinplate, zinc, gunmetal, mild steel.

SOIL PIPE, SOIL STACK

Drains that carry toilet wastes. Soil pipes are horizontal; soil stacks are vertical.

SPARROW PICKING

This term refers to the process of going over a smooth brick or concrete wall with a small pick or chipping hammer to roughen the surface to provide a key or bond for cement rendering or plastering. The introduction of PVA cement bonding agents has made this type of preparation practically obsolete.

SPIGOT

The projection at the end of a turning to fit into a corresponding recess in another turning. Also refers to a plug used for a cask.

SPROCKET PIECE

A tapered piece of wood nailed to the end of a rafter to give an upward tilt at the lower end of a roof.

SPUR

A small tooth fitted to an adjustable metal fillister plane in front of the cutter, used when working across the grain so that wood is scribed along the line of the cut. This avoids splintering the grain at each side. It can be turned to a neutral position when the tool is used in the direction of the grain.

SQUARE

This term can mean several things. First, it is a woodworking tool used mainly to mark timber before cutting.
On the other hand, it could refer to a unit of area measurement such as floors where 100 square feet of floor area is known as a square of flooring and is ordered and sold this way.
The term is also used in the checking of furniture frames which are said to be square when diagonal measurements across the frame are equal.

GLOSSARY

STANCHION

A column or pillar made of mild steel or steel pipes fitted with flanges to support a suspended floor or other structure.

STANDING TIMBER

Growing trees of suitable size and type for commercial use.

STAPLE

Double-pointed nail of U-shape for fixing wire fences, for use with a hook catch, and occasionally for fixing upholstery springs to timber battens.

STAVE

Parts forming the walls of a cask, but also applied to the parts of any similar structure. Refers to the rungs of a ladder.

STEPPING OUT

The process of using dividers to mark out a number of equi-distant positions. The setting of the dividers is ascertained by trial and error, the distance being stepped out until the legs exactly coincide.

STERLING SILVER

Sterling silver is solid silver with a very small amount of alloy added for durability.
There are rigid legal formalities connected with the manufacture of silver, and genuine articles carry the imprint of a lion. In addition, there should be a mark denoting the town from which it comes. For example silver from Sheffield bears a crown. London-made silver has a leopard's head.

STOPPERS

Basically, the term stoppers or stopping refers to such material as putty and plastic wood and the operation of using this to fill nail holes and other blemishes in timber surfaces.
With most of these materials it is advisable to allow a small surplus to stand above the surface in case there is any shrinkage.

STRAIGHT FROM THE SAW

Applied to joints such as miters and butt joints which have been cut with the saw but not trimmed with the plane.
Also applied to timber which has been sawn from the log, but not planed.

STRIKING PLATE

The metal plate fixed to the door frame and adjusted to engage the bolt and latch in the lock. A striking plate is also used with a ball catch.

STUCCO

Substance which was widely used throughout the last century, particularly for ceiling and wall decoration. It was used in place of carved wood, being molded to shape and even finished with carving tools. The basis of stucco is whiting, resin, and glue.

STUD

Is the name given to a rough upright member of a wall or partition which is to be covered with wall sheets. It is also the name given to a nail having an ornamental head.

SUSPENDED CEILING

One in which separate joists hang from girders or from floor joists. The ceiling joists are fixed to these joists.

SWEEP OF BRACE

The diameter of the circle made by the handle of a hand brace when boring holes. The greater the sweep, the less effort required to bore large holes.

TACK LIFTER

A forked and tapered tool that can be forced beneath a tack and levered, so raising the head. It is a most useful tool to have when lifting old linoleum.

TAIL STOCK

The movable stock of a lathe. It slides along the lathe bed to suit various lengths of work.

TAKE-UP

Is a term which can be used in two ways. As a verb it means to tighten or to remove any movement which may have developed. Used as a noun, it denotes an item such as a spring washer or packing used to take up the slack or remove any looseness of parts caused by wear or vibration.

TAMPING

Is the process of consolidating concrete, soil, gravel, or similar material by firmly hitting with a tool made for the purpose. As an example, the earth around a fence or other post must be firmly tamped after filling in.

TANG

Is the pointed end of a tool such as a chisel, bradawl, or file which fits into the handle. In most cases there is a shoulder at the top of the tang which prevents it being forced in too far.

TAPS

Taps are tools which are made to cut internal threads in metal. They complement dies which are used to cut external threads.
Taps are used with a special tap wrench. One end of this wrench has a chuck to grip the square shank of the tap. The other end has a rod handle to provide full leverage.

TEMPLATE

Is a board, sheet, or frame cut to an outline, shape, or profile and used as a guide in cutting or construction, especially in repetition work or where the outline of the job is complicated.

TENON

The end of a piece of timber reduced in thickness to enable it to be fitted into a mortise. The tenon may be secured by wedging, gluing, or pegging.

TENSION

Term used in connection with handsaws in which a hammering process is used to stiffen the blade. Without it, the blade would be floppy, difficult to control, and insufficiently rigid for its work. The same applies to a circular saw blade which is tensioned by hammering. In a bandsaw, tension refers to the degree of tautness given to the blade by pushing the top wheel upwards. The bearing of this wheel is usually spring-loaded to enable the degree of tension or tautness to be varied.

TENSION SPRING

Used chiefly in conjunction with loose cushions in upholstered furniture. They consist of tightly wound spring wire in the form of a cable, $\frac{1}{2}$ in. or $\frac{3}{8}$ in. diameter. They are fixed by engaging a link or hook at each end over a nail, screw, or screw eye. They are fixed at a tension approximately $1\frac{1}{2}$ in. over an 18 in. length.

TENTERHOOK

Hook-shaped nail pointed at both ends. Although connected with the stretching of cloth, the French polisher can use them to hold down loose parts when polishing the surface, driving the long end into the bench so that the cranked end bears on the wood.

TEREBINE

A light yellow liquid used mainly as a drying agent in oil paint.

TERRACOTTA

A material made from fine brick earth burned in molds and used in blocks, as a facing material, and for roof tiles.

TERRAZZO

A hard flooring consisting of a mosaic of marble chippings spread on a cement mix and rolled, then smoothed and polished. Used most commonly for walls, floors and steps.

THERMO-PLASTIC

Applied to a plastic material which can be softened and made pliable by heat.

THERMOSTAT

Instrument fitted to heating apparatus for regulating temperature.

THINNERS

Volatile liquid used to regulate the thickness of paint and varnish. In the case of French polish the thinner is methylated spirit, but for paints and lacquers, the thinner made or recommended by the manufacturer should be used.

THROATING

Groove cut beneath a window sill or other projecting member to prevent water from creeping back and running down a wall or other part.

THUMB SCREW

Small clamp similar to the G-clamp but smaller and lighter. Usual kind is made of metal strip bent to shape with the screw passing through one end. It is also known as a fret clamp.

TIE

A cross-member of a frame or other structure such as a roof truss. The rails between chair or small table legs are sometimes referred to as tie rails. In general, it is any member—usually horizontal—which serves to prevent two other members from spreading.

TILING BATTENS

Battens nailed to the rafters or roofing boards to hold the tiles. The tiles hook over them.

TIMBERING

General term referring to the use of timber for constructional or utility purposes. In particular, it is applied to woodwork used in supporting the sides of excavations.

TINNING

The operation of covering the point of the soldering bit with a thin layer of solder. It is necessary to have this operation done thoroughly, otherwise it is not possible to do soldering work.

TIPPED SAW

Circular saw teeth tipped with pieces of tungsten-carbide. Such a blade is especially useful for cutting timber of an abrasive type, and made-up panels assembled with resin glue. The tipped teeth ensure a much longer working sharpness than the ordinary saw teeth.

TOE

The front or lower end of an item such as a strut. Also used in connection with plane as distinct from the heel which is the back, or a handsaw, the toe being the narrow end of the blade, and heel nearest the handle.

TOGGLE BOLT

Special bolt for securing article to a sheet wall where there is no backing timber to receive a screw or nail.

TOMMY BAR

Metal rod used to loosen the centers of a lathe when removal is necessary and for other turning jobs with wrenches and keys where extra leverage is needed.

TOOTHING PLANE

Is a tool for scoring the surface of the base or groundwork before veneering to provide a better key for the glue. It also serves to remove any irregularities left by the ordinary bench plane. The cutter is set vertically in the plane stock, or nearly so, and its back has a series of grooves in it so that when sharpened, it presents a saw-like edge.

TOPPING

The operation of leveling the teeth of a saw which have become uneven. A flat file is run back and forth along the tops of the teeth with a fairly light but firm pressure. Topping is always done with the blade held securely in a vice of some kind.

TRACKING

Is the operation of adjusting the top wheel of a bandsaw so that the saw will keep in position centrally on the rubber cover or tire on the wheel. The term also refers to a similar operation on a belt sander or finisher to prevent the belt running off the drums.

TRAMMEL POINTS

These are a pair of special metal points which slide over a wood or metal bar and are held in any desired position with thumbscrews.
They are used to set out the distance between two points and are also to scribe circles beyond the capacity of dividers.

TRANSOM

A horizontal member between a door or window and an upper light.

TRAP

The bend in drainpipes under plumbing fixtures. Water stands in the trap and prevents sewer gas from backing up through the drain.

TRIMMER

A short joist spanning the main joists around such features as a fireplace or alcove in a room. They are needed to support the ends of floorboards or the edges of a hearth.

TRIPOLI POWDER

Fine mineral powder, also called rottenstone, sometimes used in finishing French polished surfaces. It is lightly dusted across the hard polish where the slightly abrasive action will cut back extreme brilliance.

TRUSS

A frame of timber, steel or reinforced concrete used to support loads over wide spans.

T-SQUARE

Used on the drawing board. It has a tapered blade with the working edge beveled, and screwed to a stock. Lengths run from about 15 in. to 54 in. or more, the size being chosen to correspond with the length of the drawing board.

TUCK POINTING

Type of pointing used in brickwork. The mortar is made flush with the bricks, except for a small groove in the center.
The joint is then colored to match the brickwork and the groove filled with lime putty to project slightly.

TUFT

Small items of wool or cotton passed beneath the twine when making a mattress. The twine passes through the mattress and serves to keep the stuffing in place. The tufts prevent the twine from pulling right through the covering.

TUMBLER

Is a form of movable lever in certain types of locks which prevent the bolts being operated until activated by a correctly-shaped key.

TUMBLING BOX

A box in which small items are placed with an abrasive or polishing compound. The whole is revolved so that the contents tumble against each other and become polished.

TUNG OIL

Chinese produce derived from the seeds or nuts of the tung tree. It is used as a drying oil.

TURNBUCKLE

Small metal catch to hold a cabinet door in the closed position and is operated by turning an outer knob or handle.

TWO-MAN SAW

Is a long cross-cut saw with a handle at each end. Lengths range from 3 ft. to 8 ft. and have teeth in a wide range of shapes. Good saws are ground thin towards the back to give better clearance.

ULTIMATE STRENGTH
The point at which material breaks when under a test.

UMBER
Is a tinting pigment for paints and stains. Raw umber is a fairly light brown shade, and burnt umber a darker color.

UNDERCOAT
An undercoat is designed to cover the surface well and form a base for the finishing coats. Extra pigment is incorporated in undercoats and the most common shades are white, pink, and grey. On new woodwork, especially outside, it is usual to apply a priming coat first, follow with the undercoat, and finish with paint or enamel.

UNDERCUT
This is a term used in several trades. It is applied especially to carving in which the edge of the work slopes inwards towards the underside. It also refers to the edge of an item which is planed slightly out-of-square so that it presents a tight joint on the top surface. Sometimes the shoulders of a tenon are also slightly undercut for the same reason, but this is not always advisable. Before repairing a crack in a plaster wall or ceiling, the edge should be undercut so as to form a dovetail-shaped recess for the patching plaster. This way the patch is keyed in place and cannot fall out.

UNDERLAY
Usually refers to the sheet material placed on a floor as a base for carpets, linoleum, and other floor coverings.

UNDERPINNING
This term has two applications. First it means the strengthening of a weak footing by building a new footing or support underneath. The second meaning refers to the placing of shoring timber and other temporary supports to take the loads while an opening is cut in a wall for the insertion of a lintel or frame, or for the actual underpinning.

488

UNIT FURNITURE
Items such as cupboards, cabinets, etc., made to standard sizes which can be assembled one above the other or given other arrangements.

UNIVERSAL JOINT
Is a special type of coupling which permits the free rotation of two shafts that are not in alignment.

UPTURN
Flashing or other sheet metal turned up against a vertical surface.

VACUUM BAG
Is a rubber bag in which shaped work to be veneered is placed. The air is exhausted by a pump so that atmospheric pressure forces the veneer into close contact with the groundwork.

VALLEY
The internal angle or line of intersection where two roof surfaces join. A valley rafter is fitted in this position.

VARNISH STAIN
Describes a finish consisting of a stain dissolved in clear varnish so that a natural wood color may be changed and the surface covered with a protective coating in a single operation.

V-BLOCK
A block having a V-shaped groove along its top edge in which cylindrical work can rest while being drilled or otherwise worked.

VEHICLE
It is the liquid portion of the paint used to render the base of paint workable.
It is sometimes called the medium. Linseed oil, turpentine, and water are standard paint vehicles.

VENEER
A surface consisting of a thin sheet of material applied to another surface, which is not necessarily composed of the same material.

VERDIGRIS
Is a green or black substance formed by the action of acid on copper. It may be produced to serve as a stain by subjecting copper to the action of acetic acid.

VIBRATED CONCRETE
Is a mechanical process of compacting concrete to increase its strength and density. Either compressed air or electricity is used in the process and the effect is to shake air and excess water to the surface after pouring.

WALLBOARD

The name given to a variety of boards and panels used for covering walls and ceilings. Most of them contain wood, either in the form of laminated layers, wood pulp, or compressed paper, or a combination of two or all three of these materials.

WALLPLATE

Timber laid on a wall to receive and give a fixing to other structural members such as rafters. Additionally it serves to distribute the load over the wall. It is also the name given to top and bottom horizontal members in a timber framed wall.

WALL TIES

Small pieces of metal or wire, each end of which is built into joints in the two skins of a cavity wall, thus tying the skins together.

WARDING FILE

A thin file used mainly in key cutting. They average 3 in. to 6 in. in length.

WARPING

The twisting or casting of wood so that its surface is no longer in a plane surface. It is frequently caused by faulty seasoning, though some timbers are much worse in this connection than others. Damp conditions may also cause it, or it may be the result of the wood being veneered on one side only.

WASHITA OILSTONE

A natural oilstone quarried in the Southwest, cutting at a medium rate and giving a fine edge. There is some element of luck in its choice as some stones are liable to become hard and fail to cut properly.

WASTE PIPE, WASTE STACK

Large drainpipes in the plumbing system. Waste pipes are horizontal; waste stacks are vertical.

WATER MARKS

These are sometimes found on a French polished surface. They can on occasions be removed by rubbing with a hot rag several times, or with a solution consisting of equal parts raw linseed oil and turpentine. Alternatively, comphorated oil followed by vinegar may be an effective rubbing fluid.

WATER WHITE

Is a term often used to indicate that the material is very clear and will not produce a yellowing or amber effect.

It must be understood, however, that even water applied to a timber surface will alter the color. So the term, when applied to polishes and varnishes, must be interpreted carefully.

WAVES

Refers to the undulations in a surface caused in planing or by casting. They are emphasized by the application of gloss finishes.

WEATHERBOARD

The lapped siding of a house. Clapboards or boards are nailed to form lap joints so that the surface is weatherproof.

WEEP HOLE

A hole in a retaining wall to allow water behind the wall to escape by draining away.

WINDERS

Steps in a staircase which radiate at various angles to give a change of direction.

WIPED JOINT

A joint used by plumbers to connect lead pipes. A special coarse wiping solder is used, which can be wiped around the pipe while in a plastic state with a felt pad soaked in tallow and held in the hand.

WIRED GLASS

Describes glass in which wire mesh has been embedded during manufacture.

It is used extensively in the construction of factory roof work as it will not shatter easily, and is fire resistant.

YELLOW OCHRE

A yellow powder pigment used for coloring various substances such as wood filler or cement for brickwork re-pointing jobs.

YOKE

Pieces of timber bolted together in the form of a rectangle, and used to hold the formwork when pouring concrete columns and other similar items. Their purpose is to prevent the formwork from spreading under the weight of the concrete.

ZIG-ZAG RULE

Such a rule derives its name from the way in which it is opened and closed. It is made in small sections up to 8 in. long. This makes it very compact to carry and use.

ZINC OXIDE

White pigment used in many types of paint.

ABBREVIATIONS

Apart from the extensive list of building terms listed and explained in this book, there is also a group of important abbreviations.

It is especially important to know about these when ordering timber and other materials, or when reading building plans and specifications.

Here is a selection of such abbreviations some of which, though not officially recognized by any authoritative body are in common use:

a.c.	alternating current
av.	average
bd.	board
bev.	beveled
B.T.U.	British Thermal Unit
B.V.	brick veneer
clg.	ceiling
clr.	clear
com.	common
cu.ft.	cubic foot or feet
cu.in.	cubic inch or inches
cu.yd.	cubic yard or yards

d.c.	direct current
deg. (or °)	degrees
dia.	diameter
dim.	dimension
dp.	downpipe
D.P.C.	damp proof course
E.C.	earth closet
fahr. or F.	fahrenheit
facty.	factory
flg.	flooring
ft. (0′)	foot or feet
gal.	gallon
hdl.	handle
hdwd.	hardwood
H.P.	horsepower
hrtwd.	heartwood
H.W.S.	hot water system
in.	inch or inches
kwh.	kilowatt hour
lgth.	length
lin.ft.	linear foot
nt.wt.	net weight
O.D.	outside diameter
oz.	ounce or ounces
P.C.	prime cost (Items: bath, stove etc.)
P.V.A.	polyvinyl acetate
P.V.C.	polyvinyl chloride
rd.	round

ABBREVIATIONS

rndm.	random
rfg.	roofing
rip.	ripped
R.P.M.	revolutions per minute
R.S.A.	rolled steel angle
R.S.C.	rolled steel channel
R.S.J.	rolled steel joist
sd.	seasoned
sdg.	siding
sftwd.	softwood
snd.	sound
sq.	square
std.	standard
super.	superficial (board measure)
S.W.D.	storm water drain
T. & G.	tongued & grooved (boards)
tbrs.	timbers
t.p.i.	teeth per inch (saw teeth)
V.P.	vacant possession
wb.	weatherboard
W.C.	water closet
wdr.	wider
wt.	weight
wth.	width
yd.	yard or yards

INDEX

ABBREVIATIONS 494

ABRASIVE steel wool 11

ABRASIVES papers—*sandpaper 11; glass-paper 11; garnet-paper 11; wet or dry paper 11; waterproof paper 11; aluminum oxide paper 11;* cloth —*emery cloth 11*

ABRASIVES pumice stone 11; pumice powder 11, 119

ABRASIVES wire wheels—*scratchbrush 13; soft Bessemer scratchbrush 13; bristle wheel 14;* wire brush—*brass brush 13; wire cup brush 13; buffing wheel 14*

ACCESS ROAD 400

ACCIDENTS with—*spontaneous combustion 14; flexible leads 14; overloaded wiring 14; inflammable clothing 14; blowtorch 24; power drill 15; grinding wheels 15*

ACCORDION DOOR 100

ACETIC ACID 75

ACETONE use of 75

ACETYLENE 400

ACIDS hydrochloric 123, 146, 233; muriatic 233; nitric 133; oxalic 465; acetic 75

ACOUSTIC BOARD 400

ACOUSTICS in home 17

ADHESIVES practical hints 17; P.V.A. 18; epoxy resin 18; latex rubber 18; dextrine paste 18; contact 18

ADJUSTABLE CALIPERS 69

AERATOR 245, 400

AGGREGATE 400, 462, 88

AGRICULTURAL DRAIN 400

AIR BRICK 401

AIR DRYING 401

AIR LOCK 401

ALKYD RESIN 401

ALLEN key 401; screw 22, 402; wrench 402

ALLIGATOR CLIPS 402

ALLIGATORING in painted surface 402

ALL-METAL WALLPLUG 31

ALTERNATING CURRENT (A.C.) 122, 431

ALUMINUM to protect 26; tools for working with 28; to solder 28

ALUMINUM ASSEMBLY METHODS 23

ALUMINUM EDGING STRIPS 26

ALUMINUM FOIL 184; use of 402

ALUMINUM OXIDE PAPER 11

ALUMINUM PAINT 27

AMPERE 122, 431

ANAGLYPTA PAPER 403

ANCHORS wall 31

ANGLE DIVIDER use of 32

ANGLE-DRIVE PIN wall fastening device 32

ANGLE IRON 403

ANGLES compound cuts 32

ANILINE DYE 119, 403

ANNUAL RINGS 120

ANT CAPS 326, 403; to place 34

ANTI-CORROSIVE PAINT 403

ANTIQUE FINISH on woodwork 35

ANVIL 403

APPLIANCES running costs 35; wattage chart 125; maintenance and repair 130

APRON 404

ARBOR 404

ARCHBAR use of 36

ARCHITRAVE 404

ARRIS EDGE 404

ARRIS RAIL 404

ASBESTOS CEMENT 405

ASBESTOS CEMENT ROOFING to fix 36; screw-nails for 37

ASBESTOS CEMENT SHEET WALLS to clean —*rust stains 38; wood stains 38; soot 38; dirt 38; asphalt 38*

ASBESTOS FILLING COMPOUND 405; for wall 31

ASHLAR 405

ASPHALT PAVING 38, 406

ASTRAGAL 405

AUGER 406

AUGER BIT 31

AWL (see BRADAWL) 406

AXES type of 39; to sharpen 39; side 477

AXLE PULLEY 406

BACK FILL 407
BACK FLAP HINGE 407
BACK IRON of plane 407
BACK PUTTY 407
BACK SAW (TENON SAW) 334, 407
BADGER PLANE 407
BAGGING of walls 72
BAKED FINISH 407
BALANCER VENEER 391
BALK 409
BALL BEARING CASTER 71
BALL CASTER 71
BALL PEEN HAMMER 408
BALL VALVE OR COCK 408, 422
BALL WAX for etching 133
BALUSTERS 408
BAR CLAMPS 83
BAREFACED TENON 408
BARGE BOARD 408
BARREL BOLT 50
BATHROOM FIXTURES installation 252
BATTENS 409
BATTER BOARD 409
BAY WINDOW 409
BEADS cock 409; staff 409; parting 409
BEARING WALL 409
BEAUMONTAGE 409
BEECH 305
BEESWAX 109
BEETLES in carpets 70
BELTS V-TYPE care of 43
BENCH FOR WORKSHOP to make 46
BENCH HOLDFAST 410
BENCH HOOK 410; to make 45
BENCH SCREW 410
BENCH STOP 410; to fix 48
BENCH VISE to fix 47
BENZENE 410
BENZINE 410
BEVEL 410; sliding 411
BEVELED EDGE CHISEL 77, 410
BEVELED RULE advantages of 16
BICHROMATE OF POTASH 411
BIFURCATED RIVET 411
BILL HOOK 411
BINDER in paint 411
BIRD'S EYE GRAIN 411
BIRD'S MOUTH JOINT 412
BISMARCK BROWN 412
BITS twist 52; Irwin 52; Jennings 52; center 52;
    expansion 53; countersink 53; screwdriver 53;
    auger 31; chamfer 421

BITUMINOUS FELT 88, 132, 412
BITUMINOUS MASTIC 412
BLACKBOARD COATING 412
BLEACHING TIMBER 49
BLEEDING of paint 412
BLIND BOLT 412
BLINDS to adjust 263
BLOCKBOARD 412
BLOCK PLANES 413
BLOOMING in varnish 413
BODYING UP solution 413
BOILED OIL 413
BOLECTION MOLDING 413
BOLSTER 55, 294
BOLT coach or carriage 84, 418; blind 412; expan-
    sion 433; eye 434; handrail 445; hanger 446; rag
    471; toggle 485; rubber sleeve 31
BOLTS for doors—barrel 50; tower 50; pad 50
BOND in brickwork 413
BONING ROD 414
BORERS wood 51
BORING glass 163
BOSS 414
BOX-FRAME WINDOW 328, 414; pocket in 469;
    sash 475; sash cord 475
BOX GUTTER 414
BRACE carpenter's 31
BRACKETS gutter 96, 443
BRAD 414
BRADAWL 162, 406, 414
BRASS BRUSH 13
BRASS to clean 53
BRAZING 414
BREEZE BLOCK 415
BRICK FIREPLACE to restore color 53
BRICKLAYING GUIDE 54
BRICKS 415; estimating number of 132
BRICK VENEER 415
BRICKWORK remove stains from 58; furring on
    179; repoint 57; bond in 413; concave joint 58;
    frames in 148; weather-struck joint for 57
BRIDGING 415
BRISTLE WHEEL 14
BRUISING 415
BRUSHES care of 59; selecting 59; using 59;
    camel hair 162, 418; steel 31; stencil 64; stipple
    327; pencil 467
BUFFING WHEEL 14
BUILDING LINE 416
BUILDING PAPER use of 65
BULL-NOSE PLANE 416

BUNSEN BURNER 416
BURNT SIENNA 157, 416
BURNT UMBER 416, 488
BUTT CHISEL 77
BUTTERFLY ROOF 416

BUTTERING 416
BUTT GAUGE 66
BUTT HINGES 416; fitting 180
BUTT JOINT 417
BUZZ SAW 417

CABINET FILE 138
CABINET SCREWDRIVER 282
CABRIOLE LEG 69
CALIPER GAUGE 69
CALIPERS 69; adjustable 69; outside 69; inside 69; spring-bow 70; toolmaker's 70; stiff jointed 70
CAMEL HAIR BRUSH 162, 418
CAMPHORATED OIL 75
CAPILLARY JOINT 418
CARBON TETRACHLORIDE 58, 75, 418
CARBORUNDUM POWDER 292
CARPENTER'S brace 31; pencil 467; square 204
CARPET care of 70; beetles 70
CARPET BINDING 203
CARRIAGE BOLT 418
CASEMENT WINDOW 328, 419; sash 475
CASTELLATED NUT 419
CASTERS round socket 71; square socket 71; tripod socket 71; screw socket 71; screw plate 71; ball bearing 71; swivel ball or Shepherd 71; trolley table 71; peg and sleeve 71
CAULKING COMPOUND 72, 419
CAVITY WALL 419
CEDAR 305
CEILING suspended 481; clean stains from 92
CELLULOSE TAPE use of 18, 300
CEMENT 419; epoxy 131; Portland 73, 462, 471; grouting 281, 432
CEMENT GREEN (CHROMIUM OXIDE) 422
CEMENT MORTAR 209, 419, 475
CEMENT RENDERING 238, 420, 472
CEMENT WASH for walls 72
CENTER BIT 420
CENTER PINS for dowels 73

CENTER PUNCH 31, 420
CENTERS to mark 74
CERAMIC TILES cutting 301; restoring joints 301; 420
CHAIN MORTISER 420
CHALKING in paint 420
CHALK LINE 55, 294, 420
CHAMFER BIT 421
CHAMFERING 79, 113, 421
CHAMOIS leather 156, 193
CHASES 421
CHECKING in paint 421
CHEVAL MIRROR 421
CHINA repairs to 75
CHIPPENDALE 69
CHISELS butt 77; firmer 77, 436; gouge 77; beveled edge 77, 410; cold 31, 293; plugging 468; paring 104; drawer lock 428; swan-neck 481; wood 31
CHROME care of 80
CHROMIUM OXIDE (CEMENT GREEN) 422
CHUCK 422, 482
CIRCLES use of 80
CIRCUIT 122, 431
CIRCUIT BREAKER 123, 431
CIRCULAR CUTTING 81
CIRCULAR SAW use of 82
CISSING 422
CISTERN 422
CLAMPS 83; flooring 437
CLAW AND BALL 69
CLEAN-CUTTING SAW BLADES 82
CLEAN-CUTTING TWIST BIT 107
CLEAR LACQUER 155

CLEAR VARNISH 147, 227
CLEAT 422
CLOGGED PLUMBING 242
CLOSERS 422
CLUB FOOT 69
CLUTCH HEAD SCREW 284
COACH BOLT 84
COACH SCREW 84
COARSE AGGREGATE 88
COCK BEAD 409
COLD CHISEL 293
COLD WATER PUTTY 70
COLLAR TIES 422
COLORING CONCRETE 85
COLOR-IN-OIL 423
COMBINATION PLANE 423
COMBINATION PLIERS 423
COMPOUND caulking 72; cutting 53; sealing 72
COMPRESSION FLANGES on grinder 15
COMPRESSOR PLANT 228
CONCAVE JOINT in brickwork 58
CONCRETE 423; surface finish 89; proportions for mixing 89; to color 85; curing of 425; vibrated 490; pre-cast 469; formwork 88; penetration methods 85; ready mixed 86; reinforced 87

CONCRETE PATHS to lay 87
CONDENSATION in roof 91
CONDUCTION 185
CONDUIT 424, 431
CONDY'S CRYSTALS 75; in staining 157
CONTACT ADHESIVES 18, 473
CONVECTION 185
COPING SAW 31, 104
COPPERAS 75
COPPER SULPHATE 116
CORBEL 424
CORNICE 424
CORRUGATED FASTENER 424
COTTER PIN 424
COUNTERSINK BIT 53
COUNTERSUNK HEAD SCREW 284
CRAZY PAVING 424
CREOSOTE PRESERVATIVE 92, 137, 232, 425
CROSSCUT SAW 273, 334
CURING CONCRETE 425
CURTAIN WALL 425
CUTTING COMPOUND 53
CUTTING-IN in paintwork 425
CYPRESS 305

DADO 426
DAMPCOURSE 95; faulty 96, 426
DEAD-BOLT LOCK 200, 426
DEAD WHITE 426
DEADWOOD 426
DEPTH GAUGE 97, 108
DEXTRINE PASTE 18
DIE 426
DIRECT CURRENT (D.C.) 123, 432
DISHED SURFACE 426
DISTANCE PIECE 427
DISTEMPER 427
DIVIDERS 81, 427

DOG 427
DOOR adjust to close 98; to hang 98; warped 100; flush 438
DOORBELLS AND BUZZERS 127
DOOR CHAIN 427
DOORS French 439; glazed 441; ledged 457; riverside 472; Dutch 100; louvered 100; accordion 100; screen 281
DORMER WINDOW 427
DOUBLE GLAZING 427
DOUBLE-HUNG WINDOW 328, 427; sash 475; sash cord 475
DOUBLE INSULATION 15

DOUBLE NAILING 427
DOUGLAS FIR 306, 427
DOVETAIL JOINT 102, 104, 108, 428
DOVETAIL SAW 335
DOWELING JIG 107, 427
DOWEL JOINT 105
DOWEL PLATE 105
DOWEL RODS 105
DOWN DRAFT 428
DOWNPIPES 96, 170
DRAINS clearing 242
DRAWER to make 109; to partition 110; sliding
    tray for 111; to ease 108
DRAWER LOCK CHISEL 428
DRAWER PULL 428
DRAW FILING 141
DRAW KNIFE 113

DRESSER for valve seat 246; to shape lead 428
DRIER for paint 428
DRILLING 113, 254
DRILLS masonry 114; glass 114; twist 31, 115;
    dual-speed 255; double insulation of 15; portable
    power 113; sharpening 115
DRILL STAND horizontal 114; vertical 114
DRIVE NAIL 429
DRUNKEN SAW 429
DRY-MIX 429
DRY ROT 116
DUAL-SPEED DRILL 255
DUMPY LEVEL 194
DUNNAGE 429
DUST BOARD 429
DUTCH DOOR 100

EAGLE'S CLAW 69
EASEMENT 430
EAVES 430
EBONIZING method of 119
EBONY POLISH 119
EDGE GLUING in timber 120
EDGE MARK 430
EDGE MOLDING quarter-round 72, 421; lipping
    121; L section 121; laminated plastic 121; alu-
    minum beading 121; rounded aluminum 121;
    flexible plastic strip 121
EDGES to keep square 119; treatment of 120
EDGING STRIPS aluminum 26
EFFLORESCENCE on walls 430
EGGSHELL FINISH 431
ELECTRICAL TERMS 122, 431
ELECTRICIAN'S SCREWDRIVER 282
ELECTRICITY 121; dangers 122; basic language
    122; household current 122; household wiring
    123; fuses and circuit breakers 123; appliance
    wattage chart 125; installing switches 126; re-
    placing outlets 126; doorbells and buzzers 127;
    lighting 127; lamp repairs 129; appliance mainte-
    nance and repair 130; motor maintenance 130
ELECTROLYTE METHOD to clean silver 289
EMERY CLOTH 290, 433
ENAMEL UNDERCOAT 35
EPOXY cement 131; adhesive 18
ESCUTCHEON PLATE 433
ESTIMATING bricks 132; mortar 132
ETCHING 133
EXPANDED METAL 433
EXPANSION BIT 31, 53
EXPANSION BOLT 419
EXPANSION JOINT in concrete 133, 433
EXPANSION PIPE 434
EYE BOLT 434

FACE MARK 435
FACE PLATE on lathe 435
FANLIGHT 435
FASCIA BOARD 435
FAT EDGE 435
FAUCET REPAIRS 245
FELT bituminous 142
FENCE POSTS to secure 137
FERRULE 435
FIBER BOARD 435
FIBER GLASS 167; bathroom fixtures 252
FIBER WALL PLUG 31
FIBROUS PLASTER 435
FIDDLE BACK FIGURE 436
FIGURED GLASS 168
FILE warding 491; half round 138; square 138; flat 138; cabinet 138; round or rat-tail 138; single cut 31; triangular 138
FILE CARD 31, 436
FILES use of 138, 290
FILING draw 141
FILLERS 150, 158, 436
FILLET 436
FILLISTER PLANE 141
FINE AGGREGATE 86
FINIAL 436
FINISHES antique 35; clear sealer 141; wax 142; baked 407; eggshell 431; surface concrete 89, 242
FIR Douglas 306; white 305
FIREBRICK 436
FIRMER CHISEL 77, 436
FISH PLATES 436
FITCH 437
FLAGSTONE 437
FLASHING 142, 489; damaged 97
FLAT FILE 138, 259
FLAT ROOF 437
FLATTING AGENT 437

FLEXIBLE BLANKETS 185
FLEXIBLE PLASTIC STRIP EDGE MOLD-ING 121
FLOAT wooden 234, 437
FLOOR sealer for 142; surface repairs to 144; faults 144; joists 144
FLOORING CLAMP 437
FLOUR SANDPAPER 438
FLUSH DOOR 438
FLUSH JOINT in brickwork 58
FLUSH POINTING in brickwork 58
FLUXES 146, 438
FOOTINGS 438
FORMWORK for concrete 88
FOUNDATIONS 438
FRACTURES wood 260
FRAMES in brickwork 148
FRAMES finishes for—*pickling 147; clear-varnish 147; white wax 147; gilding 147; orange shellac 147; spatter paint 147; gold leaf 147*
FRENCH CURVE 438
FRENCH DOORS 438
FRENCH POLISHING 153
FRENCH SCROLL 69
FRETSAW BLADES 439
FROG 439
FULLER'S EARTH 321
FUNGICIDE SOLUTION 148
FUNGUS on walls 148
FUR in kettles and boilers 4
FURNITURE accidents to 149; remove bruises from 150; repairs 259
FURNITURE FINISHING French polishing 153; lacquering 155; preparation for 156; staining and filling in 156, 157
FURRING strips for brick walls 179
FUSE 123, 432

GABLE 440
GADS steel 440
GALLETING 440
GANTRY 440
GARDEN HOSE as level 195
GARNET PAPER 11
GASKET 440; cutter 81
GAUGE depth 97, 108; butt 66; marking 99, 161, 210; mortise 161, 210; caliper 69; panel 162
GAUGE BOX to measure concrete 440
GAVEL 441
G-CLAMPS 83
GEORGIAN 69
GERMAN JACK PLANE 407
GERMAN SILVER 441
GESSO 441
GILDING 147, 162
GIMLETS 162
GIMP PIN 441
GIRDER 441
GLASS boring 163; cutting 164; selecting 168; wired 492; figured 168; to break 168; frosted 327; strip mirror 328
GLASS DRILL 114, 163
GLASS FIBER 167
GLAZED DOOR 441
GLAZING 442; double 427; points 442
GLIDERS furniture 441

GLUE size 443; woodworker's 109; P.V.A. 18, 184
GLUE BLOCKS 442
GLYCERINE uses of 169
GOLD LEAF 147, 162, 443
GOLD PAINT 162
GOLD SIZE 75
GOUGE CHISEL 77
GRADES timber 284
GRAIN bird's eye 411
GRAINING 443
GRAPHITE 443
GRINDING WHEELS 115, 169; glazed 441
GROMMET 443
GROUND COAT in paint 443
GROUNDING 122, 432
GROUTING CEMENT 444
GROWTH RINGS in timber 120
GRUB SCREW 444
GULLEY 444
GUM 305
GUSSET 444
GUTTER 265; 444; to make 170; down-pipes 96, 170; blocked 96
GUTTER BOX 414
GUTTER BRACKETS 96, 443; to adjust 96; to fit 170

HACKING OFF 445
HACKSAW 173
HALF-LAP JOINT 445; to make 65
HALF-ROUND FILE 138
HAMMERS ball peen 408; to secure head 175; using 176; scutch 294
HAND DRILL 31
HANDRAIL BOLT 445
HAND SAWS 334, 445
HAND VISE 445

HANGER BOLT 446
HANGING STILE 446
HARDBOARD 446; joints 179; to hang sheets 179
HARDENER 446
HARDWOODS 305
HAUNCH 446
HAWK 57, 446
HEADER brick 447
HIDING POWER 447
HINGE BOUND 448

HINGES 180; fitting 180; butt 417; narrow butt 181; rising butt 181, 472; loose-pin 181; Scotch tee 181; strap 182; parliament 182, 466; piano 182, 467
HIPPED ROOF 448
HOD 448
HOME INSULATION with—*aluminum foil 184; rigid batts 185; loose fill 185; flexible blankets 185; insulating boards 185*
HONING 448
HONING GUIDE 286

HOOF 69
HOOP-IRON wall ties 148
HOPPER WINDOWS 448
HORIZONTAL DRILL STAND 114
HOUSE INSPECTION 449
HOUSED JOINT (stopped type) 182
HOUSING 450
HYDRATED LIME 54, 209
HYDROCHLORIC ACID 133, 146
HYDROGEN PEROXIDE 227

IMPREGNATION of timber 451
INITIAL SET of cement and plaster 451
INLAY 451
INSIDE CALIPERS 69
IN SITU 451

INSULATING BOARDS 185
INSULATION 184, 432, 451; for plumbing 247
IRWIN BIT 52
ISOMETRIC PROJECTION 185

JACK PLANES steel 236, 294, 452 German 407
JAMB LINING 452
JAPAN BLACK 157
JENNINGS BIT 52
JEWELER'S SAW 31
JIG 452; doweling 107; sharpening 169
JIGSAW 452
JOINT half lap 445, dovetail 102, 428; dowel 105; mortise and tenon 210; miter 207; bird's mouth

412; housed 182; keyed 454; pegged 467; wiped 492; capillary 418; expansion 133, 433; concrete 58; hardboard 179; universal 489; lapped dovetail 104; halved 174; to tighten 186; butt 417
JOINTS to tighten 186
JOISTS floor and ceiling 453
JUMPER in tap 453
JUNCTION BOX 432

KAOLIN 454
KEROSENE 58, 133
KEY 454
KEYED JOINTS 454
KEYHOLE OR PAD SAWS 81, 146, 335, 454
KEYSTONE 454

KICK PLATE 454
KILN DRIED timber 454
KNIVES 455
KNOT timber 455
KNOTTING 455
KNURL on tools 455

LACQUER clear 155
LADDER roof 192; aids 189; use with care 190
LAGGING 456
LAGGINGS 456
LAMINATED PLASTIC 18, 456
LAMP BLACK 456
LAMP REPAIRS 129
LARRY 456
LATEX ADHESIVE 18, 203
LATHE wood turning 193; tail stock on 482
LATHING (metal) 457
LEAD sheet flashing 142
LEADED LIGHTS 457
LEAD HOLE or PILOT HOLE 457
LEAKS in plumbing 247
LEDGED DOOR 457
LEFT-HAND THREAD 457
LEVEL dumpy 194; line 194; spirit 194; garden hose 195
LEVEL improvised 194
LEVELING methods 194
LIGHTING 127

LIGHTS in window 458
LIME hydrated 54
LIME MORTAR 209, 458
LIMEWASH 458
LINE chalk 55, 294; 420; building 416; level 194
LINING PAPER for walls 321, 458
LINOLEUM tiles 195
LINOLEUM to lay 195; to patch 197
LINSEED OIL 458; raw 63, 155, 490
LINSEED OIL PUTTY 325
LINTEL 459, 486
LION'S PAW 69
LIPPING 458
LOCK-RAIL in door 459
LOCKS choice of 200; to repair 199; to fit 199; tumblers in 486; rim 199
LOCK WASHER OR SPRING WASHER 459
LONDON SCREWDRIVER 282
LOOSE FILL 185
LOOSE JOINTS 259
LOOSE PIN HINGE 191
LOUVERED DOOR 100

MACADAM driveway paving 460
MADE-UP GROUND 460
MALLET 460; plastic tipped 31; rubber 31; wood 31; rawhide 31
MANDREL 460
MANSARD ROOF 460
MAPLE 305
MARBLE to clean 203
MARKING GAUGE 99, 161; single tooth 161, 210
MARKING KNIFE 183
MASKING 461
MASONRY 461
MASONRY DRILL 114
MATCHBOARD 461
MATRIX 462
MATS floor—to repair 203
MEETING RAIL sash frame 461
METAL FITTINGS plated 204; copper 204; brass 204; bronze 204; stainless steel 205; chromium plated 205; care of 204
METAL NIBBLER 461
METRIC CONVERSION 205

MEZZANINE 461
MIRRORS arrangement of 206; cheval 421; to drill 206; screws for 206
MITER BLOCK to make 43
MITER BOX 27; to make 44, 207
MITER JOINT 207
MODULE UNITS 461
MOLDING 121; bolection 413
MONKEY 462
MORTAR 462; estimating 132; to mix 209; lime 209; cement 209, 419
MORTAR JOINTS to restore 209
MORTISE AND TENON JOINTS to make 209
MORTISE GAUGE 161, 210
MORTISE LOCK 199, 200; to repair 199
MOTOR MAINTENANCE 130
MOUTH 462
MOVING packing hints for 212
MULLION in window 462
MULTI-PLY 462
MUNTIN for frames 462
MURIATIC ACID 233

NAIL BOX to make 217
NAILING methods 218; double 427; skew 477; secret 143
NAILS to cover heads 220; wiggle 418
NAIL SET 463; use 176
NAPHTHALENE FLAKES 71
NARROW BUTT HINGE 181
NATURAL OIL STONE 463
NEATSFOOT OIL 463
NECK 463
NEWEL POST 463

NIBBLER metal 461
NICHE in wall 463
NITRIC ACID 133
NOGGINGS for walls 463
NOISE in home 221; in plumbing 247, 251
NOMINAL SIZE 463
NON-SLIP PATHS paving paint for 234
NOSING 464
NOVELTY SAW 464
NUTS to lock 221

OAK 305
OFFCUT 465
OIL boiled 413; raw linseed 63, 155; neatsfoot 463
OIL-BASE PAINT 223
OIL STAINS to remove 203
OILSTONE natural 491; case for 223; slip 290; washita 491
OPACITY in paint 465
ORANGE SHELLAC 147

ORBITAL SANDER 465
ORGANIC STAINS 203
OUTLET BOX 432
OUTSIDE CALIPERS 69
OVAL HEAD SCREW 284
OVER-ALL SIZE 465
OVERFLOW PIPE in cisterns 465
OVERLOAD 125, 432
OXALIC ACID 465

PAD BOLT 50
PAD OR KEYHOLE SAW 81, 146, 335, 454
PAINT aluminum 27; gold 162; oil base 223; bituminous 232; non-slip paving 234; anticorrosive 403
PAINT discoloration of 227; bleeding of 412; chalking in 420; checking 421; ground coat in 443; pigment 468; binder 411; hints 227; mold growth on 227; opacity in 465; runs and sags in 473; skin on 478; hydrogen sulphide blackening in 227
PAINTING with spray gun 228; with roller 254; windows 328; with brushes 60

PAINT REMOVER 11
PAINTWORK stripping methods—*with blow-lamp 231; scraper 231; butane gas 231; solutions 231*
PAIRED 466
PALING FENCE care of 231
PANEL GAUGE 162
PANEL SAWS 335
PAPER-BACKED VENEER 18
PARAFFIN WAX 133, 232
PARGETTING 466
PARING CHISEL 104
PARLIAMENT HINGE 181, 466

PARQUETRY 466
PARTING BEAD 466
PARTY FENCE WALL 466
PASTE FILLER 119
PASTE FLUX 147
PATCHING PLASTER 233; in walls 233; in ceilings 233; small tool for 289
PATHS to lay concrete 87; non-slip 233
PATINA 466
PAVING crazy 424; asphalt 38; macadam 460
PEBBLEDASH 466
PEDIMENT 466
PEG AND SLEEVE CASTER 71
PEGGED JOINTS 467
PEINING 467
PELMET 467
PENCIL carpenter's 467
PENCIL BRUSH 467
PENETRATION of timber surface 467; in concrete 85
PHILLIPS HEAD SCREW 284
PIANO HINGE 181, 467
PICKLING 147
PICTURE RAIL 467
PIER CAPS 326, 403
PIERS 468
PIGMENT in paint 468
PIN cotter 424
PINCH BAR 234
PINE 305, 306
PINK PRIMER 256
PIPES to conceal 235; to repair 325; to paint 234
PIPING 468
PISÉ DE TERRE 468
PITCH of roof and stairs 468
PIVOTED OR HOPPER WINDOW 328, 448
PLANE bull nose 417; rabbet 471; toothing 485; block 407; German jack 407; badger 407; rasp 259; fillister 141; router 183; combination 423; steel smoothing 108, 119, 156, 236; steel jack 119, 237, 294, 452
PLANING procedure 236; difficult grain 236
PLANING ATTACHMENT 119
PLASTER fibrous 435

PLASTER BOARD use of 238
PLASTERING 238
PLASTIC LAMINATE to fix 18, 150
PLASTIC ROOFING corrugated 240
PLASTICS stick-on 241; celluloid 241; acetate sheet 241; acrylic resin 241
PLASTIC-TIPPED MALLET 31
PLASTIC WOOD 150, 292
PLATE for building frame 468; dowel 105
PLATE GLASS 168
PLIERS combination 423
PLINTH 468
PLUG for wall 468
PLUG CUTTER 307
PLUGGING CHISEL 468
PLUMB 469; line 194; bob 323; rule 55, 469
PLUMBING 242; clogs 242; faucet repairs 245; noisy pipes 247; leaking pipes 247; insulating pipes and tanks 247; thawing frozen pipes 248; draining plumbing system 249; toilet malfunctions and repairs 249; installing fixtures 252
POCKET in box frame window 469
POCKET KNIFE 31
POINTING TROWEL 55, 57
POKERWORK 469
POLISH French 153; ebony 119
POLYETHYLENE 253
POLYURETHANE FOAM 469
PORTABLE POWER DRILL 113
PORTLAND CEMENT 73, 462, 471
POWER TOOLS basic operation of 253; choice of 255; drilling with 254; sawing with 255; sanding with 254
PRE-CAST CONCRETE PRODUCTS 469
PRIMERS AND SEALERS 90, 254, 286, 470, 476
PROTECTIVE LACQUER for chrome 80
PULLEY STILE of window frame 469
PUMICE stone 11; powder 11, 119
PUNCH center 31
PURLINS for roof 470
PUTTY cold water 70; linseed oil 325; Swedish 233
P.V.A. adhesives 18; glue 18, 184, 469
P.V.C. SHEETS for walls and roof 240

QUADRANT 470
QUANTITIES 470
QUARRY TILES 470
QUARTER ROUND EDGE MOLDING 72, 470

QUARTER SAWED 120
QUEEN ANNE 69
QUIRK 470
QUOIN 470

RABBET PLANE 471
RADIATION 185
RAFTERS 142
RAG BOLT 471
RAIL of frame 471
RANDOM WIDTH of timber 471
RANGEWOOD 305
RASP 471
RASP-PLANE 259
RAT-TAIL FILE 138
RATCHET SCREWDRIVER 282
RAWHIDE MALLET 31
RAWL ANCHORS 31
RAW LINSEED OIL 63, 155
READY MIXED CONCRETE 86
RED OXIDE 57, 209
REDUCING SOCKET 471
REINFORCED CONCRETE 87, 471
RELIEF DECORATIONS 321
RENDERING of cement 238, 420, 472
REPAIR PLATES use of 259
REPOINTING in brickwork 57
RESIN flux 147; core 290
RIDGE in roof 472
RIM LOCK 199
RIPSAWS 263, 334
RISERS on stairs 472

RISING BUTT HINGE 181, 472
RIVERSIDE DOOR 472
RIVET bifurcated 411; to remove 24; to use 261
RIVETING method 24
RIVING KNIFE on circular saw 472
RODS dowel 105
ROLLER BLINDS to adjust 263
ROLLER PAINTING advantages of 264
ROOF skillion 142, 478; condensation 91; asbestos cement 36; gutters 265; ladder for 190; butterfly 417; flat 437; hipped 448; mansard 460; purlins 470; pitch of 468; ridge 472; corrugated plastic 240
ROTTENSTONE 473, 486
ROUND HEAD SCREW 284
ROUND OR RAT-TAIL FILE 138
ROUND SOCKET CASTER 71
ROUTER PLANE 183, 473
RUBBER care of 266
RUBBER-BASED ADHESIVE 18, 473
RUBBER MALLET 31
RUBBER-SLEEVE BOLT 31
RUNG 473
RUNS AND SAGS in paint 473
RUST INHIBITOR 64
RUST STAINS 38, 203

SABER SAW 474
SADDLE 474
SAFE-EDGED FILE 474
SAL AMMONIAC for soldering 147
SALT uses 271
SAND BLASTING 474
SANDER orbital 465
SANDING 233; block 11; belt 474
SANDPAPER 11, 146, 438, 474
SANDWICHING 474
SARKING 253, 474
SASH 475
SASH CORD 475
SAW kerf 211; set 476
SAW keyhole or pad 81, 146, 335, 454; back or
    tenon 103, 334; coping 31, 104, 335; dovetail 335;
    hand 334, 445; scroll 31; panel 335; circular 82;
    jeweler's 31; buzz 417; jig 452; novelty 464;
    tipped 484; two-man 487; cross-cut 273, 334; rip
    273, 334; saber 474
SAW BLADES clean cutting 82
SAW DOCTOR 475
SAWDUST uses 271
SAW HORSE 272
SAW HORSE TRESTLE to make 272
SAWING 273; power 255
SAW PIT 475
SAW SET 475
SAW TEETH 278; re-shaping 277; setting 277;
    sharpening 277; jointing 277; filing 277; side
    jointing 278
SAW VICE 315
SCISSORS to sharpen 280
SCOTCH TEE HINGE 181
SCRAPER for wood 108, 156
SCRATCH COAT on wall 475
SCRATCH WHEEL 13
SCREED 475
SCREEN DOORS to fit 281
SCREWDRIVER BIT 53
SCREWDRIVERS cabinet 282; electrician's 282;
    London 282; ratchet 282
SCREW EYES 101
SCREW GAUGE 476
SCREW HEADS covering 283
SCREW NAILS for asbestos cement roofing 37
SCREW PLATE CASTER 71
SCREWS grub 444; coach 84; mirror 206; Allen 22,
    402; bench 410; countersunk head 284; round
    head 284; oval head 284; Phillips head 284;
    clutch head 284; set 98; self tapping 23; to keep
    secure 283; selection of 284

SCREW SOCKET CASTER 71
SCRIBE 476
SCRIM 476
SCROLL SAW 31
SCUTCH HAMMER 294, 476
SEALERS 286, 476; for timber 141
SEALERS AND PRIMERS 256, 286, 470
SEALING COMPOUNDS 72
SECRET NAILING 143
SELECTING GLASS 168
SELF-TAPPING SCREW to use 23
SET on saw teeth 476
SET SCREW 98
SETTING with putty plaster 248
SETTLEMENT 476
SHARPENING edge tools 286; scissors 280; axes
    39; saws 277; drills 115
SHEET GLASS 168
SHEET METAL to flatten 287
SHELLAC 256, 409, 476; use 287; orange 147
SHELLAC VARNISH 142, 144
SHIM 476
SHIPLAP 476
SHOOTING BOARD 45
SHORING 477
SHORT CIRCUIT 125, 432
SHUTTERING 477
SIDE AXE 477
SIDING (weatherboards) care of 325
SILICONE POLISH 82, 149
SILL window frame 477
SILVER care of 288; to clean by electrolyte
    method 289; polish 149
SILVER PLATE 477
SINGLE CUT FILE 31
SIZE glue 256, 443
SKARSTON SCRAPER 477
SKEW NAILING 477
SKILLION ROOF 142, 478
SKIN on paint 478
SKIRTING BOARD 478
SKYLIGHT 478
SLEEPER WALL 478
SLURRY 72, 478
SMALL TOOL for plaster repairs 289
SNAKE 244, 478
SOCKET reducing 471
SODIUM FLUORIDE 71
SOFFIT 478
SOFT BESSEMER WHEEL 13
SOFT SOLDERING 478
SOFTWOODS 305

SOIL PIPE 242, 479
SOLDERING 289; soft 478; tinning in 484; requirements for—*hydrochloric acid 290; zinc chloride 290; sal ammoniac 290; resin flux 290; tallow 147; paste flux 147, 290; resin core 290*
SOLDERING ALUMINUM 28
SPARROW PICKING of walls and floors 479
SPIGOT 479
SPIRITING OFF 155
SPIRIT LEVEL 54
SPOKESHAVE 290
SPONGE cellulose 194; sea 183
SPRING-BOW CALIPERS 70
SPRING TOGGLE WALL BOLT 31
SPROCKET PIECE 479
SPRUCE 306
SPUR 479
SQUARE 479
SQUARE roofing 290; sliding 291; builder's 65; T 486
SQUARE FILE 138
SQUARE SOCKET CASTER 71
STAFF BEAD 409
STAINING 157
STAINS organic 203; rust 203; ceiling 91; oil 58, 203; bitumen 58
STAIRS eliminate creaks in 292; winders in 492; risers on 472
STANCHION 480
STANDING TIMBER 480

STAPLE 480
STAVE 480
STEEL BRUSH 31
STEEL GADS 293
STEEL JACK PLANE 294, 452, 119, 237
STEEL RULE 163
STEEL SMOOTHING PLANE 108, 119, 156, 236
STEEL WOOL 143, 156, 290
STENCIL BRUSH 64
STEPS to repair 292
STERLING SILVER 288, 480
STIFF-JOINTED CALIPERS 70
STIPPLE BRUSH 327
STONEWORK to cut and shape 293
STOPPERS 480
STRAIGHT EDGE 54, 55, 164; testing 294
STRAP HINGE 192
STRIKING PLATE 481
STRIPPING METHODS for paint 231
STRIP SEALER 72
STUCCO 481
STUD for walls 481
SUSPENDED CEILING 481
SWAN-NECK CHISEL 481
SWEATING plumbing system 247
SWEDISH PUTTY 233
SWITCH installing 126, 432
SWITCH BOX 432
SWIVEL BALL OR SHEPHERD CASTER 71

TABLE tops 299; to square 299
TACK LIFTER 482
TAIL STOCK on lathe 482
TAKE-UP 482
TALLOW 147
TAMPING 482
TANG 482
TAP for cutting threads 482
TEMPLATE 482
TENON barefaced 408, 482
TENON SAW (BACK SAW) 103, 334, 407
TENSION on saw blades 483
TENSION SPRING 483
TENTERHOOK 483
TEREBINE 483
TERMITES 326
TERRACOTTA 483

TERRAZZO 483
THERMOPLASTIC 483
THERMOSTAT 483
THINNERS 484
THROATING 484
THUMBSCREW 484
TIE in timber frame 484
TILES to cut ceramic 301; to restore joints 281; quarry 470
TILING BATTENS 484
TIMBER faults 303; selection 304; growth rings 120; shapes and sections 308; surface finish 307; surface repairs 307; ordering 308; impregnation of 451; knot in 455; bleaching 49; edge gluing 120; grading 284; workability 284
TIMBERING 484
TINNING with soldering iron 28, 484

TINSNIPS 308
TIPPED SAW 484
TOE 485
TOGGLE BOLT 485
TOILET MALFUNCTIONS AND REPAIRS 249
TOMMY BAR 485
TOOLMAKER'S CALIPERS 70
TOOLS for working with aluminum 28—*coping saw 31; scroll saw 31; jeweler's saw 31; pocket knife 31; tinsnips 31; file card 31; single-cut file 31*
TOOTHING PLANE 485
TOPPING of saw teeth 485
TOWER BOLT 50
TOYMAKING 309
TRACKING of bandsaw 485
TRAMMEL POINTS 485
TRANSOM 486

TRIANGULAR FILE 138
TRIMMERS 486
TRIPOD SOCKET CASTER 71
TRIPOLI POWDER 486
TROLLEY TABLE CASTER 71
TROWEL 294
TRUSS 486
TRY SQUARE 291
T SQUARE 486
TUCK POINTING 486
TUFT 486
TUMBLERS in locks 486
TUMBLING BOX 487
TUNG OIL 487
TURNBUCKLE 101, 487
TWIST BIT 52
TWIST DRILL 31, 115
TWO-MAN SAW 487

ULTIMATE STRENGTH 488
UMBER 488
UNDERCOAT for enamel 35, 488
UNDERCUT 488
UNDERLAY for floor coverings 313, 488
UNDERPINNING 488

UNDERWRITERS KNOT 129
UNIT FURNITURE 489
UNIVERSAL JOINT 489
UPHOLSTERY gimp for 441; piping in 468; tuft in 486; gimp pin for 441
UPTURN 489

VACUUM BAG 490
VALLEY 490
VALVE SEAT refacing 246
VANDYKE BROWN 157, 158
VARNISH shellac 144; clear 147, 227; blooming in 413
VARNISH STAIN 490
V-BLOCK 490
VEGETABLE BLACK 209
VEHICLES for paints 490; for varnishes 490
VENEER brick 416
VENEER paper-backed 18

VENEER BALANCER 408
VENEERING 490; method 150, 313
VENTILATION under floor 313; roof 91
VERDIGRIS 490
VERTICAL DRILL STAND 114
VIBRATED CONCRETE 490
VINEGAR use 318
VISES 316; for saw sharpening 315; hinged 296; for work bench 47; hand 434
VOLT 122, 432
VOLTAGE DROP 432

WALL party fence 466; for sloping garden 323; bearing 409; cavity 419; noggings 463; curtain 425

WALLBOARD 491

WALLPAPER to clean 321; lining for 321; embossed 321; pastes 322; to remove 323

WALLPLATE 491

WALLS efflorescence on 430; fungus on 148; dampness in 95; patch plaster in 233; anchors for 31; ties for 491; fiber plugs for 31; metal plugs for 31; weep holes in 492; cement wash for 72; bagged finish 72; asbestos cement sheet 38; asbestos filling compound for 31; methods of resurfacing 324; pebble-dash 324; stipple 324; cement paint 324; concrete 88

WALL STUD 481

WALNUT 305

WARDING FILE 491

WARPING 491

WASHITA OILSTONE 491

WASTE PIPES 242; to clean 324, 491

WATER MARKS 491

WATER PIPES to repair 325

WATERPROOFING 253

WATERPROOF PAPER 11

WATER WHITE 492

WATT 122, 433

WATT HOUR 433

WAVE BLEMISH 492

WAX 80; crayon 150

WEATHERBOARDS care 325

WEATHER STRIPS 72

WEATHER-STRUCK JOINT for brickwork 57

WEEP HOLES in wall 492

WET OR DRY PAPER 11

WHITE ANTS 34, 326

WHITE PINE 305

WHITE WAX 147

WHITING 59, 158

WIGGLE NAIL 424

WILLIAM AND MARY 69

WINDERS in stairs 492

WINDING STRIPS use of 326

WINDOWS bay 409; dormer 427; mullion 462; to reglaze 330; frosted 327; how to paint 328; double-hung or box frame 328, 406, 414, 427; casement 328, 419; pivoted or hopper 328, 448; to replace cords 331

WIPED JOINT 492

WIRE BRUSH 64, 290

WIRE CUP BRUSH 13

WIRED GLASS 492

WIRING electrical 123

WOOD BORERS 51

WOODEN FLOAT 234, 438

WOOD MALLET 31

WOOD PLANES 31

WOOD PRESERVING OIL 92

WOOD TURNING LATHE 193

WOODWORKER'S GLUE 109

WOODWORKER'S RULE use of 16

WORKSHOP BENCH to make 46

WRENCH Allen 402

WROUGHT IRON 403

YELLOW OCHRE 57, 158, 493

YOKE 493

ZIG-ZAG RULE 493

ZINC use of 142, 336

ZINC CHLORIDE 147

ZINC OXIDE 493